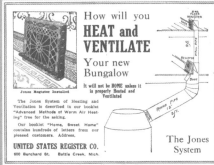

BUNGALOW DETAILS: INTERIOR

BUNGALOW DETAILS: INTERIOR

JANE POWELL &
LINDA SVENDSEN

Gibbs Smith, Publisher
Salt Lake City

First Edition
10 09 08 07 06   5 4 3 2 1

Published by
Gibbs Smith, Publisher
P.O. Box 667
Layton, Utah 84041

1-800.748.5439 orders
www.gibbs-smith.com

Designed and produced by Rudy Ramos
Printed and bound in Hong Kong

Library of Congress Cataloging-in-Publication Data

Powell, Jane, 1952–
  Bungalow details : interior / Jane Powell &
Linda Svendsen.— 1st ed.

    p. cm.
Includes bibliographical references.
ISBN 1-58685-305-8

1. Bungalows—United States.
2. Interior architecture—United States—History—
    20th century.
3. Interior decoration—United States—History—
    20th century.
4. Arts and crafts movement—United States—
    Influence.
I. Svendsen, Linda. II. Title.

NA7571.P68 2006
728'.373097309041—dc22   2005033525

INTRODUCTORY PHOTOGRAPHS:

Page 2: A basement fireplace doesn't always have to be rustic,
as shown by a fireplace in Denver. Highly glazed decorative tiles
frame the front and form the hearth, while the wood mantel
and surround features turned wood spindles and an interesting
cross-hatched decoration. The coal grate and frame, in an
oxidized copper finish, even retains the original summer cover.

Page 7: Caramel-colored art glass forms a shade fitted into a
brass ring with rectangular cutouts overlaid by diamond forms.
L-shaped holders for electric candles are riveted between the
rectangles.

Page 8: Beautiful arched double doors with diamond-patterned
glass make for a grand entrance into the dining room of a Chicago
bungalow. The doors themselves are dark-stained birch.

Page 10: A mirror on the panel that hides the hidden bed in this
Chicago bungalow also helps to make the small room seem larger.

CONTACT INFORMATION:

Author:
    Jane Powell
    P.O. Box 31683
    Oakland CA 94604
    (510) 532-6704
    www.bungalowkitchens.com

Photographer:
    Linda Svendsen
    3915 Bayview Circle
    Concord CA 94520
    (925) 676-8299
    www.lindasvendsen.com

CONTENTS:

ACKNOWLEDGMENTS

Writing is a solitary task (except for Ubu the Velcro Kitty), but a book such as this requires many people to make it happen. This book would be nothing without the stunning photographs of Linda Svendsen, which never fail to do justice to the wonder of bungalows. The words would make less sense without the judicious editing of Linda Nimori. The complexity of the book would cause it all to be a jumble of words, photographs, and captions without the design and layout sense of Rudy Ramos. I could not manage at all without the inestimable help of my friend Valerie Fahnestock, who helps sort the photos and keep track of where they go. And the information in the book would not be accurate without the help of Dennis Prieur of Through The Woods Fine Wood Flooring (floor info); Mark Neeley of Vintage Fans LLC (ceiling fan info); Cliff Popejoy of Apex Electrical (electrical info), Riley Doty (tile info); Robyn Einhorn (Murphy beds); Erik Hanson and Tim Hansen, who let me hold onto many wonderful old books and catalogs for nearly three years without ever complaining or demanding they be returned; Jim Buckley at Buckley-Rumford fireplaces; Bruce Smith of The Arts and Crafts Press; Steve Gluckman of the Old Seminole Heights Neighborhood Association; and Patrick Bulmer at Waterglass Studios. Not to mention my compatriots on the *Old House Journal* online bulletin board, whose knowledge of obscure old house stuff never fails to amaze me, including Bill Rigby, Mike Thies, Bryan Sayer, Jeff Rice, Deborah Lester, and many others who I know only by their user names. And I never would have survived the book without the sage advice, aesthetic judgement, and willingness to pitch in of my friend Jeanette Sayre, even if it was partly her fault that I bought the house.

If I had known how much clerical work was involved in writing a book, I might never have taken it up—keeping track of photos, addresses, names and phone numbers is not my strong suit, so I apologize right now to anyone I have inadvertently left out, and I am sure there are quite a few. I also apologize if I have placed a house in a different city from where it is actually located—nationwide similarities in bungalows, combined with bad note-taking on my part and the fact that there were a total of 1,100 photos probably means I messed up on quite a few of them. We would never have found houses to photograph without referrals from many people, including John Atkin and Jo Scott-B in Vancouver, British Columbia; Jennifer Barr of the Victoria Heritage Foundation in Victoria, British Columbia; Steve Ciancio of The Crafted Home, Robert Rust and Pam McCreary, Chandler Romeo and Reed Weimer in Denver; Tim Counts of the Twin Cities Bungalow Club in Minneapolis; Kathy Couturie in Southern California; Laurie Crogan, Adam Janeiro of the West Adams Heritage Association, and Suzanne Houchin in Los Angeles; Allison Freedland of the Historic Chicago Bungalow Association in Chicago; Carlen Hatala of the City of Milwaukee and Denise Hice of Historic Milwaukee in Milwaukee; John Hopkins and Marsha Oates, and Sue Williams in Memphis; Bob Kneisel of the Bungalow Heaven Neighborhood Association in Pasadena; Larry Kreisman of Historic Seattle, Clint Miller, and Laurie Taylor in Seattle; Suzanne and Dennis Prieur in Eagle Rock; John Ribovich in Pleasanton; and Cynthia Thompson in Ventura.

Most importantly, I want to thank the homeowners who opened their homes to us and allowed us to share the amazing details of their houses with the world: Mark Novakowski and Linda McCain, Janet Mark and Terry Geiser, Richard Pettler and Wanda Westberg, Lynne and Audel Davis, Roger and Jean Moss, Jeanne Franken and Fred Harder, Don and Arlyce Feist, and Homayoon Kazerooni and Audrey Shoji in Berkeley, California; Ken and Ann Katz, Cliff Cline and Julie Hardgrove, and Sally and Louis Louis in Oakland, California; John Ribovich and Lisa Alba in Pleasanton, California; Arno Grether, Ann and Andre Chaves, Tom and Nancy Reitze, Victor and Dora Smith, Phaedra and Mark Ledbetter, Suzanne and Steven Roth in Pasadena, California; Greg Gill and Rob Bruce in Altadena, California; Leonard Fenton in Hollywood, California; Suzanne and Dennis Prieur in Eagle Rock, California; Gail Howell in Santa Monica, California, Jeff Ross in Ventura, California; Kathy and Bill Couterie, and Bill Moses in Southern California; Marty and Ron Thomas, Lisa Klein, Linda and Mark Anderson, and Jim and Margaret de Laureia in Chicago, Illinois; Charlene Sloan, Christopher and Wendy Crosby, Sandy Mazarakis and Neil Burris, Kathleen

Schroeder, Gail Hadley and Bill Rickman, Barbara and Charles Reiman, Phil and Linda Lidov, and Elizabeth Wheeler in Denver, Colorado; Edith and Bob Heller, Charlotte and Sam Cantor, Michael and Melinda Wayt, Jim Rice and Linda Oxford, Davey and MJ Weakes, Rip and Nicole Haney, Genevieve Posey, Marsha Hayes, Carol Raiford, and John and Meridith Starling in Memphis, Tennessee; Keith and Denise Hice, Cathy and Steve Hoelter, Al Jacobi and Deana Ohman, Lee Ann and Mark Knippel, and Kurt and Rachel Young-Binter in Milwaukee, Wisconsin; Diane Campion in Whitefish Bay, Wisconsin; Kathy and Art Zeigler in Raymond, Washington; Larry Willits, Olivia Dresher, Carrie Schnelker and Michael Sobieck, Pamela and Gerard Zytnicki, Mary Alice Pomputious and Walter Smith, Mary Fields and John Aylward, Shelley and Michael O'Clair, Bob Welland and Mary Casey, Barbara Griffen and Judy Cherin, and Jessie Jones and Matt Johnson in Seattle, Washington; Geoff Corso and Marshall McClintock in Tacoma, Washington; Heather and Bill Andrews in Vancouver, British Columbia; and Suzanne and Patrick Bulmer, Paul and Marilynne Convey, Judith and Richard Anderson, and Sheila and Jim Colwill in Victoria, British Columbia.

It has been a distinct pleasure to be part of the Arts and Crafts Revival since buying my first bungalow in 1987. I have met so many warm and wonderful people and seen so many amazing things, and I feel honored to have been able to contribute in a small way to the renaissance of the movement.

Bungalows are all about home and family, and I would not be who I am without them—my father, Nelson Powell; my sisters, Nancy Klapak and Mary Enderle; my niece and nephew Karin and Brian Klapak; and my extended family of aunts, uncles, and cousins.

And I personally don't feel that a bungalow can be a home without cats—Ubu and Zoe, the Burmese Velcro kitties, and Milo, because there's nothing better than a large orange kitty.

LONG LIVE THE BUNGALOW!

FOREWORD:

*"It is the great excellence of a writer to put into
his book as much as his book will hold."*
—Samuel Johnson

I am a house junkie. Oh, it's true, I cover it up with high-minded terms like "restorationist" and "serial renovator," but when I see some old house that has been neglected or abused, I literally begin to twitch, I get a rush of adrenaline, my mind starts going a mile a minute with plans for what needs to be done, and I become just like a problem gambler in front of a casino, or a food addict at an all-you-can-eat buffet. I rationalize it like all addicts—I'm just keeping up on local real estate prices, I might see something interesting that I can use in a book, or I might find an interesting piece of furniture or an old stove that someone wants to get rid of, but really, I just can't help myself. I have had to ration my attendance at Sunday Open Houses. However, like many addicts, I have chosen a profession that allows me to both hide and enable my addiction. What better subterfuge than to write books about bungalows, thus making people willing to let me into their houses to see all kinds of cool things, photograph them, and then write about them? When I purchased my fabulous "bunga-mansion," I also figured that that was going to be it. No more buying houses to fix up.

Well, that worked for all of two years. Then one day I came home and found a For Sale sign on the house next door. I started to twitch, my palms got sweaty, my heart started to pound. I found myself walking over to look in the windows—it showed promise. That was bad. I called my mortgage broker and said, "So, Steve, I have no money and I can't even afford my own house, but I have a home equity line of credit I could use for the down payment and the renovation costs—could I get a loan to buy the house next door?" And he said, "Yes." And I thought, "Well, that's just wrong." So I called my real estate agent and said, "Luanne, come over and show me the house next door and talk me

out of buying it." So we looked at it—and she said she thought I should buy it. I next appealed to my friend Jeanette to talk me out of buying it. But she argued that the chance to control who lives next door was too important to pass up, and that if I did pass it up, I'd be kicking myself for the next ten years, especially if whoever bought it turned out to be bad neighbors. Which was a good point, since I have horrendously bad neighbors on the other side in a fourplex that was built on what had been part of my lot. And she added that I could possibly roll over the money I made on the house in order to purchase the apartment building. In the substance abuse world, this is known as "enabling."

So I bought the house. Of my myriad reasons for buying it, this one was the most basic—*I didn't like the color it was painted.* It had white fiberboard siding, the kind with the really fake embossed wood grain. And the trim was blue. These are two colors I believe just shouldn't be allowed on the outside of houses. There was just one problem with buying the house. I was supposed to be writing a book. Now, for those who have never done either of these things, I can tell you that either one is pretty much all-consuming. I tried to do both at once. I don't recommend this.

I did learn a few useful things in the process that are included in the book, like it's really hard to make coved ceilings with drywall, and there were many paint-stripping experiments as well, the results of which are reported herein.

The house took longer than I thought, and so did the book. In part, it's because this book is the longest I have ever written—who knew bungalows could be so complicated? As always, there are both Obsessive Restoration and Compromise Solution sidebars for each section. I have been taken to task by some people who think the Compromise

Solutions are not compromising enough. My view is that I am up against a huge propaganda machine of shelter magazines, architects and designers, and TV shows all telling people to do whatever they want and "express themselves," and I am only one (admittedly loud) voice saying, "No, don't do that. You are merely a caretaker of your home, and there are other ways to express yourself that don't impact the structure of the house." Besides, there's little point to writing a book if you don't at least get to put out your own version of how things ought to be.

Last but not least, if you've never read one of my books before, be forewarned. All the chapter headings are puns. Really bad puns. Hideously bad puns. I can't even write the chapter till I come up with an unbelievably awful pun. I realize there are many people who don't like or appreciate puns. Then ignore them. There are far more important things to worry about.

— **Jane Powell**

"In this book, the interiors of many homes are shown or described. It may be that reference was made to some scheme of decoration, or object, which is clearly set forth as being in poor taste. It may also happen that this very thing is one element in your home upon which you rather pride yourself. The writer here, at the outset, desires to state that he did not know that this thing, whatever it may be, was in your house, and begs to say that if he had known it—he would have mentioned it just the same."
—Fred Hamilton Daniels,
The Furnishing of a Modest Home

CHAPTER ONE

WHAT IS A BUNGALOW?

"Pardon me, I was using the subjunctive instead of the past tense.
Yes, we're away past tents. We're living in bungalows now."
—Groucho Marx as Captain Spaulding, **Animal Crackers**

I wish I had a snappy answer to that question, but it's fundamentally rather complicated. Dictionaries provide these definitions:

"a low house having only one story or, in some cases, upper rooms set in the roof, typically with dormer windows"

"a usually one storied house with a low pitched roof"

"a small house all on one level"

"a small house or cottage usually having a single story and sometimes an additional attic story"

"a thatched or tiled one story house in India surrounded by a wide verandah"

"a usually one storied house of a type first developed in India and characterized by low sweeping lines and a wide veranda"

It is generally agreed that bungalows descended from thatched Bengali peasant huts in India, called variously *bang-golo, bangala,* or *bangla* (depending on who's translating), possibly crossed with a hip-roofed peasant hut called a *chauyari* (literally meaning "four sides"), further crossed with the standard British Army tent. It's pretty easy to see how it was Anglicized to "bungalow." The roof could be hipped (pyramidal) or curvilinear, as described by nineteenth-century traveler Francis

Buchanan, ". . . a hut with a pent roof constructed of two sloping sides which meet in a ridge forming the segment of a circle so that it has a resemblance to a boat when overturned. . . ." Because the plinth was wider than the actual hut, when combined with the roof overhangs it formed a porch or verandah on four sides of the hut. Later the thatched roofs were replaced by tile, as some of the locals didn't subscribe to Mahatma Gandhi's nonviolence concept.

The British altered the native dwelling into something that conformed better to their idea of what a house should be, and built these Anglo-Indian bungalows in compounds outside of the cities and towns as well as in "hill stations" where the Europeans would go in the summer to get away from the heat. Eventually the bungalow was exported to all corners of the British Empire as being the proper sort of house for Europeans in the tropics. By the nineteenth century, it was understood to be a one-story house of Indian origin. In England, the first bungalow to be built and actually called a bungalow rather than a cottage was built in 1869 at a seaside resort on the English coast. This bungalow was no small cottage—there were several bedrooms, a 15- by 23-foot dining room, numerous service rooms, stables, and a coach house. But the architecture of this bungalow was amazingly simple compared to its Victorian contemporaries.

The simplicity of bungalows was both an aesthetic choice and a reaction to the increasing "servant problem." It was also bound up with Bohemian ideals about a simple rustic life, which were, in large part, a reaction to the societal changes brought on by the Industrial Revolution. Although advance-

A rather grand hip-roofed Indian bungalow is shown on this undated postcard. It was apparently in the process of reroofing, shown where the two major rooflines meet. Note the various awnings and latticework used to shade the veranda.

ments in technology and manufacturing resulted in many beneficial products, like the cookstove, the sewing machine, and indoor plumbing, the other side of the coin was pollution, sweatshops, overcrowding, social unrest, and the mass production of shoddy, badly designed goods. Most middle- and upper-class people merely wanted to get away from the cities and their problems, but there were a few who actually wanted to do something about the problems, and some of them were the founders of the Arts and Crafts movement. Although Arts and Crafts is often thought of nowadays as a style or an aesthetic, it was also a philosophical, political, and social movement.

It is impossible to talk about bungalows as we know them in America without some understanding of the Arts and Crafts movement, which began in Britain in the nineteenth century as a reaction to the Industrial Revolution. It was a reaction against inferior mass-produced goods, overwrought decorating, and appalling social conditions brought on by industrialization. The upside of the Industrial Revolution was the emergence of a large middle class, who were of course the purchasers of the mass-produced doodads, because previ-

ously only rich people could afford to have lots of stuff. Unfortunately, the widespread availability of stuff was made possible by exploitation of the lower classes in factories and sweatshops (a tradition that continues today as production is moved offshore to various Third World countries where the wages are cheap and the labor and environmental regulations nearly nonexistent). And the stuff was lavishly ornamented because machines made it possible to produce ornament that previously required a great deal of expensive handwork. And frankly, because they COULD make it. This was the world that Charles Dickens wrote about.

It's easy to think of Arts and Crafts as a style, which it is, but it was also a political movement that hoped to better the lot of the lower classes at the same time that it improved the design of buildings and the things that went in them. Many of the leaders, including William Morris, were Socialists. The main goal of the movement was to restore the dignity of labor that had been lost in factory work, thus to reform both labor and society at large, and they believed a return to handcraftsmanship, which had been a tradition

As Victorian parlors go, this one is relatively subdued; there are actually a few places you could put down your cup of tea. However, between the various wallpapers, polychromed ceiling medallions, stained-glass window, multilayer window treatments, and especially the many levels of the overmantel where the latest in Oriental and other objets d'art are displayed, there is still a lot going on. The draped fabric on the mantel is particularly scary—it's such a good idea to hang something flammable right above the firebox! And of course it would not be a proper Victorian parlor without the obligatory potted palm.

in English villages since medieval times, was the way to go about it. The movement's proponents included architects, artists, designers, and writers. The Arts and Crafts reformers believed that good design in homes and furnishings would result in an improved society. They believed that Nature was the proper source for inspiration and design motifs. The most famous of the Arts and Crafts movement founders was William Morris, a gifted designer whose textile and wallpaper designs have been in continuous production since the nineteenth century. But possibly the most radical idea of the movement was the idea that craft, or "the lesser arts," was just as important and should be accorded the same respect as "the fine arts" like painting and sculpture. It is hard to conceive from a twenty-first-century viewpoint just how radical these ideas were.

The unfortunate reality, however, was that handcrafting and the attempt to pay a living wage made the wares produced by Morris and others prohibitively expensive and mostly affordable only to the rich. This doesn't mean that Morris and the others were wrong or that the movement was a failure; it merely means that fundamentally changing society is a rather large, complex, and ongoing task.

Interestingly enough, the British Arts and Crafts movement didn't particularly embrace the bungalow, though certainly many of its architects designed some houses that fit the description. The British movement looked back to the Gothic period, or to vernacular architecture, for inspiration. It wasn't until the bungalow arrived in North America that it really became associated with the Arts and Crafts movement. Most bungalows in Britain were built after World War I, long after the demise of the Arts and Crafts movement there, and are viewed in the same way we might view the cheap tract houses thrown up after World War II in the United States.

In America as in Britain, seaside (or lakeside, or mountain) resorts comprised of hotels and summer cottages were built for the upper classes. Some of the "cottages," such as those built at Newport, Rhode Island, were not cottages at all; they were ostentatious mansions. The first named bungalow in America was built on Cape Cod in 1879. It was designed by William Gibbons Preston, a Boston architect, and being two-and-a-half stories tall, it was not really a bungalow, though it had a simple structure and broad verandah. In 1884, architect Arnold William Brunner featured a bungalow as the frontispiece in his plan book *Cottages or Hints on Economical Building.* Though that design cost $4,000, he also included designs costing between $500 and $1,000, aimed at a growing middle class. Brunner wrote, "Simplicity, elegance, and refinement of design are demanded and outward display, overloading with cheap ornamentation, is no longer in favour." Of course, he was completely wrong about that, as the recent spate of "McMansions" makes only too clear.

The bungalow's initial use as vacation architecture meant that it came to be associated with leisure and informality in a natural setting. This association continued even as bungalows were being built in cities. Architectural styles used for resort houses in the nineteenth century—such as the Shingle Style on the East Coast (so called because of the shingle siding used), the rustic Adirondack style in the mountains (featuring rustic wood and log detailing), and even the Spanish haciendas of the West and Southwest— had a lasting influence on bungalow architecture.

The Arts and Crafts movement was in many ways more successful in North America. When the ideas reached these shores around 1900, they were taken up by progressive ideal-ists in many cities and popularized by people like Gustav Stickley through his magazine, *The Craftsman,* Elbert Hubbard at the Roycrofters, and Edward Bok at *Ladies' Home Journal.* Most cities had Arts and Crafts societies or guilds, and the movement was aligned with various progressive political causes. There was just one small problem with the movement as imported from Britain: since ours was still a young country, Americans had no medieval tradition to refer to. Instead, we had to opt for incorporating various alternative ideas involving either traditional ways of building, like log cabins, Spanish missions, and Native American dwellings (though technically those had been imported as well), or things considered exotic, such as architecture and decorative arts from Japan, which had recently opened up to the outside world.

The other thing that distinguished the American Arts and Crafts movement was a more practical and democratic approach to the whole thing. Rather than throwing the machines out with the bathwater, so to speak, we viewed machines as useful tools that could be used to relieve drudgery and do the tedious and repetitive parts of the work, freeing up time and thought for the artistic part and allowing hand labor to be devoted to artistry. Having no medieval tradition, we opted to celebrate simplicity, natural (especially local) materials, and honesty of structure. Of course, much of this was lip service because a lot of things promoted as handcrafted or handmade were actually made entirely by machine, and honesty of structure, especially on houses, was often a sham, as we will see later. (Honesty of

The first house in the United States to be called a bungalow was built near Bourne on Cape Cod, probably as a vacation home for a Bostonian. It is, of course, much too tall to fit the technical definition of a bungalow, but it has many of the details that appeared on bungalows later on, including simple porch brackets, open gable decoration, asymmetrical massing, multi-light upper sashes, large decorative fascia boards, and simple corbels. But the finest detail has got to be the shark fin decoration at the ridgeline.

Although this undated photo is labeled "Van Nuys, Cal. bungalow," at two stories tall, it's not really a bungalow. But it has the same detailing: shingle siding, large brackets holding up a curved Asian-influenced gable, and a latticework front porch with what appears to be a climbing rose, topped by an open porch on the second floor. The front door and its sidelights are hidden behind the lattice.

But there was more to bungalows than that. The Arts and Crafts advocates believed that design could change people's lives. They believed that the design of objects mattered, they believed that the built environment mattered, and they believed that people living in these houses, having these objects, raising their children there, would result in a wholesome life, upstanding citizens, and a peaceful and prosperous country. It didn't quite work out that way, but it doesn't mean they were wrong. It's merely that the problem is a great deal more complicated than that. By 1900, the Arts and Crafts movement had spread to America through periodicals, lectures, books, and travel. In the last few years of the nineteenth century and the early years of the twentieth, Arts and Crafts societies were set up in many major cities. Even so, it is doubtful the movement would have taken off had it not been promoted in national magazines like *The Craftsman, House Beautiful,* and *Ladies' Home Journal.* Although these magazines publicized bungalows and other Arts and Crafts house styles, one of the main reasons for the bungalow's widespread popularity in all parts of the United States and Canada was house plan books and mail-order houses.

The hope of plan book publishers was that people would buy the actual plans from them at a price, generally somewhere between $5 and $25, so plan books were usually given away or sold cheaply. Some were nothing more than a black-and-white catalog, while others were lushly illustrated in color. There was usually a photo or illustration of each house accompanied by a simplified floor plan, and often a lot of purple prose describing the house, such as this from the 1917 Aladdin catalog:

A mass of lights and shadows softening the greens, browns, and grays of the foliage, shingles, and cobbles delights the eye. You can almost feel the touch of the sunbeams patterning the lawn, and you just want to stroll up the steps and into the inviting shade of the porch.

Descriptions of the interiors were not neglected, and the words "cozy," "convenient," and "artistic" were often employed.

There were many plan books and mail-order house books published by architects, lumber companies, builders, real estate syndicates, and, of course, the national mail-order companies of Montgomery Ward and Sears, Roebuck and Co. Gustav Stickley's *Craftsman* magazine also published

structure, known as "expressed structure" in architectural terms, basically means not hiding how the house was actually built, which is why bungalows have exposed rafters and beam-ends and such.) This hypocritical aspect of the movement in no way diminishes the beauty of both the objects and the houses. In fact, it was probably what made the movement succeed, as it allowed the middle and working classes for the first time to own houses that were economical, artistic, and practical (bungalows and other Arts and Crafts–era houses were the first truly "modern" houses, with indoor plumbing, central heating, and electricity). Before bungalows, at least in the nineteenth century, no one had made a virtue of simplicity, low cost, or ease of construction; these things had merely been viewed as cheap but not desirable.

A street of bungalows is shown in the August 1920 issue of *American Builder,* a magazine published by William Radford, who also sold plan books. The article accompanying the photo discusses the postwar housing shortage, and suggests that "the man who owns his own home is not liable to drift around the country. He is an integral part of the community." I particularly liked the photo's caption: "Contented Homeowners Take Pride In Their Citizenship And Are Immune to Professional Agitators of Discontent."

two plan books of designs. No doubt there were people who just took the photo and floor plan to a builder and had it copied, or builders who built from plan books without actually purchasing the plans. There is also evidence that many of the plan book publishers copied the designs of well-known architects and published them as their own, maybe with slight alterations.

Sears published its first book of house plans in 1908, and would also supply almost everything necessary to build the house. A few years later the company began to offer ready-cut home kits. It was not the first company to offer precut buildings; that honor goes to the Aladdin Company of Bay City, Michigan, which offered its first precut building, a boathouse, in 1906. By 1910, the company was publishing a hundred-page catalog of bungalows and other house styles, as well as garages, barns, and even small apartment buildings.

Other ready-cut companies followed suit, such as Lewis Homes and Sterling Homes, also of Bay City; Bennett Homes of North Tonawanda, New York; Gordon Van-Tine Homes of Davenport, Iowa; California Ready-Cut Bungalows and Pacific Ready-Cut Homes of Los Angeles; Robinson's Money-Saving Mill-Made Cut-to-Fit Houses of Providence, Rhode Island (a real tongue-twister, and a little hyphen-happy to boot); Ready-Built House Company and The Rice-Penne Company of Portland, Oregon; The Ainslie-Boyd Company of Seattle, Washington; and the Thayer Portable House Company of Keene, New Hampshire. There were probably others even more obscure than some of these.

Plan books evolved from the "carpenter's handbooks" of the eighteenth and nineteenth centuries. By the early twentieth century, there were probably hundreds of plan books, including Gustav Stickley's *Craftsman Homes* and *More Craftsman Homes*, which featured houses taken from the pages of the magazine. Other plan books available at the time included *Our Book of Attractive Small Homes* by the Beatty Lumber Company of Morris, Illinois; *Central's Book of Homes* by the Central Lumber Company of Reading, Pennsylvania; *Radford's Artistic Bungalows* by the Radford Architectural Company of Chicago, Illinois; *California Homes Book of Houseplans* by Dixon and Hillen of Oakland, California; *Loizeaux's Plan Book No. 7* by the Loizeaux Lumber Company of Plainfield, New Jersey; *Building With Assurance* by the

Morgan Woodwork Organization of Chicago, Illinois; *One Hundred Bungalows* by the Building Brick Association of America in Boston, Massachusetts; *Artistic Homes* by Herbert Chivers of St. Louis, Missouri; *Attractive Homes* by J. W. Lindstrom of Minneapolis, Minnesota; *Little Bungalows* by Stillwell and Company of Los Angeles, California; *The Bungalow Book* by Charles E. White Jr. of New York; *Artistic Bungalows* by the Architectural Construction Company, *Allen Bungalows* by the W. E. Allen Company, *The Bungalow Book* by the Standard Building and Investment Company, and *Bungalows* by Edward E. Sweet, all of Los Angeles; as well as plan books by The Bungalowcraft Company, Ye Planry, Stillwell and Company, of Los Angeles, California; The Craftsman Bungalow Company and the Long Building Company of Seattle, Washington; Harris Bros. of Chicago, Illinois, and the aforementioned Henry L. Wilson, who called himself The Bungalow Man. Wilson also published *Bungalow Magazine* from 1907 to 1912. In 1912 he sold it to Jud Yoho of the Craftsman Bungalow Company in Seattle, where it continued to be published until 1916.

The bungalow's popularity spread from the West Coast to the East Coast, contrary to the way that architectural styles had traveled across America in the past. The bungalow even made its way to Australia via California rather than Britain, and the style there is called "Californian Bungalow." Certainly the West Coast, particularly California, embraced the ideal of the bungalow and unquestionably ran with it. Because of plan books and precut houses, bungalows in the United States and Canada share stylistic similarities even though there are regional differences in climate, locally obtainable building materials, skills of available workmen, and innate preferences of builders and owners. Nonetheless, each city added its own flavor to the basic bungalow recipe, so bungalows across North America differ in subtle and not so subtle ways.

The real heyday of bungalows lasted from about 1900 until the end of World War I, pretty much corresponding to the demise of the Arts and Crafts movement, which is generally agreed to have ended with Elbert Hubbard's death on the *Lusitania* in 1915 and Gustav Stickley's bankruptcy in 1916. After the war, bungalows continued to be built but in a much simplified style, and the ascendance of the Romantic Revival styles (Tudor, Normandy, Spanish) cut into their popularity. Nonetheless, bungalows were still popular well into the 1930s, though by that time they were no longer trendy. Yet the plan books and precut house companies continued to offer them even as their popularity declined. (In a similar vein, ranch houses are still being built, long after *their* heyday in the 1950s and 1960s.)

Are you still confused? This is probably why: architecture isn't simple. Any given house represents the convergence of *plan* or *type* (how the house is arranged; types include four-square, I-house, shotgun, hall-and-parlor, etc.), *time period* (for instance, Victorian is a time period, not a type of house), and *decorative style* (the shape of the box and the stuff that's on it and in it—a house of the Victorian

Below: The 1909 Thorsen House in Berkeley, California—one of Charles and Henry Greene's "ultimate bungalows"—still shows the elements common to many bungalows in California and elsewhere: shingle siding, casement windows, exposed beam ends and rafter tails, clinker brick, and the integration of indoor and outdoor spaces through porches, trellises, pergolas, and landscaping.

Above: Archetypal triangular knee braces hold up the roof gable as well as a small roof over the front window of this bungalow. A stone pier topped by a tapered column defines the entry. And I have to keep harping on this: Don't paint your trim white!

time period might be Italianate, Second Empire, or Queen Anne in style). Complicated enough for most things. Then there's the fact that the interior architecture may or may not match the outside. But bungalows add another dimension: philosophy. Although bungalows have an informal plan, are of a certain time period, and come in different styles with names like Craftsman, California, Japanesque, Swiss Chalet, Prairie, Rustic, and so forth, they are also based on a philosophy that is the foundation for how they are built and furnished, for how people expected to live in them, and for how residents related to the larger society of which they were a part.

Okay, that's all well and good but it still doesn't tell you what a bungalow is. At least part of the problem is that it's a "know one when you see one" kind of thing. Of course, the good thing about being the author is that you get to make up your own definition. So here's mine: A bungalow is a one- or one-and-a-half-story house of simple design and expressed structure, built from natural or local materials, with a low-slope roof, overhanging eaves, and a prominent porch, built during the Arts and Crafts period in America (approximately 1900 to 1930).

Although there are many people who allow for Spanish, Tudor, Colonial, Cape Cod, and even ranch houses as bungalows if they are one or one-and-a-half stories, I'm drawing the line there. Well, sort of. Because everything in the above definition has an exception—for instance, the dates. There were bungalows built after 1930, and in fact the National Park Service maintained the style for park buildings long after the bungalow era was technically over. And here's another thing—there's no such thing as architectural purity. So a bungalow may have some classical detailing normally found on a Colonial Revival house—things like neoclassical columns or dentil molding. Or a bungalow may have arched windows or a Mission-style gable that would normally be found on a Spanish Revival house. Many bungalows have a medieval English influence as reflected in half-timbering or diamond-pane windows. And don't even get me started about the cognitive dissonance between the outside architecture of a house and the interior style. So I'm going with the legal requirement in a civil suit: a preponderance of the evidence. The house needs to have a critical mass of bungalow "details" (thus the name of the book) in order to qualify as a bungalow. After you see enough bungalows and learn to recognize the details that make a house a bungalow, you too should be able to "know one when you see one."

Left: The double front-facing gable is a classic bungalow design. This is a raised basement model (sometimes referred to as "high-waisted" or "high water") with decorative half-timbering in the gables and a tri-partite front window, which usually consists of a large fixed window flanked by two smaller operable windows. These are sometimes called "Chicago windows" because of their use on many Chicago office and commercial buildings.

Above: A bungalow in Memphis, Tennessee, features a large gable sheltering the full-width front porch. Red brick and limestone pillars and porch railings are typical of many Memphis bungalows. On the left is a porte cochere, also a common feature. Unfortunately, many have not survived the change from Model T's to SUV's.

Above: Because of its large lot, this Memphis bungalow is approached by a gently curving brick path leading to the generous front porch. Limestone is used for the square columns as well as the chimney.

Left: Bungalows were often set atop an embankment, which in some ways defeats their generally horizontal nature but gives them a certain stature at the same time. Concrete steps lead up to the wide front porch that has a roof supported by square wooden columns. Half-timbering and the ever-popular knee braces decorate the gable ends.

Facing below: Here are Chicago bungalows rendered in gold brick, with shallowly arched front windows, an arch over the entry, and gabled dormers set into hipped roofs. The limestone trim is typical, and the front basement window was often arched to match the windows above it. Limestone corbels projecting from the front of the bay were meant to support a window box.

Above: Chicago bungalows are in a class by themselves. Mostly built after World War I, these bungalows sacrificed the large front porch for a bay-windowed sunroom in the front, which usually featured geometric art-glass windows. They were invariably built of brick, though more expensive face brick was used on the front and cheaper common brick on the sides. Often they had tile roofs, and most were one and a half stories with a staircase to the upper floor built in, allowing families to expand into that space as needed. They were built extremely close together (five or six feet apart), with about 80,000 of them in the "Bungalow Belt" (what is now called inner-ring suburbs or streetcar suburbs). They were built as working-class housing, and they still are for the most part.

CHAPTER TWO

ROOM TO MOVE

Bungalows by and large are laid out informally, with rooms often opening into one another for the illusion of more space and a minimum of hallways. Since there is no typical plan, a lot of bungalows, especially on narrow city lots, have the living room, dining room, and kitchen on one side and the bedrooms and bath(s) on the other. Though many bungalows have entry halls, many lack them and the front door opens directly into the living room. Dining and living rooms are often open to one another, separated by an arch or colonnade, or possibly by a wide doorway with pocket or french doors, or sometimes only by half-height walls, adding to the illusion of spaciousness in a small house. Dining rooms may also have doors to the front porch or to a separate porch, part of the blurring of indoors and outdoors that bungalow designers considered essential. The kitchen is usually near the dining room, although it may be separated by a butler's pantry, even in a modest bungalow where they were not likely to have had servants. Bedrooms may open directly off the living room, dining room, kitchen, or other rooms, or there may be a hallway. In a one-and-a-half-story bungalow, the stairway to the second floor may start in the entry hall (if there is one), or in the living room or dining room. Occasionally, stairs will come up from the back of the house instead, near the kitchen. Breakfast rooms or nooks are generally off the kitchen or dining room. Other rooms, sometimes of indeterminate usage (study, library, music room, sewing room, nursery, etc.), as well as the occasional half-bath, were fitted in where space was available.

A wide doorway with tall square columns makes for a grand opening into the dining room. The small recessed squares have inserts of burled wood. The soft yellow color of the walls enhances the tones of the woodwork and the oak flooring.

Facing: Tapered columns with recessed panels atop a half wall separate the dining room from the living room and entry hall in this petite bungalow. The colonnade and trim are made of Douglas fir, the most common wood used in bungalows on the West Coast, though it was also found in many precut houses from companies with mills in the Pacific Northwest or California.

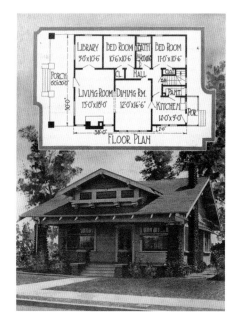

HALL AND PARTIALLY ENCLOSED STAIRCASE IN "GREYROCKS" AT ROCKPORT, MASSACHUSETTS
Frank Chouteau Brown, Architect, Boston, Massachusetts

The side-gabled bungalow with a dormer was probably the most popular style nationwide. This one, shown in the August 1920 *American Builder,* has a very typical layout as well, with the living room, dining room, and kitchen on one side; the bedrooms and bath on the other; and an extra room (here labeled as a library) opening off the living room through french doors. Note the generous size of the living and dining rooms compared with the rather tiny bedrooms. On the outside, the best thing about this bungalow is the way the clinker brick porch pillars and chimney seem to melt as they get close to the ground.

An entry hall sketched by architect Frank Chouteau Brown was published in the 1918 *Cyclopedia of Architecture, Carpentry, and Building* (first published in 1907, this sketch is labeled "06"). At one end, double entry doors open to the porch, with a view of the ocean beyond. A massive round porch column can be seen at the right side of the door. Just inside the door, there appears to be a small nook off to one side, with an unusual round window. The ceiling of the hall is beamed, and the walls have battens over plaster. Turned spindles are set into the wall separating the stairway from the entry. Note the top hat and cane on the table (I don't know about you, but I always take my top hat to the beach).

The angled hallway of a Seattle bungalow has doors everywhere you look, and a couple that can't be seen. Board-and-batten wainscoting covers the walls to shoulder height, with painted plaster above.

Coming directly after the Victorian period as they did, bungalows hadn't entirely lost the excessive numbers of doors to which Victorian houses were prone. In Victorian houses, doors allowed rooms to be closed off when not in use in order to save heat. Although bungalows had moved away from this custom as central heat became more common, they could still be pretty door-happy. Kitchens especially may have three, four, or even more doors leading into them. Bathrooms may also have a lot of doors, as they were often placed between two bedrooms (sometimes known as a Jack-and-Jill bathroom), and those may have even had a third door into a hallway. A bathroom opening off a hallway may also have a door leading into one of the bedrooms.

HALL OFF

The informality of bungalows was such that many times the front door opened directly into the living room, though this was also a space-saving device. But others were provided with a small entryway or vestibule. Often this contained a small bench or a built-in place for hanging coats, sometimes

a mirror. The stairway to an upper floor, if there was one, might be a feature of the entry hall as well.

SETTLE INN

Woodwork left in a natural finish was also a defining feature. It was second only to the fireplace in its quasi-religious significance, and it was almost taken for granted that the woodwork would be left that way. After all, it was made entirely of old-growth timber, which was part of the blurring of inside and out so prized by Arts and Crafts designers. (There were a few people who actually worried about the depletion of old-growth forests even then, but for the most part they were ignored.) Stickley wrote,

> We need not dwell upon the importance of using a generous amount of woodwork to give an effect of permanence, homelikeness, and rich warm color in a room. Anyone who has ever entered a house in which the friendly natural wood is used in the form of wainscoting, beams, and structural features of

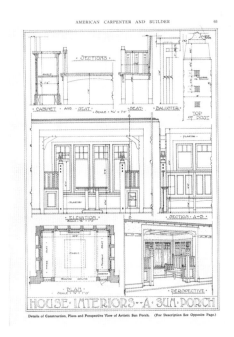

all kinds, has only to contrast the impression given by such an interior with that which we receive when we go into the average house. . . .

Often the beams and structural features were fake, but, as Charles Keeler pointed out, ". . . they are a most effective decoration with their parallel lines and shadows."

Books were important, as evidenced by the fact that almost all bungalows had built-in bookcases. After all, before television, people actually used to read books.

BUFFET THE VAMPIRE SLAYER

Difficult as it may be to believe, in bungalows, people ate in the dining room. Eating dinner together was considered an important part of family life, when news of the day would be exchanged—not like today, when the dining room is lucky to be used on holidays and for the occasional dinner party. The dining room in a bungalow was actually meant to be used for other meals as well. With the advent of breakfast nooks, however, breakfast, lunch, or tea might have taken place more informally in the kitchen, but dinner was always eaten in the dining room.

Because the dining room was often open to the living room, it shared similar décor: lots of woodwork, often wainscoting topped with a plate rail (perfect for showing off decorative objects), and almost always a built-in china cabinet or sideboard. Some bungalows had french doors leading to an outdoor porch for summertime meals in the open air. In *The Furnishing of a Modest Home,* the author remarked, ". . . the dining room should face the east, that it may have the good cheer of the morning sun to help awaken and

Left: The December 1915 issue of *American Carpenter and Builder* featured plans for a sunporch designed by architect Ralph W. Ermeling. The accompanying article mentions that the entrance to a sunporch is generally through glazed double doors, but in this case the separation is accomplished using two posts and a balustrade. He also points out that the glass in the porch can be removed and replaced with screens in warmer weather.

Right: The classic bungalow fireplace setup is shown in a bungalow in Victoria, British Columbia. High windows on either side of the chimney, bookcases with glass doors flanking the stone fireplace, an overmantel with brass light fixtures on either side of a built-in mirror, and, of course, Stickley's "generous amount of woodwork" give a cozy feeling to the small living room of this home.

arouse to activity those members of the family who have a tendency to continue unduly their dormant condition." (Personally, I like to continue unduly my dormant condition whenever possible.)

Many people tell me they never use their dining room and I always reply, "Why? Is there a force field around it?" Even if you don't eat there, it makes a fabulous library.

Some bungalows, even quite modest ones, may have had a butler's pantry between the dining room and the kitchen. This is where dishes, glassware, and silverware were kept, often table linens as well, and it frequently included a sink for washing the dishes, as it was believed to be unsanitary to have dishwashing and food preparation in the same room.

OFFICE POLITICS

In many bungalows, there would be a small room off to one side that was either set up as a study or den (always for the

Above: The dining room of a Tacoma, Washington, home built in 1901 has Arts and Crafts as well as Colonial Revival elements. The simple paneling is topped by high cabinets with glass doors for dishes and glassware. A combination gas and electric light fixture (now electrified) hangs from a star-shaped wallpaper medallion on the ceiling. In the background, an Arts and Crafts sitting room that was added to the house in 1907 features a Grueby-tile fireplace and a custom hand-painted mural as a frieze on the upper part of the wall.

Below: A large butler's pantry graces the Robinson House in Pasadena, California, designed by Charles and Henry Greene. Shown here during its (now completed) restoration, it has upper cabinets with glass doors for china and crystal, with drawers and doors below for silverware, serving pieces, and linens. At the far end is an icebox framed in nickel-plated metal.

man of the house), or else with its function not so obviously defined. If set up as a study, it usually contained more built-in bookcases, possibly a built in desk, and other built-in cabinets. Usually there were lots of woodwork and other things that would be considered masculine. This is where the man of the house might retire after dinner to read the paper, smoke a cigar, or pay the bills. If the function was less defined, it might just be a small extra room that could be used as a nursery, a sewing room, a music room, a library, or whatever the members of the household desired. It might contain a Murphy bed in case it was used for guests, another space-saving idea.

VICTUAL REALITY

Kitchens require an entire book unto themselves, which is why I wrote one. It's called *Bungalow Kitchens* (Gibbs Smith, Publisher, 2000), and it is readily available at your local bookseller and on the Internet. I encourage you to buy it, not just because I need the money, but because it will answer nearly every question you could possibly have regarding your kitchen. I am not rehashing the whole thing here, lest this volume turn into *War and Peace*. I am providing a very basic overview.

The kitchen was the most complex room in a bungalow, as it is the most complex room in a modern house. But in bungalows it was a workroom, a utilitarian space, rather than the central place in the home it has become in our century. Nonetheless, it was pretty functional even by twenty-first-century standards and compared to what had come before. Stickley wrote: ". . . the luxuries of the properly arranged modern kitchen would have been almost unbelievable a generation ago." Whether the kitchen in any given bungalow lived up to those standards depended much on the designer. Since most of the designers were men who didn't actually cook, it was often a hit-or-miss proposition.

The first "modern" kitchens—in the sense that they had stoves, refrigeration, electricity, and indoor plumbing—came about in the latter half of the nineteenth century. Though a kitchen of that era might look primitive from our viewpoint, it was still miles ahead of earlier kitchens, where cooking was done in fireplaces, refrigeration was nonexistent, and water had to be carried in. By 1900, the basic kitchen elements we have come to take for granted were in place: ranges, refrigerators, indoor plumbing, electric lighting, storage cabinets, and even concepts about efficiency we are still using, such as continuous countertops and the work triangle. Though there have been technological advances since then (undercounter dishwashers, microwaves, garbage disposals), these basic elements have remained much the same. Futuristic predictions made in the twentieth century about what kitchens would be like in the twenty-first century have mostly been proven wrong—we're not living like the Jetsons. And frankly, I don't know anyone who wants to surf the Internet while standing in front of a fridge.

The elements that make up a historic kitchen are fairly standard, and by picking a combination of appropriate elements, it's possible to have a kitchen that incorporates modern technology yet still looks right in an older home.

The right cabinets are the most important element in making a kitchen look period appropriate. Historically, cabinets were face-framed (as opposed to frameless European-style cabinets), with flush inset frame-and-panel doors (in a style now known as "Shaker" doors—square stiles and rails around a flat panel). Overlay doors (frame and panel) began to appear in the 1920s, influenced by the doors on hoosier cabinets. (Flat "slab" overlay doors, made of plywood, began to appear in the 1940s.) Panels in the doors could also be glass, either plain or with muntins. Drawers were either inset or 3/8-inch overlay, running on wooden glides. Old cabinets lacked the toe kicks of modern cabinets—the face frame extended down to the floor. (Toekicks started to appear after 1910.)

The lower cabinets were shallower than the standard 24-inch depth used today, ranging from 15 to 22 inches deep, though the upper cabinets were 12 inches deep, as they still are. However, they were often hung lower than modern cabinets, 12 to 14 inches above the countertop rather than the 18 inches that is now standard. This can make it difficult to fit small appliances underneath. Unlike many modern cabinets, the upper cabinets went all the way up to the ceiling rather than leaving the tops exposed to col-

lect that lovely amalgam of dust, grease, and combustion by-products, or by filling the gap with a space-wasting soffit. True, the top shelves can't be easily reached, but that's why they're used to store things that aren't used often.

Custom storage abounded, with tilt-out bins for 50-pound bags of flour and sugar (a popular modern usage for these bins is pet food or recycling storage), corner cabinet lazy Susans, sliding shelves, and so forth. There were also such specialty cabinets as California coolers, a ventilated cabinet with wire or slatted shelves that used the chimney effect to draw cool air up from the basement or crawlspace. These were used to store foods that didn't need to be really cold, like potatoes, onions, garlic, and even wine. Another

Left: *The Universal Design Book on Builder's Woodwork,* published in 1927, shows a complete set of prefabricated kitchen cabinets, including a built-in icebox (at right), a broom closet, a tilting flour bin, and a breadboard. By the 1920s cabinets had developed toekicks, whereas earlier cabinets had been built right down to the floor. The cabinets were supplied unpainted but are shown in the illustration with a two-tone paint job, which was a popular treatment for kitchen cabinets in the 1920s.

Above: A shallow recessed cabinet with glass doors adds some extra storage space to the kitchen of a Seattle bungalow. The back of the cabinet is beadboard (1-by-4-inch tongue-and-groove paneling), which is the traditional backing for cabinets that were built off-site rather than being built in place.

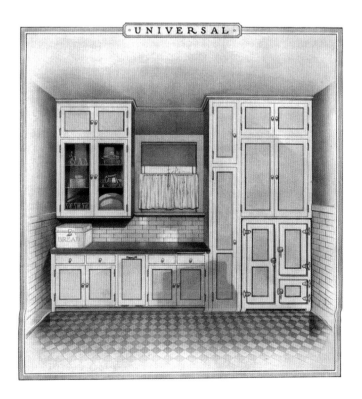

Above left: Another item offered in the 1927 *Universal Design Book* was this combination kitchen cabinet and dining room sideboard. Sliding panels, mirrored on the dining room side, allowed dishes to be passed back and forth. The doors on the upper cabinet were glass on the dining room side and solid on the kitchen side. Each side has the same layout of doors and drawers, though the kitchen side is painted and has bin pulls, while the dining room side is stained and has brass knobs.

Above right: A redone kitchen in a Pasadena, California, bungalow utilizes maple countertops over traditional cabinets with square-edge inset doors and flat panels. The upper cabinets have glass doors. In the background, a vintage O'Keefe and Merritt stove backs up to a low wall that divides the kitchen. The floor is new marbleized linoleum.

Below left: In spite of the obsession with white enamel and cleanliness, many bungalow kitchen cabinets were varnished rather than painted, like these cabinets shown in a 1915 issue of *American Carpenter and Builder*. Cabinets built all the way to the ceiling, with smaller doors on top, were a typical installation. A wall-hung sink built into the cabinets still has separate hot and cold taps, although mixing faucets had been available for more than a decade.

Below right: A built-in ironing board was often found in the kitchen. This particular one has a built-in metal rest for the iron. Most built-in ironing boards were meant to be used while sitting down, as there was a great deal more ironing in those days.

specialty cabinet was the built-in ironing board, though many of these have been turned into spice racks. And of course, the hoosier cabinet (now a generic term; Hoosier was one of many manufacturers) was prevalent in many households. Meant to be a complete food preparation center, hoosier cabinets are the Swiss Army knife of kitchen cabinets, with built-in flour sifter, canisters for sugar and spices, pull-out work surface, and utensil storage. There weren't any kitchen islands as we know them, only worktables, though many of these had built-in storage.

Most historic kitchen cabinets were made of the least expensive local wood, usually pine or fir, although other woods were used. Cabinets were either varnished or painted with enamel in shades anywhere from off-white to beige, as white was considered "sanitary"; they were really obsessed with sanitation at that time.

Cabinet hardware was also standardized. Hinges were either ball-tipped mortise hinges, surface-mount butterfly hinges, or surface-mount offset hinges for overlay doors. Doors latched with spring-loaded cupboard catches, hexagonal glass knobs, or simple wood or brass knobs. Drawers opened with metal bin pulls, glass-bridge handles, hexagonal glass knobs, or wood or brass knobs. In the Victorian period, the metal hardware often had elaborate patterns formed by lost-wax casting, but by 1900, the hardware had become much plainer. Metal hardware was usually brass or nickel until chrome became popular in the mid-1930s. The hardware was meant to be seen—the composition of hinges, knobs, drawer pulls, and such was an integral part of the design of the cabinetry.

Countertops are the most difficult element in the kitchen, since there is no perfect countertop. In the past, the most prevalent countertop was varnished wood. This was and is fine in many parts of the kitchen but problematic around the sink, where it is subject to water damage, or near the stove, where hot pots are likely to burn it.

The second most-prevalent countertop is ceramic tile. White hexagonal porcelain tiles or other small mosaics were common, although sizes up to 4 by 4 inches were used. Backsplashes tended to be 3- by 6-inch subway tiles laid in running bond like bricks, though 4- by 4-inch tiles were also employed. From the late nineteenth century through 1920, tile was white, maybe with a colored border or liner. In the twenties and beyond, wild color combinations like jadeite green and black, burgundy and yellow, lavender and peach, and even three- and four-color combinations appeared, although white continued as well. There are drawbacks to tile: a glass will break if dropped on it, and the grout gets dirty. Using stain-resistant epoxy grout, choosing a grout that's the color of dirt, and applying a sealer can take care of this last problem. Also, old tile was traditionally laid with minimal grout joints (1/16 inch or less), making for less grout to clean.

The third most-popular countertop, surprisingly, was

linoleum. Someone probably decided that if it held up well on the floor, then it would hold up equally well on the counter; and the coincidence was that, when laying a sheet of linoleum, the part that had to be cut out to allow for the cabinet was the exact same size as the cabinet itself. It was also added to a lot of previously wooden countertops. Stone countertops were fairly rare—there might be a marble pastry slab in an upper-middle-class kitchen, and occasionally a soap-

Above: A shallow cabinet with detailing that echoes the door and window trim of this Seattle bungalow showcases the owner's collection of vintage packaging. Below it, an oak table awaits use for casual meals in the kitchen.

Below: Not all butler's pantries had copper or nickel silver sinks. In this home in Berkeley, California, a white porcelain undermount sink is set into a wooden countertop. Hot and cold taps are mounted in the subway-tile backsplash.

Above: Porcelain lever handles operate a wall-mounted mixing faucet in the kitchen of a Seattle bungalow. Most kitchen plumbing and hardware was nickel-plated until the 1930s, when chrome became more popular. On this faucet some of the nickel has worn off, exposing the brass underneath. The copper backsplash was made by the owner.

Below left: Flanked by a small cabinet, a 1920s Wedgewood dual-fuel stove (gas and wood) stands on high legs on the linoleum floor of a 1906 bungalow in Oakland, California. The wood-burning side is on the left, and on the right is a high oven with a broiler beneath. Beadboard wainscoting covers the walls to a height of four feet, continuing behind the cabinets to form a backsplash.

Below right: The Monitor-top electric refrigerator was introduced by General Electric in 1927, and instantly became a best seller in spite of its $500 price tag, which was a great deal of money at the time. Advertised as having a "huge seven cubic foot capacity," it was still superior to an icebox. The round "Monitor-top" contains the compresser. They were nearly indestructible, which is shown by this still-functioning model in the kitchen of a Seattle bungalow.

stone or slate countertop would be installed, but the currently popular granite is very wrong for a historic kitchen.

I detest Corian, but some of the newer composite countertop materials aren't too bad. Products like Fireslate, Silestone, and even concrete have an appropriate look. A

fairly new product called Richlite, made from paper pulp and phenolic resins, also has the right look. Even some patterns of laminate with a matte finish and a wooden edge molding don't look too bad. It is perfectly legitimate to use different countertop materials in different areas of the kitchen—tile or stone near the sink and stove, wood or linoleum elsewhere.

Kitchen floors generally used 3/4- by 4-inch tongue and groove boards that were varnished, painted, or covered with linoleum. Occasionally, hardwood flooring (oak or maple) was installed. Fancier houses sometimes had ceramic tile floors, either hexagonal tiles or quarry tiles.

Sinks were almost always white porcelain over cast iron. There were two kinds: 1) sinks with built-in drainboards and backsplashes, which were wall-hung but often had decorative legs, or occasionally sat on top of cabinets, and 2) undermount or tile-in sinks, which were set into tiled countertops. Undermount sinks are still widely available from the major fixture companies. The currently popular farmhouse-style sinks were primarily used in the nineteenth century, and not all that often even then. Butler's pantries utilized small copper or nickel silver sinks; these softer metals were thought to be less likely to chip the fine china, which was washed in the butler's pantry rather than in the kitchen. The nickel-plated faucets were wall-mounted rather than deck-mounted as most are today. In the nineteenth century, the faucet would have had separate hot and cold taps, but by the twentieth century, mixing faucets with cross or lever handles was the norm.

Vintage stoves are popular at the moment, and you could pay up to $30,000 for a restored double-oven Magic Chef, though many vintage stoves cost far less than that. If you want more of the modern bells and whistles like electronic ignition and sealed burners, companies such as Elmira and Heartland make vintage-looking stoves with modern components. A fairly simple (and therefore inexpensive) modern stove also can be unobtrusive in a historic kitchen. The current fad for restaurant stoves can, I believe, be traced back to sometime in the late 1970s/early 1980s when MEN became interested in cooking. Naturally, they couldn't cook on those little ranges that women had been using for years; no, they required BIG PROFESSIONAL POWER TOOLS WITH LOTS OF BTUs because they weren't cooks, they were CHEFS. Of course, nowadays, people who don't cook at all insist on having restaurant stoves—I guess they're for the caterers.

Refrigerators are a little more difficult to deal with, being kind of large and hard to disguise. Only a few people want actual vintage refrigerators since they have to be manually defrosted, but they are available. (Sometimes people put a vintage fridge in the kitchen but have a modern fridge hidden elsewhere.) For lots of money, a "fully integrated" fridge that can be completely covered with wood panels is an option, as are the refrigerator drawers made by a couple of companies. There are companies that build replicas of wooden iceboxes with modern refrigeration components inside, and Mueller, a German company, makes a modern fridge that resembles a

1930s refrigerator with rounded corners and chunky chrome hardware—available in 242 different colors!

Dishwashers also come "fully integrated" with all the controls on the top edge so the front can be completely covered with wood. I would stay away from putting a wood panel on a regular dishwasher—it probably draws more attention to the dishwasher than leaving the existing panel on it. A dishwasher can also be recessed into an extra deep cabinet with a regular cabinet door to disguise it. Compact dishwashers are only slightly larger than a microwave and can fit into small spaces or under old counters that aren't deep enough for the usual 24-inch-deep unit.

Obviously there were no microwaves until recently, but it's easy enough to hide one in a cabinet.

Electricity was available, so kitchens would have had electric lights and plugs, just not as many as we are used to. There would have been a ceiling fixture in the middle of the room, possibly a light over or next to the sink, and maybe another over the range. All of these would have been simple nickel-plated fixtures with simple shades, or even just a bare lightbulb on a cord or chain, and are readily available as reproductions. The art-glass chandelier belongs in the dining room, not the kitchen. You can have as many visible fixtures as you like. Today's kitchens seem overly lit—at least I've never found myself standing in an old kitchen thinking, "Geez, I can't SEE anything." But if you want to add well-disguised under-cabinet lighting, go ahead.

Historically, ventilation tended to be passive—a plaster or painted metal hood over the range that was simply connected to a vent in the roof, using the chimney effect of rising heat to draw out smoke and steam. Electric fans mounted on an outside wall were also employed. It is possible to buy just the guts of a stove hood—the fan and light—to retrofit old hoods or to use in new custom hoods. If there are cabinets over the range, there are also retracting hoods available, which virtually disappear when not in use.

There are some things that WILL make your kitchen scream "twenty-first century": recessed can lights, which your architect or designer will tell you are unobtrusive; stainless-steel anything (appliances, sinks, countertops), which will be the avocado green of the twenty-first century; granite, not to mention tumbled marble, which is so overdone; fancy art tiles and a copper hood, which belong on a fireplace, not in a kitchen.

PLUMB CRAZY

I wrote a whole book on this subject—*Bungalow Bathrooms* (Gibbs Smith, Publisher, 2001)—as it is quite complex, and, scum-sucking capitalist that I am, I expect you to rush out and buy it if you want to know everything there is to know about bathrooms in bungalows. What I have included here is a very brief summary.

Plumbing was pretty much perfected in the nineteenth century, and the bathroom in a bungalow is still entirely functional even by twenty-first-century standards. At the time bungalows were being built, the key words in bathrooms

Left: The main bathroom at my own house, built in 1905, is typically white and sanitary except for the paint colors chosen by the previous owners. A large Roman tub with a wide rolled rim and ball-and-claw feet sits on a floor of two-inch unglazed hexagonal tiles. This tub was the deluxe model, being glazed on the outside as well, where most claw-foot tubs were merely painted. A low-tank wash-down toilet and an oval sink on legs complete the ensemble. Subway-tile wainscoting with a delicate blue border encircles the walls.

Right: Another sanitary (and very large) bathroom at the 1899 Dunsmuir House in Oakland, California, also features a Roman tub, this time with a painted exterior and gold striping. A high subway-tile wainscot with a graceful border complements a mosaic-tile floor.

Left: In a November 1918 article published in *House Beautiful* titled "Good and Bad Bathrooms," author Joseph T. Sullivan, who didn't think much of this bathroom that would have been state-of-the-art in the late nineteenth century, commented, "As much attention is paid to planning the bathroom, nowadays, as any other room in the house. This was not the case, however, when the bathroom below was equipped." The high-tank toilet, inlaid linoleum floor, exposed plumbing, wood wainscoting, and water heater above the tub had started to be replaced in the 1910s with the double-wall tub (invented in 1911) in a tiled niche, a pedestal

sink, separate tiled shower, and low-tank toilet. That being said, plumbing changes very slowly, so a bathroom like this one could have been installed well into the 1920s.

Above: Typical of bathroom layouts are the tub, sink, and toilet lined up along one wall, as they are shown here. Even allowing for the fact that people were not yet aware of the dangers of asbestos, this ad for asbestos building lumber in the March 1918 *American Builder* is kind of scary on a purely aesthetic level. Suggesting it as a wall finish for the bathroom, the ad states that "the natural gray color is pleasing and

permanent," although allowing, "it can, however, be painted or grained to match the owner's color scheme." Eventually we get to the real selling point: "As pictured it is used for artistic interior work in a bathroom, at the same time fireproofing and obviating the danger where hair curlers, alcohol lamps, etc., are used." And you know, tile is just so darn flammable.

Right: The toilet was often placed in a separate room, a civilized notion that is making a comeback today. This toilet has a round or "pillbox" tank, a style that has once again become available as a reproduction.

Yellow and black tiles mix with white fixtures, including a "ballerina" sink on a narrow pedestal, in a 1932 apartment building in Oakland, California. Four-inch hexagonal tile was used quite often on floors in the 1920s, 1930s, and beyond.

Many eras blend together in the basement bath of this Seattle home. Hexagonal floor tile and beadboard wainscoting combine with an Art Deco– influenced pedestal sink in jadite green, porcelain sconces, and a Victorian-era cabinet.

A deeply sunken shower was added in a 1920s bathroom remodel in an Arts and Crafts house in Hollywood, California. The pipes on the wall provide head-to-toe "needle spray" in addition to the regular showerhead above.

were "sanitary," "white," and "clean." People were worried about germs. According to the Standard Sanitary Manufacturing Company, "Money cannot be invested to better advantage than in a sure source of health and convenience to the entire household. . . . No other part of the house possesses the charm peculiar to the ideally equipped bathroom."

Plumbing fixtures were vitreous china or porcelain over cast iron. Claw-foot tubs were standard up until 1911, when the double-wall tub was introduced, though claw-foot tubs continued to be used after that date. Toilets generally had low tanks that hung on the wall and connected to the bowl with an L-shaped pipe. Sinks were wall-hung or pedestal, and usually had separate hot and cold taps. Showers were installed over tubs or in separate tiled stalls. All the metal parts—faucets, plumbing pipes, towel bars, window and door hardware, etc.—were plated with nickel. Floors were usually tiled, with 1-inch porcelain hexagonal tiles being the most common. There might also be tile or beadboard wainscoting. Walls and woodwork were usually painted with white or off-white enamel. (In 1926, colored porcelain was perfected, which gave rise to bathrooms with wildly colored tile and fixtures, since people realized by that point that germs were color-blind.)

The usual number of bathrooms in a two- or three-bedroom bungalow was one. (Remember, these people were still pretty excited about having indoor plumbing at all.) In a really grand bungalow, there might be a separate bathroom for the maid. Often a half bath off the kitchen or utility porch was provided, and occasionally there was a powder room off the entry hall or under a stairway. Sometimes a half bath or toilet was installed in the basement as well.

SNOOZE TO ME

In the bungalow, the function of the bedroom was primarily sleep. In an average bungalow, the bedrooms were likely to be small—12 by 12 feet is a common size, not that there weren't some that were even smaller as well as some that were larger. Everything was designed to be calm and soothing. Although the woodwork was often left natural in the bedrooms, it was just as likely to be painted, and the wall colors were usually more delicate than in the formal rooms. Built-in furniture such as window seats, dressers, benches, or wardrobes was a feature of some bedrooms. Second-floor bedrooms in one-and-a-half-story bungalows often had sloping or angled ceilings, and bedrooms

might have coved ceilings, though just as often the wall and ceiling met at right angles. Bedrooms were typically plastered, but paneling was not unheard of. The light fixtures were often more dainty in the bedrooms; one of the most popular bedroom fixtures was an oval of stamped metal with a floral or other design in relief, which had two sockets for lightbulbs.

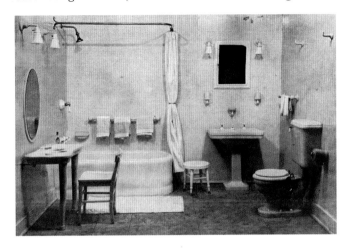

The House Beautiful for November 1918 pictured this modern bathroom with a rounded double-wall tub, large pedestal sink, and low-tank toilet. The porcelain dressing table is unlikely to be found in the average bungalow, but the other items, including sconces, medicine cabinet, towel bars, porcelain hooks, and cupholders were all quite common in bathrooms ranging from modest to grand.

Tile with a stylized Arts and Crafts motif decorates a luxurious shower advertised by the J. L. Mott Iron Works in the June 1918 issue of *House Beautiful*. In addition to the large sunflower-style showerhead, there are nine other spray heads (three on each side). Water must have been a whole lot cheaper back then.

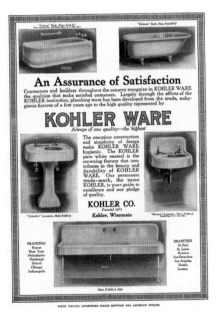

Kohler shows off its various fixtures in an advertisement in the December 1917 issue of *American Builder*. You can see that claw-foot tubs were still available in addition to the double-wall types, and although the tubs had mixing faucets, the sinks retained their separate hot and cold taps.

Sometimes the lightbulb sockets hung from short chains or links attached to the oval. These were often painted, though some were plated, and had "hand-painted" highlights. Sconces in brass or plated finishes were also used.

Bungalow floor plans often saved space by eliminating hallways, or at least making them very short. This means that the bedrooms usually opened directly off some other room—the dining room, the kitchen, the entry hall, and even the living room.

CHINK IN YOUR ARMOIRE

Closets were generally small because people had fewer clothes back then, and they often had small windows, either casement or double-hung. (A tiny double-hung window is adorable.) Some closets had built-in chests of drawers, obviating the need for a dresser; a few had built-in shoe storage; and if the builder was on the cutting edge, he included a clothes chute. In a fancy bungalow, there might be a walk-in closet, which might also have a dressing room containing a built-in dressing table and mirror. Early on, closets didn't have rods, only a few hooks of a type still readily available. These were mounted on a flat 1- by 4-inch board that, as a rule, was mounted about five feet above the floor. A shelf, if there was one, sat on top of this molding. Closets had baseboards as well, usually plain. Some closet walls were plastered, while others were lined with beadboard. Many closets had electric lights, mostly the bare lightbulb variety. Some closets were built as shallow wardrobes, rather like a built-in armoire, and had special front-to-back metal rods for

hanging clothes and sometimes a drawer underneath. Closet doors often had a mirror in place of the usual wooden panel in the center, and, on the inside, may have had a metal turnbuckle thingy (yeah, the technical term) in lieu of a doorknob. Attic hatches were often located in closets.

SLUMBER YARD

At the time that bungalows were being built, there was a lot of belief that "bad air" was responsible for disease. Tuberculosis was prevalent, and fresh air and rest were the only cure, as antibiotics had not yet been synthesized (streptomycin was introduced in 1943). An almost religious fervor had developed around the idea of fresh air and, in particular, sleeping outside in it, no matter the season. Thus was born the sleeping porch. Normally a sleeping porch was off the bedroom with a door between. But sometimes that didn't work with the layout, so the porch would be accessed from an upstairs hallway. In a big house, normally each bedroom would have its own sleeping porch, though not always. Sometimes one porch would serve two or more bedrooms. A sleeping porch was generally covered with a roof, although in climates where it didn't rain

Above: This is the closet we all wish we had in our own bungalow. Designed by Henry Greene for the 1924 Gould House in Ventura, California, a nearly wall-to-wall closet with tall paneled doors, a built-in dresser with a cabinet above, and carved wooden handles.

Right: Another closet at the Gould House features a built-in dresser and cabinet on the left, drawers at the bottom (for shoes?), and double doors in the center. Because this was a secondary bedroom, the doors have glass knobs instead of wooden handles.

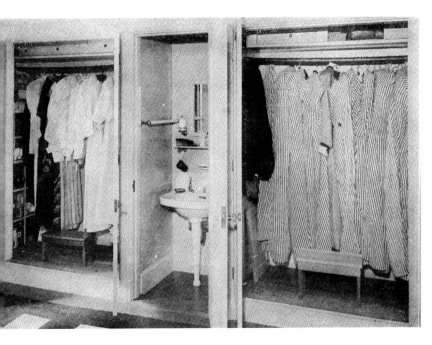

Above: The 1923 supplement to *Woman's Weekly,* called *The Home,* showed an ideal bedroom clothes closet, complete with built-in sink and mirror. Sinks were frequently installed in bedrooms, freeing up the bathrooms for bathing and, um, other matters. Note the built-in shoe storage in the left-hand closet—very civilized. Most bungalows did not have this much closet space because people did not have as many clothes as we do now.

Above right: Plans for a bedroom wardrobe to be built into a dormer were included in the October 1917 issue of *American Builder.* In the accompanying text, architect Ralph W. Ermeling explained, "This is the day of built-in furniture. This is also the day of wardrobe closets. Not everyone is familiar with them as yet, but the principle is right and progressive people demand them." The small door compartment is for hats, while the bottom drawers are actually hinged at the bottom for shoe storage. Presumably there is also hanging space elsewhere in the room.

a lot the porch might be open to the sky. Generally there was a solid railing for privacy, the porches were usually on the sides or back of the house for more privacy, and they were usually on the second floor, although a first-floor sleeping porch wasn't unheard of. It was recommended that the porch be put on some side other than the east so the sun wouldn't wake you up. Above the railing it might be open, but with canvas or bamboo roll-up shades for privacy, sometimes there would be "porch curtains," or the porch would be enclosed by sliding, casement, folding, or even double-hung windows that could be opened or closed according to the weather. Every so often, pocket windows were used, ones that could slide down inside the wall by opening a hinged slot in the sill, or slide into an adjoining wall like a pocket door, making the sleeping porch completely open. Clever bungalow designers also invented things like beds that slid out from the wall, or they used Murphy beds. Sleeping porch floors were primarily wooden, although a sheltered porch might have linoleum or a felt-base rug or possibly a carpet of some sort. On open porches, by and large, the floors were covered with waterproofed canvas or composition roofing.

As the craze grew, sleeping porches were added to houses that hadn't originally been built with them. Later on when people came to their senses and realized that sleeping outside when it's freezing cold is insane, many of the open porches were glassed in. It's still lovely to sleep out there in the summer, although many cities have become too noisy to do this.

AT YOUR SERVICE

Bungalows also had porches in back, which were generally used for utilitarian purposes such as the icebox and the laundry. They may have been glassed in or screened in, depending on the climate, although a few were completely open. Some were more like an anteroom, with only a few windows, and possibly with a small bath (sink and toilet, or just a toilet) in one corner. Every so often there would be a *kitchen porch*, which was kind of like a giant cooler cabinet; it would be screened, and there would be storage for various foodstuffs. Some of these were large enough to serve as an eating area or as a work area that could be used in the summer when it was too hot to be in the kitchen. The utility porch was almost always lined with beadboard, which was usually painted. Back porches were simpler than front

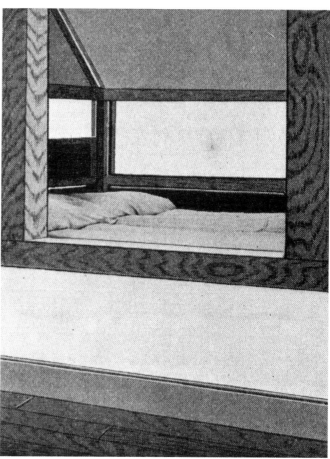

Above left: The sleeping porch of an Arts and Crafts house in Hollywood, California, provides a total of five Murphy beds for outdoor sleeping. Each one folds down from the wall, and the decorative corbels (seen at left) serve as legs.

Above right: If your house had not been provided with a sleeping porch, it was possible to cantilever one off an existing window, not unlike the sleeping berth of a Pullman car. This one, shown in the December 1917 issue of *American Builder,* was constructed of angle iron and provided with a canvas roof that could be rolled back, as well as with wire screening and privacy panels on the sides.

Right: Charles Alma Byers wrote about sleeping porches in the October 1915 issue of *Bungalow Magazine,* saying, "The bungalow usually encourages outdoor living to the highest degree and therefore the open-air sleeping place has come to be recognized as one of its natural accessories. In fact, it may be safely stated that fully one-half of the houses of this type are provided with this feature in some form or other." Shown in the article was this ground-floor sleeping porch in the rear of a bungalow, with screened openings on three sides and a striped canvas shade to control the light.

At the Pratt House in Ojai, California, designed by Charles and Henry Greene, a screened sleeping porch opens onto a roof deck with views across the valley.

porches, often lacking the pillars and other accoutrements of a front porch. A screened porch might only have a screen door, or it might have a regular door, commonly with one or more glass panes. A glassed-in or walled-off porch would have a normal door. From time to time, the back porch would have french doors leading to the outside. Generally there was only a small stoop and a set of steps, which could be wood or concrete. Frequently there was a window between the kitchen and the back porch to allow more light into the kitchen. A stairway leading to the basement might also be located on the back porch.

Sometimes there were also side porches or back porches accessed from the dining room or the bedrooms, often through double french doors. These could be quite large, and the dining porch might be a continuation of the front porch, or they could be small, like a shallow porch off a bedroom, just big enough for a couple of chairs.

For all the Arts and Crafts talk about merging the inside with the outside, and the famous quote, "landscape gardening around a few rooms for use in case of rain," one has to be clear that bungalows were oriented toward the front yard. The backyard was reserved for functional purposes like the vegetable garden, the clothesline, and the incinerator. In the majority of bungalows, access to the backyard is through the utility porch or laundry room, not the wide doors onto a deck that is typical in contemporary houses.

CHAPTER THREE

Given the fairly low roof pitch on most bungalows, the attic is bound to be a "short story." Although we all know what a story is (the space between two floors of a building), it is related to the other kind of story as well. It comes from the Latin *historia*, meaning "history" or "tale," and is thought to have evolved from the pictures or statues lining the walls of medieval buildings.

Roof pitch (or angle) is calculated by the number of inches the roof rises vertically for every foot it extends horizontally. For instance, a roof that rises 6 inches in every foot has a 6-in-12 pitch, and might be found on a bungalow. A 1-in-12 pitch would be nearly flat, and a 10-in-12 pitch would be really steep. Roof pitch not only affects the look of the house, but it may have a bearing on what kind of roof coverings can be used.

ROOF FOR THE HOME TEAM

Although bungalows in India generally had hipped (pyramidal) roofs, many different rooflines are found on bungalows in America. The gable (triangular) roof is probably the most common, consisting of two sloping sides that meet at a ridge. Bungalows may feature one, two, or more gables. A single gable might have its ridgeline parallel to the street (side-gabled) or perpendicular to the street (front-gabled). Multiple gables facing different directions (cross-gabled) are also common. Often the front porch may have a separate gabled roof of its own. A gabled roof with its point clipped is

AN EASY WAY TO FIGURE YOUR ROOF PITCH WITHOUT CLIMBING ON YOUR ROOF

Go up into the attic, with a 2-foot level, a tape measure, and a pencil. A light would be useful as well. Make a mark 12 inches from one end of the level. Place one end of the level against the bottom face of a roof rafter and hold it perfectly level. (For those unfamiliar with levels, that would be when the air bubble in the vial is exactly between the two lines.) Then measure straight up from the 12-inch mark on the level to the underside of the rafter; that measurement is the number of inches that the roof rises in a foot.

This information is useful if you are installing a dormer or a skylight, or planning an addition. You can also use it as a factoid to impress people at parties.

known as a jerkinhead (clipped) roof. Another type of gable roof is the gambrel (often found on barns), which has a lower slope that is steeply pitched and an upper slope that is less steep, allowing for more headroom on the upper

Facing: Vertical-grain Douglas fir was used for built-in bookcases, drawers, and a window seat set into a dormer of this Seattle bungalow. The top of the bookshelf follows the slant of the roof. The upholstered cushion makes a comfortable spot to take in the view of the lake in the distance.

story. The opposite of the gambrel, in which the top slope is steeper and the bottom slope less so, is commonly known as a saltbox (catslide) roof. Less common are various kinds of shaped gables, such as the Dutch gable. These were more often featured as a decorative porch roof. A one-sided gable (shed roof) can be attached either to the roof or to the side of the building. Shed roofs are popular for porches and dormers.

A hipped roof may be either pyramidal (comes to a point) or have a ridge along the top, resulting in two triangular slopes and two trapezoidal slopes. Many gable or hipped roofs may also have what are called kicked (flared) eaves.

Just to confuse things even further, many bungalows have combinations of roof styles—a gabled porch roof with a gambrel roof for the rest of the house, a hipped roof with shed roofs for dormers or porches, gable-roofed dormers set into a hipped roof, etc. The number of possible combinations is mind-boggling.

RAFTER THE DELUGE

Unless it is finished, the structure of the attic roof inside should be visible, consisting of rafters (usually two-by-fours) commonly spaced 24 to 32 inches apart, and connected to a ridge beam (if the roof has a ridge). The term *ridge beam* is somewhat of a misnomer; while there may be a large piece of wood protruding from the gable peak on the outside of the bungalow, in the attic there is probably a flat board (1 by 6 or 8 inches) serving as the ridge. It doesn't really bear any weight, although thicker boards were sometimes used. The rafter tails visible on the outside may also be larger than the actual rafters are. Each pair of rafters is often connected by a horizontal board called a collar tie, which ostensibly keeps the rafters from splaying outward under the weight of the roof. Depending on how far down from the ridgeline these are placed, they can make it difficult to get around in the attic.

A somewhat less common form of roof construction used trusses, an assemblage of wood members that form a rigid framework. Trusses have become popular again in modern buildings because they can be engineered to support the same loads while utilizing smaller and shorter pieces of lumber. Unfortunately, they usually don't leave any headroom in the attic, especially with the low slope of the average bungalow roof.

On top of the rafters there will be some kind of sheathing, either 1) solid sheathing (1-inch by something boards, plywood, or oriented strand board [OSB], depending on how recently the roof was replaced) or 2) skip sheathing (boards with spaces in between). Skip sheathing is used with roof coverings like wood shingles, tiles, or slate.

Board sheathing may be laid either at right angles or diagonally to the rafters. Laying board sheathing in this manner increases the rigidity of the roof, important for resisting damage from earthquakes, hurricanes, and so forth. Sometimes the first layer of roofing is visible in the spaces between the skip sheathing because wood shingles and, often, tiles and slates were laid without an intervening layer of roofing felt (tar paper). Or, in a reroofing job, sheet materials may have been installed directly over the skip sheathing, which will be visible from underneath.

There may also be evidence of changes to the building, such as the addition of dormers or skylights to the roof, or an increase in the square footage from an addition on the back or elsewhere. Often the new framing was made of smooth lumber and will look different from the original framing, which was normally made of rough-cut, slightly shaggy-looking timbers.

In most areas, the allowable number of layers for roof coverings is three; after that, you are supposed to tear them off down to the sheathing and start over. Often this doesn't happen, and there may be four or five roofs on top of rafters, which may be 32 inches apart. That much weight can cause the rafters to bend or even break.

The attic may also have knee walls—low walls that add support for dormers, skylights, or other roof projections. Or sometimes they're just used to close off storage space on the sides in a finished attic.

Built into an attic dormer, a window seat flanked by bookcases offers a relaxing place to read or enjoy the view from the upstairs of a Seattle bungalow. Beadboard wainscoting surrounds the seat, which lifts up for extra storage. Sconces on either side provide light for reading.

DORMER VOUS?

Dormer comes from a French word meaning "sleeping room." A dormer is a smaller roof form projecting from the main roof slope, usually containing one or more windows, or sometimes a door leading to a porch. On a one-story bungalow, dormers may be used to provide light and/or ventilation and, if the roof is steep enough, more headroom in the attic. In a one-and-a-half-story bungalow, dormers provide additional ceiling height in the attic space so it can be used as living area, generally for bedrooms. Often a dormer will be the location of a window seat or other built-in. Sometimes dormers are just there for architectural interest. Ventilation dormers may not have windows at all, only louvers or latticework. These should have screening to prevent insects or animals from getting into the attic. Dormers were frequently used instead of skylights to bring light from the attic to the lower rooms. A skylight or dormer used for this purpose requires a shaft or light well through the attic to the ceiling below.

Dormers are found in all the roof shapes used for main roofs: gable (sometimes called "doghouse" dormers), clipped gable (jerkinhead), hipped, flat, flat with parapet, gabled with parapet, curved (sometimes called "eyebrow" dormers, depending on the curve), arched (a more pronounced curve than an eyebrow), shed, and inset (set into the roof and often combined with an upstairs porch). The roof style of the dormer may not necessarily match the roof style of the house, and there may be more than one kind of dormer style on the same house.

Skylights or roof windows are not common in bungalows, but they are not unheard of. A decorative skylight might use art glass and be installed over a dining room, entry hall, or stairway in combination with a clear glass skylight in the roof above. A more utilitarian skylight would be made of wood or metal, and probably utilize wire glass for strength. Historically, skylights were likely to have been flat or pyramid shaped. Other shapes, such as domes, barrel vaulted, etc., are far less likely on a bungalow, although no doubt there is at least one of these types installed somewhere. Most skylights were fixed, although occasionally an operable skylight is found.

Skylights are useful for bringing daylight to areas of the house that might otherwise be dark. Sometimes art glass skylights would have lighting above the glass to illuminate them after dark as well. Skylights were not typically installed over kitchens or bathrooms as they are today.

A skylight was generally placed on a secondary roof that was not visible from the street, and this is a good rule to follow if adding a new skylight to a bungalow. New skylights should be as small as possible, rectangular or square, and lined up in an even row if there is more than one. Acrylic bubble skylights should NOT be used, nor should the round "sun tunnel" type of skylights.

SKYLIGHTS

OBSESSIVE RESTORATION

It is far better to use a dormer to bring light into the lower parts of the house than to use a skylight.

Old skylights may leak, the wood may be rotted, or the steel in a metal skylight may have rusted though. The glass may need reglazing as well. Stained-glass skylights may have sagged if there was not sufficient support for the leading. Epoxy consolidants may be used to rebuild the rotted parts of a wood skylight. If it is too far gone, it should be replicated with new wood. Steel skylights can also be rebuilt if only small parts are rusted through; otherwise, they should also be replaced in kind. All skylights should be carefully flashed and sealed, and some method put in place to deal with condensation from inside the house. Most new skylights have this as part of the design, but old ones may not.

COMPROMISE SOLUTION

Sometimes a strategically placed skylight can add to the livability of a bungalow, bringing light to the end of a dark hallway or stairwell. Often, new and taller buildings built next to a bungalow may cut off the light from the windows the house had when it was new, and a skylight can be a good solution for that problem. This does not mean it's okay to put a row of five skylights in your kitchen, and don't go crazy putting them in the attic either; consider dormers instead, unless that will change the roofline too drastically.

As above, put a skylight on a secondary roof that is not visible from the street, if possible. Glass is preferable, but acrylic is okay provided that it is FLAT. Bubble skylights and solar tubes are out.

JOIST DESSERTS

Below the rafters, the floor structure of the attic is made up of joists (generally two-by-fours, 16 to 24 inches apart) that support any flooring in the attic as well as the ceilings of the rooms below. The joists rest on the top plates of the perimeter walls as well as on the top plates of any interior load-bearing walls, which generally run down the middle of the house. Some bungalows were built with the idea that the attic could be finished later for more living area; these are likely to have bigger joists that are closer together and better able to support a floor since two-by-fours that are 24 inches apart aren't really strong enough for more than stored boxes. Regardless of that, the attic may or may not have a floor; if it does, it will most likely be made of tongue-and-groove softwood boards (whatever softwood was cheap in the area at the time the house was built). Only part of the attic may have flooring. Unless the attic was made into living space, these boards are commonly left unfinished.

WHY A DUCT?

Many other items may be routed through the attic, including chimneys, plumbing and other kinds of vents, furnace or air-conditioning ducts, water and gas pipes, electrical and other wiring such as low voltage wiring for doorbells and transformers. There may be an overflow tank for the boiler if the heating system utilizes hot water. Newer furnaces may be installed in the attic, especially if the house has a crawl space rather than a basement. Ducts in the attic should be insulated, including those that serve exhaust fans; otherwise, the steam they are supposed to be removing will condense inside the duct and run back down into the house.

VERMINSIMILITUDE

Unfortunately, many little creatures that you don't want in your attic would like to make their home there. Many will get in through existing holes, but others will actually chew their way in. Some may stay in the attic, but others will use the opportunity to migrate to other parts of the house as well. These varmints can be classified in various ways, but generally fall into the categories of bugs, birds, or rodents. And pigeons, of course, which many people consider to be nothing more than flying rodents. Many of the creatures are not actually pests unless they are living in your attic. Bats, which are not rodents at all, fall under the order Chiroptera. They are a fine thing to have outside, where they eat many insects that would otherwise be destroying your garden. Spiders also eat insects and are not much of a problem unless they are poisonous, not to mention providing the all-important cobwebs that no self-respecting attic should be without. This section is not for the faint of heart.

BEEHIVE YOURSELF

Honeybees are our friends. They pollinate flowers and fruit trees, and provide honey. Which is all fine when they're nesting in a tree somewhere. It's a different matter if they decide to nest in your attic or walls. They can chew their way in or enter through an existing hole. Their storage of honey can attract other bees and wasps, and their detritus (dead bees, shed larval skins, pieces of wax, and so forth) also attract beetles and moths. Bees live on stored honey, so a colony can persist for years, getting larger and larger. Bees living inside attics or walls have to be removed or killed (leave this job to professionals). The nest must also be removed; otherwise, the wax, which is normally cooled by the worker bees fanning their wings, will melt and honey will flow down through the ceiling or walls. This is not manna from heaven—it's a huge mess that will attract other insects. Wax moths will feed on the wax for years, dead bees will attract carpet beetles, the honey will attract ants, and you'll never get the honey stain out of the ceiling. Once you dispose of the bees and the nest, be sure to repair the hole(s) where the bees got in.

Bumblebees rarely nest in houses, generally preferring old mouse burrows and the like. They have smaller colonies than honeybees and die off in the winter. The prevalent belief that, according to the laws of aerodynamics, bumblebees shouldn't be able to fly, is only a myth. It's merely that how they fly is extremely complex.

Carpenter bees vaguely resemble bumblebees. They tunnel into wood, particularly the end grain of unpainted wood, and proceed to make tunnels along the grain, which they provision with pollen and use to hatch eggs. They will also tunnel into painted wood if a hole is present. They live only a year, but new females will come every year and reuse the tunnels. Obviously this is not good for the house.

Then there are Africanized bees, the "killer bees" of legend, which have made their way into North America at this point. They are actually the same species as the European bees we already have, but are adapted to a longer warm season from living in South America. The worker bees are more aggressive than their European counterparts and tend to mob intruders.

WASP WASTE

When a bunch of yellow jackets are hanging around your barbecue or buzzing around your soda, you probably ask yourself, "What good are these things anyway?" Actually, yellow jackets and other wasps need meat to feed their larvae, and usually fulfill this requirement with insects like crickets, caterpillars, grubs, or flies, or with meat from dead animals, so that's what they're good for. But they're perfectly happy to feed the larvae hamburger or chicken. The adult wasps don't eat meat—they prefer sweet liquids such as sap or nectar, but they are entirely willing to go with cola or root beer when available. At a barbecue, this is merely annoying, unless you get stung. But if they decide to build a nest in your attic, it becomes more than annoying. Why? Because the nests are built from cellulose chewed out of the wood in your house and mixed with saliva to form a kind of papier-maché; and because if you get near the nest the wasps will attack in order to defend it. Unlike bees, wasps can sting more than once, and once one is upset, it sends out a pheromone that causes all the others to become aggressive and sting anything that wanders into their path.

There are various kinds of wasps, but the most common kinds you might find nesting on or in your house are yellow jackets, mud daubers, paper wasps, and various kinds of hornets. Except for mud dauber wasps, they are all in the same family of insects, Vespidae. Mud daubers are mostly a nuisance, building their tunnel-like mud nests in attics, eaves, or porch ceilings. They are not aggressive, and will sting only if handled, but they can do quite a number on a paint job.

Paper wasps build umbrella-shaped nests that hang from a thick paper strand. The nests are not reused the next year, so empty ones can be safely knocked down in the winter; be sure to scrape off the attachment point as well, or the next year's queens will be inclined to reuse it.

The only true hornet in North America is the giant hornet, found mainly in the northeastern quadrant of the United States. These are big suckers, about an inch long, and favor construction sites and wall voids where they build large nests. They prey on yellow jackets and bees to feed their larvae, and have a very painful sting. Don't mess with them.

Yellow jackets come in eighteen different varieties in North America. Some nest in trees or the ground, but some like building overhangs, wall voids, or attics as well. This mostly becomes a problem if the nest has gotten large and the wasps have chewed their way through the wall or ceiling and into the house, or if the entrance is located next to a door or window.

Unless the nests are quite small, I don't recommend dealing with them yourself, except in the winter after they have been abandoned (and make sure they ARE abandoned). If you have a really nice looking nest you'll be pleased (or horrified) to know that there is a market for them on eBay.

PIGEON ENGLISH

I will admit right here that I used to hate pigeons. Pigeons just love bungalows—they love all the rafters and brackets and spaces under the eaves, and then they poop all over your brand new paint job. But after researching the subject, I have gained, if not fondness, at least tolerance for them. Pigeons are actually rock doves, the traditional dove of love and peace. They mate for life, care for their young together, share feeding areas, and live peacefully with each other—pretty good role models. One of their favorite foods is weed seed, and they have even helped endangered peregrine falcons make a comeback by serving as a food source (though I'm pretty sure they aren't doing that voluntarily). They are overpopulated in many areas, which is our fault because we feed them, thereby producing overpopulation. Plus, we furnish buildings with sheltered ledges and perches very much like the rocks and cliffs where they would normally nest. Nonetheless, their toilet habits are disgusting, though pigeon guano is NOT the great source of disease that it is often made out to be. They usually stay outside, but if there are pigeons in the attic, it means there must be a pretty big hole somewhere, which you might want to close up—AFTER you get the pigeons out of the attic.

(A note: Since I first wrote this part, pigeons have once again taken up residence on my house, had babies, and now my front porch is covered in pigeon poop. My hard-won tolerance is waning rapidly . . .)

Other kinds of birds can get into the attic as well, often through smaller holes than than those used by pigeons. The biggest problem is getting them out, since they tend to panic when you try to catch them. Outside of calling in a professional, the best solution is to throw a towel over them, which gets them down to the floor and allows you to gather them up and take them outside.

BAT'S ENTERTAINMENT

Too many horror movies have given bats a bad reputation. Bats are the only mammal capable of true flight, and also the only insect predator that is out at night. One small bat can eat thousands of insects each night, performing a valuable service for humans. Contrary to the phrase, "blind as a bat," they can actually see pretty well, though they locate insects using echolocation rather than sight. Unfortunately, their response to human encroachment in their environment may be to take up residence in your attic, which is easy for them to do since they can squeeze through a crack as small as three-eighths of an inch wide. Sometimes this also means that one will work its way down into your house from the attic via some crack and be flying around your bedroom trying to get out, which can be a little unnerving.

Attics are favorite bat refuges because they are warm and dark and protected. Bats need a warm place to raise their young and don't build nests for warmth like other species. The young depend on their mothers to feed them until they learn to fly and hunt on their own. If bats have taken up residence in your attic, you may be able to hear the squeaking distress calls of the babies. Usually by summer they have all learned to fly, and in the fall, the bats will travel to a winter hibernation site (they favor caves, abandoned mine shafts, and, unfortunately, wall voids and attics), where they hibernate till spring.

The good news is that bats don't gnaw on anything inside the attic, so the only real problems they bring are fleas and ticks. Oh, and bat guano.

The best way to prevent bats in your belfry, so to speak, is to make sure that holes, cracks, and voids where they might gain entry are caulked or otherwise sealed. Make sure no bats are inside before sealing up all the holes. If they have already made themselves at home, there are effective nontoxic ways to get rid of them. It's no use playing loud music, installing ultrasonic devices, putting mothballs in the attic, or setting up bright lights—these methods don't work. If they are hibernating, you may just have to wait till summer, because the only way to get rid of them is to seal up all the holes while they're out hunting. Make sure to wait long enough that the babies have all learned to fly—you don't want orphaned baby bats dying in your attic.

First you have to find the holes where they are coming and going. You can listen for squeaks, look for bat droppings (about the size of rice grains) on the ground near the house, inspect the siding for brownish stains where oil has rubbed off their coats as they squeeze through a crack, and watch the suspected holes at dusk, which is when they leave to hunt for food. Popular locations for entry include wall and roof joints, loose chimney flashing, unscreened vents, cracked fascia boards, and dormers. Once you've figured out where they are coming and going, you can close all but one hole and make it into a one-way entrance by stapling a piece of screening as a flap over the hole—they can get out but they can't get back in. Once you're sure they are all gone, close up the final hole.

You might want to think about providing them with a bat house outside—that way you get the insect-eating benefits without having them in your attic.

RAT'S ALL, FOLKS!

Eric Idle: *What's for afters?*
Terry Jones: *Well there's rat cake . . . rat sorbet . . .*
    rat pudding . . . or strawberry tart.
Eric Idle: *Strawberry tart?!*
Terry Jones: *Well, it's got some rat in it.*
Eric Idle: *How much?*
Terry Jones: *Three. Rather a lot really.*
Eric Idle: *. . . well, I'll have a slice without so much rat in it.*
    —Monty Python

Rats got a bad reputation when it was discovered that they were carriers (as well as victims) of the bubonic plague, and they've been unpopular ever since. Unfortunately for them, they also carry other diseases, including salmonellosis, Weil's Disease, typhus, and rat-bite fever.

Interesting rat factoids: they can neither vomit nor break wind, they apparently don't like punk rock, and the collective noun for rats is "a mischief."

Before I go any further let me make it clear that I am NOT referring to domesticated rats (often called fancy rats), which are kept as pets. Rat fanciers are a bit touchy, and who can blame them? There's nothing like having an unpopular pet to make one a bit defensive. Nonetheless, there are rat organizations, rat magazines, rat fashion shows, and (my personal favorite) rat haiku (or *ratku*). An example by someone known only as Jane (not me):

I love your closet!
Grinding teeth with excitement!
Do you need this dress?

Or perhaps a real rat haiku by eighteenth-century Japanese poet Taniguchi Buson:

Walking on dishes
the rat's feet make the music
of shivering cold.

Those who are squeamish about rodents should probably stop right here. There are two varieties of rats you may find in your home: *Rattus rattus* (roof rats) and *Rattus*

norvegicus (Norway rats). Roof rats prefer the attic, while Norway rats prefer the basement or crawl space (although they will happily nest in the attic if they make it up there). They can jump two feet straight up and four feet horizontally. They can get through a hole half an inch in diameter, and if the hole isn't big enough they will chew it till it is. They can survive a drop of fifty feet without being seriously injured. They can chew through wood, plastic, soft metals, fiberglass, vinyl, window screening, drywall, and even concrete. Roof rats will access the roof by climbing up the siding, using a handy vine (like that oh-so-Craftsman wisteria on your porch) or tree branch, or, lacking that, they'll come in on the power or telephone line. Once on the roof, they will enter the attic through any available hole they can find or make: exhaust vents, gable vents, holes in soffits, spaces between fascia boards and roofs, etc. Norway rats prefer to burrow, so they will burrow along the foundation and come up through the crawl space, or through unscreened vents, holes around plumbing pipes and other penetrations, and, yes, through the sewer pipes. Although rats emerging from the toilet are not common, it does happen, and, according to the Public Works Department of Everett, Washington, here's what you should do:

1. Close the lid.
2. Flush the toilet five times.
3. If the rat is still there, call Animal Control.

I'm pretty sure a low-flow toilet couldn't flush a rat. But I digress.

Once the rats are in your house, they will get inside the walls, eat and contaminate your food, and gnaw on your electrical wiring, insulation, plumbing, woodwork, clothing, holiday decorations, books, paper, and anything else they can find (rats aren't picky). A rat's average life span is eighteen months, female rats can give birth every twenty-eight days, and one pair of rats can produce 2,000 offspring per year. You do not want those 2,000 offspring in your attic.

What attracts rats? Garbage, birdseed, woodpiles, shrubbery, ivy and other vine-like groundcovers, as well as various things apparent only to rats. Getting rid of food sources is the first thing to do to discourage them.

What to do if you have rats? First, catch the rats. Don't use rat poison—you'll just end up with dead, stinking, oozing rats in your attic, walls, or kitchen cupboards. Live traps are best, but don't just take the trapped rats and release them out in the yard—take them over to the neighbors! Just kidding. Better to take them to an area that is at least semiwild. Then, plug up the entry holes using hardware cloth, concrete, sheet metal, copper dish scrubbers (steel wool will rust), etc. You can also buy a product called Stuf-It, basically a tubular form of copper dish scrubber that comes on a roll. Patching and filling compounds like Fix-All or expanding foam can also be used but only when reinforced with hardware cloth or other metal. Phone and power lines can be blocked with a round piece of metal (about the size of a pie plate) placed on the wire where it reaches the house. Better check with the utility or phone company before doing this. Cut back tree branches that hang over the roof. Then be vigilant—they'll probably be back.

MICE HOCKEY

Just about everything that is true of rats is also true of mice, except mice can only jump about two feet, and they can get through a hole the size of a pencil. Also, certain kinds of mice are carriers of hantaviruses, which cause hantavirus pulmonary syndrome, a potentially fatal disease. Mice shed the virus in their droppings, urine, and saliva. The virus is transmitted when fresh urine, feces, or nesting materials are disturbed, causing tiny droplets containing the virus to become airborne. Humans become infected by breathing in these infected droplets. Some researchers believe it may also be possible to become infected by touching something contaminated by rodents and then touching one's nose or mouth, or by eating rodent-contaminated food.

Precautions to be taken when dealing with areas that are infested by mice, include airing out the area for at least thirty minutes, wearing rubber gloves, spraying the area with disinfectant or bleach solution and allowing it to soak for five minutes, and cleaning up the urine and feces with paper towels (don't vacuum or sweep). Infected clothing or bedding should be washed in hot water and laundry detergent. Carpets and upholstered furniture should be steam cleaned or shampooed.

Besides keeping mice out of the house by plugging holes and so forth, don't give them nesting sites in the yard either. Woodpiles and garbage cans should be at least a foot off the ground. Woodpiles and compost bins should be as far from the house as possible. Mice and rats can also nest in old tires or old cars and trucks, so get rid of those too. And that antique stove sitting in the garage? Same deal: fix it up, use it, or get rid of it. (I'm in trouble—I have two old stoves on my front porch!)

SQUIRRELY YOU JEST
"So if Sunday you're free,
Why don't you come with me,
And we'll poison the pigeons in the park.
And maybe we'll do
In a squirrel or two
While we're poisoning pigeons in the park."
—Tom Lehrer, *Poisoning Pigeons in the Park*

Okay, squirrels are cuter than rats, but that's only because they have fuzzy tails. The problems they cause, and the method of entry, are about the same. Except squirrels are even better at climbing than rats. They don't reproduce as quickly, a small blessing. Squirrels need to be caught in live traps and then released outside. Squirrels are territorial, so squirrels released elsewhere will probably die, whereas the ones in your yard will keep other squirrels out of the area. Then block the holes, as for rats. There is a commercial product called Ropel that can be sprayed around the patched holes or anywhere else you don't want squirrels. Or if you prefer, you can mix a tablespoon of Tabasco sauce with a quart of water and spray that.

RACCOONTEURS

Raccoons are very intelligent animals and they have hands. If they had access to power tools, we would all be in a lot of trouble. Fortunately they don't get cable, and have yet to succumb to the hypnotic power of *The New Yankee Workshop*. They have adapted easily to urban areas, living in storm drains, ivy, dense shrubbery, and so forth. If they're in the attic, there must be a pretty big hole somewhere. (Hollow bungalow porch columns often provide an entry.) Usually they can be driven out by a combination of bright lights (they're nocturnal) and talk radio (no word on whether Rush Limbaugh works better than NPR), combined with removing their food sources (usually pet food, compost bins, garbage cans, and fishponds). They can also be trapped and relocated to somewhere more appropriate. Better lock the pet door at night, too, or they will happily come into the kitchen and make themselves at home. After they're gone, besides blocking off the opening(s) where they got in, you may have to clean up a whole lot of raccoon turds.

MARSUPIAL OF THE DAY

The opossum, or possum, is the only marsupial in North America; the rest of them having stayed in Australia for reasons known only to them. They do actually play dead under stress, but worse, they can leak a nasty smelling green fluid out of their rear, causing potential predators to go, "Eeew! Gross!" and leave them alone. They don't move very fast, so they are pretty easy to catch. But they can be nasty when cornered, so live trapping and relocation is the way to go. As with raccoons, removing food sources, blocking entry points, and locking the pet door will tend to cause them to go elsewhere.

Well, that was a cheery little section, wasn't it?

BATTING A THOUSAND

Fuel used to be cheap, so the majority of bungalows were built without insulation in the walls or the attic. Various kinds of insulation were available at the time, and there were a few builders who took advantage of them. The really low-tech insulation method was to use layers of newspaper, which is always good for providing a clue as to when the house was built or remodeled. Cellulose insulation, which today is primarily made from recycled newspapers, was used at the time as loose-fill insulation, as it still is. Mineral wool or rock wool, an inorganic fibrous material made by steam-blasting furnace slag or molten glass, was often employed, generally as loose fill, but it was also put between layers of kraft paper and stapled between wall studs or laid between ceiling joists. One of the most interesting kinds of insulation was made by Cabot, featuring eelgrass (Zostera marina), an aquatic plant, which was layered between two sheets of kraft paper. Fiberboard, first made in 1921 from a by-product of sugar cane but now generally made from wood scrap, was also utilized. Although glass fibers had been experimented with for years, and a glass fiber dress was shown at the 1893 World's Columbian Exhibition in Chicago, fiberglass insulation wasn't invented until 1938 by Russell Games Slayter at Owens-Corning. The Corning plant in Ohio produced glassware and Slayter was in charge of decorating the glassware with a thin stream of molten glass that issued from a gun. (I assume this was a mechanized process.) He had the idea that if he added air pressure to the gun, the glass would stream out faster. He was wrong about that. Instead, the air caused the glass to form thousands of tiny fibers. It takes the creative mind of an inventor to look at a mistake and wonder if there is any use for it—the same process that gave us Post-It notes.

All the materials used in a house absorb and transfer heat. Heat travels from where it's warmer to where it's cooler through radiation, conduction, and convection, processes that often occur simultaneously:

■ *Radiation* is energy emitted as waves or particles, such as the heat we get from the sun or from standing next to a fire.

■ *Conduction* is heat transferred from molecule to molecule; for example, if you heat a cast-iron skillet on the stove, eventually the handle will become too hot to hold, even though it is not over the flame.

■ *Convection* is the transport of heat through air or liquid —if you hold your hand over the aforementioned cast-iron skillet, you can feel hot air rising from it. As the hot air rises, cooler air is pulled up from below to be heated and also rise. Meanwhile the original hot air, having transferred its energy to the cold ceiling, is no longer hot, so it sinks back toward the floor to start the process again, resulting in what is known as a "convection loop." Insulation is used to slow down or resist (thus, R-value) heat transfer by trapping the heat in air pockets (so-called "dead air" resists heat transfer better than moving air—that's what defines "windchill factor"). Insulation is pretty good at slowing down heat transfer from conduction and convection but doesn't work that well with radiated heat. Radiant barriers (usually some kind of foil) are used to slow down heat transfer through radiation.

Fuel is no longer cheap, so attic insulation is the first line of defense against heat loss, because hot air rises. Insulation also helps somewhat with heat gain in the summer, when the temperature in the attic can reach 140 degrees Fahrenheit. Insulation is rated by R-value, its resistance to heat transfer. Current recommendations call for anywhere from R-38 to R-49 in attics. R-49 would require fiberglass insulation to be 16 inches thick, which would tend to cut down on the usability of the attic. Batt or roll insulation is laid between the ceiling joists, stapled between the rafters in finished attics, or both. It's important for insulation between rafters to have an airspace between the insulation and the inside of the roof if there are soffit vents; special plastic channels can be installed for this purpose. Rigid insulation boards can also be used between rafters. Loose-fill insulation is blown in by special machines, or it can simply be poured.

Fiberglass (as well as rock and mineral wool) has been identified as a possible human carcinogen. Various studies have been done, but so far results are inconclusive. Like vinyl, fiberglass is hard to avoid since there are about a gazillion square feet of fiberglass insulation installed worldwide. Fiberglass utilizes formaldehyde as a binder (also a possible human carcinogen), which can off-gas into living space. Some companies have started to offer formaldehyde-free insulation as well as insulation encapsulated in plastic, which theoretically keeps the fibers from escaping, unless of course you have to cut into it to fit it into a cavity. There seems to be agreement that, as with asbestos, it's often best to leave existing fiberglass alone, or to encapsulate it somehow. Certainly if there is no insulation at all and you are adding some, it might be good to use something besides fiberglass. Batt insulation is easier to install as a do-it-yourself job, and some of the nontoxic varieties also come in batts, though they may cost more. There is some concern that the borates used to make cellulose insulation fireproof and pest resistant are also somewhat toxic, especially to people with chemical sensitivities or preexisting lung disorders. Borate compounds are fairly benign; a 150-pound human would have to ingest about 1-3/4 pounds of borate for the dose to be lethal. But because the cellulose comes primarily from recycled newspapers, traces of toxic elements (like dioxins and bleach, dyes, synthetic resins, solvents, and printing inks also) remain in the cellulose. Certainly if you've ever been in a cellulose-insulated attic trying to run electrical wiring, you know it produces a lot of dust when disturbed—so wear a mask. And as anyone with cellulose insulation in their attic can tell you, it will escape through any available hole—the attic hatch, around the plumbing, the pocket door compartment, etc. New forms of insulation continue to emerge: products that foam, cellulose that's blown in wet, insulation made from recycled products (soda pop bottles, cotton, wool, hemp), reflective barriers with bubble wrap in between, and even radiant barrier chips (basically little pieces of foil used as loose fill in the attic—definitely the most festive-looking insulation you can buy!). There are also numerous kinds of rigid insulation boards, from fiberboard to expanded polystyrene to various kinds of closed-cell foam (polyisocyanurate, extruded polystyrene), with and without foil radiant barriers attached. You can even buy an insulating paint additive made of microscopic ceramic beads, which can be added to regular paint (interior or exterior). Some of the more obscure forms of insulation may not be carried at the local lumberyard or home center, so it may require more effort to acquire. Some kinds, like sprayed-in-place foam, require professional installation. Whatever kind you choose, you probably don't want to breathe it, so if you're doing it yourself, wear a respirator. And take my advice—learned the hard way—trying to insulate the attic in the summer is a recipe for heatstroke.

There is little agreement on what kinds of insulation are best since every kind tends to have some drawbacks. But probably the biggest drawback to retrofitting insulation into bungalows is knob-and-tube wiring. This kind of wiring, which is perfectly fine as long as the insulation on the wires is intact, was designed to have airspace around it. Surrounding it with insulation can theoretically cause heat to build up in the wires, which can cause short circuits and even fires. This prohibition is now included in the building code. Recently, however, the state of California looked at fire records over a ten-year period for any evidence of fires caused by knob-and-tube in thermal insulation and found none. Because of this, California and some other jurisdictions have relaxed their rules slightly so that the knob-and-tube can be insulated if it has been inspected by a licensed electrical contractor and found to be in good condition, and if a sign is placed in the attic warning of hidden wiring.

VAPOR CHASE

In new construction, a vapor barrier is placed toward the living space, which keeps warm, moist air inside the house from migrating and condensing in the insulation, which can cause rot and mold. For walls, another barrier called *house-wrap* is placed on the outside. Modern houses are so insulated and weatherstripped and double-glazed that they actually require some sort of mechanical ventilation to bring in fresh air. There are those who believe that these precautions are what has led to the current epidemic of toxic mold. Bungalows, on the other hand, generally leak like a sieve, and that's not all bad. The main thing about water vapor or water is not so much that it gets INTO the building, but that it has a way to get OUT. An empty wall cavity allows that to happen pretty easily.

If wall insulation is to be added to walls that don't have it, it's a bit problematic to install a vapor barrier without removing the interior wall covering. Vapor-barrier paint will solve part of the problem, and shellac on woodwork makes a decent vapor barrier for those parts, but moisture will still try to sneak through cracks and electrical outlets. About the best one can do is to try to get water vapor out of the house by other means, like fans in the kitchen and baths. You have to USE the fans, though.

Obviously if the interior of the wall is down to the framing, it's much easier to install a vapor barrier (usually plastic sheeting or radiant barrier foil stapled on top of the studs). You are not allowed to take the wall down just for this purpose.

Insulation can be blown in to existing walls by drilling two-inch holes in each stud bay from either the outside or the inside. On the outside, this is fairly easy if the siding is shingles, as individual shingles sacrificed to the process can be replaced quite easily. (Obviously, a good time to insulate is during reshingling. It's a good time to do a lot of things—run wiring, plumbing, etc., while the walls are accessible.) Wood siding will also have to be patched, and the patches are hard to disguise. Stucco presents a similar problem. Masonry walls have enough thermal mass that they shouldn't be insulated because insulation may cause water problems when moist air gets into the cavity between two wythes; normally it condenses there and runs down to the bottom, where weep holes have been provided (hopefully) for it to escape. Insulation interferes with this process. If inside walls are made of plaster, it's sometimes better to insulate from the inside since plaster is much easier to patch. In rooms with wood paneling, it may have to be removed for the purpose, which may be hard to do without damaging it.

Many different sources will tell you that most of the heat is escaping through cracks around doors and windows, electrical outlets, and so on, and that you should caulk all these cracks and weatherstrip the windows and doors. While that certainly wouldn't hurt, it is time-consuming and rather tedious. I'm not saying you shouldn't do that, but I can relate this from personal experience: I owned one bungalow that had insulated walls (blown-in cellulose) as well as an insulated attic. The double-hung windows were neither weatherstripped nor caulked, and they rattled every time it was windy. (Here in California, almost no one has storm windows.) In spite of that, this house had the lowest heating bill of any bungalow I've ever owned.

FIFTY WAYS TO LEAVE YOUR LOUVER

"Just start a new fan, Stan,
And set your air free. . . ."
    —with apologies to Paul Simon

Unlike most homes today, bungalows didn't employ soffit vents or ridge vents; rather, bungalow attics were traditionally vented through gable vents or dormers. Dormers often combine vents with windows to let light into the attic. Gable vents were often decorative, filled with different kinds of latticework or louvers. A window flanked by vents might be part of the system as well, allowing light into the attic. The vent frequently filled most of the peak of the gable, especially in warmer climates. Wire screening was installed behind the latticework to keep out insects, birds, and small dogs. As a rule, there would be a vent at both ends of the house, though not always. (Cross-ventilation is always a good idea.) Sometimes the attic wasn't vented at all. These vents are not always adequate by modern standards, which call for soffit vents paired with vents at the ridge. Rather than adding soffit vents in the eaves, which can be obtrusive (not to mention difficult to do if you don't actually have a soffit, and many bungalows don't) with exposed rafters and all, it may be better to install a ventilating fan in the roof or the gable. These may be electric, or there are solar-powered models available. Don't bother with the spinning turbine vents—they don't remove much air and they only do so when it's windy. The only problem with fans is that makeup air has to come from somewhere, and without soffit vents or other vents at the lower part of the roof, air will be sucked up out of the living space through any holes around light fixtures, plumbing vents, chimneys, or the attic hatch. Air can be sucked up all the way from the basement or crawl space, even without a ventilating fan, and this can allow moist air to get into the attic—a big problem in the winter, especially in cold climates. There is a lot of argument as to whether the primary purpose of attic ventilation is to remove heat in the summer or moist air in the winter, or whether attics need to be ventilated at all. Much depends on the climate you happen to live in, and even then, the experts don't agree. An attic can reach 150 degrees on a warm summer day, and especially an uninsulated attic can allow that heat to radiate down into the living space.

According to William Rose of the Building Research Council at the University of Illinois:

> Indoor humidity control should be the primary means to limit moisture accumulation in attics in cold and mixed climates.
>
> To minimize the danger of ice dam formation heat sources in the attic and warm air leakage into the attic from below should be minimized. The need for venting to avoid icing depends on the climate and the amount of insulation in the ceiling. However, ventilation is necessary in climates with a lot of snow to prevent icing at eaves, regardless of insulation level.
>
> Venting of attics and cathedral ceilings in cold and mixed climates [is recommended]. However, if there are strong reasons why attic vents are undesirable, unvented roofs can perform well in cold and mixed climates if measures are taken to control indoor humidity, to minimize heat sources in the attic, and to minimize air leakage into the attic from below. However, ventilation is necessary in climates with a lot of snow to prevent icing.

> Ventilation should be treated as a design option in cold, wet coastal climates and hot climates. Current technical information does not support a universal requirement for ventilation of attics or cathedral ceilings in these climates.

In other words, the jury is still out.

ICICLE BUILT FOR TWO

Icicles hanging from the edge of a snowy roof in winter are beautiful and kind of romantic—unless you know what they mean. And what they mean is the dreaded *ice dam,* a phrase that awakens fear in the hearts of homeowners in cold winter climates.

An ice dam is a ridge of ice that develops at the edge of a roof and prevents melting snow from draining off the roof. The water that backs up behind the dam can find its way underneath the roof covering and leak into the house, damaging walls, ceilings, insulation, and other areas. Ice dams are formed by a complex interaction between heat loss from the house, outside temperatures, and the amount of snow cover on the roof. For an ice dam to form, there must be snow on the roof, and the lower portion of the roof must be below 32 degrees Fahrenheit while the upper portion is warmer than 32 degrees—this can be caused by sunshine or heat loss from the house. The snow on the upper portion where it is warmer will melt and run down the roof to the colder part where it will refreeze, forming the ice dam. The more that snow melts from the top and runs down, the larger the ice dam becomes. Some of the water gets over the edge and freezes, producing icicles that get larger and larger, like hand-dipped taper candles.

There's still a lot of argument about ways to prevent ice dams, but there seems to be agreement on the following principles:

■ insulate the attic;

■ seal penetrations into the attic—such as light fixtures, exhaust fans, chimneys, the attic hatch, etc.—to keep heated air from escaping the heated areas of the house into the attic;

■ remove snow from the roof;

■ when reroofing, include a waterproof membrane (usually a self-adhesive bituminous product) that extends about a foot above the point where the outside wall of the house meets the roof; this prevents water intrusion if an ice dam does form.

There is less agreement about whether attic ventilation (usually comprising soffit and ridge vents) or mechanical ventilation (fans) is a good idea or not. Me, I'm a Californian—I just laugh and skip this part.

GARRET AND STICK

Many bungalow attics were built with the idea that they could be finished later for living space as the family grew. An attic meant to be utilized for eventual living space would have an actual stairway, albeit one that might be quite steep or winding or narrow and probably unable to meet modern building code requirements. (In contrast, the second floor of a one-and-a-half-story bungalow that was originally part of the living space will usually have a regular stairway, and an attic that wasn't intended to be living space will probably have a hatch rather than a stairway.) Generally, dormers provided the headroom on the upper floor. If the attic was finished for living space fairly soon after the bungalow was built, often beadboard (1- by 4-inch tongue-and-groove paneling) or board-and-batten paneling was used. Why? Because it's easier to get narrow boards up a narrow stairway. An attic finished somewhat later may sport knotty pine paneling (very big from the 1940s through the 1960s) or plywood with battens on the seams. Another popular choice was various kinds of fiberboard (Beaverboard, Celotex, Upson Board, etc.). Some people went whole hog and used real plaster. Later in the twentieth century, sheet materials like plywood, thin wood paneling, fake wood paneling, and drywall were used. In the 1970s, there was a spate of boards laid diagonally. (Can you picture it? The waterbed, the spider plants in beaded macrame hangers, the God's Eye, the Marimekko supergraphic, the shag rug?)

Depending on available space and layout, there might have been one large attic room, or it could be subdivided into several rooms. If there was space, a bathroom might be included. Space under the eaves was utilized for closets and storage.

An attic with enough headroom, or the possibility of adding enough headroom by installing dormers or raising the roof, can be made into living space IF there is somewhere to put a staircase. A staircase takes up quite a lot of room, so this may not always be possible, especially given the constraints of the modern building code.

White-painted beadboard lines the walls and ceiling of this attic in a Seattle bungalow. A sofa makes the best use of the low headroom near the eaves, while a comfy armchair and floor pillows provide extra seating for TV viewing or conversation. Windows in the gable end provide light and ventilation.

Architects Charles and Henry Greene extended their artistry even to the attic hatch of the Duncan-Irwin House in Pasadena, California. Not shown in the photo is the built-in ladder attached to the wall below.

On the other hand, some bungalows with very shallow pitched roofs barely have room in the attic for boxes, let alone humans.

Attic living space needs a lot of ventilation in the summer because hot air rises and the roof heats up, so it can get rather toasty unless that hot air has a way to escape. Windows that open (preferably all around for cross ventilation or operable skylights or both), combined with insulation between the rafters, ventilation for the roof, and some fans, will keep the attic at a comfortable temperature.

BATTEN DOWN THE HATCH

If the attic doesn't have a stairway, then it probably has a hatch, sometimes called a scuttle hole. The hatch may be located in the ceiling of a hallway, a closet, or, for reasons I am not entirely clear on, the bathroom. The cover is usually made of beadboard held together with a couple of battens on the top, and sits on a small lip formed by the trim around the opening. If you're lucky, the opening will be large enough to get yourself (or a box) through. If you're not lucky, it will be maybe 12 by 18 inches, only big enough for a fairly small person. In one house I owned, there was a secondary scuttle hole that was quite literally only big

enough to put your head through (to check on the bats?). If the hatch isn't big enough or if it's inconveniently located, it might be worthwhile to enlarge it or cut a new one elsewhere. The hatch cover should be covered with insulation and also weatherstripped.

TAKE ME TO YOUR LADDER

Sometimes the attic access is via a pull-down folding (or sliding) ladder. These were available when bungalows were being built, and are still available. They require a larger opening than a hatch, as well as space to unfold, so are generally installed in hallways. Sometimes an attic hatch is accompanied by a straight ladder attached to a nearby wall. Folding ladders should also be weatherstripped, though they are a little difficult to insulate.

Facing: A fashionably dressed woman shows how easy it is to use the Bessler Disappearing Stairway in this advertisement from the 1920s. They even offered a thirty-day trial period, stating, "You can have the use of the Bessler for one month, and if it does not prove to be satisfactory, return it to us at our expense." (Sure, like somebody was going to install it, decide they didn't like it, and then go to the trouble of uninstalling it, packing it back into the crate, and end up with a gaping hole in the ceiling.) Folding stairways of this sort are still being made.

THE BESSLER DISAPPEARING STAIRWAY CO.
AKRON, OHIO

BESSLER DISAPPEARING STAIRWAY IN WOOD AND STEEL

Bessler Wood Disappearing Attic Stairway

The Bessler disappearing attic stairway is a substantial, sightly and practical flight of stairs for one or two-story residences and other types of buildings, providing proper stair access to an upper floor when desired, and leaving clear the floor space ordinarily occupied by stairs when that is wanted. While not in use, the stair folds into the ceiling out of the way.

The treads are properly secured to heavy string pieces with open risers. The hand rail is strong, practical and attractive. At the top the stairs are attached to the end trimmer of an opening in the ceiling of the room or hall where the stairs are to be located. The mechanism and operation are very simple. To use the stairway a slight pull on a chain brings it into position, with very slight assistance from the operator. *Metal parts are all made of pressed steel.*

The panel is the only part visible when the stairway is closed, and this is flush with the ceiling line. There is no possibility of it coming down unassisted.

All models shown below can be furnished with either pine, oak, birch, gum or chestnut doors with one or two panels, also with flush laminated panel in pine, oak or birch.

Prices and literature furnished on request.

The Bessler disappearing stairway is guaranteed to last as long as the life of the building.

You can have the use of the Bessler for one month, and if it does not prove to be satisfactory, return it to us at our expense.

Specifications Wood Attic Stairway

Model 97
Stairway to be mounted on panel to slide on rollers. Panel to have adjustable hinges permitting edge to come to bottom of plaster. Hand rail for right or left side. One equalizing bar is to be on each side of the stairway. Double-acting spring barrel and spring drum on each side of the stair panel. The weight of the stair-stringers to bear down on the shaft which is attached to end trimmer. Adjustable cable clamps bearing against brackets attached to jambs.
Average shipping weight, 170 lbs.

Model 39
This stairway is same style and made in same sizes as Model 29 illustrated at left except it is made for a 2 ft. 6 in. wide finished opening.
Average shipping weight, 85 lbs.

Model 29
Stairway to be mounted on frame to slide through guides. Panel to be hinged on right or left side. (Mention which side panel is to be on so the proper operating parts can be furnished.) Hinges to be suitable so panel can be installed with edge flush with plaster. Spring drum attached to metal frame underneath stairway. A jointed arm for holding panel open and two coil springs for closing panel. Made in sizes up to 9 ft. 7 in. floor to floor and for finished opening 2 ft. wide.
Average shipping weight, 80 lbs.

Model 50
Stairway to be mounted on panel to slide in guides. Hinges to be suitable so panel can be installed with edge flush with bottom of plaster if desired. Hand rail for right or left side. Spring drum on each side of the stair panel at the hinged end. The weight of the stair-stringers to bear down on the guides which are attached to the hinged end of frame.
Note: This model is made for floor to floor heights up to 10 ft. 7 in. only, and for finished openings 2 ft. wide.
Average shipping weight, 90 lbs.

Model 60
Stairway to be mounted on panel to slide in guides. Hinges to be suitable so panel can be installed with edge flush with bottom of plaster if desired. Hand rail for right or left side. Spring drum on each side of the stair panel at the hinged end. The weight of the stair-stringers to bear down on the guides which are attached to the hinged end of frame.
Note: This model is made for floor to floor heights up to 10 ft. 7 in. only, and for finished openings 2 ft. 6 in. wide.
Average shipping weight, 95 lbs.

CHAPTER FOUR

CEILING GROOVY.

The majority of bungalow ceilings are lath and plaster, and generally they were flat. *Lath* (thin strips of rough-cut wood) would be nailed horizontally to the joists or wall studs, with a quarter-inch space between each piece. When the first coat of plaster was applied, it would ooze out behind the lath to form *keys*, tying the plaster to the ceiling or the wall. Later on, the wooden lath was replaced by diamond-shaped metal mesh and eventually by gypsum board (drywall). Plaster is applied in three coats. The first coat is called the *scratch coat*, because it is crosshatched before it cures to give the second coat, called the *brown coat*, something to grab onto; the third coat is the *finish coat.* Together, the three coats are about half an inch thick.

In utilitarian spaces like pantries, utility porches, laundry rooms, and some kitchens, the ceiling was often covered with beadboard (tongue-and-groove paneling), which was probably cheaper than plaster at the time. Usually the walls would have beadboard as well. On occasion, a kitchen or bathroom ceiling would be covered with ceramic tile.

The formal rooms of the house might have wooden ceilings as well. Board-and-batten, a combination of wide boards with narrower boards nailed over the seams, was the most common treatment. Occasionally even bedrooms would have this kind of ceiling.

Different rooms in the house often had different ceiling treatments—beams in the dining room, a tray ceiling in the living room, coved ceilings in the bedrooms, beadboard ceiling in the utility room, and so forth.

In a bungalow with plaster on both the walls and the ceiling, the plaster textures may have differed. If the builder had planned for the walls to be papered, the wall finish would be very smooth and the ceiling might have more texture. Conversely, if the walls were highly textured, the ceilings might be smooth. Or both walls and ceiling might be the same. Though not terribly common, molded plaster decoration showed up on some ceilings, and plaster crown molding was used more often than one might suspect.

Plaster ceilings in formal rooms could be covered with linen, burlap, or other fabric, and were sometimes painted metallic gold. Ceilings were sometimes covered with wallpaper as well. This treatment was especially prevalent in the bedrooms of one-and-a-half-story bungalows with sloping ceilings upstairs, though wallpapered ceilings in the formal rooms weren't unheard of either. Ceilings could also be decorated with stenciling, murals, or decorative paint finishes.

ROOM AND BOARD

While lath and plaster predominated as an interior ceiling and wall finish right up until World War II, inventors were working on new materials all the time. Back around 1884, Augustine Sackett and Fred L. Kane came up with a board consisting of straw paper surrounding a core of coal tar pitch, which they hoped to use as a wall and ceiling finish that could be papered or painted. Unfortunately, the pitch would soak through the paper, ruining the paint or wall-

Facing: Dark oak moldings outline the wallpapered tray ceiling of a bungalow in Milwaukee, Wisconsin. A bowl chandelier with a hand-painted porcelain shade hangs from the center. The pinkish tone of the wire-cut "reptile" brick of the fireplace is echoed by the rose color of the walls.

paper and making the room smell bad to boot. (Anyone who has ever smelled coal tar shampoo can tell you it's not a very pleasant smell.) So they went back to the drawing board. Kane suggested using manila paper and plaster of paris (gypsum) as the core. It worked, and in 1894, a patent was taken out for Sackett Board. It was slow to catch on, but enough had been sold by 1909 to attract the attention of U.S. Gypsum, which bought out the company that year. In 1917, U.S. Gypsum, after making a few improvements, took out their own patent, calling the product Sheetrock. Many other companies were marketing variations on a similar product. Most of these early plasterboards measured 2 by 4 feet rather than the 4 by 8 feet that is most common today.

After World War II, the product—whether called drywall, plasterboard, gyp-rock, gyp-board, rock, or sheetrock (still technically a trademark, though used as a generic term by most people)—took over the housing market to such an extent that it has become very difficult to find anyone who even knows how to plaster. There is a special kind of drywall called "blueboard" that can be skim-coated with real plaster rather than joint compound; this is how most "plastering" is done these days. Blueboard should not be confused with "greenboard" (moisture-resistant drywall), which is only resistant to humidity.

THE HEIGHT OF FASHION

Bungalow ceilings tended to be lower than the high ceilings of the Victorians that preceded them. Victorian ceilings could be anywhere from 10 to 14 feet high, while ceilings in bungalows tended to be in the range of 8 to 10 feet, often some in-between height like 9 feet 3 inches or 8 feet 6 inches. A lower ceiling gives a cozier feel, though generally bungalows have higher ceilings than the standard 8 feet of most post–World War II houses. It's surprising, but even 8 feet 3 inches gives a sense of vertical spaciousness lacking in an 8-foot ceiling. Some areas of a bungalow may also have had lower or higher ceilings for effect. For instance, the ceiling of a fireplace inglenook may be lower than the rest of the room for a more intimate feeling, and even the two-story living room, of which most contemporary tract home designers seem so enamored, was not unheard-of in bungalows.

MORAL FIBER

There was a great deal of advertising in the building magazines touting the benefits of fiberboard as a ceiling and wall finish, and there were probably a few builders (or remodelers) who went for it. The boards were made of wood fiber and some sort of water-resistant compound, often asphalt, fused together under pressure. Some of them even came in wood-grain patterns, which just goes to show that fake wood-grain building materials are not a recent invention, though most boards were meant to be painted or papered.

There were many different brands, but today the product is by and large known as beaverboard (brand name: Beaver Board), kind of like hoosier (Hoosier) cabinets. Fiberboard does have some insulation value as well as sound-deadening properties, which is why it is still used. Acoustical ceiling tile is probably the form of fiberboard we are most familiar with.

BEAM ME UP, SCOTTY

Beamed ceilings were extremely common, especially in living and dining rooms, and sometimes other rooms as well, as part of the whole "expressed structure" philosophy that so many bungalow designers embraced. That being said,

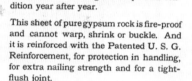
An early ad for Sheetrock appeared in the June 1920 issue of *American Builder*. According to the ad, U.S. Gypsum had apparently been advertising the product to consumers in the *Saturday Evening Post*. At the time, it was only 3/8 inch thick and came in either 32- or 48-inch-wide sheets, unlike today's standard 1/2-inch thickness and 48-inch width. And anyone who has ever leaned a piece of Sheetrock against a wall can tell you that, contrary to the claims in this ad, it does in fact warp.

many of the beams were fake. Sometimes the beams really were structural and actually held up the ceiling and/or the second floor, but just as often they were hollow "box beams" that were merely decorative. Structural beams pretty much go from one side of the room to the other because they have to. Box beams, on the other hand, can be much more fanciful, and may be diagonal or stop in the middle of the ceiling since they only have to look nice and don't have any structural limitations.

OVERFLOWING COFFERS

A bunch of box beams intersecting each other results in coffers, the recessed ceiling space between the beams. Often square or rectangular, coffers can also be diamond-shaped, lozenge-shaped, or octagonal. Moldings are applied to the edges of the box beams where they meet the ceiling, and these also intersect and are mitered inside the coffers. The ceiling portion of the coffer is typically flat plaster, though sometimes wood is used instead.

COVES AND FISHES

Although many bungalow ceilings meet the walls at right angles, coved ceilings (where the walls and ceiling are joined by a curve) are extremely common. They may be limited to the formal rooms, or most of the rooms may have them. Coved ceilings are uncommon in kitchens, bathrooms, and utility areas but not unheard of. Builders often didn't bother with coving in hallways, and closets were completely ignored. Coved ceilings are easy to do in plaster, and a lot harder to do with drywall. To make drywall curve requires either

Fibreweb wallboards were used on the walls of this bungalow living room, shown in their ad in the November 1915 *American Carpenter and Builder*. The joints between the boards had to be covered with battens, but much was made of the decorative possibilities that arose from this requirement. And, because sanitation was a major concern at that time, they had to mention that lath and plaster was unsanitary.

Fake wood grain goes way back, though the Roberd's Manufacturing Company assures us that their oak finish "is not pasted on, nor is it in any way a mechanical or imitation design of oak, but is an exact reproduction of the genuine wood, so perfect that even the most skilled observer cannot detect it." I've never seen any, so I will reserve judgment on that.

Above left: Large cutout corbels hold up the (real) ceiling beams of an Arts and Crafts house in Oakland, California, designed by architect A. W. Smith in 1910.

Above right: Crossing box beams form large coffers on the dining room ceiling of this bungalow. A four-arm chandelier with art-glass lanterns hangs over the center of the table. Mirrors on the doors and back of the built-in sideboard help make the small room seem larger. Below the ceiling, a wide wallpaper border forms a frieze, and the door to the hallway has an art-glass window set into the top panel.

Below left: Box beams can do things that real beams can't, like stop in the middle of the ceiling, as with these beams in the living room of a bungalow in Eagle Rock, California. Beam lights with exposed bulbs are located where the beams intersect. The large tiled fireplace is flanked by typical glass-door bookcases, with large casement windows above and a large front window overlooking the front porch and garden.

buying special bendable drywall or scoring the back of the drywall to make it conform to the curve, whereas in plaster, the lath can be nailed to the pieces of wood that form the curve, and the plaster can be applied to the curve in the same way it is applied to the rest of the ceiling.

ARCH ENEMY

Far less common than coved ceilings, but seen in the occasional bungalow, are arched (vaulted) ceilings. Generally confined to living or dining rooms, the ceiling usually has a fairly shallow curve rather than being like a barrel vault, and is sometimes accented with battens (narrow strips of wood) for emphasis. Vaulted ceilings could also take other shapes that were angular, commonly called tent ceilings.

TRAY CHIC

Some ceilings had a large recess in the center, surrounded by one or more bands or steps, known as a tray ceiling. Most commonly these ceilings were plaster, though they could also be rendered in wood, or may have been highlighted with various kinds of wood or molded plaster trim.

I'VE GOT A BAD CEILING ABOUT THIS . . .

The primary enemies of ceilings are water, gravity, and home-owners. Water seepage from a roof or a plumbing leak will stain and possibly rot a wood ceiling, or cause a plaster ceiling eventually to lose its grip on the lath and fall off. Of course, a long time before that happens there will probably be peeling paint, mildew, stains, or other signs of water damage.

For reasons that escape me, but probably because there is a great deal of misinformation out in the world, it seems that the vast majority of people are convinced that cracks in a plaster ceiling are a sign of imminent structural collapse, or something close to it. This is rarely the case. Cracks in plaster can have many different causes, and only a few of them are structural.

Diagonal stress cracks are caused by structural movement or the overloading of structural members (such as too much stuff stored in the attic). Stress cracks can also be caused by settlement of the foundation in areas with clay soils, or by continuing vibration from a nearby highway, train tracks, airport, and the like. In a wall, they often originate from the corners of windows or doors, though not always. Settlement cracks may run diagonally in both directions. A major structural problem will likely result in really big, deep cracks in both ceilings and walls. Smaller stress cracks caused by seasonal settlement should be less cause for worry.

Horizontal cracks are more likely to be caused by lath movement. Wood lath absorbs moisture from the air, causing seasonal expansion and contraction. These cracks will run parallel to the lath. Vertical cracks can appear where lath ends have loosened because of structural movement or loose nails. And of course gravity has been pulling at the ceiling for ninety-odd years.

The finish coat of a three-coat plaster job can also have what is called "chip cracking," caused by an inadequate amount of lime in the mix, or by this last coat over a base coat that is too dry. Chip cracking looks much like alligatored paint. A similar condition is "map cracking," a web of fine cracks that occurs when the finish coat is applied over a base coat with too much sand in it.

So what is the uninformed homeowner's answer to these cracks?

■ Occasionally: Wallpaper.

■ Rarely: Gold-veined mirror tiles.

■ Usually: Bad Patching, which can also be combined with the equally lovely Bad Texturing that is often applied by the following homeowner in an attempt to cover up the previous homeowner's Bad Patching. Random Bad Texturing can be applied by hand or it can be sprayed on for Uniform Bad Texturing.

Bad Patching aficionados seem to favor compounds like Fixall, which are well-nigh impossible to sand. But the *ne plus ultra* of Bad Texturing is the dreaded Popcorn or Cottage Cheese ceiling. And if you're really lucky, it will even have glitter in it—Red Glitter. Most of these ceilings were installed between the 1960s and the 1980s.

Let's review: a ceiling that can't be cleaned, which catches dust but can't be dusted without little pieces falling off, making it damn near impossible to edge the wall when painting, and which often contains asbestos. Yeah, sign me up for that. Even worse, sometimes people paint it after it gets dirty, and for some reason they seem to favor semigloss paint for doing so. Ooh, bumpy AND shiny—there's a good combo. The good news is, as long as there's no asbestos in it (take a sample and send it to be tested first), it's easy to get off, though incredibly messy. Just cover everything with plastic, spray the ceiling with water (add several drops of dishwashing soap), wait a few minutes, position a large garbage can directly underneath, and start scraping. It will fall off like globs of wet oatmeal.

If it does contain asbestos, you can pay an abatement company large sums of money to remove it, or you can cover the whole thing with drywall.

In this bungalow in Milwaukee, Wisconsin, a shallow arch accented by narrow oak box beams forms the dining room ceiling. On the walls, plaster panels interspersed with tall battens rise up to meet the ceiling. Both the ceiling and walls have been given a mottled paint finish that blends with the oak woodwork.

ASBESTOS

Asbestos is a naturally occurring mineral. At the time it was first used, no one was aware of the health effects of the product. Inhaled asbestos fibers lodge in the lungs and stay there, causing scarring and, eventually, asbestosis and mesothelioma (asbestos cancer). When the industry became aware of this early in the twentieth century, they did everything they could to cover it up, which is why asbestos was not (sort of) banned until 1989. (The first case of asbestos-related lung disease was reported in 1906.) The original Environmental Protection Agency (EPA) ban was overturned by a federal appeals court in 1991. Thus, while corrugated paper, flooring felt, and new uses of asbestos are still banned, asbestos-cement shingles, vinyl-asbestos floor tiles (two toxics for the price of

one!), pipe wrap, brake pads, roofing felt, and roof coatings containing asbestos are not.

As with many things that have been found to be toxic, asbestos continued to be utilized because it was a really good filler and reinforcement, it was fireproof, and, of course, there was money to be made. Besides roofing and siding, it was also used in flooring, duct insulation, flues (often called "transite" after a particular brand), joint compound, plaster, and the dreadful "cottage cheese" or "popcorn" ceilings. In fact, it continues to be mined and used in products. Many of the companies that used asbestos in the United States are now mired in class-action lawsuits, as well they should be. While asbestos is not to be taken lightly, so far there have not been any reported cases of asbestos-related disease stemming from residential exposure. Smokers face a much higher risk if exposed to asbestos, but there is no safe level of exposure for anyone.

There is likely to be asbestos somewhere in a bungalow. If not used in roofing or siding, then it might possibly be used as furnace flues, duct insulation, or fuse-box lining. The general rule for asbestos is to leave it alone unless it is friable (crumbling). Asbestos on ducts and flues can be encapsulated in various ways—painting, wrapping, etc. Asbestos removal is best done by experts, although in some jurisdictions homeowners are allowed to remove a certain amount themselves. Check with the city or county to see what the rules are. If the local government allows it, it can probably give you instructions as to the best way to go about it. The main thing is to get it wet so the fibers don't escape. All removed asbestos has to be double-bagged and sent to special landfills. And—a note from personal experience—if you want it removed from your ducts, they don't do that; they just take the whole thing, and then you have to replace all the ductwork.

There may also be asbestos in the plaster, cottage cheese ceilings, or flooring, so it is a good idea to send some samples to a local testing lab before doing any demolition. Don't be cavalier about this stuff; there hasn't been a residential exposure case yet, but you don't want to be the first.

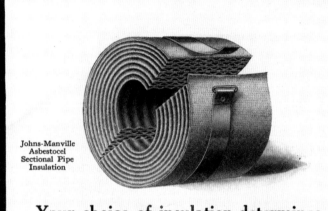

Johns-Manville
Asbestocel
Sectional Pipe
Insulation

Your choice of insulation determines your customer's coal bills

It is often as poor economy to use an expensive insulation on a hot-water heating system as to specify one inch covering for a high-pressure steam line—which means that insulation is a technical subject, and not only technical but practical, because it works right back to the coal pile.

Leave the selection of the proper insulation to us. Let us prescribe the whole installation—from the sole standpoint of maximum economy.

Our skill and experience for such work are assured by 50 years of specialization on insulation, and our line of coverings is completely standardized to meet every requirement. Just call on the Johns-Manville Branch nearest you for information and advice—you'll get it freely and fully—and increase both your profits and your customer's satisfaction.

H. W. JOHNS-MANVILLE CO.
NEW YORK CITY
10 Factories—Branches in 54 Large Cities

CEILINGS

OBSESSIVE RESTORATION

What is needed to restore the ceiling depends on how much it is damaged. Some ceilings may need to come down entirely, especially if there has been long-term water damage. If the lath is still okay, and you want to be really obsessive and either find a plasterer or learn to do it yourself, you can replaster over the existing wood lath. But the usual deal is to cover the wood lath with expanded metal lath, which actually holds the plaster better. However, it's a huge pain to take out a ceiling or wall with metal lath; often some inappropriate pre–World War II "modernizations" were done with metal lath. The somewhat less obsessive method would be to put up blueboard and then skim coat over that. It will not have quite the unevenness and handcrafted look of real lath and plaster, because any kind of drywall makes for a surface that is almost perfectly flat, whereas real plaster has very subtle irregularities.

Often the ceiling has merely sagged because the plaster keys have broken away. Push gently on the ceiling and see if it goes right back into place or feels crunchy (crunchiness means bits of plaster have lodged themselves between the ceiling and the lath). If you have access from above (in the attic), then you may be able to carefully remove these by hand or with a vacuum. (Otherwise that part of the ceiling may have to come off.) Then the ceiling can be reattached in one of two ways: 1) by using plaster washers (special washers that flatten out to hold the ceiling in place when attached with drywall screws), or 2) by injecting construction adhesive or something similar into the space between the lath and the plaster, using pieces of plywood covered with polyethylene sheeting, either screwed to the joists or propped up with two-by-fours from the floor in order to flatten the plaster back against the lath and hold it there till the adhesive dries. (See Bibliography for URL of an article discussing this method in more detail.)

Sometimes only part of the ceiling needs repair. A repair will be less obvious if the edges are uneven, as opposed to a square or rectangle. The edges of the patch, if it's large, should be reinforced with plaster washers. Predrilling the holes before screwing in the plaster washers seems to keep the plaster from pulling away as the screws go in. A patch that is more than a square foot probably needs wire lath to key into; for a smaller patch, keying into the existing lath will probably be enough. Blueboard can also be utilized for a large patch. Large patches should be done with traditional scratch, brown, and finish coats using traditional plaster; smaller patches you may be able to get away with using setting-type joint compound for the first two coats and regular joint compound for the finish coat. Setting-type compounds cure through a chemical process rather than drying through water evaporation like regular joint compound or Spackle.

The most difficult thing in a repair is matching the texture of the surrounding plaster, and some experimentation on scraps of drywall may be in order. If the ceiling is smooth, this won't be an issue; but with textures, it may require figuring out what the original plasterer used to make the texture with—brooms, brushes, specialized trowels, etc.

COMPROMISE SOLUTION

If the plaster is totally beyond repair, you may take it down and put up drywall. It's often best to take down the lath as well, especially if there is picture molding close to the ceiling, so that the same thickness will be maintained. Sometimes if the ceiling has an excessive amount of cracking or an undue amount of Bad Patching but isn't actually coming loose, it can be easier to just cover the entire thing with 3/8-inch drywall. There is a special kind of drywall made that will bend, which will be needed if the ceiling is coved. (Speaking from experience here, making a coved ceiling with drywall is a whole lot of work. The drywall has to be wet, but it can't be too wet or it turns to mush; it also can't be too dry or it won't bend; it has to be done in small pieces, making for a lot of taped seams; it's really hard to get the joint compound onto the curve with regular taping knives; it's especially hard to tape the corners. In the long run, it might turn out to be easier to either do real plastering or give up the coving entirely and just make a right angle between the walls and the ceiling.) SPRAY TEXTURING IS NOT ALLOWED! Nor is that modern "knock-down finish" where the joint compound is put on with a sponge and then flattened with a drywall knife. When in doubt, you can't go wrong with smooth, although the drywall finisher will balk, because a smooth finish is more difficult and time-consuming than a texture.

CHAPTER FIVE

Obviously a bungalow has to have walls, otherwise it would be a gazebo. Different building materials were used for walls, depending on the region of the country, locally available materials, and the skill set of the local workers. Often the prevalent building construction method had much to do with local immigrant groups and what was customary in their home country. So if there were a lot of people who knew how to do masonry, it's more likely there will be a lot of masonry. In areas where wood was plentiful, wood-frame construction was common, although it was also pervasive, thanks to kit houses. In areas with plentiful clay deposits and brick kilns nearby, brick walls were popular. Other structural wall materials included stone, concrete, concrete block, hollow clay tile, and logs.

NAIL SALON

Before the mid-nineteenth century, wood-frame buildings were timber-framed (also known as post-and-beam), a building method utilizing large structural members connected by joinery rather than nails. Partly this was because nails had to be forged by hand, and thus couldn't be used with reckless abandon the way they are today. Indeed, handwrought nails would be salvaged from burned buildings for reuse. The mortise-and-tenon and pegged joinery of timber framing has also been used for centuries in the construction of furniture, and that is probably its most familiar use. The large framing members were preassembled into *bents*, which then required quite a few people to raise into place, thus the traditional "barn raising." Some of the architectural terms used to refer to structural parts of bungalows, such as *purlins*, originally referred to parts of the timber frame. The invention of cut (or square) nails in the late eighteenth century speeded up the process of nail making and lowered the cost somewhat. The introduction of wire nail making machinery from France around the 1850s caused the round, chisel-pointed wire nail with which we are familiar to become the dominant nail in the market, mostly because it was possible to turn out zillions of them in a short amount of time and at a really low price. By the early twentieth century, cut nails had nearly disappeared except for masonry and flooring, where their superior strength and holding power (four times that of a wire nail) were still deemed useful.

Facing: Beadboard (tongue-and-groove boards with a rounded bead along one edge, and often a V-groove down the middle) came in different varieties, some wider, some narrower, but typically around four inches wide and three-quarters of an inch thick. Indoors, it was used primarily in less formal areas—kitchens, bathrooms, utility rooms, hallways, and attics. In this bungalow, white-painted beadboard forms a high wainscot in a reading nook.

PENNY-ANTE OPERATION

Nails used for attaching wood to other pieces of wood are classified using the term "penny" along with a number representing the length; for instance, a nail 3-1/2 inches long is known as a sixteen-penny nail. A 2-1/2-inch nail is known as a six-penny nail. Why? Supposedly because in medieval England, you could buy one hundred 3-1/2-inch nails for sixteen pence (pennies), whereas you could get a hundred 2-1/2-inch nails for only six pence. Thus, the shorter the nail, the smaller the number. Why then, one might ask, does it say 16d on the box and not 16p? Well, because they used the name of a Roman coin, the *denarius*.

To confuse things even further, nails not necessarily used for attaching wood to more wood (like roofing or siding nails) are referred to in inches rather than penny sizes.

A really long nail (more than 6 inches) or a really thick nail is known as a spike, while a really short nail (less than 1 inch) is known as a wire nail if it has a head, or as a brad if it doesn't.

BALLOON PAYMENT

In 1833, a man named Augustine Taylor built a church at Fort Dearborn, near Chicago, using two-by-fours and two-by-sixes set close together, all held together with nails. Old-time carpenters contemptuously referred to it as "balloon construction," and said it was so flimsy it would blow away in a high wind. It didn't. The technique was rapidly adopted, especially for rural homes on the frontier. Balloon framing involves continuous wall studs (upright framing members) that go from foundation to roof. The drawback to this type of framing was that each wall cavity formed its own little chimney, which was not good in a fire. By the 1940s, balloon framing had been replaced by platform framing (sometimes called Western framing), where the walls begin and end on each floor: after the first floor walls are built, the floor of the next level is built on top, and then the walls for that floor are built. This is the type of wood framing typically used today because it is easier to build and uses shorter pieces of wood. The wall studs were generally covered first with *sheathing*, 1- by 6-inch boards laid horizontally or diagonally to stiffen the frame. The sheathing was covered with building paper (asphalt-saturated felt), and then some kind of siding was applied to the outside.

And I may have to hit the next person that says to me (usually in the context of why bungalows are not worth saving) that they were "cheaply and badly built." Compared to tract-home building practices in the last fifty years, bungalows are incredibly well built, even the small-

est of them utilizing old-growth lumber where the two-by-fours were actually 2 by 4 inches, not 1-1/2 by 3-1/2 inches. The old-growth lumber alone makes them worth saving.

The usual practice for a wood-framed bungalow would be two-by-four walls with wood sheathing on the outside, covered with some kind of siding, and either plaster or wood-paneled walls on the inside. Wood paneling was generally fastened directly to the studs. For plaster walls, *lath* (thin strips of rough-cut wood) would be nailed horizontally to the studs, with a 1/4-inch space between each piece. When the first coat of plaster was applied, it would ooze out behind the lath to form *keys*, tying the plaster to the wall. Occasionally there would be no studs; instead the outside walls would consist of vertical boards side by side, the seams between them covered with smaller boards. This is known as *board-and-batten* construction, although board-and-batten was also used over sheathing. Often this sort of construction was used for vacation bungalows that would only be used in the summer, or for outbuildings. This doesn't present a problem unless you want to live there year round, or want to run electrical wiring, and then it becomes a challenge. A similar problem is posed by log walls, which were also used from time to time.

Brick is also a common bungalow wall material. Commonly two or three *wythes* wide (a wythe is a layer one brick thick, and you don't want to say that fast ten times), the inner wythes were constructed of softer brick since those layers would not be exposed to the weather, while the outer layer used harder bricks. Brick or stone construction was often mandated in cities where there had been huge fires, like Chicago. Unfortunately, it was also used in cities where earthquakes are common, like San Francisco. Since the only thing holding a brick wall together is gravity and mortar, a brick building will collapse in an earthquake like it was made out of stacked PEZ candy. Some bungalows may also have brick veneer, where the walls are framed with wood, but bricks are used basically as siding rather than wood or stucco.

The inside of a brick wall generally had *furring strips*, 1- by 2-inch strips of wood that allowed for the attachment of lath for plaster, or for fastening wood paneling. The furring strips also provided a space between the lath and the bricks for the plaster keys. Occasionally the plaster was applied directly to the brick, making it rather difficult to run electrical wiring, plumbing, or heating ducts.

Some bungalows were built with stone walls, which, like brick, could have furring strips on the inside for attaching lath and plaster, and/or paneling, or could also have plaster applied directly to the stone, again making it difficult to run electrical wiring, ducts, or plumbing.

Walls that carry the weight of the roof or the ceiling are known as load-bearing walls, and run at right angles to the joists. In a typical bungalow, the exterior walls and the wall that runs down the center of the house are load bearing. Walls that run in the same direction as the joists are known as partition walls.

GET PLASTERED

As mentioned under Ceilings, plaster walls traditionally consisted of lath with three coats of plaster on top (scratch, brown, finish). Depending on the intended wall finish, the topcoat might be smooth (for wallpaper or fabric) or textured (for paint).

A common wall finish was tinted sand plaster, which, as the name might suggest, had sand in the topcoat. One theory suggests that because plaster had to cure for a few months before it could be painted, it was tinted so the family wouldn't have to spend six months living with unfinished walls. Like many things born of necessity, the Arts and Crafts movement soon made this into a feature.

CHALK ONE UP

The tint was usually supplied by *calcimine* (sometimes spelled *kalsomine* or *calsomine*), and also known as *distemper*, from the French *d'étrempe* meaning "drenched with water." The root word *calc* comes from the Latin word for "chalk." Just to confuse things even further, in the early twentieth century, calcimine was also called watercolor, distemper work, or fresco, and in modern times, the British still refer to modern water-base paints as distemper. Real fresco is a technique that involves painting directly on wet plaster. Calcimine is a water-base coating made from either chalk or zinc oxide mixed with glue (casein or hide glue) and pigments for color. It came as a powder and was mixed by the painter on-site. Whitewash, a mixture of slaked lime, salt, glue, and water, though generally used on exterior surfaces, was also sometimes tinted and used indoors in a similar fashion.

Traditionally, the glue was soaked in water overnight and then heated in a small pot to dissolve it. It was then mixed with whiting (zinc oxide), pigments, and water, and applied with a special 6- to 8-inch-wide brush made of boar bristles. According to the *Modern Painter's Cyclopedia*,

> An ideal wall to work upon is one that will be sufficiently hard to have but little suction, nearly but not quite non-absorbent. The patent plastered walls left either in a stippled rough state or covered over with a skim coat of plaster paris [*sic*] make an excellent surface to calcimine upon.

But, proving that complaints about workmanship are not just a modern phenomenon, the author went on,

> With all the cheap John sort of plastering that is being done by contractors at a price which would mean a sure loss to them if they used good material, but which must be done so as to make a profit anyhow, many of the surfaces the calciminer has to deal with will be found very porous and absorbing . . . such walls are called in the vernacular "hot walls."

The difference between calcimine and water paint is explained in this advertisement in the August 1920 *American Builder*: calcimines are "glutinous compositions" and water paints are "caseinous compositions" (milk paint). Their advantage over lime wash (whitewash), and their cheapness compared to wallpaper and oil paint are also touted.

The solution, apparently, was to first give the walls (or ceiling) a coat of varnish. Lacking that, one could add glycerine, powdered alum, or even molasses, all designed to retard drying, to the calcimine so that lap marks wouldn't show.

Plaster in bungalows was often tinted in surprisingly saturated colors, including Chinese red, olive green, coral, turquoise, rust, terra-cotta, burgundy, apricot, teal blue, gold, and dark brown, though pastel colors were also used.

Calcimine was often used for stenciling or freehand decorative painting as well, though oil-base paints were also employed for this purpose.

HUE MONGOUS

"A bright color does not necessarily offend against simplicity, but an obtrusive color, or a too glaring contrast does."
—Walter A Dyer, *The Craftsman,* 1902

While an entire book could be devoted to color in bungalows, suffice it to say that they were meant to have color, not like nowadays when most everything tends to be off-white. That is fine in the kitchen or the bathroom, where

TINTED PLASTER

OBSESSIVE RESTORATION

(For dealing with plaster, see sidebars under Ceilings)

Plaster tinted with calcimine is fine until someone decides to paint over it—it was meant to be scrubbed off before recoating. Oil-base paints stick to it pretty well, as does shellac, but as they oxidize over time, they get brittle and start to let go. Latex paints don't adhere to it very well and tend to peel, and by this century and with numerous layers of paint, the entire thing may be peeling. At that point there's nothing to do but scrape off the peeling paint and then scrub off the calcimine with water and detergent. This will be extremely tedious. If you manage to get all the paint and most of the calcimine off, calcimine is still available and you can recoat with it. It has a chalky finish that is difficult to replicate with other coatings. What is more likely is that it will not all come off (the paint or the calcimine), but at that point the paint companies have stepped in with various kinds of oil-base calcimine-coating primers. White-pigmented shellac will also work. While not the perfect solution, they'll probably buy you another hundred years.

If you're really lucky, it might only have wallpaper on top. Then the only problem is removing the wallpaper paste, since water will dissolve some of the calcimine as well. Using steam to remove the wallpaper may have less effect on the calcimine, but you will still need water to remove the remaining wallpaper paste, making it sort of a moot point.

COMPROMISE SOLUTION

Pretty much the same as Obsessive Restoration, except after the calcimine coating primer, you can use latex paint instead of more calcimine.

Good Tones for Interiors

May be made by blending primary colors with white. Those shown here were made from the standard colors of "Mellotone," a washable flat finish for interiors, manufactured by The Lowe Brothers Company, Dayton, O.

The 1912 Book of Home Building and Decoration included this page labeled "good tones for interiors." The colors range from buff through ochres, taupes, browns, yellow-greens, gray-greens, and finally to a grayed blue-green. These were standard colors of "Mellotone," manufactured by the Lowe Brothers Company of Dayton, Ohio.

things were supposed to be white and sanitary, but not in the formal rooms and the bedrooms. Unpainted woodwork especially needs to be set off by color on the walls.

In keeping with Arts and Crafts philosophy, colors in the home were to come from nature. This could allow for almost any color, but what they really meant were "subdued" colors from nature. The word "dull" appeared frequently as an adjective when describing appropriate colors for bungalows. Here's Stickley describing the proposed colors for his own house at Craftsman Farms in 1908: ". . . liberal use of yellow, olive green, dull brick-red, and old blue . . . dull soft yellow of the plain plaster frieze, the warm ivory tone of the plaster panels that appear between the beams. . . ." Helen Binkerd Young of the Department of Household Art at Cornell University had this to say in the 1912 tome *Home Building and Decoration,*

All colors which can be accurately described by the suffix "ish," as greenish-gray, yellowish-green, bluish-gray, reddish brown, are tones and safe to use on large surfaces. . . . [She also mentioned that] Strong color preferences and a taste for novelty effects should be reserved for one's own bedroom or den, where they cannot offend others.

A woman after my own heart.

Much of the obsession with muted colors was a reaction to the introduction of aniline dyes in the nineteenth century. Before 1856, all color used for textiles, inks, and paints came from natural sources such as plants (bark, flowers, roots, leaves, or berries), insects (such as cochineal beetles), mollusks (the source of royal or Tyrian purple), or minerals (iron oxides and such).

In 1856, a young chemistry student named William Perkin was attempting to synthesize quinine, a cure for malaria, from a coal tar product called *aniline*. His experiment failed, yielding instead an intensely purple solution—the first synthetic dye. Not being an idiot, he realized the dye's economic potential and promptly abandoned his studies in order to pursue the marketing of his invention, which he called *mauveine*. With financial backing from his father, he opened a factory, and was so successful he was able to retire at the age of thirty-eight.

Other chemists began experimenting with aniline and, soon, other colors like aniline red, blue, and violet appeared. Soon after, both Perkin and the German company BASF found themselves in a race to synthesize indigo blue. BASF beat Perkin to the patent office by one day.

Naturally, these bright new colors—fuchsia! magenta! mauve! oh, the horror!—filled the Arts and Crafts reformers with revulsion. William Morris wrote,

> Of these dyes it must be enough to say that their discovery, while conferring the greatest honour on the abstract science of chemistry, and while doing great service to capitalists in their hunt after profits, has terribly injured the art of dying, and for the general public nearly destroyed it as an art.

The colors in the home were also meant to harmonize with the woodwork, and high contrast between the woodwork and the wall and ceiling colors was not considered desirable (and does, in fact, cause eye fatigue). Thus if the woodwork was unpainted, earthy tones like ochre, olive, rust, gold, mossy green, terra-cotta and so forth harmonized with the brown, red, or golden tones in the wood in a way that hot pink just wouldn't. Even in rooms with painted woodwork (which was generally in the white to beige range), muted tints rather than clear pastels were favored. In his book *The Furnishing of a Modest Home,* one writer warned against using blue, noting that

> Blue is the color of sky and ocean; it is nearly always associated with distances far greater than we have in the house. This is one reason why it is often unsatisfactory as a color for the walls of our modest room.

Dark-stained woodwork almost requires a deeply saturated wall color to stand up to it, as dark woodwork has an ability to suck all the color out of a shade that may have appeared quite dark on a paint chip. The main thing about paint colors is that you absolutely have to try them on the wall. You can't just pick them from a chip. A two-foot square is good, and ideally you should prime the wall with white first because the new color will look different against whatever color the wall is now. Put it next to the woodwork, too. Then you should look at the color at various times of day, under natural and artificial light, before deciding. Some paint manufacturers have wised up and started to offer small samples to be used for this purpose—otherwise you'll just have to break down and buy a quart.

In general, besides sticking with muted "ish" colors, what you want in a color is complexity. A complex color will change with the light and be somewhat difficult to pin down. What makes a color complex? Lots of different pigments. For instance, a simple pale yellow will contain only yellow coloring in a white base, while a complex yellow will also contain trace amounts of red, brown, green, black, etc., along with the majority yellow pigment. The advent of computerized color matching has been a great leap forward; now you can match the paint to the curtains, to the sample of original paint you found in the back of a closet, or to your cat (if it will allow itself to be held up to the scanner at the paint store).

PAINT SUPERSTITIOUS

In the bungalow era, paint was usually composed of finely ground pigments, linseed oil, turpentine, and white lead (later replaced by zinc oxide in some formulations, and by titanium oxide in the 1920s). Later in the twentieth century the linseed oil was replaced with synthetic alkyd resins. Premixed paint had been around since shortly after the Civil War, although some painters were still mixing their own even into the twentieth century. Oil-base paint continued to be the standard until well after World War II. Recent environmental regulations regarding allowable amounts of volatile organic compounds (VOCs) have pretty much been the death knell for oil-base paints in this century.

The color palette in premixed paint of the time was quite limited compared to the thousands of colors that are available to us now. Regardless of color, however, paint was always applied with a brush. Why? Because it was not until 1940 that Norman Breakey of Toronto invented the paint roller.

Latex paint, which is the standard now, got its start during World War II as chemists looked for substitutes for natural rubber since the war had put a crimp in the international supply and rubber was needed for the war effort. With government backing, researchers came up with a butadiene-styrene copolymer that was a good substitute. Looking for other uses, researchers came up with waterborne paint. First offered to consumers in 1948, the Glidden Company's "Spred Satin" sold 100,000 gallons the first year. Three years later, sales were up to 3.5 million gallons. Initially only good for interior use, further advances in technology, particularly the switch to acrylic binders, eventually allowed latex to become the paint of choice for most applications.

Wall and ceiling paint in most rooms should be flat or matte. Painted trim (if any) can be eggshell or semigloss. High gloss is not really appropriate for bungalows. Kitchens, bathrooms, laundry rooms, or utility areas can and probably should be semigloss for ease of cleaning.

An advertisement from Devoe and Raynolds Company in the August 1920 *American Builder* stated the contents of their paint pretty clearly, possibly overstating it a little by adding "AND NOTHING ELSE" in large letters. Devoe is still in business, now part of ICI, a French company that owns several American paint companies.

Various kinds of decorative painting were also used in addition to straight-wall and ceiling painting. All-over finishes like sponging, rag rolling, stippling, dragging, and so forth were employed. The "Tiffany finish," a polychrome finish done with glazes to resemble a really, really blurry Impressionist painting, was shown in a lot of advertisements; whether that many people went for it is somewhat questionable. Faux marble probably wasn't very common; it's just not very Arts and Crafts somehow. But murals were used—not necessarily realistic scenes, but abstracted or conventionalized landscapes. Murals were especially popular as a frieze above the plate rail in a dining room but could also be found in living rooms, entry halls, and even bedrooms.

When considering decorative painting, bear in mind this advice from *Interior Wall Decoration* regarding the living room but applying to other rooms as well: "Extraordinary or novel effects in this room might entertain or amuse the guests, but they are sure to become tiresome to the family."

STENCIL NECK GEEK

On top of the paint or the decorative finish, there might also be stenciling. Stenciled borders were particularly popular, useful near or on the ceiling, to outline panels between wood moldings, and so forth. Stenciling was also used to decorate various textile items such as curtains, pillows, table scarves, and portieres. Homeowners were encouraged to do stenciling themselves; it was a bit labor-intensive, but for lazy people it was also possible to buy wallpaper printed to look like stenciling.

Softly mottled yellow paint serves as a background for a stenciled border applied in the frieze above striped wallpaper in the entry hall of a Milwaukee bungalow.

In the same Milwaukee bungalow, plum-colored walls have been stenciled with a complex pendant border in mottled green and reddish-purple tones. Above, oak box beams crisscross to form a coffered ceiling.

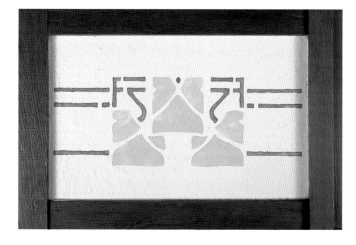

An ivy stencil designed by Helen Foster decorates a plaster panel in a bungalow in Victoria, British Columbia.

PAINT

OBSESSIVE RESTORATION

For those with unlimited money, original paint colors can be found by using microscopic analysis. For those with less money to burn, sanding down through the layers will eventually get you to the original layer, though it's important to bear in mind that color changes over time, so what you're seeing may not be quite what was originally there. (As an example, when Colonial Williamsburg was first restored beginning in the 1920s, widespread interest resulted in lines of "colonial" colors being made available to the public, and these were quite popular. These colors were based on actual paint chips as they looked after 200 years, and were rather muted. Because the technology for color analysis has greatly improved in recent years, it is now known that many of the original colors were actually rather bright, even garish by our standards.) This level of paint analysis is probably unrealistic for the average homeowner. At best, you might get a vague idea of the original color and try to replicate it with a new layer of paint.

Obviously you can paint the walls with a brush, though if there are several layers having the stippled effect that comes from applying paint with a roller, it may be slightly pointless to use a brush. On the other hand, it was recommended at the time that the paint be stippled (with a stippling brush) after application (oil paint gave one the time to do this), so maybe the point is more or less moot. For painted trim you certainly should paint it with a brush. (There is a ring of hell reserved for those who paint trim and doors with a roller, right next door to the ring of hell reserved for those who paint over sash locks!) Don't waste your money on cheap brushes—buy good ones, clean them thoroughly after use, and take good care of them. Rollers, on the other hand, I do not feel are worth cleaning. They never return to their original fluffiness, it takes incredible amounts of time, water, or solvent to get them even marginally clean, and they don't cost much anyway. Throw them out. And by the way, I've never noticed any difference between a cheap paint roller and an expensive one. Skilled painters rarely use masking tape, but if you are planning to use masking tape remember this: THERE IS ONLY BLUE TAPE! Yes, it costs three times as much as regular masking tape, and yes, it is worth every penny. It says you can leave it on seven days—I'm here to tell you, if it's not in direct sunlight, you can leave it on for months.

Oil-base paints and glazes are superior for certain kinds of faux finishes; the long drying time allows you much more leeway to manipulate the various aspects of the finish, not to mention wiping off your mistakes. It's always best to first try a faux finish on a board anyway instead of screwing it up on the wall. Or at least do it inside a closet or in a back hall first.

As oil-base paint becomes more difficult to procure; eventually you may have to give up and just go with latex. There are some alternatives, and paint companies are working on ways to make oil-base paints with different solvents that comply with new regulations for allowable VOCs. A couple of companies make environmentally friendly oil paints that use citrus-based solvents in lieu of the usual aromatic hydrocarbons. Naturally, these cost a lot more than regular paint. You can also buy environmentally friendly paint thinners for brush cleaning. It is unlikely that oil-base paint will be phased out entirely. Why? Because you just can't use water-base paint on ferrous metals—it causes them to rust.

Latex paints have improved by leaps and bounds in the last couple of decades, and are as good as oil in most applications. The one place I still think oil is better is for painting shelves, simply because once oil-base paint is dry, it's actually dry. Latex, which takes a good month to "cure," remains sticky underneath the apparently dry top film and causes things put on the shelves to stick.

COMPROMISE SOLUTION

Go ahead and use latex. Apply it with a roller if you want (except on trimwork—that special ring of hell is still waiting). You still need quality brushes, though, and you still have to take care of them. They may advertise that disposable foam brushes don't leave brush marks—they do. They're only useful for trying out colors, and even then you could just as easily use a regular brush.

Most latex paints still contain lots of nasty chemicals and VOCs, just not as much as oil-base paints. If that is a concern, there are water-base paints available with low or no VOCs, and some made with natural ingredients instead of synthetic chemicals. Naturally, these cost more than the regular stuff you'll find down at the local paint store.

ROLL MODELS

"There ought to be less promiscuous buying of wallpapers, drapes, cretonne, cushions, scarfs, pictures, rugs, pottery, and vases. When this is accomplished much more success will be gained in constructing beautiful, restful, and harmonious interiors."

—F. N. Vanderwalker, *Interior Wall Decoration,* 1924

Of course, Mr. Vanderwalker was a painter. There was continuing competition between paint manufacturers and wallpaper manufacturers to control the wall decoration in American homes. It is a competition that continues today.

Plaster walls that were not painted or tinted could be covered in various ways, utilizing wallpaper, grasscloth, fabrics such as linen or burlap, or other wallcoverings such as Anaglypta, Lincrusta, leather, or faux leather. Lincrusta is a

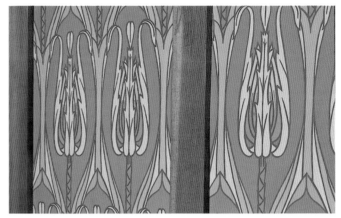

Above: Strips of Anaglypta wallpaper between oak battens add texture to the walls in the dining room of a bungalow in Milwaukee, Wisconsin. Anaglypta is generally painted.

Middle: Bradbury and Bradbury wallpaper in the Thistle pattern fills the spaces between Douglas fir battens in the dining room of a Seattle bungalow.

Below: Deep-blue faux-leather wallpaper resembling elephant hide covers the walls behind a freestanding Arts and Crafts sideboard. The plate rail above is decorated with small corbels that line up with the battens below.

Above left: Lincrusta was often finished to resemble tooled leather, though many times it was merely painted. Its nearly indestructible composition made it popular for hallways and stairways.

Below left: The walls of a bedroom in an Arts and Crafts home in Berkeley, California, are covered with a contemporary magnolia paper by wallpaper designer Carol Mead, which is based on an 1891 paper by Lewis F. Day, who, along with Walter Crane and W. R. Lethaby, were founders of the Art Workers Guild.

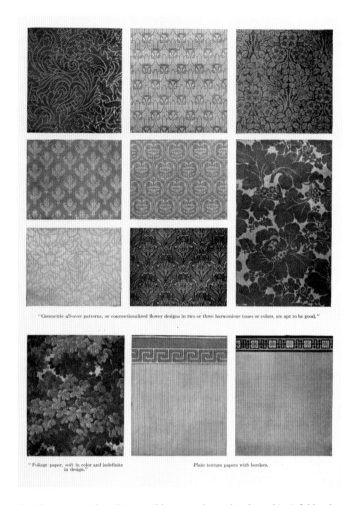

"Geometric all-over patterns, or conventionalized flower designs in two or three harmonious tones or colors, are apt to be good."

"Foliage paper, soft in color and indefinite in design."

Plain texture papers with borders.

Just in case you thought everything was always lovely and tasteful back in 1912, consider this page from *Home Building and Decoration,* showing mostly tasteful conventionalized flowers and geometrics except for the middle-right example, which is surely as bad as any flocked Mylar paper from the 1970s ever was.

In its June 1915 issue, *American Carpenter and Builder* showed a leather-paneled dining room, noting "Whether Real Alligator Hide or Not Makes Very Little Difference!" (They were very fond of capitals in those days.) The room has a built-in window seat strewn with embroidered pillows, while the windows have sheer curtains and over-curtains with a ruffled valance. The box beams on the ceiling show their complete lack of support function by both starting and ending in the middle of the ceiling.

form of linoleum with a deeply embossed pattern; Anaglypta is a similar product made from paper pulp.

The nineteenth-century concept of dado, fill, and frieze continued for bungalow wallpaper, but elaborate ceiling treatments with corner decorations, borders, and central motifs began to simplify considerably in bungalows. Ceilings might still be papered, but often with linen or other fabric, or small all-over motifs with narrow borders at the edges outlining the beams, or forming panels in the ceiling.

A subdued Arts and Crafts look was often accomplished through the use of *ingrain* or *oatmeal* papers. Invented in 1877, ingrain papers utilized cotton or woolen rag fibers that were dyed before being made into paper. Ingrain papers could be used plain or printed with a design. Early on, mineral colors were used for printing; by the 1920s, aniline dyes were used instead. Ingrain papers were available plain or

with printed designs; plain papers might be stenciled or have borders pasted on top.

Burlap was available with a backing under the name Fabrikona. There were also varnished papers (usually in tile patterns) for kitchens and bathrooms. Many papers had hints of mica or gold that added sparkle to the papers. The fill papers tended toward simplicity—stripes, diaper (diagonal) patterns, small all-over patterns, or just texture.

Realistic floral designs were frowned on, particularly those with trelliswork. Flowers were abstracted or conventionalized instead. This did not, of course, mean that wallpaper with realistic flowers was unavailable, nor did it mean that people didn't use it.

Gustav Stickley recommended leather:

As a wall-covering, it has a richness of tone, an unobtrusive character which is approached by no textile hanging. It offers with each gradation of light and each play of shadow beauties which attract by their novelty and changefulness. It is an important factor in the making of a restful and distinguished interior.

For those who couldn't afford the real thing (or maybe for the vegetarians), there were many varieties of faux leather papers.

Frieze papers were particularly popular for bungalows. *Pendant* friezes had a decorative border with stylized "pendants" dropping down at regular intervals. Landscape friezes had views of simplified pastoral scenery, often resembling a distant view through a line of trees. Floral friezes used stylized flowers, vines, brambles, and the like, although many also utilized sinuous Art Nouveau curves.

Wallpapers designed by William Morris in the nineteenth century continued to be sold, as well as papers designed by J. H. Dearle, who had taken over as the primary designer after Morris' death in 1896.

INNER PIECES

"In the simple home all is quiet in effect, restrained in tone, yet natural and joyous in its frank use of unadorned material. Harmony of line and balance of proportion is not obscured by meaningless ornamentation; harmony of color is not marred by violent contrasts. Much of the construction shows, and therefore good workmanship is required and the craft of the carpenter is restored to its old-time dignity. In such a home, inspiring in its touch with art and books, glorified by mother love and child sunshine, may the human spirit grow in strength and grace to the fulness of years."
—Charles Keeler, *The Simple Home*, 1904

Arts and Crafts designers conceived of the bungalow interior as a harmonious whole, and the integration of all of the architectural components—windows, doors, built-ins, paneling, trim, wall and ceiling finishes, fireplaces, flooring, light fixtures, and hardware—was fundamental to achieving

Above: In detail, the embossed grain of this faux-leather wallpaper contrasts nicely with the stained oak battens.

Below: The dining room of my own home, the 1905 Sunset House, shows the interplay of elements deemed harmonious by Arts and Crafts designers. The dark stained woodwork includes structural ceiling beams, board-and-batten paneling, a 4- by 6-inch plate rail, 2- by 6-inch door and window trim, and a built-in china cabinet separated from the rest of the room by a wide doorway with low walls on either side. (No sign there were ever columns there.) A set of french doors leads onto a porch, and was once matched by another set opposite that opened onto the front porch; they have since been replaced by windows for security reasons. The china cabinet has 4- by 4-inch corner posts and fake pegged through-tenons. Banks of casement windows on three sides flood the room with light, while four original pendant lights provide lighting at night. This photo was taken the day I moved in; I have a more appropriate dining table than this one.

this goal. Though the veneration of the hearth as the very heart and soul of the home was embraced with near-religious fervor, the reverence for wood was certainly running a close second. Wood has been a favored building material for thousands of years; during the Arts and Crafts movement, wood was admired for its innate qualities of color and grain, brought out by simple clear finishes, and even the less expensive softwoods like fir and pine were appreciated for their own simple beauty, bringing them out of the shadow of hardwoods like oak and mahogany. Gustav Stickley wrote, ". . . no other treatment of the walls gives such a sense of friendliness, mellowness, and permanence as does a generous quantity of woodwork."

And I think I'd better address this right here. Bungalows were and are dark. Get over it. It doesn't give you the right to paint the woodwork to make it "light and bright" like all the real estate ads always say. Those who tell you to paint the unpainted woodwork, saying "It can always be stripped later," are people who have never in their lives stripped paint off of woodwork. And don't even think of complaining to me about how dark your bungalow is—I have to wear a Tikka headlamp just to hang up a curtain rod! Come over to the dark side; it has powers you've never dreamed.

PANEL WITH CARE

Wood paneling was applied to the walls in many bungalows, but is probably most present in dining rooms. Unlike the raised panels and more elaborate woodwork of previous centuries, the paneling was generally quite simple, often 12-inch-wide boards covered with flat battens (narrow boards) at the joints. Another common kind of board-and-batten paneling utilized veneered plywood (or veneer over solid boards), which allowed wider panels and the opportunity to use a veneer with an interesting grain pattern. The battens were usually flat boards measuring 3/4 by 2, 3, or 4 inches wide. Fairly simple flat moldings were also used as battens, which were also used by themselves over plaster, the spaces between painted, wallpapered, or covered with linen,

Square corbel blocks accent the paneling, door trim, and built-in sideboard of a bungalow in Eagle Rock, California. The upper cabinet with its leaded-glass doors is supported by short square pillars. A soft yellow color on the plaster sets off the red tones of the fir woodwork, and the rabbit vase on the table is a visual pun relating to the first owner of the bungalow, the Reverend Hare. (And you know how much I like puns!)

Above: Painted paneling with small corbels gives an English Arts and Crafts look to this Memphis bungalow dining room.

Below: Paneling in a Seattle bungalow shows a grayed tone that was fairly common for bungalow woodwork, usually accomplished by tinting shellac or by brushing on diluted oil paint and then wiping most of it off.

The beautiful grain of birch is shown on this door in a Chicago bunga-low. The wide molding in the center panel is somewhat unusual for a bungalow door.

The side casing crosses the head casing with a half-lap joint held by four square pegs in this Seattle bungalow. No, I don't think they are in round holes.

burlap, or a textured wallcovering like Lincrusta or Anaglypta. Real or faux leather was also popular. Other designs for paneling depended on the whim of the designer: decorative cutouts in the boards, decorative blocks along the battens, coffers, and anything else that struck the builder's fancy. Beadboard as well as board-and-batten were also used as paneling, though traditionally their use was limited to the utilitarian spaces like kitchens, bath-rooms, hallways, and utility areas.

Paneling could cover the entire height of the wall or only part of it. Paneling that goes only partway up the wall is referred to as wainscoting. Common heights might be four feet high (usually topped with a piece of molding called *chair rail,* ostensibly to keep the chair backs from banging into the wall); five feet high (often capped by a *plate rail,* a wide molding with grooves routed into it to hold plates); or six feet high (makes the plates a little hard to get to unless you're tall). A plate rail was often supported by ornamental *corbels* or blocks.

Beadboard paneling often cov-ered the entire wall as well as the ceiling in utilitarian areas, though it was just as often used as wainscot-ing. At the time, it was a cheap alter-native to plaster. In some homes, there may be no plaster at all, and all the walls and ceilings will be cov-ered with beadboard. Although usu-ally run vertically, in certain parts of the country it was traditionally run horizontally instead.

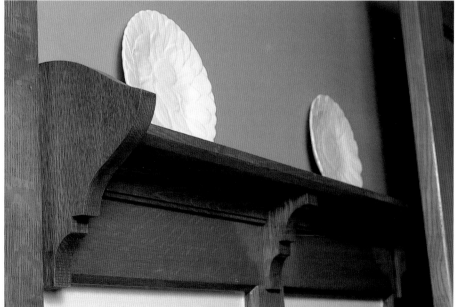

Left: Jig-sawn corbels support a wide plate rail, with larger matching corbels on the ends.

Facing: Gum Lumber Manufacturers' Associa-tion of Memphis, Tennessee, ran this advertise-ment in the June 1918 issue of *House Beautiful,* calling the wood "a joy to the eye." The room featured is somewhat grander than what would be found in a bungalow, but there are still many Arts and Crafts touches.

Above left: A wide doorway in a Memphis bungalow is cased in tupelo. Crown molding sits atop the head casing, a small fillet separates the head casing, and the transom has been filled with a decorative frieze.

Above right: Bird's-eye maple is not a common wood in bungalows, but it was utilized in this bedroom. Notice the rounded edges on the side casing, and the molded fillet.

ALL THE TRIMMINGS

The Arts and Crafts movement celebrated Nature, particularly Nature as expressed in the varied grains and hues of wood, and this is most clearly demonstrated by the plethora of wooden paneling, baseboards, casings, moldings, columns, colonnades, plate rails, and so forth found in the average bungalow. Even as bungalows became simplified in the 1920s, they still retained far more wood trim than is found in homes of later periods.

Which woods were favored for trim depended a certain amount on the location of the bungalow. In keeping with the Arts and Crafts ideal of local materials, readily available local woods were often used. In the East, this often meant oak, though oak was used everywhere. In the South, the wood might be heart pine, cypress, or tupelo (also known as red gumwood). In the Midwest, birch and maple were favored. On the West Coast (from Southern California to the Pacific Northwest), Douglas fir (also known as Oregon pine), redwood, gumwood (eucalyptus), and Port Orford cedar were the most popular. But many other woods, such as mahogany, chestnut, poplar, cherry, ash, walnut, teak, beech, butternut, etc., also made an appearance, though imported woods like teak were limited to expensive homes, not the average tract bungalow.

Wood was left natural or stained, and then given a clear finish of shellac, varnish, wax, or oil. Oak was often fumed (exposed to ammonia vapors) before installation to bring out the colors in the wood. Contrary to our modern expectation of brown furniture in brown houses with matte green pottery, they were a little more adventurous at the time, often giving the wood a transparent stain of green, grey, brown, olive, or even blue before the finish was applied. Often the pigments in these stains have not held up or have faded over time (blue is particularly unstable). On the other hand, not everyone thought that was a good idea. F. Maire, author of the *Modern Painter's Cyclopedia* (1934; originally published 1910) railed against the idea:

> It certainly is not in good taste to stain woods in colors that do not belong to them, as blues, greens, etc., and while this is a free country, etc., as long as a person is not sent to the penitentiary for committing outrages against nature, nor to insane asylums, it is very probable that the practice will go on undisturbed. But it is vulgarity, to say the least of the practice, and painters should not encourage it.

Above: Interesting woodwork with through-tenons tops a red-brick fireplace in a Seattle bungalow. The Douglas fir used has been given a slightly gray finish.

Below: Made to look like timber framing, a curved brace crosses the corner of a wide opening that separates the inglenook from the rest of the living room in this Prairie-style bungalow in Memphis, Tennessee. Held with pegs (which may or may not be real), the brace has been subtly notched into the post at the side and into the beam on top.

The Arts and Crafts designers believed that the colors of the wood, the walls, the ceiling, the floors, and the furnishings were all meant to work together to form a harmonious whole.

Wood trim in some rooms was likely to be painted, though even this was not universal. The room most likely to have painted woodwork was probably the bathroom, followed by the kitchen because it was thought to be more sanitary, and they were quite obsessed with sanitation at the time most bungalows were built. Bedrooms were the next most likely rooms to have painted woodwork.

Sometimes the woodwork would be given a painted finish, generally called *graining* or *faux bois* (French for "false wood"). If done well, this kind of finish can make inexpensive woods look like expensive woods, turning pine into mahogany, for instance. The bad news is, it often was not done well, making perfectly good fir look like bad gumwood. This sort of finish was especially prevalent in the late 1920s and early 1930s; perhaps it was an attempt to make bungalows more like the Romantic Revival homes, which often had woodwork of mahogany or other hardwoods, that were overtaking the bungalow in popularity at that point. Bad Graining of this sort causes the Obsessive Restorer to have a conniption fit, because the impulse to restore a historic finish is completely at odds with the accompanying urge to remove something that is badly done and ugly. There is no good answer to this question.

Besides its decorative purpose, trim is used to bridge gaps and joints between different building materials or architectural features. Unlike the skimpy moldings used in most contemporary houses, trim and moldings in bungalows tended to be substantial though simple in design.

Where the wall meets the floor, baseboards ranging from 4 inches high to more than 2 feet high provided a transition to the wall surface above. Baseboards could either be one piece or could be built up from several pieces of wood. The simplest baseboards were simply flat boards, usually measuring 3/4 to 1 inch thick. These were "eased" on the back side by having the center of the board slightly hollowed out, leaving a very shallow ridge on each side—this gave the board the ability to conform to uneven wall surfaces. In the days of plentiful old-growth timber, a single baseboard could be as wide as 24 inches, though 5- to 7-inch-wide baseboards were the most common. The bottom of the baseboard might be finished off with *shoe molding,* or *base shoe,* a small (3/4 to 1 inch) quarter-round molding. The top edge of the baseboard might have a *cap molding,* which was either molded into the top edge of a one-piece baseboard or added as a separate piece or pieces.

HEAD CASE

Around windows and doors, there is an interplay of several moldings, including *casings,* which cover the joint between the jambs (top and side pieces the depth of the wall, which

Above: The interplay of jambs, stops, casings, and other moldings shows off the beauty of the varnished tupelo woodwork on a doorway of a Memphis bungalow.

Left: This doorway shows what lovely things can be accomplished with simple pieces of wood. Corbels hold up a shallow shelf on top of the head casing, while a single corbel holds up a similar shelf notched into the side casing and the post below the vertical muntins of a "window." Below that, narrow battens over wood panels are decorated with small cutout diamonds.

Above: A zany take on applying moldings: these bay windows have side casings taller than the head casing and capped with crown moldings.

Above: A bookcase flanking a fireplace has a low niche above arched glass doors, and corbels ornamenting the head casing.

Below: A roomful of moldings is shown on this page of a 1927 *Universal Design Book on Builder's Woodwork,* including a head casing with crown molding and fillet, a window stool and apron, baseboards, shoe molding, side casings, and window, doorstop, and picture moldings.

Below: An even simpler set of moldings is shown on another page of the *Universal Design Book.* The head casing is plain, though cut to form a slight peak echoing the shallow pitched roof of a bungalow. The other moldings are equally plain.

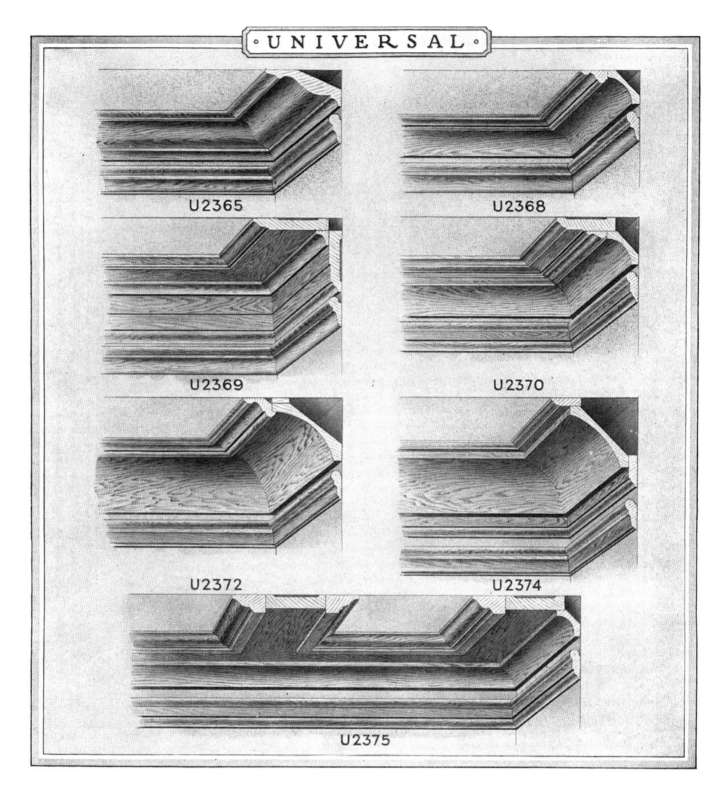

• U N I V E R S A L •

U2365

U2368

U2369

U2370

U2372

U2374

U2375

Another page from the *Universal Design Book* illustrates the various kinds of crown and associated moldings the company can supply. Except for the very small cove molding in U2369, all of the crown moldings are sprung. Picture molding is shown as the bottom element in all the assemblages.

form the frame around a window or door), and *stop* moldings (which the door closes against, or which keep the window sash in place). Windows may also have a *stool* (the interior sill) and an *apron* (a piece of molding below the stool). Not all windows have a stool, merely having another stop molding along the bottom and an apron below. (This lack of interior sills really annoys cats.) The top casing, often called a *lintel* or *head casing*, may also have *crown molding* on top, or a piece of rounded molding called a *fillet* inserted where the head casing meets the side casings. Casings may also have a molding on the outer edges called a *backband*, which may be a separate piece or may be made all in one piece with the casing. Although more common in Victorian interiors, side casings may also sit on *plinth blocks*, basically a block that is slightly wider than the casing and about as high as the baseboard.

Casings, stops, and window aprons may either be made from flat stock (generally 4 or 5 inches wide), in which case they usually have *butt joints* (ends meet at right angles), or they may be of molded stock, in which case the joints have to be mitered (cut at a 45-degree angle). A molded apron has mitered ends with a small *return*, a very small mitered piece that "returns" the molding to the wall surface.

Most bungalows also have *picture molding*, a specially shaped molding made to accept S-shaped metal hooks for hanging pictures. Why? So you don't make nail holes in the plaster. Picture molding obviously runs horizontally, and may be placed anywhere from the top of the door and window frames (which are usually lined up for continuity), to somewhere above the door frames, or right up near the ceiling (generally leaving about a 1/2-inch clearance for the hooks). Picture molding also allows for moving pictures around easily. Although the Victorians mostly used only one hook, which resulted in a V-shape for the wire, the Arts and Crafts designers insisted on two hooks so the wires would hang straight down at either side of the artwork, which naturally makes it harder to get the picture to hang straight. (The secret is to use one long piece of wire, which goes from one picture hook down through an eyelet on one side of the picture, across the back and through the eyelet on the other side of the picture, and back up to the second molding hook. This allows the picture to slide along the wire till it's straight.) Sometimes leather straps or linen cords were used instead of wire.

Many bungalows had *crown molding* at the intersection of the walls and ceiling, which could range in width from an inch or two all the way up to a foot or even more. These were simpler in profile than the crown moldings used in previous centuries. Some were all one piece, and some were built up using narrower moldings. Crown moldings, especially the wider types, are generally *sprung*, having the back side cut at an angle (which can be anywhere from 30 to 52 degrees) so that only the edges touch the walls and the ceiling. Mostly this is done to save on wood. Some nar-

rower moldings are not sprung, and have the full 90-degree angle on the back (sometimes referred to as *bed moldings*, although bed moldings can also be sprung).

Crown moldings made of plaster, though not as common as wood moldings, were found in some bungalows, either at the joint between wall and ceiling or as part of a decorative ceiling treatment such as a tray ceiling. Often these plaster moldings utilize classical motifs such as egg-and-dart, acanthus leaves, or dentils, which one might not expect to find in a bungalow.

TOTALLY COPACETIC

Moldings are usually mitered (meet at a 45-degree angle) on outside corners. Inside corners of flat moldings can also be mitered, but shaped moldings are *coped* at inside corners. A coped joint is basically a butt joint where the end of one piece of molding is carefully scribed to mimic the shape of the front of the other piece so that a tight joint is formed when they meet at right angles. We will ignore for the moment how out-of-square an old house is likely to be. Sprung moldings require a *compound miter* at outside corners, and it makes my brain hurt just thinking about it. That's because you have to deal with both the *miter* (the saw blade pivots left or right of the centerline at an angle but remains at a right angle to the bottom of the miter box or the table of the miter saw) and the *bevel* (the saw blade itself tilts to form a less than 90-degree angle in relation to the bottom of the miter box or the table of the miter saw). In a compound miter, the saw blade is both pivoted and tilted at the same time. Add to this the complexity of figuring out appropriate angles for the bevel, which depends on what degree the crown molding itself is sprung, and it inspires a whole new respect for the old-time finish carpenters who did all this without the benefit of laser-guided sliding compound miter saws.

COLONNADES

To make a small bungalow appear more spacious, the major rooms often opened to each other with wide openings, sometimes filled by a colonnade. A colonnade, as one might suspect, often involved columns. Usually these columns sat upon partial walls, which could be anywhere from a couple of feet high to five or six feet high. The walls often contained bookcases or built-in desks, adding function to the decorative aspect. The columns themselves frequently echoed the shape of the porch columns outside, being square or tapered and somewhat on the elephantine side. But they might also be simple round Tuscan columns. Sometimes the walls were so high that the columns became ridiculously short, just one more bungalow amusement. In some homes, the walls were eliminated and the columns sat directly on the floor. Colonnades were

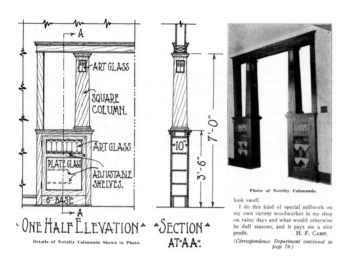

Above: A "novelty colonnade" with backlit art-glass set into the pillars was sent in by a reader of *American Builder* and published in the August 1918 issue. One assumes that one of the art-glass panels was hinged so that the lightbulb could be changed.

Below: The Chicago Grille Works advertised this very typical colonnade in the December 1915 issue of *American Carpenter and Builder*. A bookcase with leaded-glass doors anchors the left-hand side, while a drop-front desk with cubbyholes is on the right. These usually faced the living room side, while the dining room side was paneled, although shallow cabinets were sometimes placed on the dining room side.

Above: A somewhat unusual colonnade forms a partial wall between the living room and dining room of a bungalow shown in the December 1917 issue of *American Builder*. Four tapered columns, two forming a doorway and the rest connected by high partitions, form a backdrop for a lounging area with comfy pillows. The ceiling beams in both rooms are painted, though in most bungalows they would have been left natural. In the dining room, a bowl fixture hangs from chains over a round table.

Chicago Grille Works Desk and Bookcase Colonnade.

most often found between the living and dining rooms but were also used to separate the living or dining rooms from the entry hall, or to separate a nook or plus room from whatever was next to it.

A COLUMN OCCASION

Columns could appear in other places as well—as part of a built-in sideboard, at the bottom of stairways, as part of an *overmantel* above a fireplace, and so forth. Pilasters (half-columns) were also utilized around doors or fireplaces, as part of paneling, and anywhere else a designer could think of putting them.

BETTER PLATE THAN NEVER

Paneled wainscoting, especially in a dining room, though also in other rooms, was often topped with a *plate rail,* a piece of wood with grooves routed into the top to hold decorative plates. Often the plate rail was held up by ornamental corbels or blocks. If the bungalow owner didn't have plates to display, it also worked well for prints and paintings, vases, and other objets d'art that every bungalow was supposed to have. It works pretty well for flaunting your snow-globe collection or your PEZ dispensers, too.

MILLING AROUND

In spite of all the lip service given to handwork by the Arts and Crafts movement, probably the majority of millwork in bungalows was purchased from millwork shops and through catalogs. It was possible to buy all the prefabricated millwork for a house, including doors, windows, mantels, colonnades, built-in cabinetry, trimwork, inglenooks, paneling, moldings, etc., rather than paying finish carpenters to build all of it. Probably a combination of prefabricated and site-built millwork was used in most bungalows, since some aspects of the trim (such as crown moldings) were better fitted on-site.

Above: This Curtis Company colonnade, featuring short pillars and tall book-cases with wooden muntins, separates the living room from the entry hall in this advertisement in the March 1918 issue of *American Builder.* The copy notes that "Curtis Standard designs cost no more now than special woodwork cost 'before the war.'" And in case the reader wasn't clear where they should be employing the woodwork, there was a picture of a bungalow at the bottom.

Left: Dowels anchor a finger-jointed corner below the plate rail in a Greene & Greene home.

Small wooden pyramids decorate the mantel held up by wooden corbels on a clinker brick fireplace.

WOOD YOU BE MINE?

In keeping with Arts and Crafts precepts, the majority of bungalows used local woods for trim and paneling, especially modest bungalows. Large, fancy, or architect-designed bungalows were more likely to make use of imported, exotic, or expensive woods. Often the wood used in an unpretentious bungalow was whatever was least expensive locally, often a softwood like pine or fir, although in some areas of the country the inexpensive wood was a hardwood such as birch or oak. Softwoods are in no way a lesser quality wood than hardwoods—pretty much all of this wood was close-grained old-growth timber. Softwood merely refers to wood that comes from conifers (evergreens), whereas hardwoods come from trees that are deciduous. Some softwoods (like Douglas fir) are actually harder than woods classified as hardwoods (such as balsa). Popular woods for bungalow interiors ranged from Douglas fir (also known as Oregon pine) or redwood in the West, to birch, maple, and oak in the Midwest, longleaf pine in the South, and oak, maple, and other hardwoods in the East. In some places, local woods like tupelo, cypress, chestnut, etc., were used. (Chestnut was mostly wiped out by a blight introduced around 1900, and by the 1930s there were very few chestnuts left.) Gumwood, which was also fairly prevalent, comes from various

species of eucalyptus, a tree originally imported from Australia but fairly common in America by the bungalow era. Due to the popularity of kit or precut houses, which were often cut in regional factories and shipped by rail, the interior woodwork in any given bungalow may not present local woods at all. The formal rooms (living room, dining room, and so forth) might have had woodwork that utilized a more expensive wood than the rest of the house. In other homes, it was all the same wood throughout.

More exotic woods like mahogany, teak, and such had to be imported and thus were higher priced. But not all exotic woods were imported. American-grown woods like Port Orford cedar (which grows primarily along a narrow range within fifty miles of the Oregon and far northern California coasts), or variants like curly maple, curly redwood, butternut, etc., made an appearance as well. And unusual veneers were affordable and could be used as the finish layer of plywood paneling with solid wood battens of a different wood.

In point of fact, plywood had been invented by the ancient Egyptians, who had figured out that layers of thin veneer with the grain of each layer running at right angles to the previous layer was much stronger and more stable than solid wood. Veneers had been used on furniture for a long time, but plywood was first patented in 1865 by John K. Mayo as a building material. Plywood might not have happened at all if the rotary lathe had not been invented in the nineteenth century, allowing veneers to be cut quickly and inexpensively. In 1905, the Portland Manufacturing Company was asked to produce "something unusual" from wood for the Lewis and Clark Exposition in Portland, Oregon, being held later that year. Plant manager Gustav Carlson came up with Douglas fir plywood, calling it "three-ply veneer work." Initially the primary consumers of the new product were door, cabinet, and trunk manufacturers. In 1934, chemist James Nevin developed a waterproof adhesive that enabled the production of exterior plywood, but it wasn't until 1938 that industry-wide standards were adopted and plywood was approved by the Federal Housing Administration (FHA) for exterior use. Plywood in most of the uses we think of, such as exterior sheathing, subflooring, and so forth, was not widespread until after World War II.

NICE GUYS FINISH CLEAR

Because of the veneration of wood during the Arts and Crafts movement, woodwork in the formal rooms was almost always given a clear finish, usually shellac or varnish or, occasionally, just a coat of wax. Bedrooms, hallways, kitchens, and bathrooms might also have clear finished wood, although about half the time the wood in these rooms was painted. And I *will* have to throttle the next person who says to me that ". . . softwoods were cheap woods that were always supposed to be painted . . .," implying that somehow softwoods are unworthy of a clear finish. That may have been true in other periods, but during the bungalow age that was not the case. It might be good to bear in mind that vertical grain Douglas fir and heart pine are now more expensive than oak, and that Port Orford cedar, also a softwood, is now unbelievably expensive, in part because the cedars are being killed by a root fungus.

FONDUE LAC

Shellac is a finish made from resinous secretions of the *lac* beetle, *Coccus lacca,* which is collected from trees in India. It is cooked up, and then stretched into sheets. Once dry, it is broken up into flakes, which are then dissolved in denatured alcohol to form the finish. (Denatured alcohol is alcohol that has been made poisonous so you won't be tempted to drink it. You could also dissolve your shellac in vodka, but it would be kind of expensive.) Shellac comes in several colors, including platinum, yellow, orange, garnet, and various shades of brown, depending on when and where it was harvested. It can also be (and often was) tinted. The most common kinds found pre-dissolved at the paint store are orange shellac (actually kind of brown) and clear (which is bleached but still a bit on the amber side). Premixed shel-

The Murphy Varnish Company offered "Univernish, The Universal Varnish" in an ad in the March 1919 *American Builder,* claiming it could be scrubbed with hot water and soap and would not turn white nor be affected by boiling water.

lac should be used within a year of purchase—after that it will not dry properly and remain sticky. Bought in flakes, more color choices are available, and flakes don't go bad. The orange and brown colors give a certain "dipped in molasses" look to woodwork, which is quite lovely. Shellac will stick to practically anything except wax and polyurethane (and there are those who disagree on that point); it is nontoxic and even edible (it is still used for coating candies, pills, and such). It dries quickly, and although it's less durable than other finishes, it's also ludicrously easy to repair—a new coat of shellac simply dissolves into the coat underneath, so there is little need for stripping, sanding, or lengthy preparation. A topcoat of varnish applied over the "de-waxed" type of shellac will increase its durability; topcoats don't stick to waxy shellac very well, though waxy shellac is preferred for some uses like instrument restoration.

VARNISHING POINT

Varnish was made by heating various oils, combining them with plant resins or gums (typically from trees), and dissolving that mixture in solvents (also from trees, such as turpentine). Later in the twentieth century, plant resins were supplanted by synthetic resins such as the various urethanes and alkyds, and turpentine was supplanted by mineral spirits. Nowadays there are also water-based varnishes, which are basically latex paint without the pigment.

Oil finishes were used on occasion, generally boiled linseed oil mixed with turpentine. Boiled linseed oil isn't boiled at all any more—it has a cobalt additive that makes it oxidize (harden) more quickly, so it dries in a day instead of a week. Oil finishes oxidize when exposed to air. Tung oil from China was also used, starting in the twentieth century. Oil finishes sink into the wood rather than forming a film on top, and are more flexible, so they don't crack with wood movement like varnish.

Spar varnish contains more oil than resin, making it more forgiving of seasonal wood movement in exterior applications. It also contains ultraviolet inhibitors to impede the degradation of wood by sunlight.

Polyurethane tends to make woodwork look like it's been encased in plastic, unless it is put on in very light coats and sanded. The water-base polyurethanes seem especially prone to looking like plastic.

Some architects or builders even recommended no finish at all on woodwork. (Bernard Maybeck was big on this.) They were men, of course, who at that time never had to clean anything. No finish at all is not a good idea.

LACQUERED UP

Lacquer wasn't often used on woodwork, though it had been used in China and Japan for centuries. Natural lacquer is the sap of the Asian sumac tree, *Rhus verniciflua*, from whence comes the term "varnish" (from the French *vernis*). Called *urushu* in Japan, the sap contains *urushiol*, the toxic compound also found in our own poisonous plants: oak, ivy, and sumac. Nonetheless, when exposed to humid air and heat, the sap combines with oxygen molecules from the water to form a hard semitranslucent film.

In the 1920s, a new kind of solvent-based lacquer was introduced, made from *nitrocellulose* (cellulose derived from cotton and combined with nitric acid to form *cellulose nitrate*) dissolved in fun toxic solvents like acetone, toluene, and so forth. It dried so fast it could only be applied by spraying, and was first used as an automobile finish. It wasn't so much the toxic solvents that kept it from being used but the fact that nitrocellulose is explosive and also used as a substitute for gunpowder. Lacquers using acrylic resins were developed in the 1950s. Because of the toxic nature of the solvents, much work has been done to develop water-based lacquers. Brushing lacquer is also available—it contains added ingredients to retard drying so it can be brushed.

Lacquer was rarely used on woodwork, due to the difficulty of application. Paste wax was used either by itself or over shellac or varnish as an extra layer of protection. It's a bit labor-intensive, having to be renewed at least once a year.

THE STAIN IN SPAIN

Although the woodwork was often left in its natural color, it was stained just as often. Nowadays we think of bungalows as being brown houses full of brown furniture, but in reality, other colors of stain were used, though they may have faded after eighty or ninety years. Stains did tend toward earthy tones like browns, greens, and grays, but reddish tones and blue were not unheard of. Stickley stained his daughters' bedroom blue, though blue is probably the least stable of all pigments.

Colored shellac, in naturally occurring colors or tinted with alcohol soluble stains, was also used to add color to woodwork.

"Beautiful birch" was the slogan of the Northern Hemlock and Hardwood Manufacturers Association in this ad from the October 1915 *American Carpenter and Builder,* showing the dining room of a two-flat apartment building in Chicago. A wall-to-wall sideboard with windows under a shallow arch takes up one side of the room. French doors lead to what appears to be a sunporch. In the center, under a three-light chandelier, a not very Arts and Crafts lion-footed table holds court.

PAINT REMOVAL

Paint removal is probably the most tedious of all restoration tasks, but it is often necessary. This will not be a primer on paint stripping, just an overview. The choice of method boils down to hand scraping, heat, or chemicals.

Hand scraping can be used on surfaces that are smooth—obviously it won't work all that well on masonry. Scraping works well on peeling paint and somewhat less well on paint that's holding on for dear life. Different shapes of scrapers are available to use on molding and such. Scraping produces lead dust, so keep everything wet and wear a respirator. *Do not use belt sanders or orbital sanders for paint removal.*

Heat methods include heat guns, heat plates, or infrared heaters. *Do not use blowtorches!* Even with heat guns or plates, there is danger of setting the house on fire, so make sure you have a fire extinguisher handy. Heat methods cause the layers of paint to bubble up and release their hold on the substrate, at which point they can be scraped off. The upside of using heat is that it removes many layers at once, and once they cool off, they harden again, so you don't end up with toxic goop like you do with chemical strippers, though it will still be lead paint and suitable precautions should be taken. A high enough temperature (1100 degrees) can vaporize lead, but even at lower temperatures, the fumes are toxic, *so wear a respirator*. Heat will take off most of the paint, but a chemical stripper will probably be required to get the last bits of paint off. Heat really only works on wood—masonry, metal, and ceramic tile just absorb the heat and the paint doesn't come off well. Heat also doesn't work that well on clear finishes like varnish and shellac—tending to just make them gummy; chemicals generally work better for those finishes. On the other hand, when the varnish gets gummy, it tends to release the paint.

Infrared heaters (Silent Paint Stripper) work at lower temperatures than heat guns or plates, and are less likely to vaporize lead. You should still wear a respirator. And it is still necessary to protect the glass when stripping windows, or the heat will cause the glass to crack. They heat up a swath of paint about a foot long, which can then be scraped off. I found that as I got toward the end, the paint was starting to harden again and didn't scrape that easily, as opposed to using a heat gun, which allows one to move the putty knife along directly behind the heat gun so that paint can be scraped in a long fluid motion. The infrared stripper has a mechanism that can be used to prop it up to melt the next foot of paint while the first foot is being scraped off (if you're scraping something that can be laid flat). It works well on wide areas like casings or baseboards. I personally found it cumbersome to use; it's rather like trying to strip paint with a small space heater (they use the same technology), but it does really make all the layers of paint let go of the substrate, so the stripping is pretty clean. It's not too good for detail work.

Chemical methods usually involve toxic chemicals, and even the strippers advertised as nontoxic (like those based on citrus) are still strong chemicals, so wear chemical-resistant gloves. The really toxic chemicals, like methylene chloride, work faster than the citrus-based strippers, but they are poisonous and carcinogenic, so all the residue should be taken to your local hazardous waste collection point, not put in the regular trash. Actually most paint-stripping residue, whether from heat methods or chemical strippers, should probably go to the hazardous waste collection point because the paint is likely to contain lead.

Basically, you slap on the paint stripper in a thick coat, wait for the paint to bubble up, and then either scrape it off (for wood) or scrub it off (for masonry). It will probably require more than one application to strip off all the paint. After the paint is removed, usually the surface has to be neutralized with paint thinner, water, or a proprietary neutralizer made by the manufacturer of the stripper. Water tends to raise the grain of the wood, making it kind of fuzzy, and so the wood may require sanding before finishing. A lot of strippers will dry out; they no longer work if they aren't wet, so covering the stripper with a layer of plastic wrap will increase the "wet time."

There are some proprietary products on the market, including Peel-Away and Remov-All. Peel-Away uses a method where you apply the stripper, cover it with a special material, and leave it on for a certain period of time before removing it. The paint and stripper ostensibly stick to the material, so that when you peel it off, the paint comes with it. The trick with Peel-Away is to make several test patches because there is a certain ideal amount of time (anywhere from twelve to twenty-four hours) to leave it on for maximum "peelage." There are various formulations for different surfaces.

Remov-all is a product that breaks the bond between the paint and the substrate at the molecular level, causing the paint to peel off in big sheets. It's supposedly nontoxic. It also costs about four times as much as regular paint stripper, which might be worth it if it really works. It does work slowly, so it's a leave-it-on-overnight kind of product.

There is a product called Soy-Gel, made primarily

from soybeans; it is nontoxic and doesn't have a strong odor. It stays wet for a long time, and the gel formulation keeps it from dripping on vertical surfaces. It works fast (about ten minutes to remove several layers), though it's kind of sticky when you try to scrape it off. It does clean up with water, but not quite as easily as the company would lead you to believe.

No matter what method you use, there will be little bits of paint stuck in crevices and dents in the wood—this is where dental tools (picks) come in handy. Dental picks can be purchased at some hardware stores, hobby supply stores, or maybe you can convince your dental hygienist to give you used ones that would otherwise be thrown out. (Dental floss is handy for getting paint residue out of grooves in balusters, newel posts, and the like.) If the dental tools don't get all of it, sometimes putting on a coat of shellac and then stripping it off will work—shellac sticks tenaciously to just about anything, and will often take the little bits of paint with it when it is stripped off. If they just refuse to come off, a little judicious use of wood-colored paint can be used to make them disappear.

LEAD ASTRAY

As with asbestos, lead is a useful product that makes for strong long-lasting paint. Unfortunately, lead is also toxic and virtually indestructible (which is good in paint but bad in humans). At high levels, it can cause brain swelling, convulsions, coma, and even death. At low levels, it is associated with anemia, vomiting, digestive problems, and bizarre behavior, as well as damage to the brain, nervous system, and kidneys. It also poses a hazard to developing fetuses, and can affect the reproductive systems of both men and women. Because lead accumulates in bones and tissue, problems may persist over a long period of time. It is especially toxic to infants and toddlers, whose developing brains are particularly susceptible, and who are more likely to eat flaking paint chips. It's not good for adults either. The effects of long-term exposure in children are permanent. The lead companies had evidence of lead toxicity as early as the nineteenth century. By the 1920s, concerns about lead poisoning among professional painters caused one company to issue a paint in which the lead was replaced with zinc, though they continued to produce lead paint as well. Lead companies not only covered up the data, they continued to promote lead for painting children's rooms and toys, and as an additive for gasoline. Lead was not banned from paint in the United States until 1978, and was not phased out of gasoline until 1996. For comparison, lead paint was banned in France in 1917. Approximately six million tons of lead paint was applied to housing in the U.S. prior to the ban. There are approximately ten million metric tons of lead in the environment—in the air, water, and soil.

Lead paint in good condition is not a hazard. It is when the paint peels, chips, cracks, or is sanded or otherwise abraded that it becomes a problem. Most hardware stores sell a simple lead-test swab that turns pink in the presence of lead, although it's not always capable of detecting small amounts of lead.

Your local city or county will happily provide you with lots of information concerning lead paint and what to do about it. Or not do about it. Don't be cavalier about it—the dangers may have been a bit overblown, but they are still very real.

WOODWORK

OBSESSIVE RESTORATION

If your original woodwork is intact and has never been painted, keep it! Often the old finish may have darkened and alligatored, especially if it's shellac. There are those of us who are quite fond of old, crackled shellac. But if you're not one of them, judicious use of denatured alcohol will soften the top layer enough to move it around a little and get rid of the cracks. There is also a product called Restor-a-finish that does more or less the same thing. More alcohol will take most of the shellac off so you can start over. Shellac dries to a fairly high gloss—it can be rubbed out with steel wool (and a little mineral oil for lubrication) to take the shine down a notch or two, or you can buy a *flatting agent* to combine with the shellac for less shine. Using varnish as a topcoat is probably still within the Obsessive realm, and it will allow you to put something that contains ultraviolet inhibitors on your windows, which have a tendency to deteriorate from exposure to sunlight.

Sometimes the finish is just dirty, and washing it with something mild like Murphy's Oil Soap, with possibly some judicious use of 0000 steel wool (the finest grade) should get it looking decent again. If the woodwork is painted and you are not planning to strip the paint, stronger cleaning products (TSP, Spic & Span, etc.) can be used. However, the woodwork in the formal rooms should probably be stripped if they have been painted, unless there's a lot of irrefutable evidence that they were painted originally.

If the woodwork has a faux finish but some of it has chipped away or is otherwise missing, it can be replicated. If you don't care to undertake this task yourself, a decorative painter can do it for you. If there is Bad Graining, I guess it's between you and your conscience whether to fix it or get rid of it. I thank my lucky stars that so far I have not faced this particular dilemma.

The wood itself may be damaged or broken, dinged or dented. Whether it needs repair or not depends on the extent of the damage—from abuse or wear and tear, and from your own tolerance for "patina"; there can be a fine line between patina and damage. A reminder here that the goal of restoration is not "like new," it's "like old."

Clear-finished wood will require more careful repair than painted wood. Small holes or gouges in painted wood can be repaired with wood filler, water putty, epoxy putty, and the like, and then painted. Missing parts can be replicated using wood of a different species, since paint will hide the difference, though the truly obsessive wouldn't even think of doing that. I could make the argument that it would be a waste to paint now-scarce old growth timber—I would be inclined to save it for a use in which it could have a clear finish. A larger hole should be repaired using a *dutchman* (a piece of wood the same size and shape as the hole); usually the hole is cut into a more regular shape like a diamond or rectangle and the sides beveled slightly to hold the patch, which should be exactly the same size as the hole and similar in thickness to whatever is being patched. This method can be used to replace pieces that have broken off sides or ends as well. Obviously, when making a dutchman repair in clear finished wood, it becomes necessary to match the wood species and the grain pattern of the existing wood, or the patch will stick out like a sore thumb. Small holes in unpainted wood can be patched with wood putty; it comes in different colors to match various kinds of wood. No, I don't know why it's called a dutchman.

The most common place you will find a million small holes to patch is at the outer corners of window head casings, since apparently most previous owners found it necessary to drill new holes every time they put up a curtain rod.

Some or all of the woodwork may be missing entirely. Look for clues like "ghosts" in the paint, patterns of nail holes, and so forth. Sometimes the previous owners have done such a good job that even an archaeological dig won't reveal how it used to be. If there are neighboring houses built by the same builder or similar houses in the neighborhood that are still intact, those would be a good place to look for clues as to what needs to be replicated.

You may need to have new woodwork custom milled in order to match the existing woodwork (or if the existing woodwork isn't original, to match the proportion and scale of the woodwork that would have been there). Modern lumber is not only too small (two-by-fours now measure about 1-1/2 by 3-1/2 inches), but also tends to have slightly rounded edges where old boards had sharp corners. And any molding profiles you may have are not necessarily available at the local lumberyard. And if they are, they may only be available in a wood species that is different than what's in your house.

Many millwork shops, lumberyards, and molding companies will make custom millwork for you. There is usually a set-up charge, which covers the cost of making the knife that will cut the moldings. This can range from $50 to over $300. After that you only pay for the cost per foot of the lumber used to make the moldings.

The woods used in bungalow woodwork tend to darken

over time, which means replacement woodwork made from new lumber won't match. Stain will take care of some of the difference, but the truly obsessive will go for salvaged wood whenever possible. Even so, if the original woodwork was stained, it will be necessary to match the stain, which requires a lot of test samples and some obsessive record-keeping (for instance, sample A may be one part walnut stain/one part red mahogany with clear shellac, while sample B is the same stain with orange shellac, and sample C is one part walnut/two parts mahogany with clear shellac—you get the idea.)

COMPROMISE SOLUTION

You don't absolutely HAVE to strip paint. If the woodwork is painted, you can repaint it and put up some lovely William Morris wallpaper and pretend it's an English Arts and Crafts interior, as they often had painted woodwork. But in North America, generally the woodwork in formal rooms wasn't painted. Nonetheless, if you wish to skip the tedium of paint stripping, go ahead. Paint the woodwork a nice color that harmonizes with the wall color, and leave it at that. Some people paint the woodwork dark brown to resemble wood, but that doesn't work too well unless it's on the ceiling or inside a cabinet. There's always the option of some good faux graining.

If you are having moldings replicated to match the originals, they can be a different species of wood since they will be painted. You can even use *finger-jointed* wood (short pieces of wood that are joined together with zigzag joints that look like interlocking fingers) if it's going to be painted. I will go so far as to allow the use of MDF (medium-density fiberboard) for painted woodwork, with the caveat that it's better in places where you can't get too close to it, where nothing will bang into it, and where it won't get wet. This pretty much rules out its use for anything except crown molding, or perhaps the insides of closets.

If the original woodwork is all gone and you want to replace it using modern moldings, it can be done, though the proportions may be a little off. Complex moldings can be built up using smaller moldings. If there are no clues left as to the originals, you can't go too far wrong by using flat boards for everything. Resist the urge to tart up your small tract bungalow with fancy Greene & Greene–style woodwork containing cloud lifts and ebony pegs.

Left: Nor can you have this lovely carving of pomegranates, seen on a door at Greene & Greene's 1906 Bolton House.

CHAPTER SIX

OPENING LINES..

Bungalow designers did their best to open the houses to the outdoors with generous numbers of windows and doors. The interplay between indoors and out made even a small bungalow seem larger than it really was. There was also a belief that fresh air and sunshine would kill germs, prevent disease, and promote good health.

BREEDING LIKE RABBETS

There may be no more important feature of a bungalow than its windows. More than just openings for light and air, windows are the face the house presents to the street. Different architectural styles have distinctive windows: for example, the tall hooded windows of an Italianate Victorian or the leaded-glass casements of a Tudor Revival. Although sharing window styles with some other early-twentieth-century houses, bungalows have a window style all their own. The windows do not exist in isolation—their proportions, pattern, materials, and placement are some of the most important elements of a bungalow's design.

Early settlers in North America didn't have glass windows, merely openings that could be covered with shutters, maybe covered with a thin piece of oiled paper or a sheet of isinglass (mica flakes bonded with shellac, or sturgeon bladders—it's a long story). When glass did arrive, it was expensive, came in small pieces, and was even taxed. To deal with the small pieces, window sashes (the wooden frames that hold the glass) were divided into *lights*, divided by small wooden bars called *muntins*. Two or more windows side-by-side are divided by larger vertical bars called *mullions*. Wooden windows were made by hand, using molding planes and other tools. The joinery is complex, which also made windows expensive. The sash frames used *mortise-and-tenon* joinery: a *tenon* is a rectangular tab on one piece of wood that fits into the *mortise*, a rectangular slot in another piece of wood—kinda like insert Tab A into Slot B. In a window, the tenon was usually glued, although it might be held with a peg. The muntins, which had a molded profile, were joined using *cope-and-stick* joinery (coping involves cutting one piece to match the profile of the other piece) and attached to the frame with tenons. Each *light* in the sash was cut so that it had a ledge around it, called a *rabbet*, for the glass to sit on. The glass was kept in the frame with small nails, and either a small piece of molding or linseed oil putty (composed of linseed oil and chalk, although sometimes white lead or asbestos fibers were added) was also used to hold the glass in place. Somewhat later the small nails were replaced by tiny triangular pieces of sheet metal, called *glaziers points.* Wooden windows are still made this way, although now much of the process is done by machine.

Facing: Delicate art-glass casement windows designed by Henry Greene for the Gould House in Ventura, California, filter the view of the yard.

PANE THRESHOLD

By the nineteenth century, mechanization and steam-powered woodworking equipment had made it easier to manufacture windows in large quantities, putting them within reach of more people. Improvements in the manufacture of glass had resulted in larger pieces of glass being available, so window styles changed in response. Nineteenth- and early-twentieth-century glass was made by the *cylinder* method: a large cylinder of glass was blown, cut down one side, and flattened out. Because the outside diameter of the cylinder was slightly larger than the inside, when the glass was flattened, the extra glass on the outside would form tiny ridges or ripples in the glass, and there would also be air bubbles from the blowing. This is the type of glass found in most bungalows.

In 1905, a process of vertically drawing a consistent width sheet of glass from a tank was perfected, known as *drawn glass.* Commercial production using this method began in 1914. Various improvements were made in the process, and by 1928 the method had been perfected. Modern window glass is made by this process but it lacks the subtle ripples and imperfections of the old cylinder glass. Cylinder glass is still available, though it's expensive.

Another option is to buy old window sashes (or even just glass) at the salvage yard. (Make sure it's wavy, though—not all of it is.) Take some glass cleaner and paper towels with you—the glass will invariably be dirty and it's hard to tell whether it's wavy or not under all the dirt.

There were and are various styles of windows. *Fixed* windows are not movable and are simply for letting in light. *Casement* windows are hinged on the side and open either in or out like doors. *Double-hung* windows have two sashes that slide up and down in channels, balanced by counterweights. (Frank Lloyd Wright hated double-hungs—he called them "guillotine windows.") There are also *single-hung* windows with only one sliding sash, and *triple-hung* windows. Other kinds include *sliding windows* (sashes slide in horizontal tracks), *awning* windows (hinged at the top and open upward), *hopper* windows (hinged at the bottom and open downward), *austral* windows (one sash opens like an awning and the other opens like a hopper), *pivoting* windows (the whole sash tilts on two pins set into the frame), and *bi-fold* windows (two sashes are hinged together on one side, with pins that run in a track top and bottom so that they can be folded, accordion-style, to the sides of the window. There are also *pocket* windows, which slide into a pocket in the wall. Some bungalows had *transom* windows, a fixed or operable window mounted above a door or another window. Operable transom windows could be either awning or hopper style. Transom windows were used on both exterior and interior openings (such as over interior doors). *Louvered* or *jalousie* windows are a later invention and don't belong on a bungalow. And no, I don't care if you live in Florida.

Accordion windows allow the dining room of a Seattle bungalow to open completely to the front yard. The art-glass transom above picks up the colors of the foliage outside.

As noted in *Bungalow Details: Exterior,* most windows were square or rectangular, but windows with curved tops, oval and round windows (also known as *oculus, roundel,* or the particularly charming *oeil-de-boeuf* or *bull's-eye,* though I prefer the literal translation "eye of beef"), diamond shapes, and other variations.

With rare exceptions, bungalow windows were made of wood. With the advent of specialized power machinery, it was possible to make sashes with elaborate muntin patterns. On double-hung windows, the muntins were confined to the top sash, the lower sash usually being plain, a window style that started with Victorian architecture and was sometimes known as a *Queen Anne* window. Probably the most popular pattern was a nine-light design that could be described as a variation of tic-tac-toe. But if a pattern could be thought of, it was made. Geometric patterns were the most common, but patterns involving curved elements appeared on many bungalows. On some bungalows, only the front windows had muntins, and the side and back windows were plain. On others, all the windows had muntins. If the designer or builder was going hog wild, the muntin patterns might vary on different sets of windows.

On the inside, windows in the formal rooms almost always had a clear finish (shellac or varnish, generally) over stained or natural wood, making the window sashes an integral part of the interior woodwork, though the sashes may not have been made of the same wood as the rest of the woodwork, in which case they were stained to match. This may have been true in other rooms as well, though kitchen and bathroom windows were likely to be painted with enamel, and often bedroom windows were painted as well, though not always.

The upper sash of a double-hung window may or may not have *lugs,* an extension of the sides of the sash frame below the bottom rail, usually cut into an *ogee* (S-shape) but occasionally an even fancier shape. The presence or lack of lugs is entirely regional—some places they're traditional, some places they aren't. Occasionally the lower sash will have lugs at the top, though this is not very common. It is very civilized, though, as it keeps the sash lock from banging into the top of the window and making a big dent. The purpose of lugs is unclear: Less end grain to soak up moisture? To make big dents in the sill when the sash cords break and the sash comes crashing down? Because it looks nice?

Just a warning here—many bungalows were built with very plain, one-light sashes. Don't succumb to the temptation to fancy up the windows into something they were never meant to be. Embrace the plainness—it's very Zen. One-light sashes are easier to clean, too. By the same token, people with complex muntin patterns on their sashes should not replace them with windows that have snap out muntin grilles just to make them easier to clean.

Bungalow windows might also have leaded glass or *art glass* (stained glass). This was particularly common on the

Above: Another drawing shows two, one-over-one double hungs (no lugs on the upper sash on these) with transom windows above. The larger piece separating the two windows is the mullion. The dividing piece above is also a mullion.

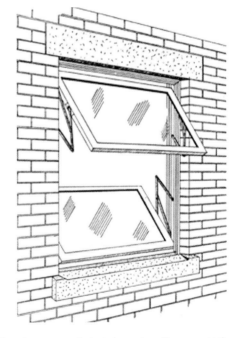

Left: A drawing from the 1915 *American Carpenter and Builder* shows a four-over-four double-hung window with muntins. Notice that the upper sash of this window has decorative "lugs" at the lower ends of the stiles (vertical side pieces). The function of lugs is unclear—possibly to cushion the glass somewhat should the sash hit the windowsill while being lowered.

Right: This illustration shows an austral window, where the upper sash opens outward like an awning window and the lower sash opens inward like a hopper window. When closed, this window resembles a double-hung window but provides far more ventilation when open. For some reason, austral windows are not common in the U.S.

An arched front window shows the geometric Prairie School–influenced art glass that is common to Chicago bungalows. Below the birch-trimmed window, plants thrive on top of a radiator cabinet.

Lugs on the lower sash are a fine idea that is hardly ever put into practice, but apparently this bungalow in Memphis, Tennessee, had a cutting-edge builder. Note that the sash hangs from chains rather than the more-common rope or cord.

Another geometric design rendered in primary-colored glass decorates a high window.

Beveled and colored glass, as well as faceted accents, is combined in this set of art-glass windows.

A row of conventionalized flowers is the motif for this art-glass window. Your guess is as good as mine regarding what kind of flowers they are supposed to be.

Multicolored stained glass brings out the best in this stylized flower design set into a background of pebbled glass.

An oriel window with panes of beveled glass highlights a bookcase in a home in Berkeley, California.

high windows that grace the walls on either side of the fireplace in many bungalows, though art glass appeared in many other locations as well. Art glass was offered in geometric patterns as well as more realistic designs of flora and fauna, scenery, and such: *obscure* glass (such as etched), *glue-chip* glass (in which the surface of the glass is chipped by the action of a particular kind of hide glue, giving the effect of ice crystals), *sandblasted* glass, as well as *patterned glass* (made by squeezing semi-molten glass between two rollers, one of which has a pattern on it). There were and are many varieties of patterned glass, including hammered (this is SO Arts and Crafts), cathedral, Flemish, reeded, seeded, and my personal favorite, chinchilla. Yup, looks like fur. Each manufacturer had their own patterns, so one company's "Rain" may be another's "Niagara."

On the front of the house, the windows were often arranged as a *tripartite* window featuring a large fixed window flanked by two operable windows (sometimes known as

a *Chicago* window, after its common use in early-twentieth-century Chicago office buildings). *Ribbon* windows, a series of casement windows in a row, were favored by the architects of the Prairie School, but also found their way onto Prairie style and other styles of bungalows. On the sides and back, windows might be positioned haphazardly according to the function of the rooms inside, or arranged more aesthetically. A chimney on an outside wall was commonly flanked by high windows, frequently featuring art glass. Sometimes a window was actually set into the chimney. *Bay* (bow) windows were much used, particularly on front facades. Other walls were more likely to have *oriel* windows (bay windows that stop short of the ground) that were rectangular, trapezoidal, curved, or V-shaped. The windows on any given bungalow might be all the same type (all double-hung, for instance), but they might just as likely be mixed, with casements in one place, double-hungs in another, and possibly other types mixed in as well.

DECEIVING LINE

Wood windows are one of the most vulnerable of historic building elements—millions are being dumped in landfills every year. And that is an absolute travesty. The multibillion-dollar window replacement industry would like you to believe that historic windows are drafty, are not energy efficient, don't work well, and require constant maintenance. Almost every day the newspaper is filled with ads for replacement windows, with headlines like, "Are your windows costing you money?" or, "Whole house window replacement—only $2,995!" Probably your local public utility will give you a rebate for ripping out your original windows to put in vinyl replacements. Often the local building code demands insulating windows in new construction or remodeling. I am always stunned when people who are otherwise quite knowledgeable will say, "Oh, and I'm going to replace all my windows with double-glazing" as though it's just a given—I guess it shows how much the window companies and their friends have succeeded in brainwashing the public. Go back and consider the phrase "multi-billion dollar." With that much money at stake, do you think these companies care whether they ruin historic buildings with their products? They are interested in one thing—SELLING YOU WINDOWS. To that end, they are quite happy to lie, and when they aren't lying outright, they are conveniently failing to mention numerous pertinent facts. Here's a list from one Internet replacement window site (which shall remain nameless):

Signs that will let you know your windows should be replaced:

1. There is condensation or frost build-up.

2. Drafts—if air is coming through a closed window.

3. Window needs support to stay open.

4. Candles do not stay lit near a closed window. [Isn't this the same as drafts?]

5. Windows show signs of deterioration.

Here's another site: "Don't bother to fix a window that has cracked glass, rotted or otherwise damaged wood, locks that don't work, missing putty, or poorly fitting sashes." And another: "Homeowners with windows over twenty-five years old should consider replacing them. . . . A home is an ideal candidate for a window replacement if its windows are sealed or painted shut. . . ."

Okay, I am gasping in disbelief, but let's take these one at a time.

1. There's condensation on the window. If there is condensation on the inside, there's too much moisture in your house. Get a dehumidifier and some exhaust fans. If there's frost on the outside, it's winter. Get a storm window. If you have a storm window on the outside and there's still frost on the inside window, the storm window leaks. Weatherstrip it.

2. There are drafts. That means air is getting in through the exterior trim or around the edges of the window. Caulk will fix the first problem, and weatherstripping and a storm window will fix the second one.

3. The window needs support to stay open. Replace the freaking sash cords! If you never want to replace the sash cords again, use sash chain—it's noisy, though. (And don't feel bad if you're propping the window open with a stick—it's a perfectly functional way to keep it open, and I did it for years before I learned how to replace sash cords.)

4. The window shows signs of deterioration. Missing putty should be replaced; rot or open joints, which are almost always at the bottom of the lower sash, can be repaired with epoxy consolidants or even just wood putty. Ditto for deteriorating sills, frames, or trim.

5. The glass is cracked. Replace it! If the putty is missing—put on some more putty! Because on a single-glazed window you can.

6. The locks don't work. ARE THESE PEOPLE KIDDING? (It wasn't even a window company site.) Go to the hardware store and buy a new lock—it isn't exactly rocket science.

7. The window is painted shut. A putty knife, a hammer, and a little elbow grease will fix that easily.

8. The windows are more than twenty-five years old. Okay, that probably means they were made with old-growth wood, which will last far longer than any wood available now.

Not one of these things will cost as much as a replacement window, even if you pay someone else to do it.

Not all claims by replacement window companies are outright lies, more like obfuscation (which means "confuse"—I like to use a two-dollar word occasionally. Oh, let's be real, I like to use a two-dollar word a lot. I need that bumper sticker that says "eschew obfuscation.")

#1 OBFUSCATION: REPLACEMENT WINDOWS WILL SIGNIFICANTLY REDUCE HEATING COSTS.
Only 20 percent of the heating loss (or cooling gain) in a building is through the windows. The other 80 percent is lost through roofs, walls, floors, and chimneys, with most of

it going out the roof. And most of the cold air is sucked in through the floor from the basement or crawl space. Reducing the heat loss through the windows by 50 percent (double-glazing) will only result in a 10 percent reduction in the overall heat loss. The average cost to replace ten windows with double-glazed units is approximately $9,500 for vinyl and $16,000 for aluminum-clad wood. And that's only ten windows—the smallest bungalow I ever owned had 20 windows. Misleading the public about actual costs is one of the sleazy tactics employed. But let's say some mythical person, obviously not me, decides to replace her twenty windows with vinyl. They pay $19,000 for them. Let's also say that their utility bill averages a ridiculous $200 a month (actually my average combined gas and electric bill here at the 3,800-square-foot bunga-mansion). A 10-percent reduction on their heating bill amounts to $20 a month or $240 a year. At that rate it would take just over 79 years to recoup the $19,000 investment. At a more realistic heating bill average of $100 per month, the payback time would be 158 years. But wait, according to the Environmental Protection Agency, 40 percent of the average household energy budget goes to heating and cooling. So at $200 per month, only $80 goes to heating and cooling. Saving 10 percent on that would only be $8 a month, putting the payback time at 197.9 years. Could I repeat that—197.9 YEARS! For the same amount of money (or less!) that replacement windows would cost, you could insulate the attic, the walls, the basement, and install a damper on the chimney and get an 80 percent reduction in heat loss. And probably vacation in Tahiti on the money you'd have left.

Or you could spend that money on storm windows. A recent study conducted at the Oak Ridge National Laboratory using actual wooden windows (removed from a house that was being demolished) showed that the addition of storm windows reduced air leakage by a considerable amount. They used a double hung window with loose sashes,

Builders were encouraged to look into installing weatherstripping in the winter when business was slow. The Pullman Company assured them that "home owners welcome anything that will make the house warmer and keep down heating costs."

no weatherstripping, gaps between the sashes and frame, missing caulk, cracked glass, and dry rot in the frame. The second window was a dual-pane double-hung with loose sashes and no weatherstripping. For storm windows, they used non-thermally broken aluminum storms with operable sashes and no weatherstripping. Interestingly enough, the addition of storm windows to both windows reduced the energy flow of the first window substantially compared to the dual-pane window. Using a measurement that took into account both air infiltration and conduction through the glass without storms, and with a wind speed of 7 mph, the single-glazed window lost about 565 BTUs per hour while the dual-glazed window lost 644. Notice that this is single-glazed versus double-glazed with absolutely nothing done to either of them, and that the double-glazed actually lost more BTUs than the single-glazed. With the storms added, the single-glazed window lost 131 BTUs per hour, while the dual-pane window lost 256. Then they removed the storm window and weatherized the first window, which involved squaring up the frame so the sashes fit more tightly, replaced rot in the frame, reglazed the panes, caulked cracks in the frame, installed a sweep at the bottom of the lower sash, and installed a new window lock to improve closure—then ran the tests again at 7 mph. Heat loss for the weatherized window was 256 compared with 131 for the unweatherized window with a storm. By comparison, the dual-pane window WITH A STORM also had a heat loss of 256. In other words, the weatherized single-glazed window WITHOUT A STORM was equal to the double-glazed window WITH A STORM. They didn't compare weatherstripping PLUS a storm window, but clearly, a storm window gives you more bang for the buck (about a 75 percent reduction in heat transmission), and weatherstripping alone gives the same reduction as a double-glazed window. And the test used a lousy storm window—a high quality storm window would work even better.

And all this talk about glazing is making me crave a nice glazed donut. With raspberry filling.

In the book *Burglars on the Job*, authors Richard Wright and Scott Decker, after interviewing hundreds of burglars, concluded that burglars avoid houses with storm windows, believing that the sound caused by two separate panes of glass breaking is more likely to alert the neighbors.

John Myers, who wrote the Preservation Brief on historic wood windows for the National Park Service, had this to say about energy-efficient windows: "Energy conservation *is no excuse for the wholesale destruction of historic windows* [italics mine] which can be made thermally efficient by historically and aesthetically acceptable means."

#2 OBFUSCATION: MAINTENANCE-FREE EXTERIOR— NO PAINTING OR STAINING REQUIRED.

No painting or staining POSSIBLE, in the case of vinyl. How will that lovely white vinyl look with your unpainted woodwork? Or if you have painted woodwork, suppose you decide to paint it a different color—the windows will still be white. And you know how I hate white windows. And you know how plastic has static electricity that attracts dirt? Not to mention that vinyl is toxic and should be avoided as much as possible. As for aluminum, even an anodized coating doesn't last that long, at which point you have to paint it. If it's not anodized, then it corrodes and turns white.

#3 LIE: EXTREMELY DURABLE AND LONG LASTING.

A vinyl window has a life expectancy of approximately 20 years, aluminum about 10 to 20 years, a new wood window from 20 to 50 years. An original wood window that is consistently maintained and kept painted can last as long as 200 years, if not more. For instance, the windows at Hampton Court Palace in England have been there since the early 1690s—approximately 315 years. Part of the reason that an old wood window lasts longer than a new one is that old windows are made of old-growth timber, which grew very slowly and is extremely close-grained and dense, whereas new wood windows are made from second-growth wood, much of it from fast-growing trees harvested from tree farms, where the growth rings are much farther apart. The softer sapwood resulting from fast growth is far less durable.

And let's talk for a moment about "springs, strings, and plastic things," as David Liberty, a window restorer in Boston, calls them. Windows used to be simple: in a double-hung window, two weights are attached to a sash cord or chain that runs through pulleys; it totals exactly the weight of the window sash so that it slides up and down effortlessly. In a casement window, there are hinges on the side (or occasionally, the bottom) so it opens like a door; ditto for awning or hopper windows; pivoting windows turn on metal pins, and all of this hardware is made of metal. It is eminently repairable, and most of it is fairly standardized. But

after the World War II, these simple and eminently repairable systems were replaced by spring balances, crank-out casements, and other "springs, strings, and plastic things." In the words of an engineer looking at modern replacement windows, "Too many things to go wrong."

For instance, a spring-loaded suspension system has a serious flaw. When the window is closed, the springs are fully extended. How long it takes for the springs to lose all of their tension depends on the quality of the metal and the weight of the sash, but they will lose their tension, and then the top sash won't stay up and the bottom sash won't GO up.

A crank-out casement has gears, and eventually the teeth fail.

And that's not even mentioning the fact that a double-glazed sash weighs twice as much as a single-glazed sash, making it even more likely to strain the springs and plastic things. And the strings and plastic things are all proprietary, which means if you want to replace one of them you have to make sure you're getting the *right* little plastic doohickey out of the 300 plastic doohickeys you'll have to choose from. And few of the doohickeys will be available at your local hardware store.

What happens if the glass breaks? In a single-glazed window, the glass can be replaced using items available at any hardware store, costing maybe twenty bucks, depending on the size of the replacement glass. In a double-glazed window, the glass is all specially sealed units, which have to be ordered from the manufacturer (assuming the manufacturer is still in business), and which cost $85 to $100 apiece (or more, depends on size), and that's if you can even order replacement glazing units—sometimes you have to buy a whole new sash or even a whole new window. And then you have to pay someone to install the new glazing because it's not really a do-it-yourself thing.

But here's the thing they're really hiding: the average lifespan of a double-glazing unit is TEN YEARS OR LESS. Let me repeat that: TEN YEARS OR LESS. The seal around the glazing can fail within ten years, causing the glass panes to fog. And the plastic and neoprene seals used to hold the panes in new windows degrade in ultraviolet light. Imagine trying to find a replacement/gasket after the window company has gone out of business.

#4 LIE: ECONOMICAL.

To whom? Let's say you went for the $2,995 ten-window special—that's $299.50 per window. Yeah, that keeps THEIR economy going. For that price you could easily pay someone to repair, reglaze, and weatherstrip all ten windows, or you could buy ten custom storm windows instead.

#5 LIE: TILT SASHES ARE EASIER TO CLEAN.

Well, it sure looks that way when the salesperson demonstrates it on that little tiny sample window. Now try to imagine tilting in and holding a sash that weighs fifty pounds and is longer than your arm, a sash that is only held up by two small plastic clips. Do you think you can hold up fifty pounds with one hand while washing the window with the other? And how long do you think the little plastic clips will last?

#6 LIE: YOUR HOME IS MORE ATTRACTIVE AND EASIER TO SELL.

Could I just repeat the first rule of real estate here? Location, location, location. Not new windows, new windows, new windows. New windows aren't going to fool anyone into thinking the house is new—people who want a new house usually buy a new house. ALL REPLACEMENT WINDOWS DO IS DESTROY THE HISTORIC INTEGRITY OF THE HOUSE! There is, in fact, a direct correlation between historic integrity and market value. Second, in a historic building, windows make up a large part of the architecture. The pattern of the sash, the window framing, and the other architectural details surrounding the window was carefully designed as an integral component of the building, and replacing the windows destroys this. Even a replacement sash that replicates the muntin pattern and trim will not look the same because it will not have the wavy glass and muntin profile of a single-glazed window, and no matter how much they try to disguise the necessary spacer, a double-glazed window just doesn't look the same. As for easier to sell, in most markets, a home that retains its historic integrity brings a premium price compared to similar homes that have been remodeled in inappropriate ways.

#7 AN OBFUSCATION: NO SWELLING OR SHRINKING DUE TO HUMIDITY AND MOISTURE.

No, only swelling or shrinking due to temperature fluctuation! Vinyl expands and shrinks at twice the rate of wood, and it expands at seven times the rate of glass—how long do you think it will be before the sealant fails that holds in the glass? Once vinyl starts to distort, it doesn't resume its original shape, as anyone with a warped vinyl record can attest.

#8 AN OBFUSCATION: INSULATES AGAINST NOISE.

Sure, as long as you never open it!!! Actually, a single-glazed window has an STC (sound transmission class) rating between 20 and 27, depending on how thick the glass is and how airtight the window is. In a dual-pane window, the STC rating is governed somewhat by the distance between the two panes—the larger the distance, the better the rating. (This suggests a storm window might be better than double-glazing, being farther away.) For each doubling of the airspace between the panes, the STC increases by about 3. If the panes are close together, the rating may actually be lower than for a single pane because the air-

space acts like a spring and transfers vibration from one pane to the other. Triple-glazing provides the same noise reduction as double-glazing, unless the spacing between panes is quite large. On an average, dual-pane windows have an STC rating of 28 to 35. A single layer of 1/4-inch laminated glass (which has a layer of plastic in the middle) has an STC rating of 33, which suggests that, if noise is an issue, it might be better to replace the glass in a single-glazed window with laminated glass instead of wasting the money on new windows.

#9 LIE: NEW WINDOWS WON'T BE DRAFTY LIKE THE OLD ONES.

Yes, they will, and here's why: Convection. Warm air in the house contacts the cold window glass and then cools, which draws more warm air towards the glass, setting up convection currents in the room. The air won't be coming from outside, but you will still feel a draft.

#10 LIE: NEW TECHNOLOGY IS BETTER.

One Web site made this claim: Glass was invented over 4,000 years ago, so single-pane glass is 4,000-year-old technology. Dual-pane glass is a 25-year-old technology, and dual-pane with Low-E and argon gas is today's technology.

The Web site argument is that today's technology is best. I would argue that 4,000-year-old technology has been tested and proven, whereas today's technology already has a very high failure rate. Also, and I can't say this enough, if no one buys into this B.S. and keeps their old windows, these companies WON'T MAKE ANY MONEY. (Cue sound of violins.)

#11 LIE: SNAP-IN MUNTIN GRILLES LOOK JUST LIKE REAL DIVIDED LIGHT WINDOWS.

Not Real but an Amazing Simulation! What's amazing is that they get away with it. Even the so-called "true divided-light" windows don't look like actual divided light windows. Even worse, they also make grilles that are sandwiched in between the glass, or the really cheapo alternative: a grid of white tape applied directly to the glass. The snap-in grilles and the grilles between the glass are supposed to make the window easier to clean. Yeah, just like a one-light sash found on many bungalows. And who said everything was supposed to be easy? It's not like window cleaning isn't still tedious, whether there is one pane or several.

Then there's the fact that replacement windows that are installed are often smaller than the existing windows. Usually both the interior and exterior trim is removed entirely, and the interior trim is replaced with some modern 2-inch-wide "colonial casing." (I just love that name—that kind of casing wouldn't be found in any colonial house either.) Interesting window shapes such as arches are made rectangular to fit the standardized replacements.

WOODEN WINDOWS

OBSESSIVE RESTORATION

Original wooden windows are eminently repairable. Repairing windows tends to be time-consuming and tedious, but it's not brain surgery. The National Park Service has a good Preservation Brief (#9) on restoring wood windows, or you can purchase Terry Meany's fine book on the subject, *Working Windows*. Or see the condensed instructions below. Few windows are so far gone that they can't be repaired, though if you don't do it yourself, it may be difficult to find someone locally who will. Epoxy consolidants and putties can work miracles, as can having new parts milled for the deteriorated parts. A sash repaired with epoxy that requires a clear finish on the interior will have to have some kind of faux graining under the varnish to match the repair to the rest of the wood. If a sash is truly beyond repair, a millwork shop can make a new custom sash or even a whole new custom window unit if the jambs and sill are also beyond hope. Be sure to make it plain to them if you want a clear finish, and you may need to specify the wood species as well, though often the windows were not the same species as the rest of the trim but were merely stained to match. And then you will have to stain it to match. If you want to be really compulsive, you can supply them some salvaged old growth wood with which to make it. If there's no one local, there are national companies that make sashes and windows as well, although I would urge you to deal locally if possible. Don't immediately call up one of the big national window companies—they will want to sell you replacement window units. Look in the Yellow Pages under "Windows—Wood," after first thumbing through page after page of window replacement companies. (We are apparently lucky here in the Oakland-Berkeley area as there are numerous custom window shops. The average cost here for a one-light single-pane sash is about $150.)

If some or all the original windows are gone, replace them with new or salvaged wood windows as you can afford to. Salvage yards are filled with zillions of old window sashes—you might want to see if you can find a millwork shop that will make new frames to put these into. Start with the front windows. If the replacement windows are smaller (Why do they do that?! Even if a smaller window costs less, surely the savings are eaten up by the labor involved in patching the siding!), you may have to try and figure out what sizes the original windows were. If they were really thorough and wiped out all the clues, look at houses in your neighborhood that still have their original windows. It's important to get the size right; the scale and proportion of the windows are the most impor-

tant aspects of a bungalow and the reasons most new "bungalows" just don't look right. Other houses may provide clues about muntin patterns as well. If there really aren't any clues available, the modified tic-tac-toe pattern is a classic. There are only one or two national companies that make a historically accurate window without all that argon/low-E, double-glazed, aluminum-clad nonsense, so you might be better off dealing with a local millwork or sash shop if there is one. Otherwise there are millwork shops that ship nationally (although you'll need to be really sure of the measurements). If you live near the Canadian border, the exchange rate for American dollars can make Canadian-made windows a good buy. If you're Canadian, it unfortunately doesn't work the other way around. (And before anybody starts writing me about "buy American" and all that, let me say this: Saving money isn't always politically correct, but it's up to each person to decide what they can or cannot do with a clean conscience. I am talking about Canada here—I didn't suggest exploitation of sash makers in Third World countries.) In replacing windows, you may run into problems with the building code, which may specify that only double-glazing is allowed. Argue with them. Show them the Oak Ridge Laboratory study, invoke your state's historic building code (if they have one). Promise to get storm windows. There is, of course, a solution to the building code problem that I would never dream of advocating. It will have to be between you and your conscience.

Windows with a clear finish can be subject to deterioration in ultraviolet light, which actually destroys the lignin in the wood. This is most obvious in the softening of the originally crisp lines of the molding profile around the glass. If the windows are to be refinished, the use of a finish containing UV inhibitors such as spar varnish can slow this process. Or it can be embraced as a sign of age and patina. Clear-finished windows are also subject to water staining, either through leakage or condensation from the glass. Refinishing will help somewhat with the staining, but the first thing to do is take care of the moisture problem, whatever it may be.

As a rule, the clear finish on the inside of a sash was either shellac or varnish, but rarely wax. Infrequently, you might encounter some other finish like tung oil or lacquer. Test the finish in a nonobvious area by using various solvents on a cotton swab—shellac dissolves in denatured alcohol, wax dissolves in paint thinner, lacquer dissolves in lacquer thinner, varnish dissolves in varnish remover. It would be best to refinish the windows using the same finish, though I could make an argument for using more than wax by itself as a finish. I guess it depends on just how uncompromising you want to be. It's always possible to apply wax over another finish.

Windows that have not been well maintained often have sustained rot and fungus damage, particularly around the joints. The bottom of the sash that sits on the windowsill is the number one location for this kind of damage. Often the damage is limited to a small area around the joint, and the rotten part can be easily dug out and patched. (Some people use wood putty or Bondo for this, but that would not be the obsessive thing to do. The obsessive would only use epoxy or possibly a dowel or other piece of wood to fill the hole.)

Naturally, the truly fanatical will use only old wavy glass should it become necessary to replace a cracked pane—either from the salvage yard or from the companies that manufacture restoration glass. (A note about restoration glass: there is much variation in the "waviness" of restoration glass, and if the distortions in the rest of your glass are particularly subtle, the restoration stuff may stick out like a sore thumb.) There is also a company that salvages old glass from old windows and ships it nationwide (see Resources).

The unbelievably compulsive will possibly mix up their own glazing putty using linseed oil and chalk, but unless you have a house museum, a can of DAP 33 glazing (or the like) is probably acceptable.

COMPROMISE SOLUTION

If you still have the original windows, see How To Fix Windows on the next page. I refuse to compromise on this. On the other hand, if some previous owner has already removed the original windows and replaced them with some dreadful vinyl or awful aluminum or something, you have my permission to replace them—with single-glazed wood windows. If you are absolutely forced (by the building inspector) to put in double-glazing, at least get true divided lights, stay away from Low-E (it makes the glass look green), and, if you have to get cladding, get aluminum or fiberglass rather than vinyl.

If the original windows are still there, you have to fix them. I will go so far as to say you can use Bondo or wood putty to repair small amounts of deterioration or rot, though the more obsessive will recoil in horror at that, but you are NOT allowed to use screwed-on L-brackets or corrugated fasteners. You can also give up a little sooner on repairing them with epoxy and just get a new custom sash or window made, all the while knowing that it most likely won't last as long as the original window. As noted

under Obsessive Restoration, be sure to specify the wood type, and if you are putting a clear finish on the inside, it will need to be stained to match. You are not allowed to just call up one of the big national window companies and order a window that is sorta, kinda the same but has double-glazing and Low-E coating and argon and aluminum cladding and vinyl jamb liners.

Besides shellac or regular varnish for a clear finish on the inside, you might consider spar varnish, Danish oil, or other oil finish (these are finishes that sink into the wood and cure, as opposed to sitting on top of the wood as a film).

It's okay to use regular (as opposed to wavy) glass to replace cracked panes—most people won't notice. Of course, if the windows were replaced with double-glazed, then, as mentioned before, you'd have to get a whole new glazing unit. The modern tendency is to bed the glass using caulk in the rabbet rather than putty, which even I have done on occasion, but I find the acrylic glazing putty (which comes in a tube like caulk) is difficult to tool, so I generally stick with the other stuff.

HOW TO FIX WINDOWS

The most common window type in older houses, regardless of the style of the house, is the double-hung window. A double-hung window has two *sashes* (a sash is the wooden frame that holds the glass) that move up and down in channels. *Sash cords* (or chains) in channels on the side of the sash run through pulleys near the top of the window, and are connected to *sash weights* in pockets inside the wall, which counterbalance the weight of the sash so it doesn't crash down on your fingers. The *channels* are formed by the *parting bead* or *strip*, a thin piece of wood that sits in a slot in the *jamb* (the side of the window frame) and separates the two sashes, and the *stop*, a piece nailed to the jamb on the interior side at right angles to the *casing* (the interior trim around the window). The most common problems with these windows are broken sash cords, painted-shut frames and sashes, cracked or broken glass, or rot and fungus damage in the wood.

Here are the tools and supplies you will need to fix a double-hung window:

—stiff-bladed putty knife (a 5-in-1 tool, available at paint stores, works well)
—flexible-bladed putty knife (for the glazing)
—glass-cutting tool
—hammer
—flat pry bar
—utility knife
—slotted screwdriver
—sash cord (1/4- or 5/16-inch diameter) or sash chain
—4d and 8d finishing nails
—WD-40 or other lubricant
—locking pliers (optional but handy)

If the window is only painted shut, it's an easy fix. Slide the putty knife in between the sash and the stop to break the paint film. You may have to hammer it in. Work your way around the sash—you may also need to break the film between the sash and the *stool* (the inside windowsill) and between the upper and lower sash at the top. If you're lucky, it was only painted shut on the inside, and you will now be able to open it. It also helps to lubricate the channels the sash slides in—anything from paraffin to soap to WD-40 will do the trick. (And by the way, when you're painting, do not paint the sash channels; eventually the paint buildup will keep the sash from sliding. In fact, if there is a lot of paint buildup, it might be a good idea to strip them while you're fixing the window.)

If the window is also painted shut on the outside, you will need to go outside and repeat the process. If it's a second-floor window, get a ladder and do it from the outside.

If the sash cords are broken, you will have to remove the sashes. Using the putty knife and/or the pry bar, pry off one or both of the interior stops. The lower sash can then be removed. Pull the sash cord out of the channels (the knot may be attached with a finishing nail—pry it out with the screwdriver). If only one cord is broken, allow the other one to ride up—the knot will prevent it going through the pulley. To remove the top sash, carefully pull or pry out the parting bead on one side, starting at the bottom (locking pliers work well for this); when you get about halfway up, lower the top sash to the bottom of the window and pull the rest of the parting bead out from the top. If you're lucky, it won't break, but if it does, go down to the lumberyard and get another piece. (Actually, if you're going to fix a lot of windows, it's probably a good idea to go to the lumberyard and buy some parting bead ahead of time, because I guarantee that one of them will break.) Then the top sash can be removed.

There are two ways to get to the sash weights. Some windows have a removable pocket cut into the jamb (usually held with a screw) for access to the weights. This can be pulled out to get into the weight pocket. If there is no pocket, the other way to access the weights is by prying off the inside casings—do this carefully to avoid damaging the surrounding plaster or woodwork or the casings themselves. Remove the nails from the stops and the casings by pulling them through from the *back;* removing them from the front will cause visible damage.

With the side casings removed, or the pocket covers removed, the weight pockets should be exposed. It's best to replace all the cords, even the ones that aren't broken. Remove the weights and cut off the old sash cords. Cut new sash cord to length, a little bit longer than the existing cord.

(Here's the super-secret formula: Measure the height of the sash + the distance from the sash bore hole to the top of the sash, which is usually 12 inches, and add 2 inches extra. For instance, a sash that is 24 inches high requires a 38-inch rope. It frays, so wrap a piece of tape around the end first.)

Tie a knot close to one end; the knot will fit into a hole drilled in the side of the sash. Run the other end through the pulley and down into the weight pocket. (With pocket covers, you will need to feed a weighted piece of string down through the pulley with the sash cord attached to the other end; this will allow you to pull the cord down from the pocket cover opening. A finishing nail makes a good weight.)

If the casings are pried off, proceed as follows: Start with the upper sash. Once the cords are through the pulleys, put the knots into the holes on the side of the sash, press the cord into the channels, fit the sash into the window, and push it up to the top (a helper is useful here). Tie the other end of the cord to the weight, using a double or triple knot. Make sure that the weight hangs just above the sill—*it should not touch.* Why? Because if there is any slack in the cord, the cord can wedge itself between the pulley wheel and the pulley housing, and it will be very, very difficult to get out. (And you will be screaming and cursing and trying to pull it out with pliers or push it out with a screwdriver and it will be wedged in so tight you think you'll never get it out and it's just really, really annoying.) Once both weights are attached, run the sash up and down a few times to make sure it slides smoothly— it should go all the way down without the weight hitting the pulley. This is a good time to squirt a little lubricant on the pulleys. Then, with the sash pushed down to the sill, reinsert the parting bead into the slot—it's a bit tricky because it has to slide between the jamb and a piece of triangular molding on the sash. It may involve some tilting and tweaking and probably more cursing, but eventually it will go back in. Once the upper sash is in, the lower sash is replaced in the same way.

If the casings have not been pried off, the procedure is slightly different. Once the cords are through the pulleys, put the knots into the holes on the sides of the upper sash, press the cords into the channels, and fit the sash back into the window. Push it up to the top. Then, reach into the pocket and pull out the weights. Tie the

SLIP HEAD SASH FRAME, PULLEYS, WEIGHTS AND CORD

SLIP HEAD frames are used principally in attics, toilets, closets, etc. This frame can be plain cap if so ordered and used for any kind of frame building. Slip head frames are also used inside between two rooms. If wanted for that purpose be sure to specify as the O. S. casing will be omitted and the sill made flat.

DESCRIPTION

U1598 — Slip Head Sash Frame, moulded cap, 1¼" O. S. casing, for Frame Building.
U1604 — Cast Iron Sash Pulley.
U1606 — Pressed Steel Sash Pulley, finished with lacquered face.

When ordering frame give opening size of sash (width first) and width of jambs. U1598 can also be made with plain cap or for Stucco or Brick Veneer Building, but order must specify.

FOR COMPLETE PRICE INFORMATION SEE UNIVERSAL PRICE SUPPLEMENT.

All the accoutrements needed for a double-hung window, including sash cord, weights, and pulleys, could be ordered from the *Universal Design Book on Builders Woodwork.*

ends of the sash cords to the weights, and then slide the sash up and down to make sure the weights don't hit the sill when the sash is up or hit the pulley when it's down. Then, with the sash pushed down to the sill, reinsert the parting bead into the slot— it's a bit tricky because it has to slide between the jamb and a piece of triangular molding on the sash. It may involve some tilting and tweaking and probably more cursing, but eventually it will go back in. Once the upper sash is in, the lower sash is replaced in the same way, except, after testing it as above, remove the lower sash again by removing the knots from the holes in the side of the sash, and put the pocket covers back. Then reinstall the lower sash.

Once the sashes are in, first nail the casings back in place using finishing nails, and then nail the stops, making sure they don't cause the sash to bind as it goes up and down. (If the woodwork has a natural finish, you may want to substitute small brass wood screws for the nails, making the stops easier to remove in the future. You can even buy *stop adjusters,* which are little brass eyelets for the screws that have slots in them and are set into the stop so that you can slide it back and forth a fraction of an inch before tightening the screws.)

A very common window problem is cracked, broken, or missing glass. A glass company will charge $80 to $100 to replace broken glass, so you can save quite a bit by learning to do it yourself. The first thing to do is remove the old glass and glazing compound (putty) that holds the glass in the sash. It is easier to do this if you can remove the sash from the window frame and lay it flat, but that isn't always possible.

The glass rests against a lip cut into the frame of the sash (called a rabbet). A thin bead of glazing compound

More!

HOW TO FIX WINDOWS, *Continued!*

cushions the glass where it rests against this lip. The pane of glass is held in by glazing points. In older windows these are small diamond or triangular shaped pieces of flat metal. One of the points is pushed into the wood of the sash frame, the rest of it lays flat against the glass. Depending on the size of the pane, there may be anywhere from one to five of these on each of the four sides. Then, glazing compound is applied over the points and tooled to a smooth angled surface, allowing water to run off and keeping moisture out of the sash frame. The glazing putty remains flexible (for many years, anyway), allowing for movement and expansion and contraction of the sash parts.

Eventually, however, it becomes hard as a rock—so hard you could probably build a patio with it. There is no particularly easy way to remove it. If you are lucky, it will crack and fall out in big chunks, but a much more likely scenario is that you will have to chisel it out tiny piece by tiny piece. One of the best tools to use for this purpose is a five-in-one painter's tool, along with a hammer. It needs to be done quite carefully, so as not to break the glass or notch the sash. A chisel can also be used, but even more care is required with this method. A glass supplier can also sell you a *hackout knife,* which is kind of a stiff putty knife with the cutting edge on the side instead of the end. You can also use a heat gun to soften the putty, although this will crack the glass unless you shield it from the heat (a piece of cardboard wrapped in aluminum foil works well for this purpose); it will also remove paint from the sash. Another option is a tool called a *putty softener,* specially made for heating window putty in order to remove it; it has a 1/2-inch-wide angled

piece of metal on two edges that heats up to soften the putty (two edges so you can do the corners). Infrared paint strippers also work. Be sure to have a fire extinguisher or a spray bottle of water on hand (I once set a sash on fire!). For those with more patience, a coat of paint remover will soften the putty, given an hour or two. There is also a tool called the Putty Chaser, more or less like a router bit that fits into a drill—*it does not work,* or at least I've never mastered it. There is also a tool called the Fein Multi-Master that can be used to remove putty—it has a blade that oscillates very fast in a small arc. I tried one—it works, but it's not the putty-removing miracle one could hope for. It's quite pricey, though it does have other uses as well, and the different blades for it are expensive.

If money is really no object, you can buy a product called Steam Stripper. It's basically a large steam chamber. You put the entire sash inside and leave it for an hour or so. The steam softens the paint and the glazing so that it can be easily scraped off. If you have a lot of windows to restore, it might be a worthwhile investment.

Once the putty is removed, pull out the glazing points with needle-nose pliers and then remove the glass. It's a good idea to wear gloves for this. If the glass is old and wavy, and the chunks are fairly large, you might want to save it in case you ever need to reglaze a smaller or multi-light window. Clean any remaining putty off the sash so that the rabbet is smooth to receive the new glass. (A carbide scraper works well for this.) Then coat the rabbet with a mixture of boiled linseed oil and turpentine (if you have lots of time to wait, like until tomorrow), or primer (such as Kilz or 1-2-3 if you are in a hurry). The purpose of the primer is to prevent the linseed oil in the putty from leaching out into the wood.

The next step is to measure for the glass. Measure the rabbet from edge to edge both vertically and horizontally. The glass needs to be 1/16 inch smaller on each side than the sash; in other words, subtract 1/8 inch from each measurement. Sashes are not standardized, so you may end up with weird measurements like 27-13/16 by 22-5/8 inches. Obey the old carpenters' adage: "Think three times, measure twice, cut once." Except I'd measure three times at a couple of different points because the sash may not be square. Use the smallest measurement because you can't trim 1/16 inch off a piece of cut glass. At this point you can either go to the hardware store or glass company and have a new piece of glass cut, or you can cut it yourself. Larger sashes require thicker (1/8 inch thick) glass than smaller ones, which only need 1/16 inch.

To cut glass, you will need a glass cutter, which will be locked up in a case at your local hardware store since young people have taken to using them to score graffiti onto shop

The H. B. Ives Company (still in business today) offered their patent window-stop adjusters in the June 1915 issue of *American Carpenter and Builder.* The slots in the adjusters allowed the stops to slide in and out so the sashes wouldn't bind or be too loose.

and bus windows. Once convinced that you are a responsible homeowner, they will let you purchase one. Make sure you wear gloves for this procedure. Lay the glass on a padded surface, such as a piece of carpeting or several layers of newspaper. Score the glass with the glass cutter, using a straightedge. Move the glass to the edge of the table or workbench so that the smaller part is hanging off the edge. Carefully bend the smaller part downward—the glass should break along the scored line. (If it doesn't, you'll have to start over with a new piece.) Old glass tends to be brittle and is more difficult to cut. Make sure it is clean before cutting it. It helps to lubricate the cutter with a little 3-in-1 oil first. Some hardware stores and glass companies will cut old glass for you, usually charging a dollar or two for the cut, which is cheaper than buying a new piece of glass.

Once the glass is cut, test fit it into the sash. If it's too big, don't try to force it in—it will crack. The smallest amount that can be shaved off is 1/8 inch; if that will make the glass too small, it's probably better to start with a new piece. Prepare the sash to receive it by laying down a thin bead of putty on the narrow lip of the rabbet to cushion the glass. If you prefer the easy way out, a bead of caulk works, too. There are two kinds of putty available—traditional linseed oil putty (DAP 33 and the like) and acrylic putty. I personally don't like acrylic putty—it doesn't tool well, and I prefer time-tested materials. Linseed oil putty has been used for hundreds of years. There is no easy way to lay down this first coat of putty. If the sash is laying flat, you can roll it into a thin snake and lay it in the groove, but if the sash is still upright in the frame, you'll just have to slap it on bit by bit with the putty knife. It should be about 1/16 inch thick once you squish it into the rabbet. Lay the glass into the rabbet and gently press it down around the edges to flatten the putty. Then, using the putty knife, carefully push the glazing points into the sash to secure the glass. Use at least one per side, more for a large window (one every 12 inches or so). Make sure they are flat against the glass.

Now for the part that requires some skill. Roll the putty into a rope about 1/2 inch thick and press it along the edge of the sash on top of the glass and the glazing points. I recommend doing one side at a time. Then, holding the putty knife at about a 45-degree angle, and using quite a bit of pressure, tool the putty into a 45-degree wedge from one corner to the next. The excess putty should fall away in a ribbon. The angled part of the wedge should be flat, and you should not be able to see the edge of the putty on the inside of the sash. In an ideal world, this would only take one pass. In reality, it will take several—there will be low spots to be filled in, it won't be smooth, or the angle will be wrong. Just keep working with it until it's even. Dipping the putty knife in paint thinner will help. The putty should be mitered in the corners. Glazing is definitely a skill, and not everyone has it or can develop it. If that applies to you, give up and let a glazier do it for you—a bad putty job is a real eyesore on a house.

Give the putty about a week to cure, and then prime and paint. Don't forget to prime and paint—often the one-week waiting period turns into two years and then the putty falls out and you have to do it over.

Repairing leaded- or art-glass windows may be more complex than most homeowners would care to tackle—much depends on the degree of damage and the complexity of the design. Some windows might be within the capabilities of a homeowner with previous stained-glass experience, or you could always take a few classes in stained glass before you tackle the repair. Art glass that is extremely complex or valuable for some reason (like your house was designed by a famous architect or the glass is by Louis Comfort Tiffany) should be dealt with by experienced restoration professionals.

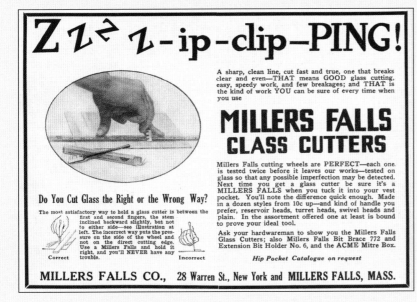

The correct way (as well as the incorrect way) to cut glass is shown in this advertisement by the Millers Falls Company in the October 1915 *American Carpenter and Builder.* Take heed.

SNEER COMPLETION

Think I've been harsh up to now? Just wait. I reserve my highest scorn for the dreadful sliding aluminum window—a window that is not appropriate for ANY building style, in my book; a window that has destroyed the historic integrity of more buildings than any other window; a window that is cheap, ugly, not very functional, easily removed from its track, making it not very secure, having no insulation value at all—what's to like? Just because this is the only kind of window sold at most home improvement centers doesn't mean anyone should buy them. The aluminum extrusion companies even have a national initiative called KAW—Keep Aluminum Windows. Do you sense their desperation? Well, at least aluminum windows aren't toxic, but that's about the only good thing I can say about them. The only proper place for ANY sort of aluminum window is on an Art Deco hotel in Miami Beach. Rip them out—that aluminum is worth money at the recycling center.

BLOCK AND ROLL

Hollow glass blocks were first patented in France in 1886. Glass blocks were not widely used in America until after 1935, when Owens-Illinois introduced Insulux. The late 1930s and early 1940s was really the heyday of glass block. Bungalows built that late might have glass block. It was often used for basement windows and for windows over bathtubs because it was mostly impervious to water, had some insulation value, and provided privacy. It was also retrofitted into the same locations for the same reasons.

IT'S A STEEL

Steel windows were only found occasionally in bungalows, but there were a few. They were available as early as 1860, but did not come into widespread use until after 1890, when technology borrowed from the steel-rolling industry made possible the mass production of rolled steel windows on a scale that made them competitive with wooden windows. In addition, devastating fires in several cities, including the earthquake and subsequent fire in San Francisco in 1906, led to the enactment of strict fire codes for multistory commercial and industrial buildings.

Rolled steel sections 1/8 inch thick and 1 to 1-1/2 inches wide were used for both sash and frame. The strength of the frame allowed for larger windows and expansive amounts of glass. The windows soon became popular for more than just industrial or commercial use because they were standardized and reasonably priced. Although many different window styles, including double-hung, pivoting, awning, and hopper windows, were used in industrial or commercial buildings, steel windows in residences were almost invariably casements, adapted from the English

wrought-iron casements with leaded glass. For this reason, they were popular for cottage-style homes in various period revival styles like Tudor, Normandy, and such.

If steel windows are not maintained, they can rust. If this goes on too long, parts can rust away. Steel windows are easily repaired—you can do it yourself or send them away. They can also be made energy efficient by the addition of storm windows.

STORM OUT

There's probably no such thing as a perfect storm window. There are only different options, and what will work best is dependent on the types of windows, aesthetic considerations, and various other factors. There are both interior and exterior storms available. Some types of windows, like outward-opening casements, awning, or hopper windows, require interior storm windows, although a storm can be attached directly to the outside of the casement sash. These same types of windows require exterior storms if they open inward. Fixed, single-hung, double-hung, or triple-hung windows may have either interior or exterior storm windows. Some types of windows, such as pivoting or austral windows, need interior storm windows that can be easily removed to operate the window if need be.

Exterior storm sashes were traditionally made of wood. They hung from special hardware (which is still available) attached to the trim at the top of the window, and were kept closed at the bottom with a low-tech hook-and-eye system. The hardware at the top allowed them to be propped open at the bottom for ventilation if necessary. Storm sashes for larger windows commonly had a crossbar in the middle for reinforcement, and some storm sashes had muntins to match the window underneath. In the summer, the storm windows were taken down and stored, replaced by wooden screens that hung from the same hardware. They were numbered using a set of dies—a blow from a hammer would indent the number in the wood. This is because even windows that appear to be the same size are not quite. The ritual of putting up the storm windows in the fall and taking them down in the spring is a long-standing tradition. Admittedly, wooden storm windows are heavy, and putting them on second-floor windows involves ladder climbing and possible danger. This led to the invention of the aluminum triple-track storm window, second only to the aluminum slider in ugliness and stupidity. A triple-track storm has two glass sashes and one screen sash, the idea being that the two glass sashes will be utilized in the winter, while in the summer, the one-glass sash can be slid out of the way and the screen used instead. That way the storms could be permanently installed. And thus, a house could be ugly all year round. They were also promoted as "no maintenance." There is, of course, no such thing as no maintenance.

Exterior storm windows have the advantage of protecting the existing window from weathering, and from damage by vandalism, burglars, or flying hurricane bricks. This may be particularly important if the windows are ornate or valuable, such as art glass. On the other hand, an exterior storm detracts from the beauty of your windows by covering them. The single sheet of glass in a storm window destroys the sense of depth that comes from the different ways each pane in a multi-light window reflects the light. It also makes the plane of the window flat and even with the trim rather than being recessed as the actual sash is, and glare off the storm window makes it difficult to see the real window underneath.

A much better solution, assuming ladder climbing is not your thing, is *interior storm windows.* These can be installed from inside, and the ladder can stay in the garage. A tightly sealed interior storm actually insulates slightly better than an exterior storm because exterior storms have to have weep holes at the bottom to let moisture escape. (Interestingly enough, experiments at Monticello, Thomas Jefferson's home near Charlottesville, Virginia, have shown that a loose exterior window that allows air infiltration is better than a well-sealed window at preventing condensation between an interior storm and the outside window. Just one more reason to give up caulking.) Interior storms can be wood-framed or aluminum, but often they are simply pieces of glass or plexiglass. Various methods are utilized for attaching them: a magnetic strip around the edges that sticks to steel channels or strips installed inside or outside the frame; spring-loaded sides for pressure fitting and a U-channel at the top; a magnetic flexible bellows like that found on refrigerator doors; pressure-fit using gaskets or weatherstripping; various kinds of clips or channels; or the ever-popular hook-and-loop tape combined with an inner gasket that provides the seal; even using foam pipe insulation around the edges.

A LOW-TECH, INEXPENSIVE INTERIOR STORM
(Summarized from an article at HammerZone.com by Bruce W. Maki)

SUPPLIES NEEDED:

—heat-shrink film
—double-sided tape
—1- by 2-inch lumber
—wood glue/brads
—paint or varnish
—scraps of polyethylene plastic
—scraps of plastic strapping
—staple gun

Build a frame about 1/8 inch shorter and narrower than the window opening (between the jambs and the sill, not the stops, unless you want it to go between the stops. Also, the pulleys of a double-hung window will either require a recess in the frame to allow for the pulleys, or the frame will need to go on the room side of the stops, so measure there instead). The joints can be mitered and joined with glue and small nails, or if you want to get fancy, joined with biscuits or dowels or even the very Arts and Crafts mortise and tenon. If you don't want to get fancy, you can simply join the corners with L-shaped metal angles, available at any hardware store. A large window will need a crosspiece in the middle. The frame can be either primed and painted with semigloss paint or stained. If stained, it will need a coat of varnish or shellac because the double-sided tape requires a nonporous surface.

Once the frame is ready, apply the double-face tape to the frame, attach the film, and shrink it with a hair dryer. If you want to go hog wild and make a "double-glazed" window, do the same on the back, although there will be more distortion from two layers. For a gasket, cut 2-inch strips of 4 or 6 mil polyethylene, fold in half, and staple to the back of the frame so that it extends about 3/4 inch past the edge of the wood (that way it will fold over the narrow dimension of the wood when the frame is pushed into the opening). Just overlap the strips at the corners. Make a handle from plastic strapping and staple it to the side of the window (makes the window easier to remove). Put a label on the back so you know which window it's for, and label the top as well because it might not fit upside down.

Push into the window opening slowly to allow air to escape (one of the stops may have to be removed for this). Replace the stop. If the storm is going on the room side of the stop, it may need some sort of retaining mechanism to keep it from blowing out on a windy day.

These windows are pretty fragile, so maybe they aren't for you if you have children and rambunctious dogs. In the off-season, they have to be stored somewhere they won't get damaged. On the other hand, even if they do, you can just go out and buy another ten bucks worth of window film.

These can be made as fancy or as funky as you wish: wood to match your woodwork and fancy brass handles are an option, or at the other end of the spectrum, cheap polyethylene instead of shrink-wrap (harder to see through but it does the trick), which would be just the thing to go with the asphalt siding. Bubble wrap works, too.

STORM WINDOWS

OBSESSIVE RESTORATION

Exterior storm windows are available with wood or aluminum frames. Wood storms have to be painted and maintained just like the wood windows of the house, although having exterior storms will cut down on maintenance of the main windows since they will be more protected from the weather. Aluminum-framed storms are available both in single units that are similar to wood storms or in the dreaded triple tracks, which you're just not allowed to have. No, not even under Compromise Solution. Anodizing has allowed aluminum storms to be offered in more colors, so it's possible to get something closer to the color of the real sash. They can even be painted, but at that point you might as well just get wood. Aluminum is less expensive than wood. If you have aluminum storm windows that are not anodized and you can't afford to replace them, at least paint them a color that matches the window sash so they won't be so silvery.

Less expensive options involve plastic film—either heat shrinkable or not. One method involves attaching U channels to the window frame, stretching the film tightly across, and securing it with a spline, similar to the way aluminum screens are made. Another method uses double-stick tape applied to the window and heat-shrink polyolefin film, which is then heated with a hair dryer to shrink and tighten it—this is a one-season-only solution, although it is possible to use heat-shrink film with a rigid frame made of wood. (I experimented with heat-shrink film this winter, and while California is not exactly Minnesota, it did make an appreciable difference in my comfort level, if not the heating bill.)

THE BIG SCREEN

Screens are pretty much the same as storms except they have an opposite purpose, which is to let air in and also to keep bugs out. As with storms, they can be exterior or interior, though most are exterior. Outward-opening casements, awning, or hopper windows require indoor screens, which are usually hinged on the side so that they open inward in the same way that the casement opens outward. This allows the screen to be opened so that the window can be opened or closed. Another screening mechanism is the roll screen, invented by Pella in 1925. (It was patented as Rolscreen. The company name was changed to Pella when the company moved to Pella, Iowa.) This is a screen that unrolls like a window shade and rides down two metal channels attached to the sides of the window. Several other companies now make versions of these, and if you're really lazy, motorized versions are available too.

Wooden screens had wire screening stapled to one side and covered with half-round molding, screen molding, or some other kind of small molding that was tacked on with small nails or brads. The screening (or wire cloth) was made of bronze or copper, galvanized steel, black iron, and, later, stainless steel or aluminum. The iron screening had to be painted periodically. Naturally, this tended to clog up the holes. All these kinds of screening are still available (except iron), with the addition of vinyl-coated fiberglass. Like storm windows, screens were numbered using dies to indicate which screen went on which window. Aluminum-framed screens use a flexible spline to hold the screening in a channel. There are also new systems involving hook-and-loop tape and magnets, similar to the systems used for interior storms. And of course there are both wood and metal sliding adjustable screens available at every hardware store and home center—good in a pinch but not that efficient

A 1912 ad in *House Beautiful* for Pompeiian Bronze screen cloth proclaimed: "People who own homes like this . . . ," i.e., a big honkin' bungalow at the beach, ". . . invariably select Pompeiian Bronze for all their screening . . ." and just so no one would miss the point, two close-ups of flies in the border hammer the message home. But what I want to know is, what does window screening have to do with Pompeii?

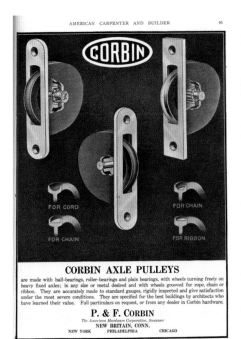

The P. and F. Corbin Company featured their various sash pulleys in the November 1915 *American Carpenter and Builder.* At the bottom, the different pulley profiles for cord, chain, or ribbon are shown. (Ribbon, usually flat steel, was used primarily for very large sashes that would be too heavy for rope or chain; they were more likely to be found on a commercial building, school, or church, rather than a residence.)

A less satisfactory kind of sash pulley is shown in a 1917 advertisement. It is held in by teeth rather than screws, which works fine until you might need to replace it for some reason—then you will completely mess up the window jamb by trying to remove it.

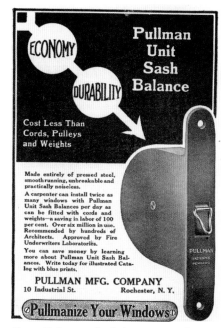

Above: Pullman spring balances were advertised as less expensive and quicker to install than traditional weights and pulleys. Pullman has now become a generic term for this kind of spring balance.

since bugs can still creep in around the edges. Some bungalows even had decorative screens with "muntins."

It's not that hard to make wooden screens—the only difficulty is that the bottom rail has to be angled to match the angle of the windowsill, which requires a table saw. The hardware for hanging them is still available at any well-stocked hardware store or by mail order. Yes, they have to be painted, and priming and painting the screen molding is tedious, but they look so much better than aluminum-framed screens that it's worth it. Wooden screens can also go on the inside, although they need to be operable somehow so that the window can be opened easily.

NEED A LIFT?

Depending on the type of window, various sorts of latches, locks, pulleys, lifts, and hardware for keeping the window open or closed were used. Unlike their Victorian predecessors, all this hardware tended to be quite plain. Window hardware could be made of solid (cast) metal, which was more expensive, but more often it was made of spun or stamped metal, which is thinner, and, of course, cheaper. This is not to say that it's low quality, merely that it is less

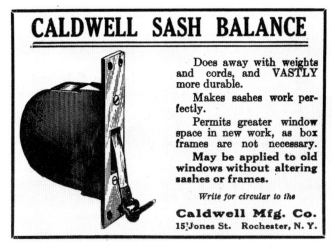

Caldwell was another manufacturer of spring balances. As you can see in the illustration, the loop at the end of the steel ribbon simply screwed into the side of the sash.

expensive. Double-hung windows require pulleys for the sash cords or chains, sash locks where the two sashes meet, and sash lifts or hook lifts to aid in raising and lowering the sash. Pulleys meant for sash chain have a squared-off profile to the groove in the pulley, while pulleys for sash cord have a rounded groove. Most pulleys were made of steel (sometimes plated) although higher-quality ones were made of solid brass, and are mortised into the side jambs and held with

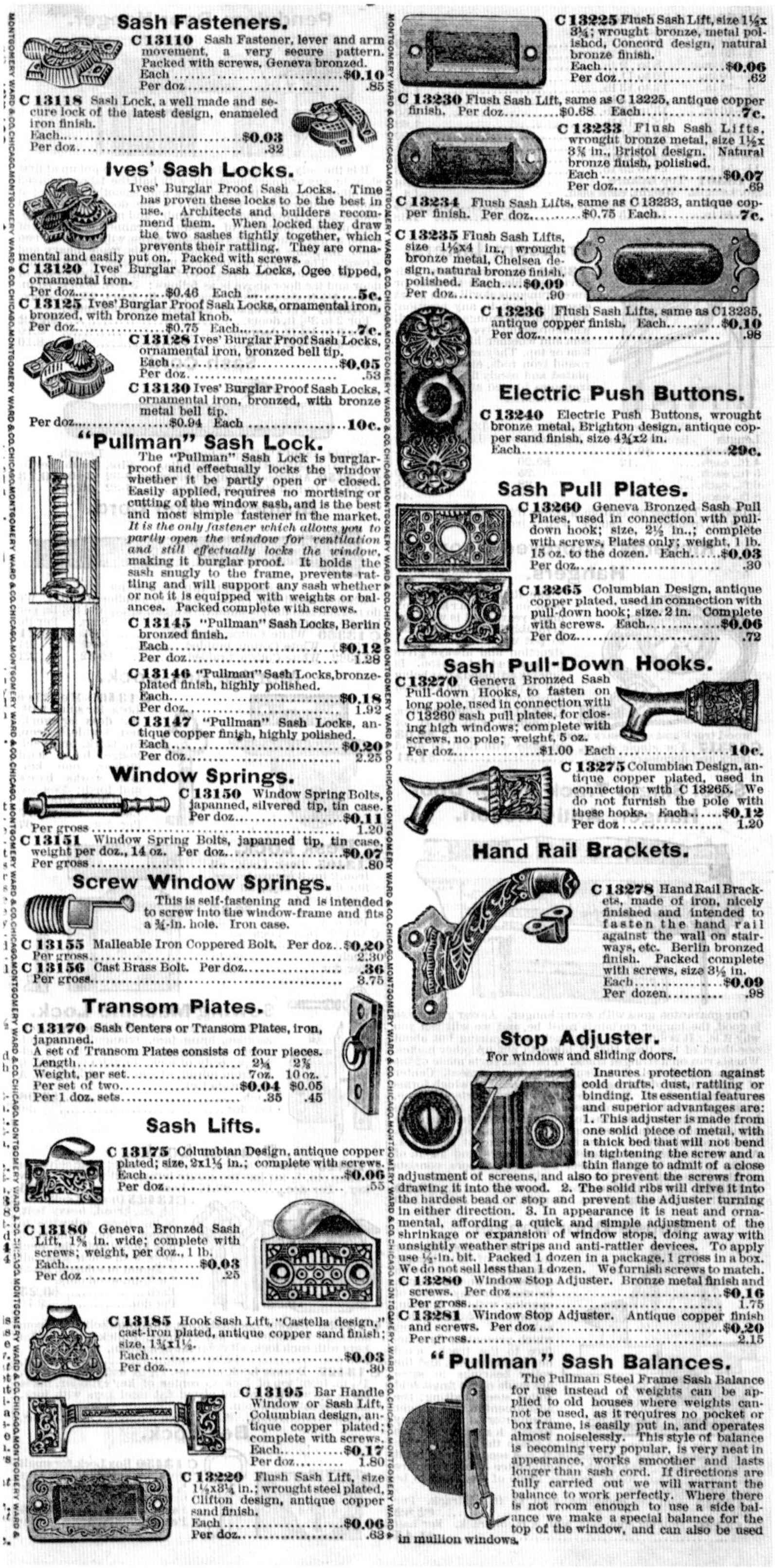

MONTGOMERY WARD & CO. CHICAGO.

Sash Fasteners.

C 13110 Sash Fastener, lever and arm movement, a very secure pattern. Packed with screws, Geneva bronzed.
Each **$0.10**
Per doz .... .85

C 13118 Sash Lock, a well made and secure lock of the latest design, enameled iron finish.
Each **$0.03**
Per doz .... .32

Ives' Sash Locks.

Ives' Burglar Proof Sash Locks. Time has proven these locks to be the best in use. Architects and builders recommend them. When locked they draw the two sashes tightly together, which prevents their rattling. They are ornamental and easily put on. Packed with screws.

C 13120 Ives' Burglar Proof Sash Locks, Ogee tipped, ornamental iron.
Per doz........ $0.46 Each .... **5c.**

C 13125 Ives' Burglar Proof Sash Locks, ornamental iron, bronzed, with bronze metal knob.
Per doz........ $0.75 Each........ **7c.**

C 13128 Ives' Burglar Proof Sash Locks, ornamental iron, bronzed bell tip.
Each **$0.05**
Per doz........ .53

C 13130 Ives' Burglar Proof Sash Locks, ornamental iron, bronzed, with bronze metal bell tip.
Per doz........ $0.94 Each .... **10c.**

"Pullman" Sash Lock.

The "Pullman" Sash Lock is burglar-proof and effectually locks the window whether it be partly open or closed. Easily applied, requires no mortising or cutting of the window sash, and is the best and most simple fastener in the market. *It is the only fastener which allows you to partly open the window for ventilation and still effectually locks the window*, making it burglar proof. It holds the sash snugly to the frame, prevents rattling and will support any sash whether or not it is equipped with weights or balances. Packed complete with screws.

C 13145 "Pullman" Sash Locks, Berlin bronzed finish.
Each........ **$0.12**
Per doz........ 1.28

C 13146 "Pullman" Sash Locks, bronze-plated finish, highly polished.
Each........ **$0.18**
Per doz........ 1.92

C 13147 "Pullman" Sash Locks, antique copper finish, highly polished.
Each **$0.20**
Per doz........ 2.25

Window Springs.

C 13150 Window Spring Bolts, japanned, silvered tip, tin case.
Per doz........ **$0.11**
Per gross 1.20

C 13151 Window Spring Bolts, japanned tip, tin case, weight per doz., 14 oz. Per doz........ **$0.07**
Per gross .... .80

Screw Window Springs.

This is self-fastening and is intended to screw into the window-frame and fits a ¾-in. hole. Iron case.

C 13155 Malleable Iron Coppered Bolt. Per doz.. **$0.20**
Per gross........ 2.30

C 13156 Cast Brass Bolt. Per doz........ **.36**
Per gross........ 3.75

Transom Plates.

C 13170 Sash Centers or Transom Plates, iron, japanned.
A set of Transom Plates consists of four pieces.

Length........	2¼	2⅞
Weight, per set........	7oz.	10 oz.
Per set of two........	**$0.04**	$0.05
Per 1 doz. sets........	.35	.45

Sash Lifts.

C 13175 Columbian Design, antique copper plated; size, 2x1⅛ in.; complete with screws.
Each........ **$0.06**
Per doz........ .55

C 13180 Geneva Bronzed Sash Lift, 1⅝ in. wide; complete with screws; weight, per doz., 1 lb.
Each........ **$0.03**
Per doz .... .25

C 13185 Hook Sash Lift, "Castella design," cast-iron plated, antique copper sand finish; size, 1¾x1½.
Each........ **$0.03**
Per doz........ .30

C 13195 Bar Handle Window or Sash Lift, Columbian design, antique copper plated; complete with screws.
Each........ **$0.17**
Per doz........ 1.80

C 13220 Flush Sash Lift, size 1¼x3¼ in.; wrought steel plated, Clifton design, antique copper sand finish.
Each **$0.06**
Per doz........ .63

C 13225 Flush Sash Lift, size 1½x 3¾; wrought bronze, metal polished, Concord design, natural bronze finish.
Each........ **$0.06**
Per doz........ .62

C 13230 Flush Sash Lift, same as C 13225, antique copper finish. Per doz........ $0.68 Each........ **7c.**

C 13233 Flush Sash Lifts, wrought bronze metal, size 1½x 3⅝ in., Bristol design. Natural bronze finish, polished.
Each **$0.07**
Per doz........ .69

C 13234 Flush Sash Lifts, same as C 13233, antique copper finish. Per doz........ $0.75 Each........ **7c.**

C 13235 Flush Sash Lifts, size 1½x4 in., wrought bronze metal, Chelsea design, natural bronze finish, polished. Each.... **$0.09**
Per doz........ .90

C 13236 Flush Sash Lifts, same as C13235, antique copper finish. Each........ **$0.10**
Per doz........ .98

Electric Push Buttons.

C 13240 Electric Push Buttons, wrought bronze metal, Brighton design, antique copper sand finish, size 4¾x2 in.
Each........ **29c.**

Sash Pull Plates.

C 13260 Geneva Bronzed Sash Pull Plates, used in connection with pull-down hook; size, 2½ in.,; complete with screws, Plates only; weight, 1 lb. 15 oz. to the dozen. Each..... **$0.03**
Per doz........ .30

C 13265 Columbian Design, antique copper plated, used in connection with pull-down hook; size. 2 in. Complete with screws. Each........ **$0.06**
Per doz........ .72

Sash Pull-Down Hooks.

C 13270 Geneva Bronzed Sash Pull-down Hooks, to fasten on long pole, used in connection with C 13260 sash pull plates, for closing high windows; complete with screws, no pole; weight, 5 oz.
Per doz........ $1.00 Each .... **10c.**

C 13275 Columbian Design, antique copper plated, used in connection with C 13265. We do not furnish the pole with these hooks. Each..... **$0.12**
Per doz 1.20

Hand Rail Brackets.

C 13278 Hand Rail Brackets, made of iron, nicely finished and intended to fasten the hand rail against the wall on stairways, etc. Berlin bronzed finish. Packed complete with screws, size 3½ in.
Each........ **$0.09**
Per dozen........ .98

Stop Adjuster.

For windows and sliding doors.

Insures protection against cold drafts, dust, rattling or binding. Its essential features and superior advantages are: 1. This adjuster is made from one solid piece of metal, with a thick bed that will not bend in tightening the screw and a thin flange to admit of a close adjustment of screens, and also to prevent the screws from drawing it into the wood. 2. The solid ribs will drive it into the hardest bead or stop and prevent the Adjuster turning in either direction. 3. In appearance it is neat and ornamental, affording a quick and simple adjustment of the shrinkage or expansion of window stops, doing away with unsightly weather strips and anti-rattler devices. To apply use ½-in. bit. Packed 1 dozen in a package, 1 gross in a box. We do not sell less than 1 dozen. We furnish screws to match.

C 13280 Window Stop Adjuster. Bronze metal finish and screws. Per doz........ **$0.16**
Per gross........ 1.75

C 13281 Window Stop Adjuster. Antique copper finish and screws. Per doz **$0.20**
Per gross........ 2.15

"Pullman" Sash Balances.

The Pullman Steel Frame Sash Balance for use instead of weights can be applied to old houses where weights cannot be used, as it requires no pocket or box frame, is easily put in, and operates almost noiselessly. This style of balance is becoming very popular, is very neat in appearance, works smoother and lasts longer than sash cord. If directions are fully carried out we will warrant the balance to work perfectly. Where there is not room enough to use a side balance we make a special balance for the top of the window, and can also be used in mullion windows.

A page from the 1904 Montgomery Ward catalog lists a whole variety of sash locks, balances, lifts, and other hardware. Two kinds of sash pins, here called window springs, are shown in the center of the page.

screws. Inexpensive pulleys didn't have screws—instead they had serrated teeth top and bottom that bit into the wood to hold them in the jamb. Hooded pulleys, introduced in the 1940s, prevent the really annoying tendency of the sash cord to wedge itself between the pulley and its casing, which happens when the sash cords are too long, and which is really aggravating to fix. Most pulley casings are shaped like a racetrack oval, though a few are squared off. Another system, the *spring balance,* first appeared in the 1880s. Think of a small version of a retractable carpenter's measuring tape and you've got the idea. Often these are referred to as *Pullman balances,* after a particular manufacturer, who is still in business. These came in different sizes depending on the weight of the sash. Since they don't require a weight pocket, they were particularly useful in single wall or plank construction. They were also retrofitted onto a lot of windows. Duplex pulleys were introduced in the 1940s. These consist of a metal box set into the jamb containing spring-loaded cables, which were connected to L-hooks screwed to the bottom edge of the sash.

Sash lifts, hook lifts, or recessed pulls were used on the lower rail of the bottom sash to help raise and lower the sash. Sash lifts are basically handles and are more likely found on larger sashes. Hook lifts are screwed on singly or in pairs (for larger windows), as are recessed pulls. They could be made of stamped steel or pot metal, plated to match the finish of the other hardware, or sometimes they were solid brass, copper, bronze, or iron. Sash locks not only locked the window but also served to pull the meeting rails of the sashes closer to prevent air infiltration. Sash locks were generally made of thicker metal than the other window hardware. A few windows, especially ones that weren't likely to be opened often, such as closet windows, dispensed with the whole pulley system and instead used *sash pins,* spring-loaded bolts attached to the sashes that insert into holes drilled in the jamb every

Whitney casement window hardware, advertised here in the January 1918 *American Builder,* could make your windows open and close like an accordion playing a really fast kopanitsa. (Okay, that's a really obscure reference that few people will get, but I don't care.) Shown here on a lovely shingled bungalow in Minneapolis, another example is shown on page 90.

six inches or so. Pulling in on the bolts released the sash so you could move it. (It gives a whole new meaning to Frank Lloyd Wright's description of double-hungs as "guillotine windows." And just so you know, Dr. Joseph-Ignace Guillotin did not invent the guillotine, he merely recommended its adoption. His descendants, understandably, decided to change their surname when it became associated with the device). Similar to sash pins are *ventilating bolts,* which are sliding, spring-loaded bolts that attach to the top or front of the lower sash and lock into small strike plates set on the stop, the jamb, or the front of the upper sash, depending on where and how the bolt is mounted. These were intended more as a security device, allowing the window to be open for ventilation but not allowing it to be raised any further.

If you are suffering under the illusion that complaints about lousy building materials are a twenty-first-century phenomenon, consider this harangue in the 1918 *Cyclopedia of Architecture, Carpentry, and Building:*

In all the range of house hardware, there is none so unsatisfactory as that used in connection with window-sashes. This is not altogether the fault of the hardware, as the customs regulating the manufacture of the sashes themselves make them the most flimsy part of house construction. The glass is wide, and the meeting rails narrow. Sooner or later someone tries to force up the lower sash when "stuck," by pushing violently on its top rail, or tries to pull down the top sash by pulling on its bottom rail; these operations pull the rails away from the glass, and if, when "fitted," there was not considerable play, the sashes never come together again. Any sash-lock adapted to such a position must necessarily be far from exact in its working. All work perfectly in the model; few work at all on the real sash. Most of the locks are safe, at least, little attention need be paid to representations that certain kinds can be opened by means of a thin blade inserted between the sashes from the outside; for, after one has seen the difficulty of working them from the inside by the usual means, he will never be troubled by the thought of anyone working them from the outside with a putty knife.

Casement windows opened in or out on either butt hinges or *friction hinges* (sometimes called scissor hinges, or these days, Whitco hinges, after one company). Friction hinges are mortised into the bottom of the window. One would think that butt hinges on outward opening casements, being exposed to the weather, would be brass or bronze so they wouldn't rust, but they are actually more likely to be galvanized (coated with zinc) steel. Butt hinges on inward-opening casements were more likely to match all the other hardware since they can be seen from inside the house. Outward-opening casements with butt hinges require some sort of *casement operator* or *stay* to keep them from blowing shut, although many casement windows don't have them. There were various kinds, but by and large they had some kind of rod or bar that attached to the bottom rail of the sash, and a mechanism affixed to the interior stool. The mechanisms varied—a rod that slid through a round carrier with a knurled nut to tighten it; a rod with a pin on one end that attached to a square piece of metal running in a track attached to the stool, which

Above: A hidden casement operator is installed through the window apron at the 1924 Gould House in Ventura, California. The groove in the vertical stop is the track for a rolling screen, which unrolls like a window shade.

Left: The problem of screening an outward-opening casement could be neatly solved with this adjuster from the Casement Hardware Company, which was installed in the apron. And apparently the coinage of previously nonexistent words by adding the suffix "ize" started as early as 1912, since they are advising "Postalize us today."

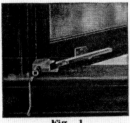

Above: The Rixson Company offered a slightly different casement operator in the October 1915 *Bungalow Magazine*. Their model could be installed on top of the stool or through the apron.

could be tightened with a wing nut (and which is practically guaranteed to gouge a big trough in the window stool); a flat bar with holes drilled every inch or so that it fits over a pin in the mechanism; and the really low-tech version—the giant hook-and-eye, where the foot-long hook was screwed to the sill and several eyes were attached to the bottom rail side by side (depending on which eye you chose, the window would stay open that far). This is by far the simplest and most effective method, one that was employed by Frank Lloyd Wright on his own house in Oak Park, Illinois.

Casement fasteners were generally located on the stiles about halfway up, and the strike plate was located on the stop. Some casements had the fastener at the bottom instead (the top as well on a tall window) with the strike plate set on the stool. Double casements might have fasteners at the bottom and top as well as one in the center where the two windows met—this required a different sort of strike plate. The strike plates were usually set into a mortise so they were flush. The fasteners themselves had various sorts of arms or loops that pivoted. The ubiquitous casement fastener for bungalows had an oval loop about an inch in diameter.

Awning, hopper, or austral windows had similar hardware, as they were basically casements turned on their sides. Awning or hopper windows, since they had gravity to keep them open, employed chains to stop them from flopping too far, although some used hinged hardware akin to the lid support hardware used on fold-down desks and

trunks. Awning and hopper windows were often used as transoms, and could be fastened with a *transom catch*, a spring-loaded catch with a round loop that allowed it to be opened using a hook on the end of a long pole if it was too high to reach.

Occasionally you may come across weird windows or hardware; they were very inventive in the early twentieth century, and all sorts of stuff were tried that didn't catch on for various reasons.

CURTAIN CALL

"Another advantage is that, if curtains were required, these central casements offer precisely the right dimensions for a sash curtain, which is, after all, the only natural curtaining of the window itself. Long outside draperies are a part of the decoration of a room, but if a window is to be curtained at all it should be with some sheer material that, while screening the room from the outside, admits the light and tints it the color most in harmony with the general scheme of the room."
—from Home Department, *The Craftsman*, July 1907

This is not really a decorating book. However, since window coverings are attached to the house, they walk the fine line between decoration and architecture, and are worth mentioning. In the Victorian era, window treatments were as ruffled and flounced and layered as the ball gowns of the period, and seemed purposely designed to keep out as much sunlight as possible. By contrast, the Arts and Crafts era embraced sunlight, often opting for no curtains at all or very simple window treatments.

The layer closest to the glass was often a simple curtain of netting, muslin, voile, scrim, or some other sheer fabric, referred to as *sash* or *glass* curtains. This was mounted either directly on the sash itself or just inside the window frame. Usually the curtain rod was threaded through a pocket at the top of the curtain to form soft gathers, the curtain itself being maybe one-and-a-half or two times as wide as the sash itself. Fabrics for these curtains might be plain or printed. Plain fabrics could be decorated with hemstitching or embroidery or occasionally some sewn-on tape or braid trim in a simple design. Net curtains might have a border of very simple crocheted or tatted lace. There were occasional lace curtains with simple designs, unlike their Victorian predecessors. Colors like ivory, cream, straw, or yellow

Typical of Charles and Henry Greene's attention to detail, glass curtains of a printed design on sheer linen are attached directly to the casement sash on a rod held by small wooden blocks. Above the sash curtains, square wooden rods mounted on the head casing are held by wooden brackets—these would hold the over-curtains if there were any.

were favored, as well as natural or unbleached linen. Part of the reason for sash curtains is to filter the light because the contrast between the surrounding unpainted woodwork and bright sunlit glass causes glare.

Sash curtains were made to cover the entire window or sometimes only part of it (café curtains). Occasionally these were paired with a valance (basically a really short curtain) at the top of the window. Sash curtains hung to the sill.

Inside, somewhat heavier curtains (called *side* or *over-curtains*) were installed. These could be closed for privacy or warmth, and so were often hung on brass rings sewn onto the top to make them easier to open and close, although they could also just employ a rod pocket like the sash curtains. Sometimes they were pleated at the top, though not generally with the triple pleats that are the most common in draperies now. These utilized various fabrics, including linen, canvas, denim, duck, burlap, velvet, velveteen, pongee, and so forth. Fibers could be cotton, linen, silk, jute, hemp, or wool. There was no polyester. In fact, the first manufactured fiber was *viscose* or *rayon,* made from cellulose and patented in 1894 but not commercially available in the United States until 1910 (the name "rayon" wasn't used until 1924). It was the result of many attempts during the nineteenth century to come up with artificial silk. Polyester wasn't invented until 1941. But I digress.

Overcurtains generally stopped at the sill or just below, although they could hang all the way to the floor for a more formal look. Sometimes a valance was used at the top; this was often a good device for making a set of windows look unified. Overcurtains were often stenciled or appliqued or otherwise tarted up; they could also be printed.

ANY PORTIERE IN A STORM

Many bungalows also had *portieres* (door curtains) on interior doors. These served to soften the doorway and add privacy when closed, as well to block drafts and so forth. They also were a really good way to show off nice fabric and embroidery and other kinds of embellishment, and since they were not exposed to constant sunlight like window curtains, they were more likely to have been decorated. As they would usually be seen from both sides, each side could be completely different. The most common place they were found is between the living room and dining room, or the

Above right: In an article in the February 1912 issue of *House Beautiful,* this dining room was given as an example. Behind the brass-and-slag glass pendant over the dining table, portieres with an appliquéd geometric design hang in the doorway separating the dining room from the living room. Built-in glass-door cabinets in the colonnade face the dining room, and the plate rail is at the top of the door and window casings.

Right: A set of simple portieres softens the doorway between the living and dining rooms in this June 1915 advertisement for Fiberlic wallboard. In this case the joints in the wallboard have been artistically worked in with the moldings, beams, and other woodwork.

living room and the entry hall, much depending on the layout of the particular bungalow. An opening with a pocket door might even have two sets of curtains—one on either side of the door. Portieres normally were hung on rings because, as contemporary author Fred Hamilton Daniels noted in his book *The Furnishing of a Modest Home* (1908),

> From the nature of the service expected of them it should be seen at once that they should be hung upon rings so that they may be easily moved. They should not be swathed about a pole (as if the pole was suffering from tonsilitis), thus rendering their moving aside a matter calling for a step-ladder. . . . Portieres made from ropes, beads, bamboo, shells, spools, buttons, or string beans serve no purpose, and merely illustrate the craving for novelty associated with an untrained mind.

One of my distant ancestors, perhaps.

HOT RODS

Most curtains hung on the ubiquitous curtain rod of the period—a 3/8-inch-diameter brass rod (solid brass or plated steel) cut to length and held up by gooseneck brackets (sometimes called *barrel* brackets because of the shape of the part that unscrews to hold the rod) The brackets were available with different protrusions, depending on how far from the window casing one wanted the curtain to hang, and were also made with more than one bracket on the same mounting plate so that the sash curtain, overcurtain, and valance could all hang on separate rods attached to the same mounting plate, which cuts down the number of drilled holes in the woodwork. There were also spring-loaded, rubber-tipped ends made for 3/8-inch rods so that the rod could be held by tension; thus, holes weren't needed at all.

For larger windows, heavier curtains, or portieres, a brass-covered wooden pole, a brass tube, or a wooden pole up to 1-1/2 inches in diameter was used. If mounted inside the casing, simple sockets or sometimes even simple L-shaped wire brackets that screwed into the frame were employed. For outside mounting, a simple metal or wooden bracket was used, and very plain finials could be added to the rod. Doors meant to have portieres sometimes had

Above: Simple wooden brackets support square rods at the Henry Greene–designed Gould House. A subtle stepped detail adorns the ends of the head casing.

Below: Stenciled linen café curtains with brass rings hang on the ubiquitous 3/8-inch brass rod mounted on the window stops in the dining room of a Seattle bungalow. Above the plate rail, a piece of art hangs in the proper way from the picture molding on two hooks. The V-shape resulting from hanging on one hook was considered undesirable, though it's a lot easier.

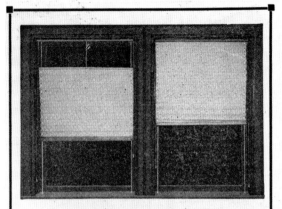

It's the Little Things That Sell A House or Apartment to a Woman, And Women Have a Lot to Say

sliding hooks that ran in a metal track attached to the top of the door frame. Occasionally wrought-iron rods and brackets were used for curtains, but this was more common after World War I with the increasing popularity of period revival styles.

Although Charles W. Kirsch invented the telescoping flat curtain rod in 1907, these rods did not seem to have come into common use until the 1920s. They were touted as being stiffer and less likely to sag. Kirsch also invented the traverse rod in 1928, but before that, a draw system had to be rigged up using cord and screw eyes.

MADE IN THE SHADE

In addition to or in place of sash curtains, many bungalows used roller shades. These were made of stiffened fabric (unlike the vinyl of most roller shades today) attached to a wooden roller, and finished with a wooden slat inside the hem at the bottom and a simple round crocheted pull. They generally didn't have fancy scalloped hems or tassels or trim, and if they weren't ivory-colored, then they were dark green.

In addition to fabric shades, sometimes blinds made from bamboo, paper, or various grasses (referred to as "matchstick" shades) were used. These were especially popular for sleeping porches and sunrooms, as the natural materials helped to "bring the outdoors in." A version of paper accordion-pleated shades, similar to modern ones, was being advertised in 1920.

Wooden shutters made an occasional appearance as well, partly due to the influence of the Colonial Revival.

Facing: Apparently Charles W. Kirsch must not have done much to defend his flat curtain rod patent, since by 1923, the Gould-Mersereau Company, a competitor, was running this advertisement for pretty much the same thing. They mentioned that it had been awarded a Certificate of Approval by *The Modern Priscilla,* a popular women's magazine at the time.

Left: Perhaps you thought accordion-pleated shades were a recent invention? Not so, as this ad from the August 1920 *American Builder* demonstrates.

ENTRY LEVEL

They were still pretty door-happy in the bungalow era. Besides conventional front, back, and side doors for entry to the house, there may have been french doors to the outside as well. French doors often opened onto porches on the front, sides, or back of the bungalow. French doors were usually double, but single multi-light doors also made an appearance. Inside, numerous doors also opened the rooms to one another, since many bungalows had been built without hallways. It's not uncommon for a kitchen to have four or five doors opening off of it.

The front door was meant to impress. The other doors were meant to function. These included the back or side doors; french doors (a door with glazed panels extending the full length, usually paired but not always); cellar or basement doors; and doors for milk, ice, coal, or package delivery.

Back or side doors tended to be much more utilitarian than the front door. They were generally frame-and-panel, with varying numbers of panels. A typical back or side door would have a high window for light and panel(s) below, although eight or ten light doors weren't unheard of either. Sometimes the door would be solid with no window. These doors could be varnished but were more likely to be painted than the front door.

In keeping with the blurring of indoor and outdoor spaces so prized by Arts and Crafts designers, bungalows often had wraparound porches, or porches on the side or back, that were accessed through french doors, either single or double.

Front doors on bungalows ranged from the very plain to the very fancy, and there wasn't always a correlation between the elaborateness of the house and the fanciness of the door. The front door was usually wider than other exterior doors, which were commonly 30 or 32 inches, but that could mean a width anywhere from 36 to 60 inches. Some doors also had *sidelights*, essentially narrow windows on one or both sides of the door. In general, sidelights were fixed, but if you wanted to get really fancy, they could be operable for ventilation. If you wanted to get even more elaborate, and this was especially true if the main door was really big, the sidelights could actually be narrow doors that could be used in lieu of the main door. There might also be a transom—a window above the door, which might be fixed or operable.

No. M-169—Morgan Front Door
Solid metal bars used in glass design, and genuine Polished Bevel Plate.
— See Morgan Millwork Handbook

Doors That Sell
By Reason of Their Beauty and Quality
MORGAN DOORS
stay sold and each day give the owner more pleasure and satisfaction. Morgan Doors are guaranteed—don't forget that and we are telling about ten million readers of National home magazines about them every month by our advertising. May we have your co-operation to use them on your jobs?

Your dealer can supply MORGAN DOORS without delay from our immense stock.

Morgan Sash & Door Company
Department A-23, CHICAGO
FACTORY: Morgan Co., Oshkosh, Wis.
Eastern Warehouse and Display:
Morgan Millwork Co., Baltimore

DISPLAYS: 6 E. 39th Street, New York
309 Palmer Building, Detroit
Bldg. Exhibit, Insurance Exch., Chicago

Facing: Two vertical panels of flat-grain Douglas fir form the lower part of this door, which also features a geometric art-glass window.

Above: Featured in this November 1915 ad, a front door from the Morgan Sash and Door Company has two vertical art-glass panels with a geometric pendant design inspired by the Prairie style.

Above: Beautiful arched double doors with diamond-patterned glass make for a grand entrance into the living room of a Chicago bungalow. The doors themselves are dark-stained birch.

Above right: A small door for milk delivery resides in the back hall of a bungalow in Milwaukee, Wisconsin. On the outside of the wall, an insulated box kept the milk cold. A cabin latch (so-called because it keeps cabin doors closed on boats) prevents burglars from using small children to break into the house.

Right: Various bolts to keep the fixed door of a pair of french doors closed were illustrated in the 1918 edition of the *Cyclopedia of Architecture, Carpentry, and Building.*

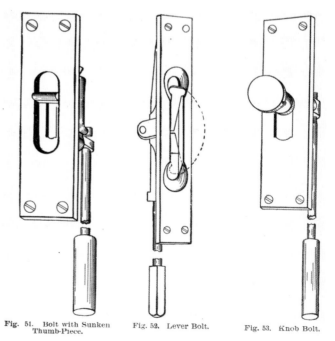

Fig. 51. Bolt with Sunken Thumb-Piece.   Fig. 52. Lever Bolt.   Fig. 53. Knob Bolt.

Doors were made of almost any wood imaginable: soft-woods like pine and fir or hardwoods like oak and birch. The door itself could be solid or have one or more windows. Front doors were often covered in *veneer* (a thin layer of wood, often a more expensive wood or one having a more interesting grain pattern), which allowed the inside to be a different wood than the outside. Traditionally, the inside veneer matched the wood of the interior trim. Other exterior doors could be veneered as well. Because of the Arts and Crafts reverence for wood, bungalow doors were not usually painted; instead they were varnished.

There were different ways of constructing doors. The most common was *frame-and-panel*. In a frame-and-panel door, a frame of *stiles* (vertical members) and *rails* (horizontal members) surround one or more wood panels. The panels sit in channels in the edges of the frame but are not glued, which allows for movement as the wood expands and contracts seasonally. Panels were generally flat, though some had a simple raised panel design. The edges of the frame around the panels could be cut square, or they could have a molded profile. Another type of construction was *board-and-batten*, where vertical boards, usually tongue-and-groove, were held together by Z-shaped or X-shaped battens (boards) applied to the surface. This was one of the earliest forms of door construction. Of course, in another triumph for faux structure over real structure, a frame-and-panel door could be made to look like a board-and-batten door by using tongue-and-groove boards for the panel and applying thin boards on top to look like battens. Although *flush* or *slab* doors are thought of as a later (post–World War II) invention, they were often used on front doors for bungalows, frequently with a decorative veneer. *Dutch doors*, which are split horizontally, allowing the top and bottom halves to be opened separately, were a less frequently used door type. Doors weren't always rectangular either; arch top or round top doors were also used.

On top of the basic door, whatever its construction, all sorts of decorative things could happen. Interestingly shaped panels or windows were common. Window glass might include beveled, leaded, etched, or art glass. Windows could be operable for ventilation or for talking to someone outside the door without opening it (this is often called a *speakeasy*); applied moldings, blocks, or carvings added more decoration. A slab door might be covered in an exotic veneer and/or have inlay work, or *marquetry*. Decorative butterfly-shaped keys might be used to join the boards of a slab door. Brass or bronze hardware might be simple or intricate.

French doors by definition are double, but multi-light single doors have also come to be referred to as french doors. The lights in a french door are commonly rectangular, though many french doors may have a muntin pattern that matches the windows. French doors were also used in the opening between living and dining rooms, and some-times between other rooms as well. French doors separating a living and dining room are mostly decorative, seeing as how no one ever closes them. In its 1921 catalog, *Building with Assurance,* The Morgan Sash and Door Company commented, "The average Home will be made doubly attractive if French doors are used between all the rooms on the ground floor, with the exception of the kitchen." But then, being a manufacturer of doors, perhaps they weren't as objective as they might have been.

The kitchen often had an outside *icing* door, by which the iceman could put ice directly into the back of the icebox without coming into the house. This prevented dirt and water being tracked into the kitchen. In addition, the outer door could be left open during cold winter months to save on ice.

A similar setup was used for milk or package delivery doors. The deliveryman opened the outer door to place the milk or package inside. An inner door that could be locked allowed the goods to be retrieved from inside the house.

Before air-conditioning was common, any ventilation one could get in a hot climate was important. These partial doors, screened with loosely woven fabric, were used to provide visual privacy for the bedroom while still allowing air circulation.

INSIDE JOB

Interior doors take the same forms as exterior doors, though they are thinner (generally 1-3/8 inches thick where exterior doors are 1-3/4 inches). Measuring anywhere from 24 to 32 inches wide, the most common widths are 28 inches and 30 inches. The majority of interior doors are a standard 80 inches tall (6 feet 8 inches). Narrower doors may be used on closets, bathrooms, and the like. There were many different styles, but the most common are one-panel doors (with one vertical panel) and five-panel doors (with five horizontal panels). The panels were generally flat, though some had a very simple raised panel design. The stiles and rails usually had a simple molding along the edge, though square-cut edges were also fairly common.

Glass panels were used on some interior doors, often to bring light into an adjacent room or hallway. It was fairly common for a bathroom door to have an obscure glass panel to allow light into an adjoining hallway.

IF YOU POCKET, IT WILL NEVER HEAL

The rooms in a bungalow were often divided by pocket doors that slide into a cavity in the wall. This is particularly true of rooms that open off the living room, such as the dining room or study. Another common location for pocket doors is between the entry hall and rooms that open off it. A wall containing a pocket door is thicker than an ordinary wall (which generally measures about 5 inches deep), since it is made up of two walls separated by the pocket. Pocket doors may take the same forms as other doors: one or more panels that may be wood, glass, or art glass, or a combination separated by stiles and rails. There may be one single door, or there may be double doors that emerge from pockets on each side to meet in the middle. Pocket doors commonly hang from a rail installed inside the wall, while some may run on a track mounted on or recessed into the floor, although the floor track was more common in the nineteenth century; top-hung doors had mostly superseded floor tracks by the twentieth century.

SILENCE OF THE JAMBS

Any door (or window, for that matter) is set into a rough opening that has doubled studs (vertical framing members) on each side, and a *header* (a short beam) across the top, ostensibly to distribute the load since there aren't any studs in the opening. (There is some controversy right now regarding whether headers are actually necessary.) The header is usually made from two pieces of framing lumber nailed together—this can be anything from a couple of two-by-fours up to a couple of two-by-twelves; the wider boards just mean that the space between the top of the

Pocket doors WITH portieres are highlighted in this ad from the August 1922 issue of the *Home Designer*, a magazine published for a few years in Oakland, California. The main selling point for these particular doors was that they did not require an extra thick wall, which most pocket doors do.

rough opening and the top of the wall doesn't have to be filled in with short studs (called *cripple studs*). This opening is usually about 2 inches bigger all around than the actual door; for instance, the rough opening for a 30- by 80-inch door measures 32 by 82 inches. Why? So you have wiggle room in order to make the door frame level and plumb. The door frame is made up of the *jambs* (the side and top pieces), the *stops* (a small piece of molding about 1/2 by 2 inches that the door closes against, although sometimes the stops are made all in one with the jamb), and the *casings* (decorative molding that attaches to the edge of the jamb and the wall to finish off the door opening. *Shims* (thin pieces of wood) are placed between the jambs and the rough framing to keep the jambs square and level; if the frame isn't square, the door won't hang or close properly. The door hinges and the strike plate for the lock are mortised (set into recesses) into the jambs.

DOORS

OBSESSIVE RESTORATION

If a bungalow was well taken care of, the front door is usually in good shape and may only require paint-stripping or a new coat of varnish (which should be some kind of varnish based on natural resins, NOT polyurethane or other synthetic varnishes; spar varnish works well and contains UV inhibitors that protect the wood from breaking down). If the house was not well taken care of, the door may have been abused. Typically this means veneer separating, paint peeling, trim elements missing, hardware missing or replaced with some cheap modern substitute, glass broken or gone, and the door drilled for numerous deadbolts. In addition, the door may have sagged or the joints separated. Sometimes the door is missing altogether and has been replaced with some cheap door from the home center. (I swear, those six-panel "colonial" doors should just be banned.) Sometimes the replacement door isn't even cheap, just inappropriate. (Those replacement doors with beveled glass and brass "leading" spring immediately to mind.) In that case, a more appropriate door from a salvage yard or a newly built door of suitable design should be installed. If the original door has been abused, it's still best to try to save it, though it's up to you to decide when to take it off life support. Veneer can be re-glued or replaced; if parts of it are missing (often at the bottom of the door), it may be easier to cover up the missing parts with a brass kickplate. Glass can be replaced, but one of the big problems with old doors is that the glass is essentially held in by the door structure rather than being held in with putty or molding as it would be in a window; this requires taking the door apart in order to replace the glass. Not all doors are like this; some use small molding instead, and these are obviously easier to reglaze.

Missing trim elements often leave "ghosts" that provide clues as to their shape and size. A custom millwork shop can replicate these, or simple ones like corbel blocks can be made using commonly available power tools. Cheap hardware can be replaced; the biggest problem will be what to do about the numerous 2-inch holes drilled for deadbolts. You can try patching them with 2-inch plugs cut from the same species of wood, trying to match the grain as closely as possible, though it will still be pretty obvious. A better option might be to enlarge the hole to some geometric shape that could almost be considered decorative, and to fill that with contrasting wood like it was done on purpose. It may also be possible to find door hardware with a really large backplate that will cover the hole(s). Sometimes paint is the only option—it's much easier to hide the various patches that way. Sagging doors, or doors with joints that have opened up, can be taken apart and re-glued. But often the previous owner's solution to a sagging door was to plane it, sometimes severely. Sometimes the door frame has been hacked up as well. (Obviously if the door frame is out of square, both that and whatever structural problem might have caused it need to be dealt with first.) Once the structural issues have been dealt with, a piece of wood can be attached to the edge(s) where the door was planed to make it square again. (You can use screws, biscuits, dowels, mortise-and-tenon, whatever strikes your fancy, and glue.)

Replacement doors are available in many wood species, including oak, mahogany, fir, cedar, ash, alder, cherry, birch, and others, as well as tropical hardwoods like teak and nyatoh.

If by some unbelievable chance the original storm or screen door is still there—same deal. Fix it. If it's not there—get a new one. There are many companies and shops that manufacture wooden screen and storm doors.

French doors between the living and dining rooms are often missing altogether. I guess the reasoning was that no one ever used them anyway. Not really an excuse, but there it is. It's easy to tell if there were french doors if the previous owners left the mortises, but sometimes they go to the trouble of filling them in. But unless they did a really good job on the filling in, it should still be possible to tell. Yes, they're mainly decorative and take up wall space, but they're supposed to be there. If you're lucky, they just stuck them in the attic or the basement or the garage, but often they got rid of them. In that case, get new or salvage ones and put them back.

Pocket doors that work are a wonderful thing, but quite often after 80-some years they don't. Instead they stick, bind, scrape the floor, gap in the middle, or refuse to come out at all. In some cases they can be easily fixed; in other cases it will be a little more difficult. The clearances around a pocket door aren't much, so any settlement in the building or debris in the pocket or the track (such as broken plaster keys or blown-in insulation filtering down from the attic) may cause the doors to stick or refuse to come out at all (or conversely, refuse to go all the way back in). Or the explanation may be even simpler than that—someone has toenailed it to the floor. If a look with a flashlight shows debris, lift the door and try to inch it forward while a helper clears the debris using a vacuum cleaner crevice tool, a broom handle, or some other long skinny device. If most of the debris seems to be at the back of the pocket, sometimes

More!

DOORS, *Continued!*

making a hole in the plaster wall on one side of the pocket allows the debris to be vacuumed out (or prying off the baseboard, if the walls are paneled).

The first thing to ascertain is what sort of mechanism the door has—floor track or top-hung. Regardless of type, the rollers are attached to a metal bracket that is (usually) screwed to the top of the door. By shining a flashlight up into the pocket, you should be able to see what kind of hardware is there.

In top-hung doors, there are three basic types: single-roller, double-roller, or trolley style. A single-roller door has wheels that roll in a flat metal track attached to one side of the framing inside the wall, a double-roller door has two wheels attached to a single axle that roll on wooden tracks attached to both sides of the framing, and a trolley-style has two wheels on a single axle that roll in a two-sided metal track attached to the header (the framing member) that runs across the top of the doorway. Most top-hung doors have a slanted adjusting screw located at the top of the door at the leading edge that can be used to raise or lower the rollers. Stick a couple of shims under the door to hold it about 1/4 inch off the floor, and then adjust the screw (don't unscrew it completely—the door will fall off if you do). Sometimes one or more of the rollers on a top-hung door falls off the track, and this is why it scrapes the floor—often if you can get the door out of the pocket, you can lift and tilt it to get the wheels back into the track. (This is a job that often requires two people.) Also check to make sure that the roller mechanism is securely attached to the door.

Floor-track doors that won't move may have jumped the track. Try lifting and rocking the door to get it back on the track. Settlement may also cause doors to scrape on the floor or gap in the middle when closed. Floor-track doors that gap in the middle can be helped by shimming under the track—at the center of the track for doors that gap at the

An adjustable trolley-style roller offered by the Lane Brothers Company in 1920 claimed to make it impossible for pocket doors to scrape or bind. Oh, how wrong they were!

bottom, and under the back edges for doors that gap at the top.

Sometimes the door may be rubbing on the stops along the jambs because they have warped or loosened—the stops can be pried off and re-nailed, or replaced if too far gone. If the door itself is warped, you may be able to widen the opening between the jambs to allow for it, but it may also involve getting inside the pocket to shave some material off the studs to allow for the warp in the door; this will involve taking out the wall on one side. Sometimes the studs inside the pocket are warped; fixing this will require, yup, taking out the wall and either replacing the studs or shaving them down. Sometimes the door has warped so much that, if you can get it out at all, it will just have to be replaced. If the house has settled so much that no amount of adjustment or shimming will make the door function, you probably have a much larger and more expensive problem (foundation and structure) that needs to be dealt with first.

Sometimes the door needs to be removed for repair or refinishing. For a single-roller door, if you can get it all the way out (most have a retractable wood or metal finger on the back edge of the door that catches on the jamb; this needs to be flipped out of the way), then the bottom can be swung out (away from the side the track is bolted to) and the wheels lifted out of the track. As with many things in life, this is better with two people. Have a couple of padded sawhorses waiting to put the door on. If that doesn't work, try removing the stop, casing, jamb, and wood track from the side opposite the track—that should give you room to get the door out or at least to unscrew the roller assembly from the door. Then pull the door out farther so you can get to the back roller as well.

Double-roller or trolley-style doors usually have an access panel—a small piece of wood that is screwed into the top of the door framing, not unlike the pocket cover in the side jamb of a double-hung window. Above this there is generally a small section of track that is also removable, which should then allow you to access the flange that holds the roller and unscrew it from the door, and then to pull the door out farther and undo the back roller as well. As an alternative, sometimes it's possible to unscrew the track from the framing in the center of the door opening (two sections usually join there) and swing it to one side (you may need to loosen the other side as well), which allows you to pull the door off the open end of the track. (Again, this probably requires several people—two for the door, at least one to hold the loose track out of the way, and probably another to question your sanity for even attempting the job.)

COMPROMISE SOLUTION

Existing original doors may have been damaged in various ways, most often by being drilled for umpteen different deadbolts, but they can also fall victim to dog chewing and scratching. Deadbolt holes are difficult to patch, especially in a clear-finished door, but make the attempt anyway. It may also be possible to find door hardware with a really large backplate that will cover the hole(s). Dog scratches may sand out, but chewing can be more of a problem; repair may involve removing the damaged part and inserting a *dutchman* (a wooden patch). In addition, the original mortise lock may have been replaced with a modern tube lock; often the mortise is still there to accept a new mortise lock in a more suitable style. Veneered doors may have loose or missing veneer; loose veneer can be re-glued, but missing veneer will have to be replaced somehow. Generally veneer is damaged near the bottom, but replacing only that part and making it look aesthetically pleasing can be a challenge. Much of this patching is easier to disguise on a painted door, but

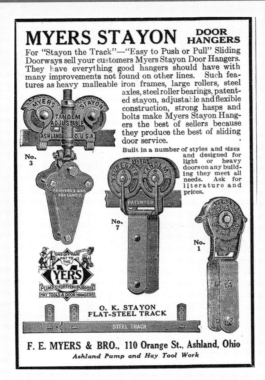

Stating the obvious, Myers "Stayon" door hangers "Stayon the Track," according to this ad in the August 1920 *American Builder.* Three different kinds of single rollers are shown, as well as an illustration of the sectional flat track the rollers run on.

Once the door is out, the rollers can be cleaned and lubricated (a squirt of machine oil into the bearings). Some rollers have a fiber or leather core to make them roll quietly; don't get oil on that part. If the rollers are damaged or broken (dirt in the track can result in flat spots on the rollers, among other things), you will either have to find salvage rollers to match, find new replacement rollers to match, or have a machine shop fabricate new wheels.

If the top track is damaged it will be necessary to take out a strip of wall in order to access the track so it can be repaired or replaced. If a floor track inside the pocket is damaged, same deal, only lower down.

The reward for all this tedious work? Pocket doors that glide like Brian Boitano.

that is no excuse to paint a previously unpainted door. In fact, you should strip it.

Glass can be replaced, but one of the big problems with old doors is that the glass is essentially held in by the door structure rather than being held in with putty or molding as it would be in a window; this requires taking the door apart in order to replace the glass. Not all doors are like this; some use small molding instead, and these are obviously easier to reglaze.

Sagging doors, or doors with joints that have opened up, can be taken apart and re-glued. Of course, often the previous owner's solution to a sagging door was to plane it, sometimes severely. Sometimes the door frame has been hacked up as well. (Obviously if the door frame is out of square, both that and whatever structural problem might have caused it need to be dealt with first.) Once the structural issues have been dealt with, a piece of wood can be attached to the edge(s) where the door was planed to make it square again. (You can use screws, biscuits, dowels, mortise-and-tenon, whatever strikes your fancy, and glue.)

More!

DOORS, *Continued!*

Another atrocity visited upon doors is the covering of frame-and-panel doors with thin pieces of plywood to make them into slab doors; in this case the plywood can be pried off and the door restored to its original appearance. But often the doors have been removed entirely and replaced with either hollow-core slab doors or the modern equivalent: fake six-panel doors with embossed "wood grain." If you're lucky, whoever took out the originals just put them in the garage, attic, or basement. But if you're not that lucky, there's nothing for it but to replace them, either with salvaged doors or new doors. (The hollow-core slab doors make great bench tops and such in the garage or basement.) Of course, you have to find a salvage door that is the right style, the right size, and if clear finished, the right wood. Although the majority of interior doors tend to be 30 by 80 inches, salvage doors always seem to be in sizes like 78-1/2 by 29-3/4 inches, probably because someone hacked off the bottom to allow for really thick carpeting or something.

Pocket doors often get buried in the wall by another board nailed over the door slot, which seems kind of pointless to me. If you don't want them, just leave them in the wall. But occasionally people actually go to the trouble to remove them altogether—again, seems like an awful lot of trouble. But often they got walled up because they wouldn't open and close anymore, either from coming off the track or the house shifting so that the doors rubbed on the floor. (See instructions for fixing pocket doors under Obsessive Restoration.)

If original doors have been removed or too badly abused, replacement is an option. It may be less expensive to use a door from the salvage yard, although the cost savings may be eaten up in the labor required to hang it. But with new wood doors costing anywhere from $200 to $1,000 or more, it may still be the less expensive choice. Also you have to find one the right size that's in decent condition. Environmentally it's the better option, reusing existing resources instead of consuming new ones. There are also numerous companies and shops manufacturing craftsman- or bungalow-style doors. In wood doors, there is generally a choice of solid wood or engineered wood. In solid wood, the stiles and rails are solid wood, whereas engineered wood can be anything from built-up solid wood

pieces, *finger-jointed* wood with veneer, MDF (medium-density fiberboard) with veneer, and probably particleboard with veneer as well (which I would avoid). I have mixed feelings about engineered wood. It does make use of scrap products and sawdust that would otherwise be thrown away, and it can utilize smaller trees instead of old-growth timber—all a good thing. But I question the longevity of some of these products, especially for an exterior door. I just can't see that an MDF-core door is going to hold up that well in the face of moisture. For interior doors it would probably be fine.

I probably need to mention that there were no sliding doors (except for pocket doors), only sliding windows (which were primarily limited to sleeping porches). I know it is possible to buy sliding doors with divided lights and all, but that doesn't mean you should. If there's no room for an in-swinging door, then get an out-swinging door. If you absolutely insist on having a slider, then get a wooden one and put it on the back where no one can see it.

There are also fiberglass, steel, and carbon (similar to fiberglass but without the fiber reinforcement) doors. Although the manufacturers trumpet their resemblance to wood doors, the fact is they have to be painted. So to get them to resemble wood, they require a faux finish. I've got nothing against faux finishes, but it does kinda go against the whole Arts and Crafts "honesty of materials" thing. It amuses me that not a single Web site for fiberglass or steel doors dared to show them close up. The fiberglass doors also suffer from the fake "wood grain" embossing, although a smooth finish is available. The steel doors dent and corrode if exposed to moisture (wouldn't be good for a bathroom, for instance). Steel and smooth fiberglass doors don't look too bad when painted a solid color, and they certainly cost less than wood doors. It might be an okay choice for side, back, or interior doors, and even the front if you're on a very tight budget. Just stay away from the six-panel "colonial" doors and the brass "leading."

And I've got to keep saying this: Don't fancy up a modest little bungalow by getting a teak/art-glass/carved Greene & Greene–style door with sidelights and a huge surround, no matter how much you might want one. Invest in some nice Greene & Greene reproduction furniture instead. It will cost about the same.

LATCH OF THE MOHICANS

Doors would just be flapping in the breeze unless some provision was made for keeping them closed, and thus was born the latch. The earliest latches were surface mounted, and this kind is still used on the interior of some doors for a very rustic look. This kind of latch was activated by a thumb latch on the exterior, which raised a small bar on the interior, releasing it from its resting place on a U-shaped metal catch that was attached to the door frame. Most bungalows have a doorknob or lever. Turning the knob or pressing the lever activated a spring-loaded bolt, pulling it back from the *strike plate,* which was recessed into the door jamb, or from the catch of a *rim lock,* which was surface mounted. The mechanical parts that made this work were mounted inside a flat metal box that could either be surface-mounted like a rim lock or inserted into a mortise (recess) in the door. The doorknob or lever fit over a square *spindle* and was held on by a *set screw.* A contributor to a 1918 building encyclopedia didn't think much of this method, writing,

> The old scheme of making a solid spindle which was secured to both knobs by screws through the shank of the knob running into the nearest hole in the spindle, the play being taken up by thin washers, was always bad, inasmuch as when enough washers were put in to make the knob feel solid and to prevent its

rattling, it was usually so tight as to bind. The screw always works loose, and being small is lost as soon as it drops out. Before a new screw is found, some of the washers very likely disappear; and if new ones are not obtained, the knob remains permanently loose.

He was absolutely correct, yet he was mostly ignored. Yeah, welcome to my life. Nonetheless, that is what many bungalows have, so you might as well learn to embrace rattling doorknobs as part of the old-house charm. Later, spindles were fluted in different ways and had threads that allowed the knobs to screw onto the spindle (though these still had set screws to immobilize the knob once you got it where you wanted it). The same bolt mechanism could also be activated by a thumb latch. Often a large mortise lock would have both a spring-loaded bolt and a deadbolt, which required a key for locking and unlocking from the outside and usually had a thumb-turn on the inside.

Left: The anatomy of mortise locks and rimlocks is demonstrated in this illustration from the 1912 volume of *Home Building and Decoration,* including a lovely Arts and Crafts illustration in the upper right corner for no apparent reason.

Middle: Brass is used for this thumb-latch entry set with a large backplate decorated with ornamental cutouts.

Right: A cast alligator provides the thumb-latch on the oak entry door of a home in Whitefish Bay, Wisconsin.

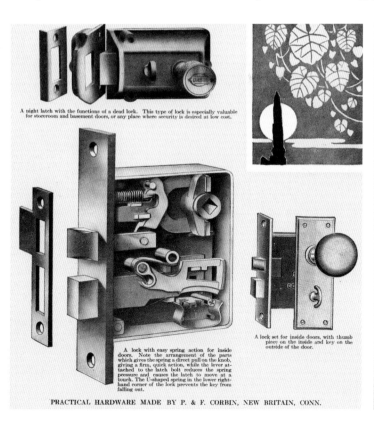

Right: Nickel-plated hardware with hexagonal doorknobs and back-plates is shown on a bathroom door. Below the inside knob is a turn that operates the privacy lock.

Below right: P. & F. Corbin illustrated a few of their available knob and backplate designs in this advertisement from the December 1911 *House Beautiful*. Any one of these designs could have been found in a bungalow, though some would be more common than others, especially the upper right example, the one just below it, and the upper left example as well.

Below: In 1915, the Gordon Van-Tine Company could sell you all the hardware you might possibly need at half price, including window, door, and cupboard hardware.

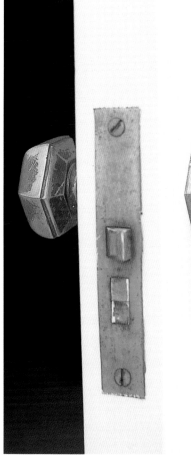

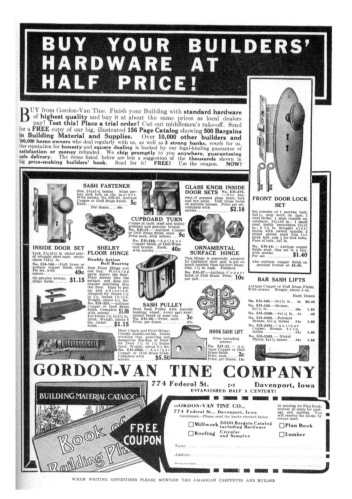

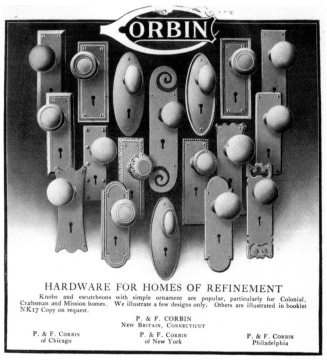

ENTRY LEVEL

Separate deadbolts were also made, as they still are. Old deadbolts do not have the same *throw* (how far the bolt penetrates the jamb) as modern ones—an original deadbolt may only have a 1/2-inch throw as opposed to a 1-inch throw for a modern deadbolt. Early locks used skeleton keys, which are still available at well-stocked locksmiths. Mortise locks usually had push buttons on the door edge that could be used to lock or unlock the knob without requiring a key. This feature is handy to avoid locking oneself out when going outside to fetch the newspaper.

In 1833, a man named J. A. Blake patented the grandfather of today's tubular lock, but it was Walter Schlage (pronounced "shlag" with a long "a") who took Blake's idea and came up with a different spring-loaded mechanism in 1920 for doorknobs that only required a couple of round holes instead of a full mortise; it is the more common door lock or doorknob sold today. The door could be locked using a push button that was part of the knob. This kind of lock had a *rosette* (small round backplate) rather than the larger backplates of mortise locks, and a separate small plate, called an *escutcheon,* for the keyhole. The escutcheon is, as one writer put it, "the lineal descendant of the escutcheon of chivalry borne by knights and persons of distinction." He went on to say, "Careful study of escutcheons on the doors of houses, will show that much of the character of the owner is still indicated thereby." Tubular locks were used more often on interior or secondary doors while front doors continued to use mortise locks. Mortise locks are still commonly available, though, and are the standard for high-end entry sets.

Mortise locks had *backplates* attached to the door on both sides. These ranged from extremely simple to extremely elaborate. Brass, copper, bronze, or iron were the favored materials, and the plates might be cast or stamped from sheet metal, or they might be hand hammered. Less-expensive entry sets might have plated steel or plated *pot metal* (metal of unknown pedigree). Electroplating had been invented in the mid-nineteenth century, and by the late nineteenth century, chemists had come up with finishes that chemically altered the base metal as well. Naturally, in true nineteenth-century fashion, these finishes were given elaborate names like "Statuary Bronze Verde Antique." Plated hardware could be had in different finishes such as lacquered brass, brushed brass, nickel, copper, or what was known as *japan* (basically painted black) but often used to refer to a tiger-striped copper and black finish, also called "Old Copper" or "Mottled Copper" or something of that ilk. Large mortise locksets with deadbolts were used for the front door while side or back doors had the simpler mortise locks or sometimes rim locks. Screen or storm doors, especially those that didn't use spring hinges, had small mortise locksets of their own, and these often had a button allowing one to lock the screen door from the inside.

The main nationwide lock companies at the time were Russell and Erwin (known as Russwin—they used to be

Though not original to this 1910 home in Oakland, California, a doorknob salvaged from a public school makes an amusing addition.

two separate companies), Corbin, Yale, Schlage, Simpson, and Stanley.

And just so you know, the key-duplicating machine was invented in 1909. Before that, keys had to be filed by hand.

HANDLE WITH CARE

Doorknobs were made of spun or cast metal that matched the rest of the lockset and could be solid or hollow. Glass knobs were molded and attached to a metal base for strength. They came in various shapes—plain, fluted, or faceted—and in various colors as well. Clear glass knobs were the most common. Porcelain, mineral (made from colored clays), and Bakelite knobs were also found in bungalows. Mineral knobs came in plain colors (brown or black) or swirly agate or granite-like colorations (often called "Agate" after Josiah Wedgwood's pottery). Some knobs were also glazed to resemble this look rather than being made from mixed clays. Bakelite knobs came into being after Leo Baekeland invented Bakelite in 1907. The substance was considered to be the first synthetic plastic, made by combining phenol with formaldehyde. He was trying to come up with a substitute for shellac, which was being used for electrical insulation. Bakelite was formally introduced in 1909, and soon was being used for all sorts of things besides electrical insulation, including billiard balls, knife handles, jewelry, radio parts, and doorknobs. Regardless of what they were made of, doorknobs could be round, oval, hexagonal, octagonal, or whatever, though round is the most common. Some metal knobs featured beading, hammering, casting, or other ornamental features, though Arts and Crafts door hardware was far simpler than its Victorian antecedents. Thumb latches were generally quite simple, though the handle that accompanied the thumb latches could be fancier.

Swinging doors, usually found between the dining room and the kitchen or the butler's pantry, often had push plates of either metal or glass. French doors usually had flush or surface bolts to keep them closed and secure, along with the door latch. Really fancy french doors had cremone bolts that ran the whole length of both doors. French doors required special mortise locks that were stepped to fit the rabbet on the edge of the door; they usually had smaller knobs than regular doors, or had a knob on one side and a lever on the other.

Of course, it wouldn't be good if the doorknob banged into the wall when the door was opened, so the doorstop was invented to stop the door before the knob hit the wall. Traditionally installed on the baseboard but occasionally on the floor, doorstops were made of either turned wood (a reproduction is still available) or metal with a rubber tip on

REPLACING LOCKS

OBSESSIVE RESTORATION

An original lock that is broken may be able to be fixed; take it to a local locksmith who is experienced with old locks, if there is one. Sometimes the lock may be beyond hope unless custom parts are replicated by casting or other methods. It's conceivable that the lock guts may be able to be replaced, otherwise you'll have to buy a whole new lockset or at least the part that goes in the mortise. For simple mortise locks, these are readily available; for a more elaborate front door lock, they may be harder to come by. Often an old lock that doesn't work may simply need a shot of lubricant like WD-40.

Contrary to popular belief, a skeleton key will not open every kind of lock; there are actually different shapes for different locks. If none of the standard ones fit your locks, you can have one custom made. If the existing locks use modern keys, a locksmith can also rekey them. If this is being done, you can have all your locks rekeyed so that one key will open all of them.

Locks had a certain *backset,* meaning the distance from the edge of the door to the center of the bolt mechanism. Generally this was 2-3/8 inches (then and now), but on some locks it can be as much as 4 inches.

If the knobs are missing, salvage doorknobs are widely available, so unless the knob is unusual, it shouldn't be too much trouble to find a replacement. Glass knobs that have detached themselves from the metal base are difficult to repair; it may be easier to get a new one. No doubt the truly obsessive will try melting the glass near the base with a torch to try and reunite the two parts. It might work. Reproduction knobs are also being made in both metal and glass.

Salvaged backplates are also widely available, though reproduction styles are more limited than what was available at the time. They can be custom made as well, for a price. A mortise lock that requires a skeleton key does allow air infiltration through the keyhole on an exterior door. If you're not using the key, this can be plugged by removing the lock from the mortise, opening it up (there's a screw to remove—take the top off carefully because if the spring goes *sproing* it will be hard to put it back together), and covering the holes with thin pieces of cardboard or sheet metal held down with small pieces of foil tape.

Antique locksets are also available, though it would be a good idea to make sure the lock actually works before buying one. An antique lock can be paired with a modern deadbolt for extra security on exterior doors.

COMPROMISE SOLUTION

There are many fine reproduction locksets to be had, and even a home center will have a few that are simple enough to be acceptable. Try to avoid really shiny lacquered brass, and stay away from "colonial" or very contemporary locksets. As noted above, an antique lockset can be paired with a modern deadbolt (in a matching finish) for more security. Many modern locksets utilize modern spring-loaded bolts while still having the appearance of a mortise set, especially useful if the door itself is new and has been predrilled for a modern lockset rather than having a mortise. It is also possible to buy a tube latch with a square hole that will accept old-style square spindles and knobs.

There is one modern doorknob that has a concave face—this is probably the ugliest doorknob ever invented. Don't buy a set that has this knob, and if it's already on the house, remove it. Often you can replace just the knobs. If the front door has modern knobs and a separate deadbolt, it would be better to replace these with a lockset that looks like it's mortised, since the separate knob and deadbolt were usually reserved for secondary doors.

one end and a screw thread on the other, just like the ones you can still buy at the hardware store. There were also various *doorkeepers* that could be used to keep the door open so it wouldn't slam shut in a sudden breeze.

BUTT IN

One generally doesn't want to pick up the entire door and shove it aside, which is why hinges were invented. Doors had mortise hinges, strap hinges, or surface-mounted hinges. The earliest hinges were strap hinges, which are attached to the face of the door and the frame. Mortise hinges (by and large referred to as "butts") were set into shallow recesses chiseled into the doorjamb and the edge of the door. These hinges were invariably ball-tipped, with one ball attached to the bottom of the hinge and the other one fastened to the end of the pin that slipped through the *knuckles* attached to each leaf of the hinge to hold the hinge together (these are called *loose-pin hinges*). Each door had at least two hinges, and the larger the door, the more hinges it required. Front doors usually had at least three and possibly more. Exterior doors traditionally opened inward, with the possible exception of french doors. Hinges were made of brass, cast iron, bronze, or plated steel. Plated butts came in the same finishes as the door hardware.

Surface-mounted hinges were customarily strap hinges, at least on exterior doors, although there were also surface-mounted butt hinges as well as half-mortised hinges where one leaf was mortised into the jamb while the other, which often had a decorative shape, was applied to the face of the door rather than to the side of it. Brass, copper, bronze, or wrought iron were the usual materials for strap hinges. The shape of the strap could be simple or exceedingly complex. Frequently the straps would be adorned with decorative nail-heads or screws. These may or may not have had a structural purpose, like fastening the strap to the door. Strap hinges were used when a more rustic effect was desired.

Above: The swinging door between the dining room and the kitchen usually had a spring hinge so it would close automatically after someone went through. Some kinds of spring hinges, such as these by the Chicago Spring Butt Company, had a mechanism that allowed the spring to be disengaged, keeping the door open if desired.

Below: The Shelby Spring Hinge Company claimed their hinge (with a door attached) had been hooked to a machine that swung the door back and forth 1,560,000 times without wearing out the hinge.

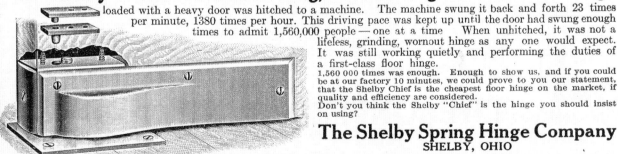

Screen doors traditionally used surface-mounted spring hinges so they would slam shut, but sometimes they had regular mortise hinges, requiring one to actually make an effort to shut the door.

Honesty of structure notwithstanding, there were a lot of fake strap hinges attached to exterior doors that actually had mortise hinges. James C. Plant, writing in the 1918 *Cyclopedia of Architecture, Carpentry, and Building,* decried the practice, saying,

> The attempt of the manufacturers to supply the appearance by making the plates separate, has led to the production of unduly elaborated face-plates of thin metal, which are often screwed on without reference to their suitability to the location or sur-roundings, so that, instead of having the appear-ance of being a minor item for use in swinging the door, they give the impression that the door is for the special purpose of exhibiting the hardware.

And you thought I was prone to sarcasm. Strap hinges were far less common on interior doors unless the designer of the bungalow was really trying for rusticity.

Swinging doors had special floor-mounted hinges that were spring-loaded in such a way that the door would stay open if you opened it fully but would swing closed if you didn't. The floor hinge was accompanied by a metal pin on the top of the door that fit into a hole in the upper doorjamb.

MAIL OF THE SPECIES

Mail slots were installed either in the front door or through an outside wall. With a front door slot, the mail would just be laying on the floor inside when you got home, as there was rarely a receptacle on the inside, although a kind of wire cage that fits the inside of the door to receive the mail is available. A through-the-wall slot typically had a recep-tacle of some sort, often with a small door on the inside. This might be in the living room, the entry, or a closet.

A front door might also have an operable window (gen-erally a casement) or a metal grille, allowing you to speak to someone outside the door without opening it—often called a speakeasy after the advent of Prohibition in 1919 (so you could give the password that allowed you inside to drink the illegal hooch).

KNOCK IT OFF

When arriving at some bungalows, you just had to knock on the door with your bare knuckles. But at most homes, there was a doorbell or a door knocker. Doorbells were either elec-tric or mechanical. A mechanical doorbell was mounted directly on the door and involved turning a knob or other protrusion that activated the bell on the inside of the door.

REPLACING HINGES

OBSESSIVE RESTORATION

If the original door is still there, the hinges are usually there with it—people rarely bother to replace the hinges unless they're replacing the door. Hinges can pull away from the jamb over time if the screws work their way loose; sometimes the fix for this is as simple as jamming a few pieces of wooden matchstick (no matchheads, please) into the screw hole so that the screw threads have something to grab onto. A short piece of hardwood dowel glued into the hole serves a similar purpose. If that doesn't work, longer screws of the same diameter can be substituted; these will be capable of reaching through the jamb and into the studs of the door frame. Hinge pins can bend, especially on a heavy door. These can be straightened in a vise or, if that doesn't work, replaced with new ones.

The fake part of faux strap hinges may have been removed. If so, there should be ghosts or a pattern of holes where the nails or screws were that may give some idea of the shape (assuming there is no historic photo or original drawings to go by). Conjecture may still be involved.

Try never to remove a swinging door if you can pos-sibly help it—it is very difficult to put them back, though it can be done. It is absolutely a two-person job.

Hinges were made of brass, bronze, cast iron, or plated steel. As with other plated hardware, finishes such as brushed brass or a japan finish were used on hinges. Although the finish usually doesn't wear off hinges, they can always be replated if it does.

Only slotted screws were used—Phillips screws weren't invented until 1936. And they weren't even invented for res-idential use—Henry Phillips intended his screws to be used with automatic screwdrivers in the auto industry. Their ability to grab and center the tip of the screwdriver made them better than slotted screws in this application, and the annoying tendency (to us) of the tip to slip out or strip the screw also meant that the screws couldn't be over-tight-ened, which was also good on the assembly line.

Phillips wasn't the first to come up with an alterna-tive to slotted screws—that honor goes to a Canadian by the name of Peter L. Robertson, who invented a screw with a square recess in 1907. It caught on in Canada, but Robertson refused to license the technology, so it was not universally adopted, even though, frankly, it's a far more sensible design than the Phillips screw. Robertson screws, now called "square-drive," are still available.

COMPROMISE SOLUTION

Okay, you can use Phillips screws. If you live in Canada, you can even use Robertson screws. But you still have to get ball-tip hinges.

Electric doorbells ran on low voltage, so there was a transformer installed somewhere (the attic was a common place for it). The transformer converted alternating house current to the low-voltage direct current used by the doorbell. Often the transformer served both front and back doorbells, and the chime or buzzer was installed in the kitchen. Electric doorbells were mounted in the door trim or on the wall next to the door. The push button itself was encircled by a brass, copper, or wrought-iron surround, and often had a decorative backplate as well.

ILLUMINATING DISCUSSION

Since most bungalows were built during the era of electricity, the light fixtures tended to be electric, although some builders hedged their bets by also installing gas because early electrical power was somewhat unreliable. This also led to a certain proliferation of combination gas/electric fixtures, easily identified by their mixture of upturned shades for gas and downturned shades for electric bulbs; these continued in production well into the 1920s. The earliest electric lights tended to be nothing more than a bare lightbulb on a cord—a conspicuous display of new technology—but these soon morphed into simple pendants, sconces, chandeliers, and so forth. Arts and Crafts–design influence on light fixtures was wide-ranging. In some cases, it led to simple, often squarish fixtures with square tubing and simple shades; in other cases, it resulted in fixtures of hand-hammered copper

Made to look like a combination gas and electric fixture, this brass wall sconce has a keyed electric socket pointing down and an electrified candle pointing up, though it also has the square key that would be used to turn on the gas if this were a real combination fixture.

Clearly influenced by the sinuous plant forms of Art Nouveau, a silver-plate-over-brass chandelier hangs from three ornamented rods in the dining room of a bungalow in Milwaukee, Wisconsin. Both the ceiling canopy and the pan of the chandelier are embellished with metal tassels.

Four art-glass lanterns hang by triangular loops on the arms of a chandelier in the living room of a bungalow in Southern California. Each side of the central post of the fixture features a cast "smiling monk" face. There were also "frowning monks" (see page 134), and monks sticking out their tongues (which is not very pious behavior if you ask me).

A fixture with multiple lights hanging on chains is called a "shower." This fixture at the Greene & Greene–designed Duncan-Irwin House in Pasadena, with a total of eleven lights, is more like a torrential downpour. The lights hang from an elaborate pegged wooden ceiling canopy.

that ranged from rustic to refined, Art Nouveau fixtures with sinuous curves, severe geometric fixtures inspired by the Prairie school, fixtures that combined wood with metal and glass, and so forth. At the same time, and often in the same bungalow, were fixtures that borrowed motifs from classical design or the Colonial Revival. As there is no such thing as architectural purity in the architecture of bungalows, so there was no such thing as design purity in bungalow light fixtures.

INDIE PENDANT

Fixtures that hang from the ceiling include pendants, chandeliers, showers, flush-mounts, and bowl fixtures. Early electric fixtures tended to hang from pipes, a holdover from gas fixtures, which required pipes, although chain-hung fixtures appeared after cloth-covered electric wire was perfected around 1915. Pendant fixtures ranged from the basic bare-lightbulb-on-a-cord to those that were quite elaborate. Chandeliers, evolving from something that originally held candles (thus the name), were basically a more elaborate form of pendant, with multiple arms, sometimes multiple levels, or numerous lights that hung from chains (known as a *shower*). And of course many fixtures actually had fake candles, often complete with fake dripping wax, and still do today, which is why you can buy decorative bulbs shaped like flames. A flush-mount fixture stuck close to the ceiling; these were more often found in rooms outside the formal rooms—kitchens, bathrooms, hallways, etc., although they appeared in the formal rooms as *beam lights*, mounted on the real or fake ceiling beams. Beam lights could also be pendants. The introduction of brighter tungsten filament bulbs in 1910 allowed for indirect lighting from bowl fix-

Pebbled green glass overlaid with a wire grid forms the sides of a rustic-looking wrought-iron ceiling fixture. Riveted strapping embellishes the truncated pyramid-shape shade while more curved straps form a sort of large finial underneath the shade.

Just in case you were under the impression that all bungalow light fixtures were simple and linear, here's quite a frou-frou brass pendant to prove otherwise.

Left: A molded shade in an oak leaf pattern is paired with a narrow cast-brass fitter in a pattern of overlapping leaves; it hangs from its ceiling canopy by a single chain.

Green slag glass panels the shade of a ceiling-mounted lantern fixture made of cast iron. Note the subtle twisting in the ceiling canopy as well as the top part of the lantern.

A brass shade with Gothic cutouts, lined with mica, hangs from a simple ceiling canopy. A pull-chain and ball for turning it on and off hangs on the right side.

Lovely hand-painted molded glass forms the shade for a simple pendant fixture, located in the bedroom of a Chicago bungalow.

Flame-like slag glass lines a flared brass shade on a pendant fixture in a bungalow in Denver, Colorado. An amber glass panel on the bottom hides the lightbulb.

A round molded shade decorated with hand-painted landscapes filters the light on a chain-hung pendant fixture.

Curved hammered straps ending in spirals surround the opalescent glass shade of this pendant fixture. The shade has swirls that resemble draped fabric.

The same brass fitter as the oak leaf shade on page 132, suspended from a pipe, has a molded shade in an Art Nouveau floral pattern with painted highlights; it hangs in the dining room of a Chicago bungalow.

A grapevine motif with hand-painted highlights decorates the shade on a ceiling-mounted indirect fixture in the living room of a Milwaukee bungalow. The stamped brass canopy is embossed pattern around the edge.

Another molded bowl shade is hand-painted with roses and hangs on three brass chains from a simple bell-shaped ceiling canopy.

Layered colored glass forms the tendril-like design on bell-shaped glass shades, suspended from a wrought-iron ring with riveted accents. This fixture hangs in a bedroom of a bungalow in Victoria, British Columbia.

Four shades of flared and ruffled iridescent amber glass are attached to chains that seem to pierce the embossed brass ring they are hanging from. A fifth light hangs from a chain in the center.

Hammered copper forms the flat ring base for these four cylindrical shades. The shades are formed of hammered and riveted copper surrounding amber-colored glass. Short chains attach the whole thing to the ceiling canopy.

tures that hung from pipes (and later, chains). After the 1925 L' Exposition Internationale des Arts Decoratifs in Paris, what we now term Art Deco–styled (known then as Art Moderne) fixtures started to make an appearance. Many of these had what are called *slipper shades*, which are kind of clamshell shaped and slipped into slots on the body of the fixture. A bungalow with an upper floor might also have a newel post light at the bottom of the stairs. This could be anything from a post lamp to an upside-down pendant (obviously it had to be on a pipe, although I suppose a really stiff chain *might* work) to an elaborate figural light, generally involving a young maiden in diaphanous draperies with a couple of lights worked in for effect.

O'ER THE LAMP PARTS WE WATCHED

Now for a brief digression into light-fixture nomenclature. The part that covers the electrical box is known as the *canopy;* the part that holds the shade, not surprisingly, is known as the *shade holder.* Shade holders come in standard sizes: 2-1/4,

"Frowning monks" ornament the ring on which the four filigree-decorated lanterns hang. The chains attach to a ball on the pipe just below the canopy, and the pipe ends in an inexplicable finial in the center. There are also matching beam lights of similar design in this Memphis living room. (See "smiling monks" on page 131.)

Hanging in the dining room of a home in Oakland, California, is a brass four-arm fixture with a square center post and tapered art-glass shades suspended from straight arms. This was a common sort of fixture in the bungalow era, and is the kind of straight-lined fixture that most people associate with Arts and Crafts lighting.

This slightly wacky four-light shower hangs in the breakfast room of the Gould House in Ventura, California.

3-1/4, 4, and 6 inches for most fixtures. (Anything bigger than that is probably too big for a bungalow and belongs on a fixture in a public building.) These correspond to the *fitter* on the shade, the rimmed part of the shade that fits into the holder. Bowl shades and slipper shades (for Art Deco fixtures) are not necessarily standardized and are not always interchangeable between fixtures. The part that the lightbulb screws into is known as the *socket*, which often had a square (usually Bakelite) *turnkey*, which allowed the light to be turned on and off at the fixture, since the fixtures were not always wired to an on/off switch. (Some had pull chains instead.) They often had the turnkey even if they were wired to a switch. Because of this, period fixtures were often hung lower than modern ones so one could reach the switches. With knob-and-tube wiring, there was often no electrical box for light fixtures; instead the two wires just emerged from a hole in the wall or ceiling, and the fixture was attached to a *hickey* (a metal doodad—yup, that's the technical term) attached with screws, with a hole in the center for a threaded rod. And just to confuse things even more, while we may think of a lamp as that light fixture that sits on the end table or the floor, technically lamp refers to the lightbulb.

Light fixtures were most often made of metal, and as with other hardware, the metal came in various finishes, either inherent in the metal itself or else plated or painted. All the finishes found on metal hardware were also found on light fixtures. Some light fixtures were also painted either in one color or polychromed. Some of the multicolored ones could be pretty cheesy since the "hand-painting," probably sprayed on by machine, didn't always line up with the elements that were supposed to be highlighted. But they have a certain charm because of that.

Because my house was designed by a Norwegian and somewhat resembles a Viking ship, I totally lust after this light fixture. Attributed to a German Arts and Crafts metalwork company called Goberg, it features a three-dimensional Viking ship in full sail on an "ocean" of hammered copper in the center oval, complete with a pennant flapping in the wind, a dragon on the bow, and shields along the sides. The ship is surrounded by four shadeholders in the shape of Viking helmets. As a final touch, an anchor-shaped finial is suspended from the underside.

RAGING BULB

The fixtures used incandescent bulbs invented by several people, none of whom were Thomas Edison. Henry Woodward and Matthew Evans of Toronto took out a patent for a lightbulb in 1875 but were unable to garner enough financial backing to commercialize their invention. Meanwhile, in 1878, English physicist Joseph Swan received a patent for an incandescent bulb with a carbon filament, though he had actually publicly unveiled his invention for the first time in 1869. Edison bought the rights to Woodward and Evans' invention, and after messing with it for a few years, unveiled his carbon filament vacuum bulb in 1879. It burned a whole thirteen hours. Nonetheless, Edison decided to electrify his laboratory. Lewis Howard Latimer, a member of Edison's team, made improvements to the carbon filament for which he took out patents in 1881 and 1882. In 1903, Willis R. Whitney invented a treatment for the filament so that it wouldn't darken the inside of the bulb, and in 1910, William David Coolidge invented a longer-lasting tungsten filament. Tungsten is what we are still using, though carbon filament bulbs continued to be sold well into the 1920s. Incandescent bulbs are, of course, completely inefficient, giving off only a small portion of the energy they use as light.

But it wasn't just the bulb. The bulb was not going to be practical for home use without a system to make it safe, economical, and widely available. What Edison did (and he should get credit for) was invent a more durable lightbulb (Edison bulbs would eventually last 1,200 hours), and then safety fuses and insulating materials, followed by light sockets with on/off switches, plus the parallel circuit, and then basically the power grid. This had to include the invention of devices for maintaining constant voltage, improved dynamos for generating the electricity, and a system of distribution for the electricity. Edison's system used direct current (DC) power, and eventually lost out to Nikola Tesla's alternating current (AC) system, which we are still using.

Reproduction carbon-filament bulbs hang from maroon cloth-covered wire on a ceiling-mounted fixture. An X-shaped metal piece is held with pyramid-head screws to the wooden block that acts as a ceiling canopy, and then there's a weird metal thingy in the middle. (Yes, thingy is the technical term.)

And there's a matching (and equally zany) sconce.

In 1901, Peter Cooper Hewitt invented the mercury vapor lamp, used for years in streetlights until it began to be phased out in favor of sodium vapor lights (the orange ones). Mercury vapor lives on as a dreadful form of security light that no one should be allowed to have.

In 1911, Frenchman Georges Claude invented the neon light, which was far more amusing but still unlikely to be found on a bungalow.

In 1927, the first fluorescent light was invented in Germany, which was less amusing. Strides have been made in the color of fluorescents, and they are energy efficient, but even the full spectrum variety and the modern compact fluorescents have a weird cast to them that just does not seem right for a bungalow.

GLASS WARFARE

Although carbon and tungsten filament bulbs didn't give off as much light as we are now used to, maybe the equivalent of a modern 25-watt incandescent, to people coming out of an era of gaslight and kerosene they seemed pretty darn bright. But very soon there were complaints about glare, which soon led to the early bare-lightbulb-on-a-cord needing to have a shade. The most common material for shades was glass, which could be etched, cut, hand-painted, bent, leaded, molded, or even all of these things at once. Glass could also be combined with metal or wood in various ways. Another popular material used in shades was mica (from a group of minerals known as phyllosilicates, which form thin translucent flakes, combined with shellac to form sheets). Other shade materials included paper, alabaster, and leather.

All-glass shades came in a huge variety of shapes and sizes, but some shapes were more common than others, and a lot of them are still used even in modern fixtures. Shades could be open or closed. Popular shapes for closed shades include globe or ball, schoolhouse (hard to describe but you know one when you see one), mushroom (for bowl fixtures), and teardrop or "stalactite" (applied to any elongated shade). There was even more variety in open shades, which could be round, square, flared, ruffled, crimped, fluted, ribbed, etc.

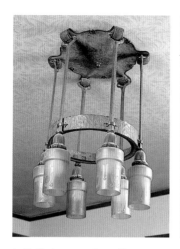

Left: Six loops on the ceiling canopy hold the rods that suspend the shadeholders of this fixture. The rods pass through riveted holders on a ring just above the shades. Compared to the heavy wrought-iron look of the fixture, the orange glass shades are etched in delicate designs

with a Vienna Secessionist influence. This bungalow is located in Denver, Colorado.

Mid-left: Ruffled ombré glass shades on chains hang from straight arms fastened to a tapered center post with rivets. The chandelier, made of ham-

mered copper, hangs from a square canopy on a large chain. The matching shade is on page 137.

Mid-right: Matching flared shades are an addition to this bowl fixture, hand-painted with lovely landscapes on each shade. The metal parts of the fixture have a painted

gilt finish, and in the background is one of the tupelo beams of this Memphis bungalow's dining room.

Right: Simple cylindrical shades are painted with an autumnal-looking landscape, and hang from a hammered wrought-iron disc.

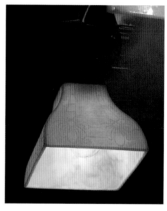

Above: A variation on the fixture shown on page 7, the same caramel art-glass shade fitted into the same ring lacks the candleholders, substituting female faces surrounded by grapes and leaves. The pieces to which the chains are attached are also different on this fixture.

Above: There is an extremely subtle pattern to the glass in this four-sided shade.

Above: A shield-shaped canopy covers the electrical box on this bedroom sconce in a Victoria, British Columbia, bungalow.

On top of the basic shape the glass could be molded, faceted, etched, cut, pressed, hand-painted, colored, overlaid with decorative cutouts of metal or wood, etc. And besides the basic shapes there were weird shapes, my personal favorite being a closed shade made of ruby glass in the shape of a pointing index finger. No doubt this was meant for exit signs but I'm picturing a bunch of them on a chandelier.

The glass itself could be colored—ivory, amber, and green were popular (green with white inside was particularly common for desk lamps and "billiard fixtures," a two- or three-light pendant for hanging over the pool table)—

but other colors like pink, red, orange, citron (yellow-green), straw, and blue were also offered. Colored glass could also be layered and then cut or etched for a two-tone (or more) effect. Or the glass might be tinted only on part of the shade, called *ombré* (from the Latin *umbra*, meaning "shade," also the root of *umbrage*, something I like to take on a regular basis).

One specialized type of glass shade was made from prismatic glass, which could direct and magnify a light source. Prismatic glass was invented in 1893 by French scientist Andred Blondel and Greek engineer Spiridon Psaroudaki. They named their product "holophane," from

Greek *holos* (entire) and *phane* (a torch). The product was a success, and in 1895, an entrepreneur named Otis Hygatt bought the rights and opened the Holophane Glass Company in New York, as well as a branch in London. Here's a description from a period lighting catalog:

> Glass of particular quality is molded into globes, the faces of which are made up of tiny prisms, which are calculated with the greatest exactness to reflect, diffuse, and deflect light rays so that these rays are redirected into useful directions and the intrinsic brilliancy of the light sources greatly reduced.

Depending on the design of the shade and the prisms, the light could be concentrated downward or dispersed outward or sideways for maximum illumination. Naturally other companies began producing prismatic glass as well, often less expensively, so Holophane had to defend its patents, noting:

> Although Holophane is constructed upon the principle of the optical prism, our product should not be confounded with the so-called "prism glass." The Holophane system is protected by letters patent and no imitation, unless it be an infringement upon our rights, can be made to give the results we advertise.

Above: Ombré shades go from yellow to red-orange on a four-light pan fixture. The pan has a neoclassical egg-and-dart motif.

Above: A brass wall bracket attached to a window frame suspends a socket and shadeholder with a ruffled holophane shade.

Above: A round pan with a finial has three pyramid-shaped art-glass and brass shades suspended on chains. Besides

being decorative, the main purpose of the finial was to attach the chandelier to the threaded rod that holds it to the electrical box.

Above: A cast-brass lion's head mounted on the backplate of a sconce holds a hook for hanging the pink slag glass and brass lantern. The backplate is fastened with pyramid head screws.

Above: Some Art Nouveau influence is seen in this sconce with hammered backplate and fluted bell-shaped art-glass shade. (This shade matches the chandelier on page 136.)

Above: Slag-glass shades with brass filigree hang from square shadeholders on chains connected to a square pan embellished with repoussé ornament. A large protuberance fills the center of the pan.

Above right: As many bungalows suffered from architectural cognitive dissonance (actually they didn't suffer—they enjoyed it thoroughly), so too did the light fixtures, sometimes to an even greater degree. For instance, this chandelier—which has a square canopy and pipe, square shadeholders, and even a square pan (that's the metal thing in the middle), as well as lovely flared shades with a stylized floral filigree in the Arts and Crafts style—also sports classical swan-neck split pediments with finials on all four sides.

Fleurs-de-lis ornament the corners of a four-light pan fixture. Pyramidal and triangular prisms suspended from the shadeholders shield the lightbulbs.

Well, they tried. The Holophane Company is still in business, but "holophane" is now the generic word for a prismatic glass shade. Still, the shades were a success and are still used in all kinds of fixtures, from residential chandeliers to the metal halide lights at the local warehouse club.

Various kinds of art glass blown into various shapes were also prevalent. Flat or bent pieces of art glass (nowadays often called *slag* glass, which is basically glass with two or more colors in a marble-like pattern) were combined with metal frames to form rectangular, pyramidal, cylindrical, faceted, or other shade shapes, including leaded glass. Or the previous three types could be combined on one shade. Blown art-glass shades came in the same shapes as the plain glass shades mentioned previously but had decoration in and on the glass, such as swirls, *millefiore*, iridescence, and so forth. Leaded glass used lead or zinc *cames* (channels) to hold the glass or utilized the copper-foil method, where the edges of each piece of glass were wrapped with copper tape and then the pieces were soldered together. Art glass could also be combined with decorative metal overlays, or *filigree,* which could be something like conventionalized florals but often was some kind of scenic design like trees or maybe the "camels-and-palm-trees-at-the-oasis," which was quite fashionable. What exactly that has to do with bungalows I don't know—a bungalow is an oasis in an urban environment?

And then there are the things you don't expect to find on a bungalow light fixture—things like prisms and fringe. And grapes. Prisms (holophane shades excepted) are what one expects to find on crystal chandeliers. Yet many bungalow light fixtures had shades that consisted of several prisms suspended from the shadeholder to surround the bulb and diffuse the light. Slightly more common than prisms was multicolored glass-bead fringe, used either by itself to shield the bulb or attached to the bottom of some other sort of shade as a decorative element. And yes, you could purchase bunches of glass grapes that fit over a lightbulb.

The look of any given fixture will completely change, depending on the shade(s). For example, a pendant with a square canopy and a square pipe will look totally different with an etched-glass globe than it will look sporting a slag-glass open pyramid with multicolored fringe. A hand-blown glass shade with swirls of color will give a completely different impression than a shade delicately etched with twining vines.

CAN DON'T

Okay, I'm just going to keep harping on this until the lighting designers give up. DO NOT ALLOW RECESSED CAN LIGHTING INTO YOUR BUNGALOW! There is nothing, NOTHING that screams "late twentieth century" more than a recessed can light—I don't care how many lighting designers tell you they are "unobtrusive." Architect Robert A. M. Stern began referring to them as "ceiling acne" in the 1970s, and he was absolutely correct. I was amused and horrified to discover a company making decorative medallions for can lights—talk about putting lipstick on a pig!

There was no track lighting either, nor were there fancy Italian-designed halogen lights suspended on wires.

CEILING ALRIGHT

In the hot climate of the original Indian bungalows, they had ceiling fans to provide cooling. These fans were powered by servants, and it probably was not cool for them. In early-twentieth-century America, servants were harder to come by, but conveniently, electricity was available instead; so, in addition to electric lighting, electrically powered ceiling fans came into being in the late nineteenth century. They were either driven by belts and pulleys or by a motor in a housing like modern ceiling fans. As with modern fans, they came with or without lights and with various numbers of blades.

The blades were generally wooden. They were seen more often in commercial locations like hotels, stores, and factories; these were large fans, 52 to 60 inches in diameter. Smaller fans, 32- or 36-inch diameters, more suitable for residential use, were introduced in the early twentieth century. But at an average price of $50 to $70 at a time when a bungalow might cost anywhere from $1,000 to $3,000, they were a high-end item that only a wealthy bungalow owner could afford to install. Likely locations for those rich enough to buy a ceiling fan included the kitchen, bedroom, or hallway.

And if you want the authentic Indian look, albeit without the servants, you can get a fan with side-to-side motion and palm fronds. If you have a big fancy bungalow in a hot climate that might have had them originally, you can buy restored vintage ceiling fans; the old ones were built to last, unlike many modern ones that are made inexpensively overseas, and like so many things now, expected to be thrown out in five years.

REPLACING LIGHT FIXTURES

OBSESSIVE RESTORATION

Original light fixtures may need to be rewired or have broken or missing glass replaced. If the original fixtures are missing, salvaged fixtures are readily available at salvage yards, antique stores, estate sales, antique lighting shops, and on eBay. Many fine reproductions of fixtures and shades are being made as well. Keep in mind that the original fixtures may not have been strictly Arts and Crafts, so even a "transitional" sort of fixture could still be appropriate. (Ideally, you would have photos showing the originals, but that isn't always going to be the case, and an educated guess is the best you can do.)

Occasionally you may have the original fixtures, except as it turns out, they are really, really, REALLY ugly, because in spite of our viewing the past through rose-colored glasses, it turns out a lot of people back then had execrable taste, just as they do now. In that case, you may either set new parameters so you view them as so ugly they've crossed the line over to fabulous. Or you may take them down, pack them very carefully into boxes that you will clearly label "original light fixtures for house"; they will then will be stored in the attic or somewhere and left with the house when and if you sell it, with instructions to the new owners to do the same. (If they then choose to try and sell them on eBay, at least you will have done your part.)

Reproduction carbon-filament incandescent bulbs that cost ten times as much and give off a third as much light as regular bulbs are available for the truly fanatical. Naturally, these are known as "Edison bulbs." But there is no substitute for the golden glow they provide—in fact, the colors in your bungalow may not look quite right under modern lightbulbs. The reproduction bulbs look especially nice in fixtures with exposed bulbs since they are the bulbs the fixtures were designed for. Otherwise, appliance bulbs or small globe-shaped bulbs (usually sold for vanity lights) look the best. Decorative bulbs, often shaped like flames, can be used, though they really should be pointing up, for obvious reasons, but also because they burn hot. All that being said, I still use flame-tip bulbs pointing down because I'm just a really contrary person.

Compact fluorescent bulbs save energy, but the truly obsessive will find some other way to save energy rather than sacrifice the quality of light.

COMPROMISE SOLUTION

Many reproduction fixtures are available, and even a home center may have a few decent Craftsman- or Mission-style fixtures that are reasonably priced, though these will be pretty generic. They won't be terribly well made either, and the plating on them will be really thin. But they'll certainly do in a pinch to replace the horrible 1970s chandelier put in by a previous owner, at least until you can afford a better fixture. Usually the shades they come with will be pretty bad too, so sometimes just getting better shades will make a big difference.

Compact fluorescent bulbs save a lot of energy and last a long time (particularly important if there's a fixture that's hard to get to), but they are kind of pinkish, which is still better than how they used to be—a kind of bluish or greenish. A fixture with art glass or mica does a pretty good job of hiding the weird light of fluorescents, and you can even get a compact fluorescent bug light (yellow bulb) for that amber Arts and Crafts glow. Fluorescents are obviously better in a fixture with a closed shade because they really don't resemble old lightbulbs at all, especially because of the bulky ballast they require.

CHAPTER EIGHT

HEARTH OF THE MATTER

"There is no substitute for fire."
—**Christopher Alexander, et al, A Pattern Language**

Fire fulfills a deep and primal role in the human psyche, such that even today, when fires are no longer needed for heating or cooking (let alone for protection from saber-toothed tigers), fireplaces are routinely installed in homes and thought of as a desirable feature and a focal point in a room. In Arts and Crafts homes, the fireplace took on almost religious significance, and even bungalows in warm climates such as California and Florida were still built with fireplaces. Although in some bungalows they were used for heating (again, they weren't often needed for that purpose in warm climates), mostly it was just assumed that one would be installed, and a bungalow without a fireplace is hardly a bungalow at all. Stickley wrote,

> The big hospitable fireplace is almost a necessity, for the hearthstone is always the center of true home life, and the very spirit of home seems to be lacking when a register or radiator tries ineffectually to take the place of a glowing grate or a crackling leaping fire of logs.

Almost always a feature of the living room, fireplaces were also found in dining rooms, bedrooms, dens, and basements.

Quite a large inglenook is shown in this photo, published in the March 1918 *American Builder.* The brick fireplace has insets of terra-cotta tile, and the same tile is used for the floor of the inglenook. The larger square tiles have some sort of molded design that is difficult to make out. The paired ceiling beams have a decidedly Japanese look about them, not that the brothers Heineman would have dreamed of knocking off the brothers Greene. Very Art Nouveau– looking wall sconces hang over each bench as well as on the frieze on either side of the opening.

Facing: Clinker bricks plus assorted other bricks make up a fireplace in the living room of a Memphis bungalow. A corbeled shelf with a stone top on the chimney breast holds candles. Just above the shallow arch of the firebox, the bricks have been formed into the letter "A" (the initial of the first owner). High multi-light windows on either side of the chimney let in light but lack the usual built-in bookcases below.

Chimneys were of masonry construction (brick, stone, concrete block, etc.), but the fireplace itself could be faced with a wide array of materials, provided they weren't flammable. Frequently the fireplace was surrounded by built-in benches or settles to form an *inglenook* (from two words of Scottish origin: *ingle*, meaning a fire on a hearth, and *nook*, meaning a corner). Often the ceiling in this space was lowered to set it off from the rest of the room and provide a feeling of coziness. Coziness was big in bungalows. The fireplace, whether in an inglenook or not, was usually surrounded by built-ins of some sort, most often bookcases, but a drop-front desk on one side was pretty common as well. The most typical bungalow fireplace was flanked by glass-doored bookcases with high windows above, the whole surmounted by a continuous wooden shelf and, quite often, a pair of sconces or other light fixtures thrown in for good measure.

There is endless variety in fireplace facings, including brick, stone, ceramic tile, cast stone, concrete, stucco, metal, or plaster—anything that won't burn. Brick (which comes in many colors and varieties) was much favored, especially *clinker brick,* which has become vitrified and misshapen by being too close to the fire in the brick kiln. Before

the bungalow era, these bricks had been thrown away as rejects. This made them available cheaply or even for free, which no doubt made the eyes of many a speculative bungalow builder light up. But they were also rather organic and interesting to look at, so the Arts and Crafts designers embraced them, and soon they became, well, trendy. But many other kinds of brick were used as well, from basic red or gold bricks, to various kinds of wire-cut (textured) bricks, to bricks that were multicolored, spotted bricks, even decorative molded bricks.

Brick sizes are standardized, and have been for centuries, at 4 by 4 by 8 inches, except for *Roman brick* (which was a favorite of Frank Lloyd Wright), which measures 4 by

Above: Stained-glass windows above a fireplace of purplish brick are featured in this inglenook. The brick facing extends to the walls at the ends of the benches. A cast-iron surround accentuates the firebox opening.

Right: Brownish brick makes up this simple fireplace with a recessed inset and ledge, and brick corbels holding up the mantel. Two sconces with iridescent glass shades light a collection of art pottery and the ever-popular Parrish *Daybreak* print. A hammered copper fender protects the floor from any burning logs that might escape the firebox.

Buff-colored brick outlines the top, sides, and firebox opening of a redbrick fireplace. The hearth is made of red tile with a buff-colored stripe. The fireplace is filled with multicolored candles instead of the usual logs.

2 by 12 inches. Even clinker bricks started out being that size before they warped and swelled from the fire. There are many colors and textures of brick, and many ways of laying them, called *bond*. Familiar to most people is *running bond*, where the joints in each row are staggered by half a brick. *Flemish bond* features one brick turned on end every other brick. Use of multicolored brick in patterns was called *tapestry brick*. Brick could also be laid unevenly and randomly, known as *eccentric brickwork*. In bungalows, brickwork was sometimes combined with river rocks to form what is generally referred to as *peanut brittle* because of its lumpy appearance. Occasionally some use was made of *glazed bricks*, which are just what they sound like—bricks that have been fired, then glazed and fired again like pottery.

Stone, including fieldstone, river rock, cobblestone, or rubble stone, had the rustic look esteemed by bungalow designers, and *split-face ashlar* (rectangular cut stone with an irregular face), though a bit more formal, was also used on fireplaces.

Cast stone, a molded product made from concrete and fine aggregates, was often used in place of real stone on fireplaces. Since the aggregates used were real stone, it could resemble whatever sort of stone was required, although

Cast concrete blocks are used for the fireplace above shown here in a photo accompanying a 1915 article in *American Carpenter and Builder*. According to the article, "by means of a special composition, with which it is possible to make face plates direct from the cut or chipped stone, the Hobbs Cement Block Machine turns out blocks in which all the fine edges and sharp detail of the original cut stone are retained." The photo shows a fireplace built using the machine by George W. Edgecumbe of Benton Harbor, Michigan.

An arched river-rock fireplace is installed in an unusual location in this bungalow in Pasadena, California—on a curved corner between the living room and the dining room. Both the mantel and the hearth are curved, with the mantel continuing on one side to form a plate rail in the dining room and the top for a bookcase in the living room. The wall above the fireplace is angled because pictures don't hang well on a curved wall.

Large blocks of granite give a solid presence to the living room fireplace of a bungalow in Victoria, British Columbia. The Douglas fir mantel is accented with square corbels, and a small cabinet built into the side of the fireplace can be glimpsed on the left.

No. 96.

No. 42.

No. 34.

102

No. 82.

Henry L. Wilson of Los Angeles, who called himself The Bungalow Man, showed a variety of cast-concrete fireplaces in the back of one of his plan books.

sandstone and limestone seemed to be quite prevalent. Another concrete product was pressed concrete, molded into panels about 1-1/2 inches thick, which was large enough to constitute the entire front of the fireplace. These were molded and colored to resemble tile or stone, and sometimes real tiles were set in as accents.

Ceramic tile was also much in favor as a fireplace facing, from plain 6- by 6-inch field tiles to decorative art tiles from now famous Arts and Crafts potteries like Grueby, Rookwood, and Batchelder, among others. Many fireplaces combined decorative accent tiles with field tiles. Accent tiles were usually set into the center above the firebox, in the corners, or down the sides. Landscape tiles were particularly favored as accents, with scenes of medieval castles, Spanish missions, English villages, and such. Most companies could also supply matching ceramic corbels to hold up the mantel, ceramic keystones for arched fireboxes, as well as various trim tiles. It was possible to order the whole fireplace front so the firebox could be constructed to fit the tiles instead of the other way around.

Some bungalows had transitional fireplace facings—kind of a Victorian holdover—which featured highly glazed majolica tiles, usually a smaller version of subway tiles, generally measuring 1-1/2 by 6 inches or 1-1/4 by 6 inches but sometimes as small as 1 by 3 inches. These had semi-translucent glazes with color variations from light to dark within each tile.

Some fireplaces were simply faced with plaster or stucco, although plaster was also combined with brick, stone, or tile as an accent. Some designers may have been influenced by Spanish Revival styles, particularly after the 1915 Panama-California Exposition in San Diego, which was designed in a Spanish Colonial style by architect Bertram Goodhue. A Spanish-influenced fireplace tends to feature a monolithic plastered firebox and chimney, often with built-in niches for art objects. But plaster was also used with the regulation bungalow fireplace, possibly because it was cheaper.

Many fireplaces were available in kit form; a builder could simply order a fireplace and it would arrive with the masonry, the facing, the damper, and some directions.

Malibu tile is used for the fireplace, hearth, mantel, and baseboards in this home in Ventura, California. Typical 1920s candle sconces are located on either side of the chimney.

Mottled square tiles surface the fireplace in a Memphis bungalow. Above the mantel, the chimney is faced with book-matched veneer and a corbelled shelf.

Stunning 6-inch bluish-green tiles form the surround and hearth of a small fireplace, probably meant to burn coal. The tile is bordered by large flat boards of dark-stained wood that merge into the board-and-batten paneling. A black iron frame around the firebox supports a small hood with a flowing pattern and spade-like shapes.

An image of tall trees formed by four landscape tiles decorates the sides of this fireplace. Decorative border tiles, including curved corner pieces, outline the firebox.

New Arts and Crafts tile in a pinecone pattern surrounds a gas fireplace in a Milwaukee bungalow.

Trees situated by a flowing river with plowed fields in the background form a bucolic scene on a landscape tile.

Rare and beautiful wisteria tile by Ernest Batchelder fronts a large fire-place in a bedroom at Artemisia, an Arts and Crafts home in Hollywood, California.

Four pilasters (half-columns) topped with pyramid-shaped blocks give a sturdy presence to the mostly wood surround of this fireplace. A band of mottled 6-inch tiles outlines the firebox and is also utilized for the hearth.

Ships on tile waves ornament blue-green Grueby tile surround in a 1907 fireplace in Tacoma, Washington.

Right: Highly glazed tiles like these, often called Minton tiles after one manufacturer, were a Victorian holdover still found on many bungalow fireplaces. Notice the variation in color on each tile. These tiles were generally laid with staggered joints. The oak woodwork surrounding the tile features interesting corbels supporting the mantel, which has two tiny cabinets with art-glass doors on either side of a mirror that mimics the shallow pitch of a bungalow roof.

The builder could then turn the whole thing over to the mason to build.

Naturally, in some misguided attempt to "modernize," later owners may have painted, covered up, or removed the original fireplace facing. Painting seems to be the most common; my favorite is when someone has painted the bricks bright red and the mortar bright white, usually with semigloss paint, to make it look like one of those cardboard fireplaces you can buy as a Christmas decoration. In fact, invariably the paint chosen to paint a fireplace facing is glossy, and ninety-nine times out of a hundred it's white. On a stone fireplace this often gives the effect that the fireplace was constructed out of marshmallows—mildly amusing in a Hansel and Gretel kind of way, but so, so wrong. And often, people who choose to paint the facing also choose to paint the inside of the firebox as well—yeah, there's a good idea. After paint, the most popular refacing material seems to be the dreaded "used brick," often not really used, instead tumbled after manufacture, and consisting of mixed colors, mostly red but with a lot of white and black on the surface of some bricks. This is possibly the ugliest brick ever invented, though everyone is welcome to propose their own candidates. "Used brick" also comes in a thin veneer version, often called "Z-Brick" after a certain manufacturer who particularly marketed their products to do-it-yourselfers. More recent "modernizations" may find the fireplace being refaced with 12- by 12-inch stone tiles. Granite and marble seem to be the most popular, but slate is up-and-coming because it looks kind of rustic, and people misguidedly think it is therefore appropriate for a bungalow. It's not.

HOOD ORNAMENT

Some fireplaces had metal hoods of copper, brass, bronze, or cast iron over the top of the firebox. Often merely decorative, some also served the purpose of lowering the top of the firebox, making for a better draw. If you're just dying to have a hand-hammered copper hood in your bungalow, this is where it should go, NOT in the kitchen. Coal-burning fireplaces had a cast-iron surround and grate (basket for the coal), and often had *fenders* on the hearth to prevent any coals that escaped the fireplace from rolling out into the room and starting a fire. These fireplaces came with *summer*

Narrower 2- by 6-inch tiles in turquoise blue are paired with painted woodwork for this fireplace. There are essentially two mantels: a narrow lower mantel held up by corbels, and a wider one above.

Massive dark-stained oak woodwork surrounds a fireplace faced with deep red high-glaze tiles. Tall Tuscan columns on plinths flank each side, while the thick (though probably hollow) mantel rests on curved corbels. Above the mirror, two more corbels support another substantial shelf.

covers, a matching cast-iron piece for covering the fireplace when not in use; few of these have survived the scrap metal drives that took place during World War II.

MANTEL ILLNESS

Without a mantel, how could one display one's tasteful collection of art pottery? And where would one hang the Christmas stockings? The mantel over the fireplace ranged from a simple shelf on brackets or corbels to a wide shelf spanning the adjoining built-ins. Generally made of wood, mantels could also be made of the same material used to face the fireplace, whether that was stone, brick, tile, or concrete. The area above the mantel might be filled by an *overmantel,* which, although much simplified from the excess of Victorian overmantels, still could be quite a festival of moldings and mirrors. Barry Parker and Raymond Unwin, writing in *The Craftsman,* gave their opinion of probably Victorian overmantels, saying,

> . . . the final touch of senseless incongruity, some form of that massive and *apparently* very constructional and essential thing we call a mantelpiece is erected in stone, wood, or marble, towering it may be even to the ceiling. If we were not so accustomed to it, great would be our astonishment to find that this most prominent feature has really no function whatever, beyond giving cause for a lot of other things as useful and beautiful as itself, which exist only that they may be put upon it, "to decorate it."

Often the mantel itself was either a thick piece of wood, or a box built to give the illusion that it was a thick piece of wood.

FIRE AWAY

The inside of the firebox was most commonly brick—firebrick was recommended although that doesn't mean everybody went with the recommendation. Fireboxes came in different shapes, depths, and heights, depending on the fuel to be used, among other things. A coal-burning fireplace has a shallow firebox compared with a fireplace meant to burn wood. The opening was most often square or rectangular, but arched openings of various varieties were also quite common. Typically, the firebox would include an ash dump or ash trap, a metal door in the floor where the ashes could be shoveled into, leading to the ash pit that had a clean-out door located in the basement or near the base of the chimney outside so that the ashes would not have to be carried through the house for disposal. The firebox narrowed at the top into the throat, and above that was the smoke chamber, which had a shelf at the back that was supposed to stop downdrafts from forcing smoke back into the room. If the fireplace had a damper, it was usually located in the throat and operated with a lever. Retrofitted dampers, which are a good idea for fireplaces that don't have them, are installed on top of the chimney, operated with a steel cable or chain that hangs in the flue, and anchored to a bracket on the side of the firebox.

Extending out into the room from the firebox, the hearth kept stray burning embers from setting anything on fire, at least in theory. Traditionally constructed of masonry, the hearth was supported by a shallow arch underneath the floor. Like the front of the fireplace, the finished surface of the hearth could be brick, stone, tile, or concrete. Typically the hearth was constructed to be level with the rest of the floor, although raised hearths are not unheard of.

The space over the mantel in this Denver bungalow came complete with a built-in frame containing the Maxfield Parrish print *Daybreak.* Unfortunately, a previous owner took the original print; this one is a modern version.

In 1915, $27 would get you this complete mantel in oak or birch, with tile facing and an oxidized copper coal grate and frame.

Fireplaces, for all that they've been in use for centuries, are quite complex and often don't work all that well. The interaction between the size and shape of the firebox, the size and shape of the throat, the height of the chimney, and various other factors make the difference between an efficient fireplace that burns cleanly and one that smokes and draws badly. In the 1740s, Benjamin Franklin developed a cast-iron fireplace with a hood in the front and an airbox in the rear, and called it a "Pennsylvania Fireplace," what we now know as a Franklin stove; however, his original idea had a few inherent flaws that had to be ironed out by later inventors. In 1796, Benjamin Thompson, known today by his title Count Rumford, applied his studies of heat to improving the design of

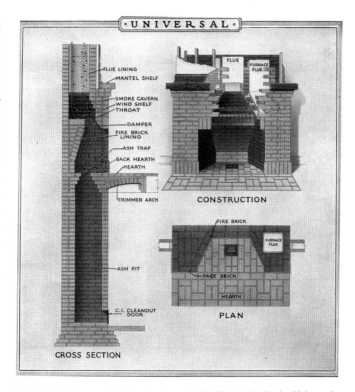

Typical fireplace construction is shown in this illustration in the *Universal Design Book on Builders Woodwork*. Often the furnace flue was part of the kitchen chimney rather than the main fireplace chimney, although it depended on where the furnace was located.

advertised various devices for recirculating warm air from the fireplace.

Around the turn of the nineteenth century, another fireplace option appeared—the gas fireplace. Although gas lighting had been around during the nineteenth century, it used primarily manufactured gas that was a by-product of coal. The first naturally occurring gas was discovered in Pennsylvania in 1859, but up until the turn of the century, it was used primarily for lighting, and couldn't be transported very far because there was no pipeline infrastructure. The 1885 invention of the Bunsen burner, a device that safely mixed natural gas and air in the right proportions to create a flame that could be used for cooking and heating, led to the invention of gas stoves and

fireplaces. He realized that the only useful heat emanating from a fireplace was radiant heat, as any air that was heated by the fire simply went up the chimney. So the fireplace he designed had a tall, wide opening with a shallow firebox and splayed sides to reflect as much radiant heat into the room as possible. He also streamlined the throat in order to "remove those local hindrances which forcibly prevent the smoke from following its natural tendency to go up the chimney." His ideas were adopted almost immediately and became state of the art in fireplaces from the 1790s to the 1850s.

Starting around 1850, the Industrial Revolution led to metal products becoming cheaper and easily transportable by railroad, which contributed to the development of metal heating devices—cast-iron stoves and furnaces as well as a variety of patented coal-burning fireplaces that gradually took over the job of heating the home. Coal was a lot less work than wood, not needing to be cut or split, and was viewed as "modern." Fireplaces remained, but there was less concern about efficiency because they were no longer the main source of heat. Stickley promoted the "Craftsman fireplace-furnace," a complicated metal box set into a regular fireplace opening that somehow recirculated warm air and burned coal or coke. He installed five of them in his own home at Craftsman Farms. Other companies also

heaters. And the introduction of electricity for lighting also had industries that were dependent on gas looking for new uses and products as electric lights came to dominate.

In 1901, Alfred Humphrey invented an inverted gaslight and started the General Gas Light Company in Kalamazoo, Michigan. Soon after, when it became apparent that electric light was going to take over, he used the same technology to come up with the Humphrey Radiant-Fire heater, which used gas to heat ceramic inserts to incandescence. Many of the heaters were designed to be installed in a fireplace. There were other companies that manufactured radiant heaters as well, including Reznor and Dearborn.

Eventually this led to other kinds of faux fireplaces, like gas logs or, my personal favorite, the electric fireplace that consisted of a red lightbulb and a rotating cylinder of crumpled tinfoil to simulate the flames, generally combined with a really fake-looking log. At least the technology of log fakery has improved in the present-day gas fireplaces.

By the time of the American Arts and Crafts movement, enough time had elapsed since the heyday of fireplaces that actually served to heat the house that masons had forgotten how to build them. But enough time had also elapsed for people to become nostalgic about "hearth and home," at least the people in cities who were no longer chopping and carrying wood every day to heat their houses and burn in

The pull that operates the damper has been artistically worked into the design of a speckled brick fireplace; it hangs like a tassel between two tiles featuring jousting knights.

their cookstoves. Thus, many bungalow fireplaces, though they may be lovely to look at, don't draw well, tend to smoke, and basically suck all your expensive central-heated air up the chimney.

Depending on the location of the fireplace, the chimney may be on an outside wall or come up through the middle of the house. The kitchen usually had its own chimney, serving the stove and the water heater and possibly the furnace. (Kitchen and furnace chimneys sometimes used "patent chimneys," consisting of round terra-cotta flue pipes wrapped in a galvanized metal skin.) Or the furnace might share the main chimney. Each chimney could have more than one flue. Although stove and furnace chimneys could be made of metal or asbestos (usually referred to now as "transite," after one particular brand), the main chimney was always masonry. It might be brick, stone, river rock, clinker brick, concrete block, or some combination of these. If the house had stucco siding, the masonry of the chimney might be covered with stucco as well, or it might not. Bungalow chimneys are often shorter than what is required by modern building codes, which dictate a certain height above the roof surface for the chimney top, but the good news is that if you don't mess with it, it's grandfathered in. (Minimum is three feet above the highest point where the chimney penetrates the roofline, or two feet higher than any portion of the structure within ten feet of the chimney. You can see how this means the steeper the roof, the higher the chimney has to be.) Chimneys may be lined with terra-cotta flue liners, though some are just brick. It was recommended that there be two thicknesses of brick if a flue liner wasn't used. Flue liners often fail at the joints. Retrofit flue liners of stainless steel and/or concrete can be used to strengthen existing chimneys.

The top of the chimney should have a cap, usually made of concrete, that is sloped to shed water, which is known (at least in Britain) by the amusing term *flaunching*. All chimneys should have a spark arrester on top and a damper that will keep all your heated air from escaping out the chimney in winter. A damper can be retrofitted into chimneys that don't have them—and you might as well get an energy-saving damper that has a gasket like a refrigerator. It will also keep birds and squirrels from nesting in your chimney, and has the additional benefit of keeping water out, which keeps the chimney from deteriorating.

Masonry chimneys can fail in an earthquake, and there are differing points of view on what to do about this. Some advocate bracing the chimney above the roofline with metal braces, while others think the entire chimney should be replaced with stainless-steel triple-wall flue, and the visible parts faced with brick or other masonry veneer. At the very least, installing plywood on the attic floor all around the chimney will keep it from crashing down into the living space below should it fail in an earthquake. All of the above is also true of hurricanes and other major windstorms.

Burning wood causes creosote deposits in the chimney, which can lead to chimney fires. This is not something to be taken lightly—creosote burns at about 2,000 degrees Fahrenheit, which can crack masonry and destroy mortar, allowing the flames to escape and reach the combustible wooden parts of the house. One chimney fire may not harm the house, but a second one could burn it down. This is why you should have your chimney inspected every year and cleaned when necessary.

BURNING AMBITION

Given the near-worship of the fireplace by the American Arts and Crafts movement, what I am about to say may seem like heresy. Burning wood pollutes the air and you should keep it to an absolute minimum. Even at the time that bungalows were being built, there were already pollution problems, primarily related to coal burning in industries and homes. Though coal burning fell from favor after World War II and was replaced primarily by natural gas, pollution increased due to larger numbers of automobiles and trucks. Unlike the Rumford fireplaces of the eighteenth and nineteenth centuries, the fireplaces built in most bungalows do not burn wood efficiently, and the less efficient the combustion, the more pollution is produced. Wood burning produces fine particulates (soot) that bypass human defense systems and lodge deep in the lungs; particulates have been linked to lung cancer, respiratory problems such as asthma, and heart disease, along with other cardiovascular problems. Wood smoke also contains toxic compounds including formaldehyde, benzene, toluene, methyl chloride, dioxin, dibenzofuran, and methyl ethyl ketone. There are also VOCs (volatile organic compounds) and nitrogen oxides—precursors to smog. And then there's carbon dioxide, a greenhouse gas adding to global climate change, and carbon monoxide, a poisonous gas that can kill you in high enough concentrations and isn't exactly good for you in lower concentrations either.

What's an environmentally responsible bungalow owner to do? Well, if you are going to burn wood, make sure you burn well-seasoned dry wood. Don't burn garbage or wrapping paper, and use newspaper only to start the fire. A tipi-style fire, with the logs vertical, burns more cleanly than a fire of horizontal logs. Make sure the fire burns hot—go outside and check the chimney: if there is smoke coming out, you are not getting complete combustion. A hot fire should result in nothing but heat waves emanating from the chimney. Somewhat surprisingly, manufactured logs (Duraflame, Pres-to-Logs, etc.), which are made from compressed sawdust (sometimes with wax added), burn about 70 percent cleaner than real wood. There is even a product that crackles; the crackling, caused by pockets of moisture in a real log, is an important aspect of a wood fire. You can also get a special grate that uses a motor and fan to provide air at the base of the fire, which causes it to burn hotter and more completely. Another clean-burning option is gelled alcohol fuel, although it needs to be combined with fake logs in order to look like a fire since it comes in cans. On the other hand, it doesn't need a chimney or any kind of ventilation, so it's perfect for fireplaces that were originally electric or ornamental. It also has a crackle feature. There are gas logs or wood-burning inserts as well. The problem with either of these is that the box or insert that comes with them frames the firebox in a way that makes it look like the fire is on television, at which point you might as well just stick the TV in the fireplace and put on the video log. There is one company that has come up with a way to eliminate this effect by producing a gas fireplace with no visible metal louvers or framing, and a flush hearth—but it's expensive ($6,000 to $9,000 as of this writing). Interestingly enough, it has a firebox shaped rather like a Rumford fireplace. Natural gas burns cleanly, but it keeps going up in price, and given the current discussion regarding peak oil production, it may not turn out to be sustainable over the long term.

A Rumford fireplace is another option—they can be retrofitted into existing fireboxes, are EPA approved when used with glass doors, and are also allowed by the Uniform Building Code. Local areas may have their own regulations; it's best to check with the building department first.

GRATE EXPECTATIONS

Okay, I admit it. I'm only writing this so I could use that pun. And I never read the Dickens book either. And it's hard to think of a pun for "andirons," the metal supports for the logs in a wood-burning fireplace. Anyway, as one would expect with Arts and Crafts fireplace worship, andirons were a big Arts and Crafts metalwork item. Andirons are not

all that practical as a support device, serving primarily as a decorative function now, while the logs are held up by a more practical grate. The coal grate, by comparison, was more of a basket.

STOW-ICISM

"The question of built-in fittings is one that I feel is an essential part of Craftsman idea in architecture. I have felt from the beginning of my work that a house should be live-in-able when it is finished. Why should one enter one's dwelling and find that it is a barren uninviting prison-like spot, until it is loaded with furniture and the walls hidden under pictures and picture frames? I contend that when the builder leaves the house, it should be a place of good cheer, a place that holds its own welcome forever. This, of course, can only be accomplished by the building in of furnishings that are essentially structural features, and by the planning of the finishing of the walls and the woodwork so they are part of the inherent beauty of the house, and not mere backgrounds for endless unrelated decorations. In no other way can a house be made beautiful, or the architecture of the interior be complete and homelike."
—Gustav Stickley

A large tree motif anchors the center panel of a riveted firescreen.

FIREPLACES

OBSESSIVE RESTORATION

One of the most common fireplace problems is deterioration of the firebox—missing mortar or damaged bricks. Most regular bricks were not made to stand up to the thermal shock of being heated to upwards of 1,000 degrees on one side while the other side is still at room temperature. This tends to make them crack. If the fireplace didn't originally have firebrick, just be prepared to replace cracked and spalling bricks from time to time. Mortar joints can also deteriorate over time and may need re-pointing, just like other masonry. It's best to use *refractory mortar* for joints, which is designed to withstand the heat. Older fireplaces were built using *fireclay mortar,* which is fine, but it probably doesn't hold up as well as the refractory mortar. A fireplace with a damaged firebox should not be used—you could burn the house down. In general, firebox repairs or rebuilding are best left to professionals.

Original fireplace surrounds may have cracks or other damage. Minor damage can be embraced as patina; major damage may require repair or replacement. Replacement depends on whether you can get matching materials, be that brick, stone, concrete, or tile. Cast-stone or cast-concrete elements can be custom made if replacement is required. Dealers in antique or salvaged brick may be able to match existing brick. Tile, especially art tile, may require some searching at salvage yards, antique dealers, auction houses, and eBay to find tile that matches. There are also companies that reproduce tile in various historic styles.

If the original fireplace was ripped out and replaced with something really horrid like a nasty 1970s woodstove, please remove it and build a proper fireplace. The rebuilt fireplace will have to comply with current codes unless your state has a historic building code or you have a house museum or you can get some other sort of dispensation. It would probably be good to use firebrick for the firebox—it comes in several colors, not just the buff color that one normally associates with firebrick. If the fireplace facing has been painted, see the earlier Paint Removal sidebar. Paint is easy to remove from tile; it's harder to get off brick or stone, but it can be done. It will involve chemicals, scrubbing, and probably dental tools. If the facing has been covered, it depends on how they did it and how much it damaged what was underneath—hard to say until you rip it off. Sometimes you find nothing underneath because they ripped the original facing off first. At that point, you'll have to figure out what to use for refacing (for suggestions, see Compromise Solution).

There has been a trend, which is likely to continue, of municipalities banning open-hearth wood-burning fireplaces altogether in an attempt to decrease air pollution (so much easier than getting people to give up their cars). Existing fireplaces are grandfathered in—they can't force you to remove them. At least not yet. Some ordinances don't even allow existing fireplaces to be repaired. Most ordinances do allow for gas or wood-burning inserts that comply with Environmental Protection Agency standards.

Smoke or draft problems can be complex, but here are a few things that sometimes work, starting with the easiest—opening a door or window in the room before starting a fire. Making the top of the firebox lower can help—this is part of the reason for fireplace hoods. A cheapo (and experimental) hood involves taping a strip of aluminum foil or sheet metal over the top of the firebox; no use spending money on a hood if it isn't going to help. Making the chimney taller by adding to the top of the flue or installing a chimney pot can also help.

Given that the chimney is probably the heaviest thing in your bungalow, if it was not built on a large enough footing, or if there have been other settlement problems, it may now be sinking and taking the fireplace, the hearth, and that side of the house with it. A little bit of subsiding is probably nothing to worry about, but if your living room floor resembles a roller coaster, something should be done. And that something is to jack up the chimney and put in a new footing. This will be expensive and not at all glamorous. Sometimes only the hearth is sinking, possibly because of the failure of the arch that is supposed to be holding it up. Again, if it's only sinking a little, consider it part of the old house charm, but when it becomes a tripping hazard, think about getting it repaired.

A fireplace with old gas logs should get a safety check, but like vintage gas appliances, they can probably be made to operate safely. Radiant heaters in fireplaces should also be checked for safety; Humphrey RadiantFire and similar brands can be rebuilt, and parts are available. Some radiant heaters contained asbestos and should possibly not be used, or you should have the asbestos abated.

Old fireplaces were open—they did not have glass doors, nor did they have sliding "chain mail" curtains. What they did have is freestanding firescreens, generally made of metal.

Okay, every now and then an original fireplace is, um, not as attractive as it might be. Or perhaps you personally dislike that color of tile or brick or whatever. Or you were really hoping for art tile and there isn't any. Get over it—this is Obsessive Restoration.

COMPROMISE SOLUTION

Most of the information under Obsessive Restoration still applies, especially in regard to structural issues. Areas for compromise are primarily aesthetic or environmental. For instance, a fireplace meant to burn coal is, as a rule, too shallow to successfully burn wood. Burning coal isn't really a good idea either, so this is an instance where gas is useful, as there are several companies that make gas burning inserts that mimic coal fireplaces, thus giving the look of the original fireplace without the pollution. As I mentioned before, log fakery has improved greatly, so gas logs now look pretty realistic, although the flames still don't have quite the randomness of burning wood. And the fact that most of the gas inserts still have a metal frame all the way around, not to mention glass doors, has the effect of making the whole thing look like a TV screen. On the other hand, real logs rarely come with a remote control.

As mentioned under Obsessive Restoration, many municipalities have banned open-hearth wood-burning fireplaces, so gas logs or a wood-burning insert may be your only option if you are having to rebuild the fireplace or are adding a fireplace. At that point it's mostly an aesthetic choice, although I do draw the line at pellet stoves. If, for some reason, the house never had a fireplace to begin with, then you have a choice of inserts that vent straight through the wall, inserts that require a flue (which is metal and requires some kind of disguise to make it look like a proper chimney), or alcohol-burning fireplaces that require no venting at all. And just because they require no venting doesn't mean you should place them somewhere that a real fireplace could never go, like under a window—strive for plausibility.

If the fireplace facing has been painted and you just can't face stripping it (or maybe plan to strip it later but just can't stand the way it looks right now), there is always the option of repainting it, perhaps in a more brick-like or stone-like or tile-like color. (Don't use semigloss! Bricks aren't shiny, stone isn't shiny, and most Arts and Crafts fireplace tile isn't shiny.) If you don't ever want to strip it, faux painting it to look like brick, stone, or whatever can be a good solution, although if you've never done faux painting before, you might want to practice (a lot) on a board before attempting the fireplace. Or it might just be worthwhile to hire a decorative painter to do it for you because unskilled faux painting may make it look even worse. But you are not allowed to paint an original fireplace that isn't already painted just because you don't like the facing or it doesn't match your color scheme.

If the fireplace has already been rebuilt or refaced with something inappropriate, it may be possible to simply cover it up, depending on the fireplace's design. Many brick manufacturers make thin versions of brick for use as veneer (unfortunately no clinker brick veneer that I know of!), and tile is another option. It's important that fireplace tiles look like they belong on a fireplace and not in a bathroom. Most tiles in the bungalow era were glazed by hand, even if the tiles were machine made, and that results in less uniformity in the glaze than modern tiles. And because a fireplace surround is U-shaped, tiling a fireplace is less straightforward than tiling, for instance, a countertop. And if the firebox is arched, it complicates things further. A fireplace that was tiled originally also had a firebox sized so that the surround could use full tiles, which may not be the case in a retrofit. Careful designing will be necessary. In any case, tiles bigger than 6 by 6 inches tend to read as modern. Fireplace tiles tended to have wider grout joints than the minimal ones used in kitchens and bathrooms of the era, especially if the tile was handmade or irregular. Joints up to 1/2 inch were common, although narrower joints (generally not less than 1/8 inch) were also used.

If you absolutely have to have glass doors, at least get the simplest, most unobtrusive ones you can find. And don't get the chain mail curtains, either by themselves or with the glass doors.

A shallow cabinet with leaded-glass doors is built into the colonnade of a Seattle bungalow. An immense but short square pillar is apparently not enough to support the load of the open doorway since it is accompanied by a similar large pilaster at the wall.

The space left by the narrowing of the chimney above the fireplace of this bungalow is put to good use by the installation of a small cabinet. The purpose of the cabinet, however, is unclear. Liquor? Extra matches?

An L-shaped bench forms a cozy nook next to the fireplace of the Bolton House by Charles and Henry Greene. The back of the bench has two of the cloud-lift patterns that the Greenes used extensively; above it, a set of casement windows provides light.

Although typically a built-in desk was a small drop-lid affair, this desk, located on one side of the fireplace in a bungalow in Vancouver, British Columbia, also has cabinets on either side, a larger writing surface, and actual legs in the front.

Much more typical, a very basic drop-lid desk above a cabinet forms one side of a colonnade topped by a tapered column.

Leaded beveled glass makes up the panels in the upper doors of a dining room china cabinet. The lower part of the cabinet has raised panel drawers and doors, a less-common style for bungalows.

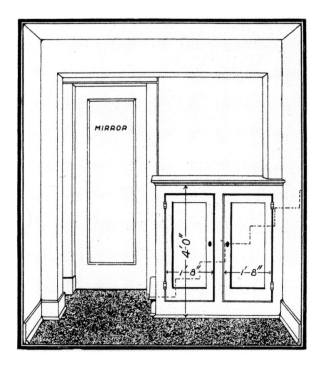

At least part of the reason that bungalows can be small and still "live large" is because of the amount of built-in storage they contain. As common to bungalows as low-pitched roofs, built-in fittings of all kinds provided storage, seating, workspace, and even places to sleep. Before one even entered the bungalow, there might be built-in benches on the front porch, often with seats that lifted up for storage beneath. Upon entering the house, the entry hall might contain a built-in hall tree, perhaps with hooks for coats, a mirror, and possibly an umbrella stand included; a simpler coat rack with hooks and a shelf for hats; or perhaps a bench to sit on in order to remove wet shoes or to put down packages. In the living room, benches around the fireplace, a window seat, bookcases (sometimes with drawers above or below), a writing desk, a liquor or smoking cabinet, a niche for firewood storage, or even a disappearing bed might make an appearance. A built-in mirror or piece of artwork above the fireplace was quite common. The colonnade that often separated living and dining or other

Left: A diagram for building a cabinet into the newel at the bottom of a stairway was illustrated in the February 1919 *American Builder.*

Square pilasters with somewhat elaborate capitals and a hint of classical detailing in the cornice-like moldings above lend a dignified air to the china cabinet of a Seattle bungalow. Beveled glass in the upper doors is combined with simple inset drawers (including a shallow drawer at the bottom for tablecloths) below. The greenish cast to the wood is achieved by using tinted shellac.

Angled like a bay window, the china cabinet of this home in Milwaukee, Wisconsin, is entirely separated from the built-in sideboard below. The battens over plaster that line the walls of the dining room continue behind the sideboard, which has legs in front that make it appear like a piece of furniture although it is built in. The corner posts break through the top surface and are beveled into pyramids. Ornamental brass strap hinges decorate the lower doors, while inset drawers open with typically Arts and Crafts pulls.

Art-glass doors hide the contents of the cabinets in the upper part of this built-in made of tupelo wood in a Memphis dining room. The upper cabinets sit directly on the much-deeper lower portion, which has three sets of doors providing an abundance of storage.

This bungalow in Albany, Oregon, features a dining room built-in with a mirrored back, which is counterweighted like a window sash and lifts up so that items can be passed to or from the kitchen on the other side.

Now this is what I call a built-in. Taking up an entire wall, a sideboard with glass-door cabinets (in the nearly universal modified tic-tac-toe design) and a plethora of drawers (especially the very civilized shallow drawers for table linens) provides enough storage even for a china and linen freak such as myself. The sideboard is ornamented with pyramid-shaped blocks and a mirror in the center; a large picture window flanked by operable casements brings in light and views.

rooms frequently contained bookshelves, cabinets, or a desk. The dining room invariably had a sideboard, buffet, or china cabinet either recessed into a wall or projecting into the room. Occasionally this was actually a freestanding piece of furniture made of the same wood as the rest of the trim-work, or else it was built to look freestanding, having the back attached to the wall but still having legs. Dining rooms may also have been home to window seats or benches. Rooms like dens, libraries, or music rooms usually had bookcases and often had desks if the room was meant as a den, and were also a likely location for disappearing beds, which allowed the room to be used for guests. Hallways were the likely location of a telephone niche, often accompanied by a foldout seat. Foldout seats also found a home in bathrooms and bedrooms. The underside of stairways was often the location of closets, drawers, or cabinets (and even the occasional bathroom) constructed in the space beneath. Laundry chutes, with openings in the bathroom, the hallway, or near the kitchen, made it easy to get laundry down to the basement. For obvious reasons, these were more common in bungalows with an upper floor. In a civilized world, laundry chutes would have been accompanied by a dumbwaiter for getting the clean laundry back upstairs, but in reality that didn't happen much—although there were dumbwaiters available. Laundry hampers were also built in to many bathrooms. Ironing boards recessed into the wall were a common feature in many kitchens, utility rooms, or, if the bungalow's designer was very cutting edge, near the bedrooms. It would have made even more sense for ironing boards to be IN the bedrooms, at least from my point of view. (The majority of built-in ironing boards in kitchens have been turned into spice racks.) Closets or cabinets for linen storage were included in hallways and bathrooms. Bedroom closets, if they were large

Built-ins with glass doors were not limited to the formal rooms, as this set of cabinets and drawers in one of the bedrooms of a Milwaukee home demonstrates. Set into an arched niche, the side cabinets are taller with tops supported by corbels. An Arts and Crafts stencil with roses encircles the room.

The Peerless Built-in Furniture Company offered their "conbination [*sic*] table and ironing board" (there was no spell-check back then) in an advertisement in the August 1922 issue of *Home Designer.*

A built-in breakfast nook featuring windows and cabinets with mirrored doors above the benches was showcased in *The Home,* a 1923 supplement to the magazine *Woman's Weekly.* The benches have beadboard backs and come complete with pegged thru-tenons. The accompanying article mentioned that "High-backed built-in seats are a further convenience provided in many breakfast nooks. If well-designed, such seats can be made more comfortable than chairs, although their chief purpose is to economize space."

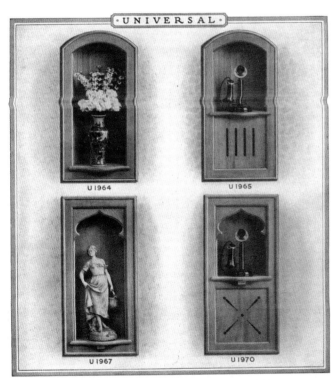

TELEPHONE AND STATUE NICHES

Niches for telephones or statuary were offered in the *Universal Design Book on Builders Woodwork.* In the telephone niches the lower part dropped down for phone book storage.

According to the April 1919 *American Builder,* the ceiling bed is "a handy piece of furniture in the sun parlor." What they did not make clear is exactly how it operates. Are there gigantic counterweights inside the walls? Is it on springs? Is there a block-and-tackle somewhere that is used to raise it up and down? I'm not saying it's a bad idea—just needed a little fleshing out.

Sometimes the designers went a little overboard in their attempts to save space. This particular "housing device," highlighted in an article in the June 1920 *American Builder,* is a round platform 6 feet 10 inches in diameter with a four-section cabinet 7 feet 6 inches high. The section shown is the kitchen, which supposedly contains a refrigerator (where?), a sink hooked up to a water supply and drain (okay, somebody explain to me how plumbing would be able to revolve?), food compartments (the drawers above the sink?), an ironing board, and an electric stove with portable oven (looks more like a fold-down hotplate to the left of the sink—where are they hiding the oven?). Oh, and there is NO counter space unless you fold down the ironing board. On the side opposite the kitchen is a folding bed, while on one side is a dresser and on the other side is a library with a bookshelf on top of a folding desk. In the very center is a closet, accessed from the dresser side. The whole thing could be rotated using handles on the corners of the sections.

Reddish Douglas fir is the wood used for this small built-in cabinet. Simple art-glass in the doors is set off by brass pulls with decorative backplates. Ball-tipped hinges, which are normally mortised, are applied here as surface hinges instead.

enough, frequently had dressers built in, or a dresser could be recessed into the wall of the bedroom.

In addition to all these, a few bungalows had secret panels (most often a section of board-and-batten paneling that was hinged) leading to closets or compartments behind. A few homes may even have had a safe set into the wall, and some even had special rooms or closets for off-season fur storage (these would be the homes of people who could afford furs, so these would tend to be larger bungalows). Some homes also had a "trunk room" for storing luggage when it was not in use, although the difference between a trunk room and other rooms of nebulous purpose is not always entirely clear.

Then there are built-ins that aren't all that common and some that are downright goofy. In the uncommon category are things like a hinged paneled wall on one side of a stair landing that could be swung out of the way in order to take large items up the stairs—items that it might be hard to get around a corner; another is a shoe-shine cabinet containing an angled surface to put your foot on and a place for all the supplies, all of it recessed into the wall to fold out when you need it. Under goofy we have things like beds that slide through the wall onto the sleeping porch, dining rooms where a round platform could be pivoted into the kitchen, where the complete meal could be set on the table before being rotated back to the dining room.

GLASS ACT

Many of the built-in cabinets had glass doors, whether their purpose was storing books, china, liquor, or something else. The glass was set into a *rabbet,* a lip on the inside of the door frame, and was held in by small quarter-round or other shaped moldings. Glass doors could simply have plain glass, or they might use beveled or etched glass. Some doors might have a muntin pattern that matched the windows of the house, or they could have leaded or art glass. Art-glass doors were common for china cabinets, sideboards, buffets, and bookcases. Sideboards frequently had mirrored panels set into the space between the top and bottom cabinets, and often these panels were designed to slide aside so that food and plates could be pushed back and forth between the dining room and the kitchen. Some sideboards were even constructed so that the doors and drawers opened on both sides (into the dining room and into the kitchen) as a step-saving feature.

Built-in cabinets, whether bookcases, sideboards, or whatever, were always built with *face-frames,* a wooden frame nailed to the front of the cabinet box, and with *flush inset doors,* doors that are set into the face-frame and flush with it when closed. Drawers could be either flush or *overlay* (having a lip, usually 3/8 inch, that overlapped the face-frame and also served as a stop). Doors were invariably *frame-and-panel,* consisting of vertical *stiles* and horizontal rails around a usually flat panel. Most often the edges of the frame were squared off around the panel, a style known today as *Shaker doors*. Sometimes the perimeter of the frame around the panel would have a simple molded edge, but in general the doors were very plain. The drawer fronts could also be frame-and-panel but most often were plain. Drawers typically ran on wooden glides installed inside the cabinet on either side of the drawer or running down the middle. (These work better with a little lubrication—candle wax, soap, WD-40, silicone spray, whatever. You can even install the self-adhesive plastic corner strips that are sold to protect wallpaper corners on the bottom edges of the drawer.) Basically they are just strips of wood—hardwood was preferred but not always used. Wooden drawer glides are still available from woodworking supply companies. A drawer box assembled using dovetail joints is the best, and is used in quality furniture, but a drawer box with dovetail

joints is practically unheard of in bungalows, where it was far more likely to simply be glued and nailed together. Don't look down on this; most of them, if not abused, have managed to last for 80, 90, or 100 years.

VANISHING ACT

Disappearing beds were an important part of many bungalows. William L. Murphy of San Francisco began experimenting with a hide-away bed in the late nineteenth century and took out a patent for his folding bed around 1900. Why? Because he was living in a one-room apartment where the bed took up a large part of the room. And he had met a "fine young lady." In those days, a lady was not permitted to enter a gentleman's bedroom. His new invention allowed him to safely stow his bed in the closet, transforming his apartment into a parlor in which he could properly entertain a female caller. It must have worked, because he ended up marrying the young lady in question. And he also started a business manufacturing fold-away beds, which incorporated as The Murphy Wall Bed Company. In 1918, he invented the pivot bed, which pivoted on the doorjamb of a closet, and then lowered into a horizontal position for sleeping. He called it the Murphy "In-A-Dor" Bed. The 1920s and 1930s were the heyday of Murphy beds, and the company moved to New York

In an advertisement in the December 1917 *American Builder,* the Curtis Companies showed some of their available woodwork, including a built-in china cabinet, colonnade, swinging door, and window seat (in the living room).

A cabinet with glass doors is built into the bottom of a stairway, as shown in the *Universal Design Book* in 1927.

Installation No. 4
Murphy Recess Type

Murphy Recess Bed—Standard Type—Two-piece End

Fastened to floor in shallow recess—lowers straight to floor, does not pivot. When on floor, ready for use, bed is projected forward so head end is in line with door opening.

Note: When closet can not be provided, a canopy rod can be furnished which permits concealing bed behind draperies

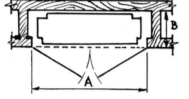

Width of bed	A	B
4′ 6″	5′ 0″	19″
4′ 0″	4′ 6″	19″
3′ 6″	4′ 0″	19″
3′ 6″	3′ 0″	19″

One of the numerous models of Murphy In-A-Dor beds is shown in an undated brochure (probably from the 1920s). This type did not pivot but merely folded straight down. Notice the different bed widths; 4 feet 6 inches corresponds to a modern double bed, but the other widths are no longer standard and can only be obtained from the few custom mattress manufacturers still in business.

A mirror on the panel that hides the disappearing bed in this Chicago bungalow also helps to make the small room seem larger.

The same bed in the down position has a wooden panel that acts as a headboard and hides the opening.

The mechanism of the bed uses wooden pins that slide in wooden tracks, similar to the mechanism used in most built-in ironing boards, albeit on a larger scale.

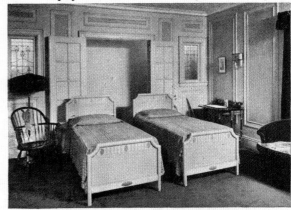

In-A-Dor Type, Custom Design No. 17931

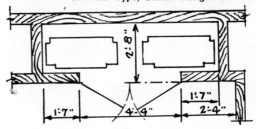

Both beds through same opening. Beds independent of doors. At the left are shown minimum closet dimensions for Murphy Pivot Bed—twin arrangement, for standard 3 ft. 0 in. beds

A contemporary disappearing bed hides behind built-in cabinetry and bookshelves in a Seattle bungalow. The bottom cabinet doors in the center are false.

Two twin beds pivot out of a single closet in this particular installation. These beds are 3 inches narrower than modern twin beds, which are 39 inches wide rather than 36 inches.

The All-One Cabinet Bed
A REAL SPACE SAVER

To the Living and Bed Room what the Kitchen Cabinet is to the Kitchen. Is designed to meet the Great Demand for More Room and at the same time give More Convenience and Comfort.

As a Couch. Also note large Divided Drawer

As a Luxurious Bed. Finest Steel Springs

Showing Large Wardrobe—Adjustable Reading Lamp

SOME of the Features of an **ALL-ONE** are Bed, Dresser, Chiffonier, Desk, Wardrobe, Dressing Table and many others.

An **ALL-ONE**, Table and Chair will furnish a Room Complete.

Adds at least **30%** to your Floor Plan.

Ideal for Small Apartments, Bungalows and Hotels.

We Want Your Co-Operation and will pay well for it.

We want you to figure them in your Floor Plans, recommend them to your Customers, show them where they can Save Money by Using an **ALL-ONE**. Explain to them that you can build a Smaller House and get the same amount of Floor Space.

An **ALL-ONE** in an 8x10 room gives you more Floor Space than 10x12 the old way.

Get in touch with us. We'll send **ALL** Details and Catalogue. It's Profitable.

THE CABINET BED CO.
830 Consumers Bldg.
Dept. G.   CHICAGO

Showing Commodious Desk. Note Desk Light

Dressing Table. Triplicate Mirror. Adjustable Light

Shoe, Rubber and Slipper Space

Left: The Cabinet Bed Company of Chicago proclaimed their All-One Cabinet Bed was "To the Living Room and Bed Room what the Kitchen Cabinet is to the Kitchen." And it is pretty much the hoosier cabinet of beds, including options like a closet, dressing table, desk, dresser, bookshelf in the headboard, and even a built-in reading light. Pretty civilized, actually, though apparently it didn't catch on—at least, I've never seen one still extant.

WHEN WRITING ADVERTISERS PLEASE MENTION THE AMERICAN CARPENTER AND BUILDER

Another manufacturer, the W. L. Van Dame Company, advertised its version of a disappearing bed in the April 1919 *American Builder,* noting that it had been awarded the Gold Medal at the Panama-Pacific International Exposition, which took place in San Francisco in 1915.

in 1925, becoming the Murphy Door Bed Company, which is still in business. Other companies jumped on the bandwagon as well. Most of the beds were metal, considered more "sanitary." Most raised and lowered by using springs or pistons, but some used a wooden mechanism where wooden pins attached to the bed frame slid in a wood groove cut into the sides of the opening—the same mechanism that many of the built-in ironing boards also used.

(Much thanks to Robyn Einhorn, Murphy Bed expert, for the above information.)

SHELF IMPROVEMENT

The various kinds of cabinets came with either fixed or adjustable shelves. Several kinds of shelf pins that fit into holes drilled in the sides of the cabinet were available, similar to the varieties we use today. But it was far more common for the ends of the shelves to sit on thin wooden cleats that fit into notches cut at intervals into uprights nailed at the front and rear of each cabinet side. The notches were variously square, rounded, or cut at an angle, and the ends of the cleats were shaped accordingly. The corners of the shelves also had to be cut to fit around the uprights. The notches were about an inch apart, so the shelves could be adjusted in 1-inch increments. Shelves were mostly solid wood, usually 3/4 inch thick by whatever the depth of the shelf needed to be. Sometimes two boards were edge-glued to achieve the needed depth, because a really wide board has a tendency to cup, whereas two boards glued together is less likely to do so.

TOTAL FABRICATION

Many of the built-ins, whether benches, cases, or colonnades, were built in place by carpenters. A cabinet with a back wall that is plaster is likely to have been built in place. But this was inefficient, and soon American ingenuity (not to mention capitalism) caused the millwork companies to expand from making sashes, doors, and molding to making just about everything wooden that might go into the house: staircases, colonnades, mantels, bookcases, sideboards, cabinets, linen cases, freestanding closets, dressers, paneling, kitchen dressers, box beams, breakfast nooks—you name it. A builder could just pick up the catalog and order colonnade A-317, combined with staircase T-111, fireplace surround B-438, sideboard C-583 with optional art-glass doors, and then go on and pick doors, window sashes, moldings, and all the other millwork to match. Then when he began building the house next door, he could choose completely different built-ins, a different window style, and so forth, put them all into a bungalow that was otherwise identical to the first one, and have it look completely different. This is how many of the bungalow neighborhoods developed. There were enough choices to make each bungalow unique.

CATCH OF THE DAY

All the various sideboards, bookcases, desks, and whatnot required hardware: hinges, knobs, pulls, catches, latches, and handles. Hinges fall into two categories: mortise hinges and surface-mounted hinges. Mortise hinges are set into mortises chiseled into the edge of the door and the face-frame of the cabinet, and are most commonly about 2-1/2 inches high, though they come in various sizes from 1 inch on up. Usually these were ball-tipped, loose-pin hinges. Surface-mounted hinges are attached to the face of the door and the face-frame, and are sometimes called *butterfly hinges* because of their shape; these are generally loose-pin as well, which makes door removal easier. Surface-mounted strap hinges were also available, and unlike the fake strap hinges often found on entry doors, these were real hinges. Many of the strap hinges for cabinets had L-shaped straps to accent the corners of the door. There were also half-mortise hinges, where one leaf of the hinge was set into a mortise but the other leaf (sometimes decorative) was attached to the surface. Linen cabinets often had drop-down doors (sometimes called *drop-front drawers*) that were kept in place by spring hinges similar to those used on screen doors, although some used regular hinges combined with some mechanism to keep the drawer from dropping too far; these ranged from a length of chain to various sorts of scissor-motion devices mounted inside the cabinet. (These methods were also used on the built-in drop-front desks.) A writer at the time mentioned that "Stay-chains should be put on each end of these fronts, to prevent them dropping below a horizontal position, in order both to prevent straining the hinge and to provide a strong extension to the drawer when open, whereon to lay linen."

Catches are divided into decorative varieties that go on the outside, and others that are mounted on the inside to keep the doors shut. Among the most common inside-mount types are spring-loaded ball catches and elbow catches. The outside sorts include cupboard catches and cupboard turns, the difference being that on one the spring-loaded knob turns to release the catch, and on the other it slides to one side. Both of these range from the very basic sort that is nearly universal in bungalow kitchens, to fancier models with interesting shapes or backplates.

There are approximately a zillion kinds of knobs and various sizes of each—that's why most decorative hardware catalogs are so big. A knob is defined by having only one screw—anything more than that is a pull. Or maybe a handle. Mostly. Because there are drop pulls—they only have one screw and yet they are not knobs. But that doesn't matter because drop pulls are mostly a Victorian thing. The head of the one screw could either be on the inside, in which case it screwed into a threaded shaft on the back of the knob, or it could be on the outside, in which case the screw went through the middle of the knob and there was a nut on the inside that threaded onto the screw. You will no doubt gather from this that these were machine screws. Although some tiny knobs just had wood-screw threads that went straight into the door. Knobs were used on drawers as well as doors. Wooden knobs came in simple shapes like round, oval, square, or pyramidal, and could be stained to match the woodwork. Metal knobs came in similar shapes, usually made of brass or bronze but also plated in other metals. Knobs also could have metal backplates—usually combined with metal knobs but sometimes with glass. Glass or crystal knobs included the ubiquitous hexagonal knobs with a screw through the middle, as well as others where the screw wasn't visible. These came in shapes including hexagonal, octagonal, faceted, round, oval, etc. Clear glass was the most popular, but glass knobs also came in colors. The difference between glass and crystal? Crystal is glass with more lead in it.

Pulls and handles are pretty much interchangeable, although some only go on drawers while others can be used for doors OR drawers; but in any case, they both have more than one screw, usually two if they attach from the back, sometimes more if they attach from the front. The most common pull is the *bin pull* (called that because of their original use on bins in retail stores), a cupped pull mounted to the face of a drawer. Typically half-moon shaped and very plain, there are also squarish varieties. The ubiquitous sash lift/drawer pull/door handle is also common, though used as a drawer pull more in utility areas. Glass knobs have a pull equivalent, sometimes called a *bridge handle*. Benches with lift-up seats and fold-down doors for linen closets used *recessed pulls*, which were set into a mortise; most often these had round rings. The occasional sliding door on a cabinet would also have a recessed pull. Pulls or handles are sized by their *boring*—the distance between the screws. This can vary, though something in the 3- to 4-inch range is prevalent. This doesn't matter much unless the pulls are missing and you want to use the same holes. Pulls can be rigid or they can be floppy—the floppy ones are known as *bail pulls* (like a bucket handle). The floppy parts come in different shapes—round, curved, square, diamond, triangular—you name it.

All the hardware discussed above might be found in any early-twentieth-century home, not just in a bungalow. But there was some hardware that was pretty specific to bungalows, and it's a festival of hammered metal, pyramid-head screws, quatrefoils (four squares arranged in, yes, a square!), acorns, twigs, sinuous Art Nouveau curves, and whatever else they could think up. It's the hardware you're all dying to put in the kitchen (on the fumed oak kitchen cabinets), except that I won't let you. But in the formal rooms—go for it! Because the bungalow designers did. Though the plainer hardware is much more prevalent, they did use the fancy stuff on many occasions. (Bedrooms, bathrooms, kitchens, and utility areas—stick with the plainer stuff.) Most of the hardware companies offered an entire suite of matching hardware, from the front-door entry set to the window hardware, from drawer hardware to escutcheons; it was easy for a builder or designer to just order the whole shebang—possibly a different design for each house they were building. And do I need to mention that the "hammering" was probably fake?

Rendered in brass, an Arts and Crafts bail pull is anchored to a drawer front with pyramid-head screws, though unfortunately one is missing.

All the (metal) hardware came in different finishes. Some hardware was solid metal (usually cast or wrought) like brass, bronze, copper, iron, or steel; other hardware was stamped or spun. Brass and steel were often plated with other metals—nickel was always used for hardware in kitchens and bathrooms until it was superseded by chrome in the 1930s. Which is ironic in a way, because chrome won't stick to brass, so brass has to be plated with nickel before it can be plated with chrome. Many of the finishes used then are still available today, and one had a choice of bright, brushed, or antique in brass, copper, and nickel, as well as specialty finishes.

And, as mentioned previously—no Phillips screws!

FLIGHTS OF FANCY

"The stairs are an important feature of a building. On entering a house they are usually the first object to meet the eye and claim the attention. If one sees an ugly staircase, it will, in a measure, condemn the whole house, for the first impression produced will hardly afterwards be totally eradicated by commendable features that may be noted elsewhere in the building."

—from the *Cyclopedia of Architecture, Carpentry, and Building*, 1918

Bungalows may theoretically be one story, but a bungalow with an upper level or a basement required a staircase or two. Or more. Stairs to the upper floor might begin in the entry hall, the living room, or the dining room. Basement stairs most commonly originated in the kitchen, utility room, or back hall, but might start off the main hallway as well, and under the main stairway was also an option. Not all

The stairs of the Greene & Greene–designed Duncan-Irwin House in Pasadena are enclosed by a railing of panels and alternating wide and narrow slats that echo the extremely narrow windows that step up the stairway. The newel post is very plain and decorated only with a couple of pegs.

bungalows have inside stairs to the basement—sometimes the only entry is from outside. Bungalows with a roof pitch steep enough for an attic might also have attic stairs. Some bungalows (larger ones, mostly) even have back stairs (for the servants, you know)—these usually ended up in the kitchen and were either an entirely separate stairway or a branch of the main stairway that came off a landing partway up, usually with a door. Often the stairways were stacked as a space-saving measure, with the stairs to the basement installed directly under the main stairway.

Stairways can be closed or open or a combination. Many stairways are built with a wall on one side and a railing on the other, at least until it reaches the ceiling of the lower floor; but some have walls on both sides, and a few are completely open. Some may be open up to the first landing, and then turn and be walled in on both sides. Stairways that are built against an outside wall usually have windows; these range from a single window or set of windows over a landing (often art glass), to windows that step up the wall along with the staircase. If the landing is unusually large, there may even be a window seat installed there.

The walls of the stairway may be covered with paneling, plaster, or wallcovering. Paneling generally matches the paneling in other parts of the house—board-and-batten or whatever. Some complex finish carpentry is involved, since due to the inclination of the stairs it all has to be parallelograms, and uneven ones at that. Lincrusta was a favored wallcovering for stairways that dated back to the Victorian era; it could take the bumps resulting from people carrying things up and down the stairs. Usually the paneling, the Lincrusta, or what have you was used as a wainscot, and above that there was plaster, which was painted, wallpapered or tinted.

Staircases are complex, and to be able to build a good one is a greatly admired skill. Seventy-four pages were devoted to stair building in the *Cyclopedia of Architecture, Carpentry, and Building,* and they were only scratching the surface. But there are a few terms one ought to be familiar with:

well-hole: the opening in the floor through which one ascends or descends between floors;

rise and run: rise is the distance from the top of the lower floor to the top of the upper floor, and the *run* is the length of floor that the stairs will occupy. If the rise and the run are two legs of a right triangle, then the hypotenuse of the triangle is the pitch—the inclination of the stairway. In modern parlance, rise usually refers to the height of an individual step above the step below, and run refers to the depth of each step from front to back, not counting any overhang at the front;

tread: the part you step on;

riser: the vertical part;

landing: a platform between flights where the stairs may

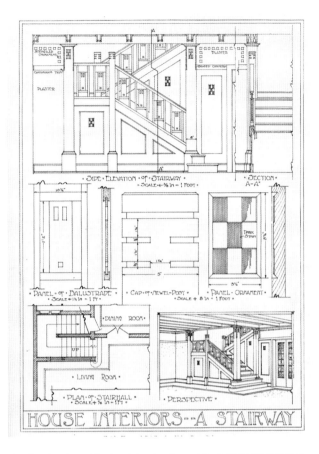

Another lovely architectural drawing by architect Ralph W. Ermeling was showcased in the November 1915 *American Carpenter and Builder.* Not surprisingly, given that the magazine was based in Chicago, the stairway shows a great deal of Prairie School influence, particularly in the balustrade panels. The columns and panels along the stair are decorated with 3-1/2- by 5-1/2-inch rectangles with the center and corners stained dark and the rest in a lighter stain, surrounded by a beveled groove. The newel posts at the landing have horizontal grooves that are 1-1/4 inches apart. At the bottom of the stairway, french doors lead to the dining room.

turn to the right or left or even run in the opposite direction;

flyers: treads that are the same width at both ends;

winders: treads that are wider at one end and are used to make turns. No more than three winders could be used in a turn—it was considered too dangerous otherwise. Many old winders basically come to a point at the narrow end, making it easy to miss one's footing.

Stairs are the most dangerous thing in a building, which is why the building code has more regulations pertaining to stairs than anything else. Many stairways in bungalows probably don't meet current code, especially basement and attic stairs, which tend to be overly steep or have shallow treads. But the basic safety rule for stairs is that the steps must be uniform—uneven steps cause people to trip and fall. Codes also govern the dimensions of railings, and the amount of headroom required (another place where bungalow staircases, especially attic and basement stairs, don't measure up).

The ratio of rise to run has much to do with whether the stairs are, as they used to say, commodious. Nowadays the rise and run combined generally has to equal 18 inches, with the rise being smaller than the run. I suppose you could make a staircase with a 2-inch rise and a 17-inch run, but it would take up the entire length of the average bungalow. An ideal rise and run is an 11-inch tread with a 7-inch rise (indeed, that is what is decreed in the current Uniform Building Code), but conditions in the real world are rarely ideal. Back in 1918, the recommendation in the *Cyclopedia of Architecture, Carpentry, and Building* was that the tread should never be less than 9 inches wide and the riser should never be more than 8 inches high (for a total of 17 inches), but even they admitted that the dimensions "cannot always be adhered to, as conditions often compel a deviation from the rule." That's because, given that the steps have to be uniform, you have to come up with some

These flat balusters are pierced with a design of leaves and subtly curving stems.

Closely spaced slats in this simple railing match the battens on the walls.

Simple cutouts adorn the slats of a stair railing, while a simple newel post with a mitered crown holds a round lantern.

In a home in Oakland, California, tall dark-stained newel posts, subtly tapered balusters, and a curved ceiling form part of a complex set of woodwork on the entry hall stairs.

combination of rise and run that equals the exact distance between the two floors—you can't put in a half step just because it didn't come out to an even number. For instance, if the distance between floors is 100-1/2 inches, and you put in twelve steps, the rise will be 8-3/8 inches and the run will be 9-5/8 inches, which will be just a bit steep. Thirteen steps will result in a rise of 7-3/4 inches and a run of 10-1/4 inches—somewhat better. Fourteen steps result in a rise of about 7-1/8 inches and a run of 10-7/8 inches—closer to the ideal. But that may take up too much space on the floor because that extra step is adding almost 11 inches to the length of the stairway. So it's always a balancing act. If you have a stairway that is too steep or narrow to meet code, I would advise you not to mess with it, as you will just be opening a huge can of worms—just put in some handrails and be careful.

Another feature of many bungalow stairways that has been banned by modern code (and for a pretty good reason) is doors that open directly over the stairway (nowadays if there is a door that opens toward the stairway, there has to be a landing at the top that is as wide as the door). Two different people have fallen down my basement stairs because they opened the door and, not realizing there was no landing, put their foot down expecting to hit solid wood and found only air, causing them to lose their footing and tumble down the stairs. (Fortunately for me, they're not the litigious type.)

There are also many rules in the code about railings—currently railings are required on BOTH sides of the stairway (though codes vary by city), and they have to be at least 30 inches high, measured from the front edge of the tread, and 34 inches high for horizontal railings on a landing. The railing itself has to be "graspable." Some bungalows probably have railings that meet these requirements—others have no railings at all. Railings are a good idea, so if one can be installed without unduly impacting the look of the stairway, it would probably be worthwhile. Railings generally have upright supports called *balusters,* although one tends to think of balusters as being turned, so square uprights are commonly called *spindles* (spindles can be turned as well, making the difference between a baluster and a spindle usually one of diameter—spindles are thinner). Flat boards or slats were also used, sometimes with cutout designs. The whole railing assembly could also be solid, usually paneled in some way. The balusters, whatever they were, either sat directly on the treads, with two balusters per tread generally, or were set into a bottom rail that was parallel to the top rail.

Railings normally terminated in a newel post at the top and bottom of the stairs and also on any landings. Newel posts took many shapes, including square, round, hexagonal or octagonal, battered (slanted sides), or turned. Although newel posts were always bigger than the balusters, sometimes they were massive, echoing the massive columns outside holding up the front porch roof.

At the top of the stairs shown in 168, the newel posts are topped with turned finials that rather resemble doorknobs.

Upstairs in the same Oakland home shown on page 166, the railing in the hall traces the curve of the ceiling below. Substantial square newel posts anchor the railings.

Stair Rods and Grips.

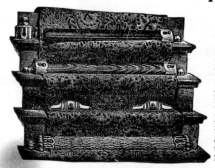

We offer a variety of the most popular rods and grips for fastening carpets to stairways. The use of these fastenings limplifies the saving and taking up of the Carpet which has heretofore been the most difficult carpet to lay properly.

THE ABOVE CUT REPRESENTS THE NEW STYLE, QUARTER-ROUND ROD, ALSO SHOWS THE WAY GRIPS ARE USED.

Acorn End Stair Rod.

Oak Stair Rods (stained), 27 in. or 30 in., acorn ends, with fixtures.............each **$ .05**

Oak Rod (stained), 27 in. or 30 in.,with **nickel ends** and fixtures ....each **.07**

Nickel End Stair Rod.

New Style Rod, quarter round, **oak** or **cherry,** heavy oxidized trimmings, complete (best cheap rod made, like large cut above), for 27 in. carpet.............................each **.11**

New Style Rod, same as above, for 36 in. wide carpet, each **.15**

Brass Oval Rod with fixtures, 24 inch, for 22 inch carpet, highly polished.........each **.10**

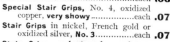

Brass Oval Stair Rods.

Brass Oval Rod with fixtures, 30 inch, for 27 inch carpet, see cut ....each **.12½**

New Stair Grip, No. 48, made of French gold or oxidized silver, see illustration below ....each **.06**

Special Stair Grips, No. 4, oxidized copper, **very showy**.................each **.07**

Stair Grips in nickel, French gold or oxidized silver, **No. 3**..............each **.07**

Stair Grips, walnut, oak or cherry, **No. I,** see illustration...............each **.05**

Gilt Corners, to be used in corners of stairs to prevent collection of dust— see illustration.......................dozen **.18**

Gilt Corners.

No. 1 Grip.   **No. 4 Grip.**   **No. 48 Grip**

Brass Stair Nosing, for the protection of stair carpets and rubber treads where there is an unusual amount of wear; can furnish any length desired up to 12 feet long, 1½ inches wide, per foot .... **.15**

Brass Nosing.

Our Heavy Corrugated Rubber Matting.

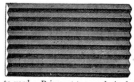

A very satisfactory floor covering for halls, stairs, passageways, and wherever a noiseless and sanitary carpeting is wanted. 36 inches wide. **Can be cut any size** desired,for stair treads, landings, etc. $\frac{3}{8}$ in. thick, 1 yard wide, about 7 lbs. to yard; or, $\frac{1}{8}$ in. thick, 1 yard wide, about 9 lbs. to yard. Price cut to any desired size, **20c** per pound. We handle only a superior quality of this Rubber Matting. The cheaper grades we have found unsatisfactory.

A page from the 1908 catalog of the Frank Betz Company of Indianapolis shows the various styles of stair rods and holders that were available, as well as dust corners.

A built-in bench next to a telephone niche anchors the bottom of a stairway as shown in the *Universal Design Book on Builders Woodwork.* A closet with a mirrored door is set on the landing (although the drawing doesn't actually match the floor plan).

What newel post could possibly be complete without a fixture featuring a nymph-like woman in diaphanous draperies, holding a light in the shape of a flower? Other than that, the post is quite plain, with only a line of dentil molding and a small fillet.

Sometimes the newel post at the bottom of the stairs included a light fixture.

The bottom step(s) were often wider than the rest of the stairs for effect, as if to funnel people up the stairway. These steps frequently had rounded corners, though not always.

The wood used in the risers and treads was sometimes the same as the other woodwork, or else matched the flooring, usually oak. The treads were solid boards with a bullnose edge, and usually overhung the riser by 1-1/2 inches. A small piece of cove or other decorative molding was nailed underneath the lip. The landings, if any, had strip flooring that matched the other flooring. All the wood (treads and risers) was given a clear finish rather than being painted, at least for the main stairway. A decorative carpet runner could be used, leaving the wooden treads exposed on either side. Brass *stair rods,* which were brass rods that fit into small brackets attached to the stairs, were used to keep the runner in place, although if the owner couldn't afford that, the carpet was simply held in place with carpet tacks. Many stairways also had *dust corners,* triangular pieces of sheet metal that were nailed into the corners to make it easier to sweep.

Basement, attic, or service stairs tended toward the very basic—softwood treads and risers, and simple or no railings—and often had treads covered with linoleum for ease of cleaning. They are more likely to have inadequate headroom and to be steep and narrow.

Many times people desire to add a second story to a bungalow or turn the attic into living space, and the biggest obstacle that stands in the way of doing this is where to put the stairway. Stairways take up a lot of space, and spiral stairs, while solving the space problem, are inappropriate and also make it awfully hard to get a mattress to the upper floor.

It is entirely unlikely that the average bungalow would have an elevator. However, this bungalow in Seattle, situated on a steeply sloping corner lot, somehow manages to be one-and-a-half stories tall in the front and four stories in the back. The owners, tired of walking up and down four flights of stairs, stole some space from an existing service stairway to put in an elevator. The interior of the elevator is paneled to match the wainscoting in the rest of the house (some is visible just to the right of the door), and even has a mica-shaded ceiling light for a certain Arts and Crafts ambience.

FLOOR WORD

As one might expect, given the Arts and Crafts reverence for wood, bungalow floors were, with rare exceptions, finished with either hardwood or softwood. Both types of floors could be laid directly on the floor joists, though often hardwood floors had a softwood subfloor underneath. Hardwood was primarily used in the formal rooms, with softwood being reserved for kitchens, bedrooms, and utility areas; but some bungalows had softwood floors throughout, and a few had hardwood floors throughout. Hallways could have either type of wood. Flooring practices varied widely in different parts of the country, depending on local wood availability, milling practices, building practices, personal preferences of the owner or builder, and even whether the house was a precut house, which would use woods typical of where it was cut, not where it ended up.

Probably 99 percent of hardwood floors were oak—either white oak or red oak. Other hardwoods used for flooring were maple, birch, ash, and tupelo. Hardwood traditionally used boards ranging from 1-1/2 to 2-3/4 inches wide, with 1-1/2 and 2-1/4 inches being the most common, although "matchstick floors" with narrower boards were sometimes installed. Later bungalows (late 1920s up to World War II) occasionally had "pegged" plank floors, probably due to the influence of both the Colonial Revival and the Romantic Revival. Parquet floors were rare in bungalows. The best floors used quartersawn oak, which produces coveted "flake grain"—glistening splotches of lighter colored wood that verge on iridescent, although even a plain sawn floor usually had a few quartersawn boards mixed in (and vice versa). The floors came in 3/4-inch-thick tongue-and-groove, or 3/8-inch- or 1/2-inch-thick strips (not T&G) that were meant to be installed over existing softwood floors when the owners wanted to upgrade to hardwood. (These

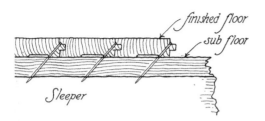

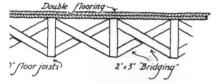

Above: An article in *House and Garden's Second Book of Houses* showed the proper construction of floors, with diagonal subflooring and tongue-and-groove finish flooring. This would have been the high-quality and expensive method. Most bungalows got by with a tongue-and-groove softwood subfloor laid at right angles to the joists, with a hardwood floor on top in the formal rooms and a softwood subfloor often used as the finish floor in the rest of the house.

Right: Dark-stained inlay outlines the oak floor in the living room of a Seattle bungalow. This sort of "knot-work" inlay is quite common. A corner window seat looks out over the porch to the view beyond.

were cheaper, and probably installed as new in low-cost bungalows, as well as being a retrofit.) In modern parlance, all wood floors that are not plank floors are called strip floors, but at the time these houses were built, the term *strip floors* referred to flooring that was not tongue-and-groove. Sometimes hardwood was installed only around the perimeter of the room, the center being filled in with softwood on the theory that there would be a rug covering that part. At times, the center portion was even recessed slightly, so the surface of the rug would be flush with the rest of the floor; of course, that meant you had to buy a rug *exactly that size*. As you can imagine, dining rooms were a likely spot for this treatment, but other rooms were not immune. Tongue-and-groove floors were installed with nails driven through the tongues (yeah, like the barista at your local coffeehouse), whereas strip flooring was face-nailed. It was considered a good idea to lay down rosin paper between the finish floor and the subfloor, but that dictum was mostly ignored.

Softwood floors generally utilized whatever inexpensive softwood was available locally—in the West, that was Douglas fir (Oregon pine), elsewhere it was what was termed *hard pine*, a term "used to designate any pine which is not white pine," according to one source, adding that, "only five [pines] are of practical importance in the building industry . . . the long-leaf southern pine, the short-leaf southern pine, the yellow pine, the loblolly pine, and the Norway pine." These days, it's pretty much all known as "heart pine." In some areas of the country, maple was inexpensive enough to be used as flooring in kitchens and other less formal areas of the house. Softwood floors usually had wider boards than hardwood floors—mostly 3 to 4 inches wide, occasionally 6 inches, and sometimes 2-1/4 inches like hardwood, though all were 3/4 inch thick.

There were various ways of laying wood floors, but most often the boards were laid in one direction, usually parallel to the longest wall in the room. Occasionally the board floor was surrounded by a border so that two sides of the border were at right angles to the rest of the floor. The corners could be mitered but usually were stepped or staggered, which is known as "log cabin corners." The boards could either be installed in long lengths that

Above: An interesting border of diagonal strips and triangulated squares is set into a face-nailed oak floor.

Left: In the master bedroom of my own home (the 1905 Sunset House), narrow 2-1/4-inch Douglas fir flooring rather than the usual 3 or 4 inch is laid with extremely wide borders, leaving rather short boards in the middle. All of the upstairs floors are laid in this pattern, including the hallway. Unlike many bungalows, the upstairs ceilings in my house are only 8 feet high, though the vertical thrust of the window and door trim makes them seem higher. This photo was taken the day that I moved in; the walls of this room are no longer white but are a lovely shade of goldenrod.

spanned the room or random lengths with staggered joints. It's true that the floors in Greene & Greene's Gamble House were installed on the diagonal, but this would have been much too wasteful for the average bungalow. In addition to the regular border, decorative borders were frequently installed around the perimeter of the room. These borders ranged from simple 1-inch strips of darker or lighter wood to Greek key or other geometric designs. A double border with knotwork designs in the corners is very common. Decorative borders could be cut and fit by carpenters on-site, or they could be ordered prefabricated.

In the bungalow era, many floors were still being prepared for finishing or refinishing by scraping, although things had progressed from hand-scraping to machine-scraping with a giant scraping blade on wheels, which made the job go a little faster. Electric drum sanders (as are used today) were beginning to appear as well. After the initial sanding or scraping, a filler was applied, followed by more sanding. If the floor was to be stained (though they usually weren't, because though tastemakers all thought it was a good idea for the floors to be as dark as the woodwork, the

workmen were of the opinion that natural was a lot faster and easier). Then the stain was applied, followed by shellac or varnish, and then paste wax. The shellac was often colored as well, giving a certain depth to the finish. The shellac could also be pigmented, making it resemble paint. And softwood floors were often painted. Occasionally the floors were finished with a penetrating oil, generally boiled linseed oil combined with turpentine for penetration, or tung oil from China, which began to be imported in the early twentieth century. Urethanes and other synthetic resin varnishes weren't introduced until the 1950s.

RESISTANCE IS FEW TILE

Ceramic tile found its way onto many bungalow floors, particularly in entry halls, sunrooms, and of course, bathrooms and kitchens. Naturally, the bathroom is the most likely place for a tile floor, and the unglazed 1-inch white hexagon is the most likely tile you will find, often with colored insets or borders. In some areas of the country, 1-inch-round "penny" tiles were used instead.

WOOD FLOORS

OBSESSIVE RESTORATION

Wood floors last a very long time if well taken care of, but all too often they aren't. Water damage, whether from roof leaks, plumbing leaks, plant watering, or floods, can result in cupped boards and black stains (caused by a reaction between the iron in the nails and the tannins in the wood, and nearly impossible to remove). Odors and stains from pet urine are another serious problem. And just like walls and ceilings, wood floors are often subject to the dreaded Bad Patching, generally involving a big piece of plywood inserted where a floor furnace used to be.

When it comes to wood floors, wall-to-wall carpeting can be your friend—that gold shag from the 1970s may be protecting lovely wood floors from damage, and it also makes an excellent drop cloth while you are patching plaster, painting, and doing other renovation tasks, if you can stand to leave it there. On the other hand, sometimes when the previous owners decided to do some redecorating and put in wall-to-wall, they figured they didn't need to protect the floors from paint drips, joint compound, or even gouges because, after all, they were going to cover it with carpet. So an unpleasant surprise may await you when you pull up the carpet. And naturally, carpet installers seem to feel it's necessary to secure the padding with an unbelievable number of staples, all of which you are now going to have to remove with pliers. Along with the tack strips. I hate tack strips.

Then there's the issue of urine stains and odors, which are very difficult to get rid of. Here's some scary information about urine from Mister Max, a manufacturer of Anti-Icky-Poo (yes, that's really the name):

> When urine is allowed to dry and remain in the carpet or other material, it begins bonding itself to the fibers. Proteins physically bond to the fibers while other portions of the urine crystallize into salts, forming ionic (electric charge) bonds. At this point it has become impossible to completely remove by cleaning alone. Given average carpet/pad thickness and levels of absorbency, 1/2 cup of hot urine will penetrate clear to the hard floor beneath and spread into a circular pattern nearly a foot wide. Recurring urination in the same area tends to spread these hidden spots in ever widening circles, contaminating more of the pad, the hard floor, and the backside of the carpet. The process of decay results in bacteria consuming the waste while converting it into gases.

While feeding on these wastes the bacteria produce obnoxious vapors, releasing primarily ammonia, sulfur, and methane gases in various combinations which we perceive as a bad odor.

Swell. These odors can be dealable or they can be so bad you have to rip up the floor, the subfloor, and the lower part of the walls as well. There are many products sold for getting rid of odors. Most are based on enzymes or on the mineral zeolite. Zeolite-based products work by *ad*sorption, where negatively charged molecules in the zeolite bond with the positively charged odor molecules—in simpler terms, like a magnet, or, as one site described it, like "odor-sucking rock." Enzymes basically speed up the natural decay process to remove the odor source. I've found a combination of both works the best. Whether the stains can be removed depends on how deep they've gone. Sometimes they will sand out, sometimes not. Bleaching doesn't help much—the stain will get lighter, but it still won't look like the surrounding wood, and inevitably bleach will get onto the wood around the stain, causing a halo effect. If you're very lucky, perhaps the end result will be a religious image, causing people to make pilgrimages to your bungalow, getting you on national TV, and allowing you to sell the piece of stained floor (which you are going to have to replace anyway) on eBay for enough money to re-do your kitchen. But this is unlikely.

Bad Patching will have to be, well, patched. As will other damaged or stained areas. Strip floors (non-T&G) are easier to patch, not having any tongue-and-groove to deal with, and random-length boards are easier to patch than boards that cover the full width or length of the room because the end joints of the patch can be staggered to blend in with the other random lengths. Closets are an excellent place to find boards to use for patching because wood tends to darken over time, so new boards may not quite match. (The boards in the closet can be replaced with new boards.) In the case of softwood, sometimes boards can be taken out of the attic if it has a floor. Salvage boards can work too. In the case of oak, it's important to know if you have white oak or red oak—red oak has a pinkish tinge while white oak is straw-colored. Tongue-and-groove floors are more difficult to patch, and you have to resign yourself to destroying at least one board in order to get the others out.

If the entire floor has to be replaced, there are companies that mill flooring from new or salvaged wood. If the floor being replaced is not a typical size, such as matchstick flooring or narrow softwood, it may have to be custom milled.

Most floors these days are refinished by sanding to remove the old finish, which also removes some of the wood. Old floor finishes can contain lead, so it's advisable to do a lead test beforehand just in case. Tongue-and-groove floors can only be sanded a limited number of times (about four to six, according to the Wood Flooring Manufacturers Association), since eventually the tongue is exposed. That goes for non-T&G strip floors as well, since they're not that thick to begin with. If the floor only needs a new coat of finish and is otherwise in good shape, it can be stripped with paint and varnish remover, or with denatured alcohol if it's shellac (see Paint Stripping). A shellac-coated floor can often be redone just by wiping gently with alcohol and then applying another coat of shellac, since each new coat bonds easily with the one beneath it. And it never hurts to test a floor that appears to be painted to see if it's really pigmented shellac, which is much easier to strip. All of this will be time-consuming and incredibly tedious, which is what all we obsessive types live for. It will also preserve the patina of the wood. On the other hand, if the floor has damages like cupped boards, scratches, or stains that are mostly on the surface, sanding will usually take care of a lot of that.

Floor sanding is generally done with drum sanders, starting with coarse grits of sandpaper and progressing to finer grits. Then the edges are sanded with an edger because the drum sander would totally mess up the baseboards. Corners and underneath obstacles (radiator valves, etc.) have to be scraped by hand. Many people have done this themselves, but it is easy to end up with a roller coaster effect if you don't know what you're doing, especially with softwood floors. (For some reason, people who have messed up this way like to highlight it by using a high-gloss finish on the floor, complete with big puddles of finish in the low parts.) Somewhere between the coarse and fine grits, a filler is applied to the floor to fill holes and cracks. Cracks between floorboards caused by shrinkage and wood movement are nearly impossible to fill successfully—the filler just pops out at some point. Learn to think of them as patina. Really big holes should be dealt with by either replacing the board entirely or patching it with a dutchman, unless you really want to faux-paint wood grain onto the filler to make it blend with the rest of the floor.

In any case, once the floor is stripped or sanded, stain (if any) can be applied. Stain requires careful application in order to avoid lap marks and blotches. Softwoods like pine and fir as well as maple tend to stain unevenly. Stickley, while admitting it wouldn't be practical to fume interior woodwork with ammonia, nonetheless gave directions for doing it:

> . . . shutting up the room in which the woodwork is to be fumed, stuffing up all the crevices . . . and then setting around on the floor a liberal number of dishes into which the ammonia is poured last of all. It is hardly necessary to say that the person to whom the pouring of the ammonia is entrusted will get out of the room as quickly as possible after the fumes are released.

Stickley also recommended applying diluted sulfuric acid to birch or beech floors to change the color, but he cautioned that a hog-bristle brush should be used since the acid would eat up other brushes, and that great care should be taken to avoid getting acid on the face, hands, or clothing. Yeah. I don't care how obsessive you are, I don't think you should try it.

At this point it's time to make a decision about finish. If you know what the original finish was, go back to it. Even if the floor has been refinished since, original finish may still be lurking in a closet, inside a window seat, or some other out-of-the-way place. If no vestige of the original finish is left, then there are choices to be made. Finishes that (mostly) sit on the surface (shellac, varnish) are considered to be "reversible" while penetrating oils (tung oil, linseed oil, etc.) are not. Surface finishes are more difficult to apply, especially on large areas like floors, while penetrating oils are easier to apply and allow for doing the finish one small area at a time; with shellac or varnish the whole floor has to be done at once, which is particularly true of shellac because of its fast drying time. Then there is the issue of varnish. Old varnish was made with plant resins (tree sap), sometimes called *phenolic resins,* drying oils (linseed or tung, mostly), and turpentine, whereas modern varnish primarily uses synthetic resins like urethanes and alkyds. But then it gets complicated, as many modern varnishes may also contain linseed or tung oil and phenolic resins in addition to synthetics. Proprietary formulas make it difficult to ascertain just what you're getting, and the ingredients are often not listed on the can—you have to get the Material Safety Data Sheet (MSDS) from the manufacturer, which you can't exactly do while standing in the finish aisle at the paint store. Think you'll get around that by going

More!

WOOD FLOORS, *Continued!*

with a penetrating oil? Many of the penetrating oils have synthetics added as well. What's an obsessive person to do? Well, interestingly enough, the best place to get varnish or penetrating oils made with traditional ingredients is from the few "natural" or "green" paint products companies, thus being obsessive and environmentally responsible at the same time. In any case, whatever finish you decide on probably shouldn't have a high gloss—you don't want your bungalow to look like a gymnasium. In the case of shellac, which dries glossy, adding some "flatting medium" is a good idea. For varnishes, use satin or semigloss.

A note from personal experience: the best time to refinish the floors is before you move into the house. I realize this is not always possible, but once you move in, you'll be reluctant to remove all the furniture in order to do the floors, and it's hard to do them one room at a time, though it is possible. Newly refinished floors can be protected from further depredation by covering them with red rosin paper secured with blue painter's tape. (I used to joke that I was going to redo all of my décor so that it went with rosin paper.) I have left blue tape on the floor for as long as nine months and still it came off leaving very little residue.

There is much of interest to study in this illustration from the April 1918 *American Builder* besides the nice collection of Arts and Crafts furniture. According to the accompanying article, "This alcove contains, besides the fireplace, a single long window seat and considerable built-in shelving for books. Designed somewhat in the shape of a letter V with the point cropped off by the group of four casement windows, one of the diagonal-running end walls possesses both a wide and a narrow section of book shelving and the other includes the fireplace and a single narrow book case. Beneath the window group is the built-in seat, which, designed with a hinged top, is of the box type and is used as a fuel receptacle." (Note: This is a bad idea that invites termites into your house.) The author goes on, "An interesting detail of the corner is the lantern-like lighting fixture suspended from the casing above the reading chair." There is another lantern over the chair next to the bookshelves. On the floor there is both an oriental rug and a Native American rug lying at odd angles, which was common. But what I love about this photo is that it looks like people actually live there—there are books scattered everywhere, there is food on the side table next to the chair in the alcove, and the pictures are hung kind of randomly. Apparently no one explained the concept of cleaning up for the photo shoot.

COMPROMISE SOLUTION

I don't care how bad the existing floors are, don't even think about Pergo! Actually, most of the info under Obsessive Restoration still applies, except that I suspect you will not choose to finish the floor with shellac. Go for it—use oil- or water-based polyurethane or tung oil or Swedish finish or whatever. And I also suspect that you may not want to stain the floor, as we seem to like things lighter these days, so that is certainly an option. And you may want to cover your softwood floors with hardwood since the latter is less prone to dents and dings and gouges from dog claws and so forth. I personally don't care for most of the commercial prefinished hardwood flooring, as it tends to come in really short lengths, and it always has a little V-groove between each board, which I realize is so that cracks between the boards don't become obvious, but to me it's just a place to collect crud and it makes these floors look obviously new. A lot of modern flooring is now just wood veneer over an engineered core, which looks okay when you install it but which will probably not be able to be refinished.

White oak is harder to find these days than red oak, but white oak is more durable. I do draw the line at bamboo flooring—they weren't making bamboo into flooring until quite recently. Nor were they importing exotic woods like bubinga, padauk, or wenge, to name a few. And they most certainly did not have laminate flooring (Pergo, Formica, Wilsonart, etc.), which is nothing more than a photograph of wood under a melamine wear layer on top of some particleboard. Laminate floors cannot be refinished nor can they be easily repaired when damaged, and if you sell your house, the buyers will mentally be subtracting the cost of installing wood floors from your asking price.

There seems to be a modern tendency to want to fancy everything up, including floors, so if you just can't resist doing that, here's the good news: Stickley featured an oak floor with inlaid butterfly keys in a 1905 issue of *The Craftsman,* as well as a floor with a fairly elaborate border using Native American motifs, so there is actually precedent for this sort of thing. Just try to refrain from putting it in the kitchen.

Hexagonal 2- and 4-inch tiles were also used—the 4-inch ones were usually glazed. Other kinds of mosaic tiles, including 1-inch squares, oblong tiles set in herringbone or running bond patterns, combinations of 1- and 2-inch squares and 1- by 2-inch rectangles, and basketweave tiles were also fashionable. The 4- by 4-inch matte-glazed square tiles were also common; the matte glaze made them less slippery. These were primarily white until the 1920s, because of the obsession with sanitation and cleanliness. Colored tile began to appear when everyone realized that germs were colorblind, though white tile continued to be used. Art tile really wasn't used in bathrooms until the late 1920s and beyond; before that it was confined mostly to fireplaces. Tile was somewhat less common in kitchens, but if it was used, either white hexagons or 6-inch red quarry tile was pretty much the deal. Sunrooms often had tile floors, usually hexagonal or other mosaic tile or art tile, that not only served as thermal mass to collect heat but also were easier to clean if one overwatered the plants that were often kept there. Entryways were another customary place for tile, and probably the second most likely place for art tile after the fireplace. Occasionally there is a bungalow with tile floors practically everywhere, but that's generally because it belonged to somebody who owned a tile company.

FLAX OR FICTION?

Linoleum, a resilient flooring made of oxidized linseed oil, cork dust, wood flour, chalk, and pigments on a burlap backing, was invented by Frederick Walton in 1863. LINOLEUM IS NOT VINYL! (Vinyl was invented much later and didn't become the predominant resilient flooring until the 1960s. Vinyl is also highly toxic, whereas linoleum is a totally nontoxic product.) Popular in kitchens, bathrooms, and other utility areas because of its ease of cleaning and its resilience, after 1910 linoleum began to be used in other rooms as well, due primarily to an advertising campaign launched by the Armstrong Cork Company in 1913, with the slogan "Armstrong's Linoleum For Every Room in the House." At about the same time, the Congoleum Company was formed and marketed a competing product called "feltbase," which had designs printed in enamel on asphalt-impregnated felt. Although not too many people really went for linoleum in every room of the house, it did prove to be popular for hallways (special "passage linoleum" was manufactured for that purpose), sunrooms and enclosed porches, breakfast rooms, children's rooms, attics, the occasional entry hall, and, of course, kitchens and bathrooms. What proved to be more popular than sheet goods were linoleum

TILE

OBSESSIVE RESTORATION

Ceramic tile flooring on a mortar bed will pretty much last forever, as long as the wood underneath remains intact. It may develop cracks, the glaze may wear, and the grout may get stained and dirty, but most of this is easily dealt with. Start by cleaning the floor. Use basic household cleaners first—if that doesn't work, go for something stronger, like an acid-based tile and grout cleaner. Use a stiff bristle toothbrush on the grout. If the grout turns out to be white (usually only in bathrooms) but it's still a little dingy, there are grout whiteners available that, surprisingly, actually work. They usually come in a bottle with a sponge applicator—it's basically paint, which sticks to the grout but can be wiped off the tile once it dries. If there are very large cracks in the tile, it might be good to fill them—use white thinset mortar with a latex additive. If the tiles are colored, the right color of nail polish can do wonders for touching up, or appliance touch-up paint also works for the more basic colors. There's not much to be done about worn patches except to learn to think of it as patina.

Sometimes the ceramic tile has been covered with some other kind of flooring such as linoleum, vinyl, or asphalt tile. Usually this was glued directly to the tile and is fairly easy to pull up. (It would be wise to have a sample of it tested for asbestos first—if it tests positive, removal might be best left to experts.) But after pulling up the other flooring, a lot of glue residue and other gunk may be left. This will generally dissolve in the right solvent—try hot water, mineral spirits, lemon oil, citrus-based strippers, or floor-adhesive remover (this is usually methylene chloride—a known carcinogen; be sure to wear a respirator as well as hand and eye protection, and dispose of the residue at a local hazardous materials collection center). Some serious scrubbing may be required to get the residue out of the grout. After it's all cleaned up, it probably wouldn't hurt to seal the floor. Tile stores sell many kinds of sealers, and floor or paste wax also works.

If the existing floor is beyond saving because of irreparable damage to the tile or rot in the wood underneath, then a new floor can be installed. It's probably best to rip out the existing floor and start over, especially if rot is involved. Sometimes some of the tiles can be saved, and it is possible to get custom-matching replacements or figure out a new design that makes use of the remaining tiles

while adding new ones to make up for the damaged ones. The rule of thumb when removing existing tiles is that you'll probably lose about 25 percent of them. A reinforced mortar bed is the traditional way to go, although plywood and cement backer board will also work. There is also a new product made of plastic that greatly resembles a gigantic waffle and serves as both a backer and an isolation membrane. There are some things to consider when using new tiles. Most old tiles were flat rather than having eased edges as modern tiles do (although it is still possible to get flat tiles). Most modern tiles also have spacing "lugs" on the sides that give a wider grout joint (usually about 1/8 inch as opposed to 1/16 inch for old tiles). The spacing lugs will have to be cut off for smaller joints. An exception to this is art tiles, which were meant to have wider joints, up to 1/4 inch. Also, mosaic tiles now come on sheets with 1/8-inch joints—if the joints are to be smaller, the sheets will have to be cut apart. Some companies will assemble custom borders or sheets based on your designs. You can also assemble your own designs at home. It's best to lay out the whole thing dry first and label it very carefully. Floor tiles should be unglazed or matte glazed—shiny glazes are too slippery for floors. Unglazed tiles should be sealed, especially if they are not vitreous or porcelain. It is also possible to tile over an existing floor, assuming the substrate is in good condition. (Be sure to use latex admixture in the thinset.) This will make the floor higher, though, and may require adjustments at plumbing fixtures or doorways. Tile floors can be cold—it would at least be worthwhile to install insulation under the floor, especially if it is over an unheated basement or crawl space.

COMPROMISE SOLUTION

Eased-edge ceramic tiles will be fine for the floor. Avoid 12- by 12-inch tiles (unless they're stone) as they look too modern. Stick to mosaics and try not to get anything bigger than 8 by 8 inches. As mentioned above, custom borders can be ordered or you can make up your own. There are many companies and artisans making art tiles, either reproductions of vintage tiles or new designs in an Arts and Crafts style. Try to avoid the currently trendy glass tiles—they are lovely, but they're wrong. Either a mortar bed or cement backer board can be used as a substrate for the tile.

and felt-base rugs, which were printed in designs ranging from geometrics to imitations of Oriental rugs; these continued to be popular well into the 1950s. There was also a thinner linoleum product for walls called Lino-wall (Armstrong) and Congo-wall (Congoleum), which was used as wainscoting mostly in kitchens and utility areas and occasionally in bathrooms.

Linoleum came in solid, marbleized, granite, jaspé, and inlaid patterns, which were all an innate part of the material. Linoleum was also available in printed patterns. Felt-base used patterns that were similar to linoleum, but all felt-base patterns were printed. In both materials, a lot of the patterns were an imitation of some other material: tile, stone, wood, straw, brick, carpets. Most of them were not particularly Arts and Crafts, and there were not a lot of conventionalized flowers, though Congoleum did have one rug that was very Charles Rennie Macintosh.

There's a great deal more to it than that, which is why I wrote an entire book called, not surprisingly, *Linoleum* (Gibbs Smith, Publisher, 2003). If you want to know more, you'll just have to buy the book. (It's a cult favorite, you know.)

Periodically there will be some other sort of floor in some part of a bungalow, things like stone, concrete, or magnesite (magnesium carbonate, asbestos, sand, and sometimes wood fiber, mixed with magnesium chloride solution instead of water). Terrazzo, composed of stone chips set in concrete and then polished, was used once in a while, though it was fairly expensive, especially before the electric polishing machine was introduced in 1910.

CUT A RUG

By the bungalow period, wall-to-wall carpeting had fallen into disfavor as being unsanitary, mostly because no one had invented a decent vacuum cleaner. Area rugs could be taken outside and beaten to remove dust, but with wall-to-wall carpeting that was kind of difficult. In any case, the Arts and Crafts movement tended to favor area rugs. Oriental carpets were used by those who could afford them. Native American rugs were also thought to be appropriate. Other flat-woven rugs such as *drugget* (a rug with cotton warp and wool filling) and *ingrain* (a reversible flat woven wool carpet, also known as Kidderminster) had a simplicity that went well in a bungalow.

Machine-woven rugs such as Wilton (a sheared pile carpet made in 27-inch-wide strips that were sewn together to form rugs), Brussels (a looped pile carpet also made in 27-inch strips), and Axminster (a thick pile carpet that could be woven into a room-size rug without seams) were more affordable than hand-knotted rugs.

Bouquets of flowers are printed on a felt base rug installed in a bedroom in a bungalow in Raymond, Washington. This rug likely dates to the 1940s.

CHAPTER NINE

SUPPORT GROUP

You know, they don't call it "laying the groundwork" for nothing. The foundation is the first part of any building to be built. The foundation ties the house to the earth and keeps it there. Although a foundation may be as simple as some flat rocks just sitting on the ground, as a whole, permanent foundations were generally set below the ground. Brick, stone, poured concrete, or concrete block were and are the commonly used foundation materials.

FANCY FOOTWORK

The foundation starts with *footings*, an area wider than the wall above it that spreads the weight of the house over a wider area so it won't sink into the ground (much like the theory of snowshoes). Generally the footings are concrete, even if the wall of the foundation uses some other material. The foundation (footing and wall) is shaped like an upside-down T. The main reason that homes in cold climates have basements is that the footings have to be below the *frost line* (however deep the ground freezes in winter), otherwise the foundation walls will be subject to *frost-heaves*. You know how water expands when it freezes, like when you overfill the ice tray? Well, when it freezes in the earth and expands, it can actually lift up whatever's on top, be that a road or the wall of your house. By keeping the footings below the frost line, the house will stay put. For a similar reason, bungalows in areas with a high *water table* (the level below the ground where the ground is completely saturated with water) are

often built on poured concrete slabs that sit on top of the ground or are raised up on piers above the ground. Conveniently, most areas with high water tables seem to be warm weather areas, or it might be a problem. Most bungalows meant for year-round use were built with full perimeter foundations. These days, foundations are built with a drain at the level of the footing to carry off any water that might make its way down there, but a lot of bungalows lack this item.

PIER REVIEW

In some areas, mostly in the South or in areas with high water tables, bungalows were built on brick, stone, or concrete *piers* (really short structural columns) rather than continuous foundations to allow ventilation underneath the structure (and give the animals somewhere to hang out on hot days). Bungalows with perimeter foundations also had piers as secondary structural support within the perimeter foundation. Even the smallest bungalow had a beam down the center supported by posts resting on piers or on a continuous piece of foundation (*grade beam)* and possibly other posts and piers for additional structural support.

JOIST DESSERTS

However tall the foundation happens to be, the *sill plate* or *mud sill* (generally a 2 by something like 8, 10, or 12 inches) sits on top of it. The horizontal *joists* (usually 2 by 10 or 12

Facing: Builders often used the base of the chimney to provide a fireplace in the basement, like this one on the lower level of a Prairie-style bungalow in Memphis. The stone basement fireplace is far more rustic than the arched fireplace in the living room above it. The owners use this space as a family room.

inches) that hold up the floor may sit directly on the sill, or there may be a *cripple wall* between the top of the foundation and the first floor, and the joists sit on top of that. They are attached to the *rim joist* (sometimes called a *ribbon joist*) either with nails or with metal *joist hangers*. Down the center of the bungalow, the other ends of the joists rest on the beam held up by the aforementioned piers, the joists from opposite sides of the house overlapping on top of the beam. The ceiling joists upstairs generally run in the same direction as the floor joists. Upstairs in the house, any interior partition wall that is at right angles to the direction of the joists is known as a *load-bearing* wall. (Why do you care about this? Because you have to provide alternate means of support if you want to take out a load-bearing wall.) Joists may have diagonal or straight *blocking* or *bridging* in between to keep them from bowing to one side or the other. Often pieces of tin were placed between the joists and over the sheathing to prevent rodents from getting in. (Of course they get in somewhere else—see the vermin chapter.)

CELLARS MARKET

A full basement was usually given a concrete floor, although I am sure there were exceptions. This essentially doubled the available space of the house, and many owners took advantage of that to add bedrooms, bathrooms, workshops, offices, laundry rooms, wine cellars, fruit rooms, summer kitchens, and even ballrooms in the cellar. Later in the century it became fashionable to turn the basement into a "rec room," which usually involved knotty pine paneling, although occasionally it was something more amusing like a tiki theme. In many places, builders took advantage of the chimney's foundation in the basement to put in a basement fireplace. Depending on the depth of the frost line, basements could have quite high ceilings, although the ceilings were often somewhat lower than those in the house, especially after allowing for plumbing, heating ducts, and so on. There was normally a staircase leading to the basement from somewhere inside the house, often near the kitchen, though sometimes the basement access was from outdoors, down a series of steps. This was either a regular door or sometimes a *bulkhead door,* actually a set of doors on top of triangular walls sticking out from the back of the house.

Depending on the slope of the lot and the design of the bungalow, very little or a lot of the foundation walls might show on the outside. A California bungalow on a flat lot might have only 6 or 8 inches of foundation showing, with a crawl space. A crawl space can be anything from a slither-on-your-belly height to a crawl-on-your hands-and-knees height to a walk-like-the-Hunchback-of-Notre-Dame height, at which point it's become a *raised basement*, basically like building a basement aboveground, which means it's not really a basement at all, but, hey, I don't make up the terminology. A raised basement has only a few inches of foun-

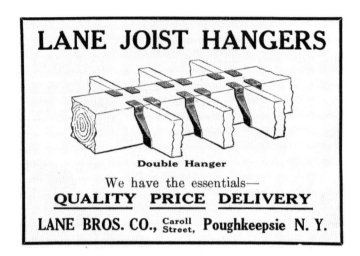

Perhaps you thought joist hangers were a recent invention? Not so, as this ad in the March 1919 *American Builder* illustrates.

Stunning green tile with a crystalline glaze, accented by riveted iron straps, makes this fireplace the focus of the room. Stained-glass windows in a stylized floral pattern feature a subtle dentil molding along the apron. The oak mantel has a similar detail between its three corbels, as does the box-beam ceiling. An Arts and Crafts textile is set under glass in a small tray atop the table in front of the fireplace.

dation showing; the rest of the wall is constructed just like a regular wall, only shorter. Many bungalows with crawl spaces have a partial basement dug out that provides space for the furnace, the laundry, and some storage. A sloping lot also provides space for a partial basement. And, if the owner was willing to pay extra to get one, bungalows can have full basements even in warm climates where they may not be necessary. Full basements also have the top of the foundation wall above *grade* (the ground).

Ventilation was provided by metal or wooden vents. There is much disagreement about whether vents are necessary, particularly in southern climates where they introduce hot, humid air into the crawlspace. But it is generally agreed that covering the ground with 6 mil (0.006 inch) polyethylene to restrict the evaporation of moisture from the soil will help prevent condensation and wood decay. It should be run up the inside of the foundation wall as well, stopping about three inches from the top (this has to do with termites—more on that later). Basements generally don't have vents, though basement windows were often included for light, and could be operable. Windows could be above ground level or completely or partially below the surface in *window wells*, which still allowed some light in.

Basement or crawlspace cripple walls should also be insulated (if you're going to insulate), and insulation should be installed between the floor joists as well. The vapor barrier on the insulation should face the warm-in-winter side of the wall or floor.

Damp basements are a subject so complex it makes my brain hurt. Basically you want to keep water away from the foundation in any way possible. Water is insidious. The first line of defense is to make sure the ground outside slopes away from the foundation, since this is often not the case after eighty to a hundred years. Then you want to make sure the gutters aren't overflowing, that the downspouts empty away from the foundation, that there's no vegetation too close to the house, and that any water coming down a hillside toward the house is diverted before it gets there (by swales, french drains, etc.)—you know, I totally passed up the opportunity to use a pun like "Prince of Swales"; I'm proud of myself—anyway, then you have moisture from leaking plumbing, dryers not vented to the outside, hanging clothes to dry in the basement, and moisture that comes up through the concrete floor or the walls as vapor, or for that matter, as liquid. In the old days they generally didn't bother to put any kind of waterproof barrier under the concrete, and concrete is not actually impervious to water. Then you have bungalows that were built in areas where there are springs or seeps in the ground (a geologist friend described the composition of seeps as "a pile of dinner plates and sponges"— when the sponges are dry, they hold up the plates; when the sponges are wet, the weight of the plates squeezes the water out)—not much you can do about these if they are under your house except to put in a sump pump. Many basements

have floor drains; these may be connected to the sewer line, they may go to the storm drain, or they may be so filled with crud at this point as to be totally useless. But if you can smell sewer gas in the basement, it's a good bet the drain is connected to the sewer, and you need to pour some water into it occasionally to keep a seal in the trap.

Small amounts of moisture can be dealt with by using ventilating fans or dehumidifiers. Large amounts of moisture are a more difficult problem and too individualized to go into here, but suffice it to say that waterproofing the inside walls is probably not going to do the trick, and that it's best to try dealing with grading, downspouts, leaking plumbing, and other inexpensive fixes before you start digging up the foundation.

CHUTE FIRST, ASK QUESTIONS LATER

Many furnaces burned coal until after World War II, and this involved having a lot of coal on hand to shovel into the furnace; so the coal bin was located in the basement, handy to the furnace, with an outside door or window so the coal truck could deliver the coal through a chute directly into the bin. The bin itself could have walls of wood or concrete. After the furnace was converted to gas or oil, or was replaced, many people cleaned out the coal bin and used it for something else—a wine cellar, storage for preserved fruits and vegetables, and so forth. (When I was a kid, my father used the former coal bin of our Indianapolis house as an office.)

Another chute terminating in the basement was the laundry chute, since that was often the location of the laundry. The chute may terminate in some sort of a receptacle— a cupboard, a wooden bin, or the like—or the laundry may just end up on the floor if you don't put a basket under the opening. If it doesn't have one, you might want to put a spring-loaded door over the opening since a laundry chute can act like a chimney in case of a fire in the basement, allowing the fire to easily reach the upper floors.

Before the introduction of the washing machine, laundry day involved *laundry trays,* large deep sinks made of fired clay, porcelain over cast iron, soapstone, or concrete. These may still be in the basement, and often a modern washing machine still drains into the sink. Concrete sinks have been replaced in our time by fiberglass or plastic versions that don't weigh as much. Laundry had to be hung outside to dry, or hung in the basement to dry in winter since the automatic clothes dryer wasn't introduced until the late 1930s.

Whole-house central vacuum systems were also introduced early in the century, and the vacuum motor and dirt receptacle were located in the basement. Each room had a small, hinged brass outlet near the floor for connecting the hose. The systems were expensive and not common in the more humble sorts of bungalows.

Thurman No. 2 Electric-Driven Stationary Vacuum Cleaner Installed in Basement of a Residence. The machine is started by pushing electric button on each floor. These machines are made in all sizes.

Above: In this 1915 advertisement by the Thurman Vacuum Cleaner Company, the servants clean in the living room while the gentleman of the house shows off his built-in vacuum in the entry hall to impress a friend. The machinery sits below in the basement.

Right: Guilt was clearly used to sell vacuum cleaners, as amply demonstrated by this ad proclaiming, "DEATH RIDES ON EVERY CLOUD OF DUST" in the back of the 1912 *Book of Home Building and Decoration*. It went on, "DUST breathed into the lungs spells DISEASE—often DEATH—AND THE BABY, PLAYING ON THE FLOOR, GETS THE WORST OF IT!" Yeah, parental guilt gets them every time.

Far right: In a 1915 article about vacuum cleaners clearly aimed at men, author F. W. Eichorn states, "The vacuum cleaner is, emphatically, here to stay, and the time is not far distant when to be without an air cleaner in your home will be equivalent to being without a bathtub!" He goes on, "You ask, perhaps: Why do I require a cleaner in my house, which is kept spotlessly clean by my wife or my maid or my twenty servants?" The author goes on for a few paragraphs about "unnamable [*sic*] filth," Petri dishes, and public expectoration, before noting the laborsaving aspects of vacuum cleaners and why you should provide such conveniences for your wife. Meanwhile, the illustrations show the maid vacuuming various parts of what is apparently the bungalow shown at the top, including the bearskin rug.

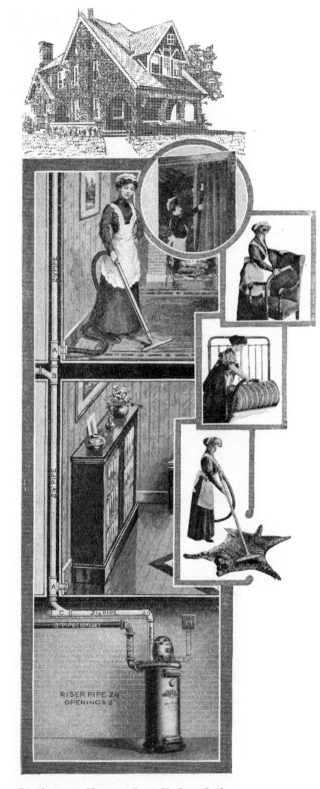

Stationary Cleaner Installed and the Many Ways in Which It Can be Used. The Tuec Company Have to Their Credit Over 7500 Installations of this kind.

Basements that had rooms turned into living space may have dropped ceilings (to hide ducts and pipes) and were often finished similarly to attic rooms, with beadboard, wood paneling, fiberboard, etc., occasionally even plaster. All this was usually attached to *furring* strips (one-by-two's) fastened to the basement walls. The floor could be left concrete and painted, or covered with asphalt tile, or built up on *sleepers* (furring strips for the floor, essentially) and then covered with wood or linoleum. The piers and posts were sometimes boxed-in to look more like columns.

DON'T BUG ME

The basement or crawl space is one of the most likely locations where you will find the various "wood-destroying pests and organisms," including termites, wood-boring beetles, and the ever-popular fungus (sometimes called dry-rot, which is kind of a misnomer). An infestation of any or all of these almost always has to do with excessive moisture, or with "earth/wood contact," which means framing lumber or wood siding in contact with the ground, or both.

Here's more than you ever wanted to know about termites. They are related to cockroaches but resemble ants, though lacking the narrow waist typical of ants. Flying termites, which are often called "flying ants," are differentiated from flying ants by having four equal-sized wings. There are three types of termites: damp-wood termites, found mainly in coastal British Columbia, the Pacific Northwest, and cool coastal areas of California; dry-wood termites, found mostly in the southwestern parts of the United States and Mexico; and subterranean termites, found nearly everywhere, although the farther north one goes, the less they are a problem (thus most of Canada, Maine, northern Minnesota, etc., don't have to worry much). Formosan termites, a particularly voracious species of subterranean termite introduced into the United States after World War II, has become a major problem in the Southeast. Termites feed on cellulose, and in nature they feed on roots, dead trees, and such, performing a useful service. Unfortunately, they can't distinguish between your bungalow and a dead tree. They will eat any wood that has more than 20 percent moisture, as well as cardboard and paper. Subterranean termites live underground but are happy to build mud tubes in order to get from the ground up to your very tasty framing lumber. It's not that they target your house on purpose, it's just that any kind of moisture makes them go "Hmm, I wonder if there's any wet cellulose around here?" So a damp basement or crawlspace, especially one with earth-to-wood contact or "cellulose debris" (wood, cardboard, or paper in contact with the ground), is pretty much an "all-you-can-eat" termite buffet.

Then you have your wood-boring beetles: the powderpost beetles (Lyctidae), the false powderpost beetle (Bostrichidae—those are the ones wearing the Groucho glasses), furniture and deathwatch beetles (Anobiidae), and the long-horned and old-house borer beetles (Cerambycidae). It's not the beetles that are the problem, really, it's their children. The beetles lay their eggs in wood (some kinds prefer hardwood, others prefer softwood), and after the larvae hatch, they proceed to tunnel their way out, leaving a fine powder *(frass)* and a tiny exit hole in their wake. They are called powderpost beetles because a large infestation can literally reduce a piece of wood to powder. As with termites, the best bet is prevention since there does not seem to be much agreement on the best way to treat an infestation.

There are many types of fungus—mushrooms and yeast are a couple we probably find nice to have around. In nature, dry-rot fungus serves the purpose of breaking down wood and plant fibers, and releasing carbon dioxide, which supports the photosynthesis of green plants. You just don't want it doing that to your house. There are two main kinds of wood-decaying fungi—brown and white. As with the beetles, white rot prefers hardwood and brown rot prefers softwood. Brown rot fungi have the ability to transport water from wet areas to the wood surface in order to facilitate the decay process. Fungi reproduce using spores. When the spores come to rest in a favorable environment, they begin to grow. A favorable environment includes high humidity, warm temperatures (68 to 86 degrees F), stagnant air, and low light—in other words, a basement, a crawl space, or under a sink—which is not to say they don't grow outside in the light, because they do. But they can't survive in wood with less than 20 percent moisture, and simply drying out the wood will kill them. They also don't care much for borates, so treatment and prevention often involves borate solutions.

There is a common thread to all these pests: water. If you keep the water where it belongs (in the plumbing or outside the house), you stand a better chance of keeping the pests away as well.

PUT YOUR DUCTS IN A ROW

With the exception of bungalows that were built strictly for use in the summer as vacation homes, most bungalows had some sort of heat. In a warm climate it may have been nothing more than the fireplace, but even mostly warm climates like Florida or Southern California have days where the temperature gets down to freezing, so you might want to have another option. And when bungalows were first built in cold climates, heating was clearly required and was primarily provided by piped furnaces with ducts and registers, pipeless furnaces, floor furnaces, or radiators connected to boilers.

Here's a description of a piped furnace from the publication *Modern Conveniences for the Farm Home,* published by the Department of Agriculture in 1906:

A furnace is a stove within a casing of galvanized iron or brick. Air is admitted to the space between the two and when it becomes heated passes through pipes to the different rooms of the house. The furnace may be constructed of cast iron, wrought iron, or steel. . . . Where natural gas is available the furnace can be arranged to burn it, but it is well to have a coal grate also in case the gas should be shut off.

There were a few furnaces designed to burn wood, but the great majority burned coal. These furnaces used large pipes from 8 to 12 inches in diameter—the larger the room, the larger the pipe. (These ducts are often covered in asbestos.) Because the furnace depended on gravity, the cold air return was also large—2 feet or more in diameter. To save money, some builders only ran heating ducts to the formal rooms, with bedrooms, bathrooms, and kitchens remaining unheated. Each duct was equipped with a damper near the furnace to regulate the heat. This was the dominant furnace type until the 1930s. It had the advantage of being quiet and simple to operate, and many are still in use.

After the invention of electric fans in the 1880s, experiments in attaching an electric fan to the furnace began to take place. By 1908, Emerson Electric was marketing a fan designed to be added to the furnace, and General Electric was advertising a booster fan for furnaces as early as 1910. These continued to be added to existing furnaces, but it was not until the 1930s that forced-air furnaces with built-in blowers were offered as a package. Forced-air furnaces are now the standard installation. Because of the fan, they are noisier than gravity furnaces, especially the inexpensive models. And yes, they used furnace filters, made of cheesecloth, as early as 1902.

The other type of furnace was the "pipeless furnace." These used a large, centrally located floor grate (the one in my house is 30 by 36 inches) set directly above the furnace. In the center of the grate, a large pipe about 2 feet in diameter allowed the hot air from the furnace to rise into the house. Around the central pipe, the remaining spaces of the rectangular grate formed the cold-air return. The idea was that convection would cause the warm air to circulate

throughout the house. Convection is the transport of heat through air or liquid—if you hold your hand over a pot being heated on the stove, you can feel hot air rising from it. As the hot air rises, cooler air is pulled up from below to be heated and also rise. Meanwhile the original hot air, having transferred its energy to the cold ceiling, is no longer hot, so it sinks back toward the floor to start the process again, resulting in what is known as a "convection loop." This works pretty well within one room, but as a method for heating the entire house, it was less than sat-

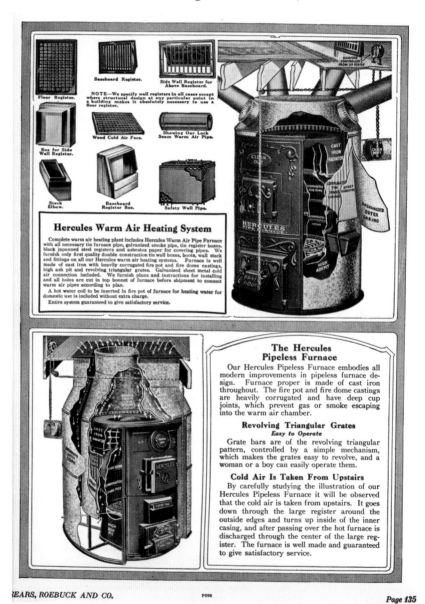

Sears Roebuck showed the different furnaces you could purchase to heat your Honor-bilt precut home. At the top is a coal-burning furnace for piped systems, with all its various accoutrements, and below is a pipeless furnace, also coal burning, with arrows showing the hot air rising through the center of the register while the cold air returns through the corners to be heated again.

isfactory. If there was an upper floor, registers were sometimes installed in the ceiling to allow the heat to pass through to the upstairs. Pipeless furnaces still burned coal. Although gas furnaces and boilers had been available since around 1900, a coal shortage during World War I increased their popularity. With the advent of reliable natural gas supplies in some areas, another kind of pipeless furnace—the floor furnace—began to be used. These consisted of a metal box with a burner that was suspended from the floor joists and a grate set into the flooring above. Floor furnaces didn't bother with the cold air return, letting the cold air chips fall where they may, as it were. They were installed in a central location such as the entry hall, the hallway, the dining room, the living room, and sometimes in the archway between the living and dining rooms. There might be more than one unit, and some were installed directly underneath the main wall that runs down the middle of many bungalows, with slanted registers opening to one of the formal rooms on one side and usually the hallway on the other. Most of them operated manually with a pilot light, and a metal key fit a square shank to turn on the gas. There were other natural gas options, including freestanding gas heaters, the various gas heaters that fit into the fireplace, and the extremely nasty rip-it-out-if-you-have-one gas wall heater favored by cheap landlords everywhere. Perhaps I have not yet recovered from the trauma of the badly installed wall heater in the dining room of my first bungalow, right next to the built-in sideboard where you couldn't possibly miss it. Many of these were used to replace floor furnaces, which are considered to be dangerous. More on that later.

The other heating options were steam or hot water heat. Although steam heat had been proposed as early as 1745, it didn't take off until the nineteenth century. It was used primarily in factories and other commercial buildings. Stephen Gold invented the first radiator in the late 1840s, using two

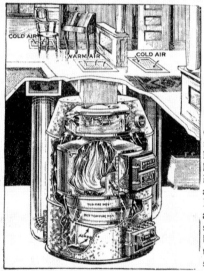

Bovee's Pipeless Furnace used a slightly different method, with cold air returns separate from the hot register. Whether this worked any better is difficult to say.

The Hart and Cooley Adjustable Ventilator allowed heated air to pass from the lower to the upper floor without ductwork, although it mostly allowed dirt and debris from the upper floor to filter down to the room below. Still, it was probably better than no heat at all.

This behemoth boiler once provided heat for "Artemisia," a 10,000-square-foot Arts and Crafts home in Hollywood, California. No longer in use, it is too large to go through the door to the basement.

Electric wall heaters like this one were most commonly installed in bathrooms, which often didn't have heating ducts run to them. Some were installed as a retrofit later on.

The ceramic cylinder in the center of this wall heater is wrapped with coiled copper wire that glows red-hot when the heater is on.

sheets of dimpled iron riveted together at the dimples, which soon became known as the "mattress" radiator. After the Civil War, a number of manufacturers began to produce boilers and radiators, and there were patents aplenty taken out for various steam systems. The first popular cast-iron radiator was introduced in 1874. Some of these radiators were built only for steam or for hot water while some could be used for either. But steam heat never became terribly popular in single-family homes because of fear of explosions, though it came to be used in a great many apartment buildings.

Hot water heat became popular after the 1880s. Perceived as much safer than steam heat, it was also simple and easy to maintain. Most early systems operated on gravity, based on the principle that hot water is lighter than cold water—the heated water rises in the pipes to the radiators, where it gives off its heat, becoming cold water that then falls back down to the boiler to be heated again. Because heated water takes up more space than cold water, these systems had expansion tanks in the attic with a vent to the outside. Each radiator had two pipes—one at the top for the hot water to come in, and one at the bottom for the cold water to get out. The boilers mostly burned coal, and later, natural gas, and occasionally oil.

Because the cast-iron radiators took up a lot of space, they were being replaced by the 1950s with copper-fin baseboard radiators and with radiant heat installed using pipes in the floor or ceiling. Let me digress for a moment. Heat RISES—why on earth would you put it in the ceiling? Radiant heat in floors involved burying the pipes in a con-

A portable hot water radiator was advertised in the October 1915 *Bungalow Magazine.* They used all the buzzwords of the time: "safe," "sanitary," "reasonable in cost," and, most importantly, "artistic." Everything meant for a bungalow had to be "artistic."

crete slab—a fine idea until the pipes corroded and started leaking. Radiant floor heating, now generally known as *hydronic* (although all heat involving hot water is hydronic), is enjoying a resurgence in popularity with the introduction of PEX tubing, made of cross-linked polyethylene that supposedly lasts longer when embedded in a slab. Radiant floor heat can also be retrofitted under wood floors (at least on the first floor; if there's an upper floor, you may have to use radiators there unless you want to rip out all the first-floor ceilings). Hydronic heat of all sorts has always been more expensive to install than hot air, but it does make for very even heat and doesn't introduce dust into the home.

In a few places where electricity was really cheap, electric heat was used, though most of it dates to the 1940s and after. Electric baseboard heaters or electric wall heaters were the usual installation.

Another option now used for heating as well as cooling is the *heat pump*. It works like an air conditioner in reverse. In an air conditioner, the cold coils and fan are placed somewhere inside the house, usually near the furnace, and the cold air is blown through the same ducting used for heat. The hot coils of the air conditioner are placed outside in a unit known as the *condenser*. In a heat pump, there is a valve that switches the direction of the coolant in the coils so that heat can be directed to the inside coils. When it's hot outdoors, the process can be reversed and it goes back to being an air conditioner. Heat pumps are more commonly used in warm climates.

CONTROL FREAK

One would think that everyone would have been so grateful to have central heat that they wouldn't have minded running down to the basement several times a day to add more coal and adjust the various drafts and dampers to control the heat. But that would not be human nature. Shortly after central heat became popular, devices were introduced to control the furnace remotely. Some of these were mechanical—the 1906 publication *Modern Conveniences for the Farm Home* mentioned the following: "An alarm clock with a ratchet or gear arranged to trip a lever and allow the weighted damper to open is often used to turn on the drafts in the early morning." Warren Johnson taught at a school in Wisconsin where the only means of controlling the temperature in the classroom was to call the janitor and send him to the basement to adjust the steam valves. First Johnson developed an *annunciator* system to signal the janitor, and then in 1885, he patented a thermostat that used compressed air to operate the steam valves. In 1905, he patented the *humidostat,* used to control humidity in buildings. Meanwhile, Albert Butz, a partner in the Mendenhall Hand Grenade Fire Extinguisher Company (which manufactured thin glass vials filled with carbon tetrachloride that were designed to burst when thrown into a fire; the carbon tetrachloride

smothered the flames), patented a thermostat-controlled damper in 1886. They were first advertised in 1895 but did not find much favor in the residential market. Efforts continued, and the invention of better electric motors allowed the first electric coal stoker controlled by a thermostat to be placed on the market in 1912. By the 1920s, there were many brands of electric coal stokers. Perhaps you thought night-setback thermostats were a recent thing? Nope, one was produced by the Jewell Thermostat Company in 1905. Today, of course, we have programmable thermostats that can be set to turn the heat on and off at different times of day and different days of the week. This is a fine thing except they are all made of white plastic—not quite right for installing on the glorious wood paneling of your bungalow. Thermostat manufacturers have apparently not gotten on the retro bandwagon, although you can still buy the classic round gold thermostat that's been around for years, but not quite back to the time of the bungalow. About all you can do with the white plastic ones is paint them or put them inside a lovely wooden (ventilated) box.

REGISTER FOR THE DRAFT

Concurrent with the rise of furnace and boiler makers in the mid-nineteenth century, companies that manufactured registers for heating systems began to proliferate as well. By the middle of the century, cast-iron registers in white, black, bronze, and nickel finishes were being produced. The first damper-style register was patented in 1895, and steel registers began to be produced in 1899. As with all things Victorian, they tended to be fancy, with elaborate scrollwork patterns. Although many bungalows have simple registers with a square grid design, there seem to have been a few Victorian holdovers, so some relatively ornate registers still

This polished cast-brass register is seriously ornate for a bungalow, though it makes a nice contrast with the dark wood around it.

showed up in bungalows. Floor, wall, and baseboard (wedge-shaped) registers were all used. There were many sizes, but 8 by 10 inches seems to be quite common. Most were of the damper type, with louvers or a metal plate that could be used to regulate the heat. Ceiling registers, when used, were often rectangular, but round registers made an appearance as well. Steel registers were generally plated and often matched the rest of the hardware in the home.

Cold air returns could have metal registers or be covered with "eggcrate"-design wooden grilles set flush with the floor. Some cold air returns were set into interesting places like stair risers, but were more likely to be in some central part of the house such as the entry hall or dining room. Grates from old pipeless or floor furnaces are often turned into cold air returns when central heat is installed, which keeps one from having to patch the floor.

Cast-iron "column" radiators had become the standard for hot water and steam heating, and, indeed, it was a literal "standard" because the American Radiator Company had bought up most of the competing firms (what? you thought mergers and acquisitions and hostile takeovers were a recent thing?), and in 1929, they merged with the Standard Sanitary Manufacturing Company, which was eventually shortened to American Standard. Cast-iron radiators were modular—the number of columns depended on how big a space had to be heated; thus, a living room radiator is apt to be much longer than a bathroom radiator. They could be tall or short—a shorter one is usually longer to provide the same amount of radiation. Actually, *radiator* is kind of a misnomer since it works primarily by convection. Traditionally radiators were placed under windows when possible, as the cold air coming off the window helped with the convec-

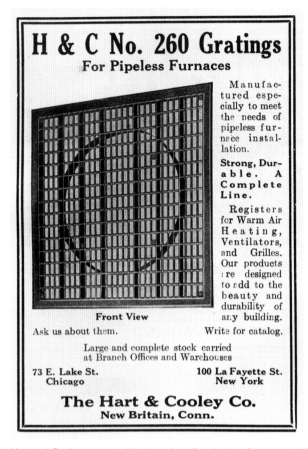

Hart and Cooley presented their gratings for pipeless furnaces in this ad from the August 1918 *American Builder.* The round area in the center is for the hot-air pipe.

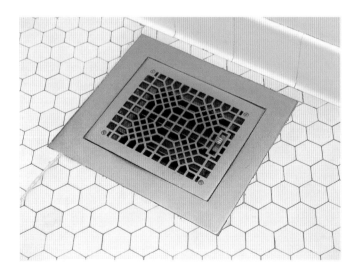

A nickel-plated register set into the hex-tile floor of a bathroom has a simple design that is more customary for bungalows.

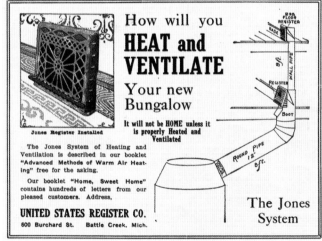

The United States Register Company showed quite a lovely register design in their ad in the October 1915 *Bungalow Magazine,* while insisting "[your bungalow] will not be HOME unless it is properly Heated and Ventilated." (Have you noticed how fond all these companies were of Using Capital Letters?)

tion loop. (The top should stay below the window stool for best results, and the radiator should be 2-1/2 inches from the wall.) But the exigencies of available wall space for the radiators or the limitations on where the pipes could be run meant that some radiators were installed on inside walls as well. This is especially true if the system was a retrofit installed after the house was built. Radiators either sat on the floor (they had legs, allowing enough space for small cats to get underneath—I have photographic proof!) or hung on the wall. The castings can be quite plain or quite elaborate. In the Victorian era, a lot of them were polychromed or bronzed or gilded or otherwise tarted up—it was a conspicuous display of new technology. By the bungalow era, that had died down some, although radiators continued to be painted or bronzed (actually, it's more likely they were "coppered"). It was no longer such a new thing, and some people started to cover them with radiator covers of various sorts. Often they were built into window seats or cabinets.

A wooden cover with a grid pattern disguises a low radiator set under a window. The top panel lifts off for access.

The argument over whether paint on radiators decreases the heat output has been going on for years. A circular called *Painting of Steam and Hot Water Radiators*, put out by the National Bureau of Standards in 1935, addressed the issue. Here's what it had to say:

> We will state at the outset the principal conclusion, which will be explained in more detail later, that *the last coat of paint on a radiator is the only one that has an appreciable effect.* And that a radiator coated with metallic paint will emit less heat, under otherwise identical conditions, than a similar radiator coated with nonmetallic paint. In order to obtain the same amount of heat from the two radiators just considered, the temperature of the one painted with metallic paint must be somewhat higher. Under these conditions, exactly the same amount of heat is being supplied to the two radiators. And since neither the boiler efficiency nor the heat wasted in the pipelines is appreciably affected by small changes in radiator temper- atures, practically the same amount of fuel is required to supply the heat in each case. In other words, while it may be desirable for various reasons to avoid the use of metallic paints on radiators, *no appreciable saving in fuel will result from the use of non-metallic rather than metallic paints* [italics added].

Some more recent information from the Institute of Heating and Ventilating Engineers in Britain shows that if perfect emissivity in a radiator equals 1, then paint brings it down to .95, not a big difference. This affects only radiation, not convection, and radiation only accounts for about a third of the heat output. They added that the texture of the paint (matte rather than glossy) also makes a small difference. In any case, radiator paint needs to be heat-resistant, and it needs to be oil-base because latex will cause rust.

MANY ARE COLD BUT FEW ARE FROZEN

Before air conditioning, keeping cool involved open windows, high ceilings, outdoor porches, lightweight fabrics, and fans (human-powered by self or servants). The fan aspect improved with electric fans, introduced in the late nineteenth century, but it was not until the mid-twentieth century that residential air conditioning even became an option for the middle and lower classes.

Back in 1842, Dr. John Gorrie of Apalachicola, Florida, had become convinced that he could save the lives of his malaria patients if only he could reduce the room temperature in the hospital. He began by rigging up a system to blow air over buckets of ice, but the ice had to be brought by ship from Boston and New York, and delivery schedules were a bit chancy, not to mention the ice was expensive at ten cents a pound. Ice in those days could only be had by cutting it out of frozen lakes in the winter and storing it in icehouses. Gorrie decided there had to be a better way, and, armed with some knowledge of the laws of thermodynamics,

set out to figure a way to cool air by mechanical means. He wrote in the local newspaper in 1848,

If air were highly compressed, it would heat up by the energy of compression. If this compressed air were run through metal pipes cooled with water, and if this air cooled to the water temperature was expanded down to atmospheric pressure again, very low temperature could be obtained, even low enough to freeze water in pans in a refrigerator box. . . . This principle of producing and maintaining cold might be made instrumental in preserving organic matter for an indefinite time and thus becoming an accessory to the extension of commerce [this statement showed a lot of foresight].

Unfortunately, due to ridicule from the very much entrenched ice industry, he was unable to secure financial backing to produce his machine, and so he died broke. Fortunately for us, however, others took his idea and ran

HEATING AND COOLING

OBSESSIVE RESTORATION

It may be a true sign of obsessiveness if you are willing to keep your old and possibly not-very-efficient furnace or boiler just because it's old or you like the way it looks. And it's even more a sign of obsessiveness to live in a hot climate without air conditioning. But I respect this. I like gravity furnaces—they're quiet, the heat is even, and they can be reasonably efficient. And there's the fact that a new furnace is going to set you back a few thousand dollars, not to mention that it's going to be difficult to get that old metal behemoth out of the basement.

Floor furnaces are another matter. They're quite common here in California because it doesn't get very cold, and one or two floor furnaces do a perfectly adequate job of heating a bungalow. The best thing about a floor furnace is that you can straddle it in your bathrobe until it's become a little tent of warm air—a regular heat register just doesn't do that job. But because the grille gets very hot, there is also a danger that it will start a fire if anything flammable is too close, and there is also a chance that someone (often a child) will get burned, not that this doesn't happen to adults; a friend of mine burned his foot by stepping on his floor furnace while stumbling to the bathroom in the middle of the night. Often people with children will build some sort of wall around the floor furnace to keep the kids away, at least until they're old enough to understand the danger. For others, when children appear is the time they change the floor furnace to central heat. Floor furnaces have not been banned entirely, but they are

frowned on in a lot of jurisdictions; so if you want to replace one that isn't working, it may be an uphill battle.

I've never seen a pipeless furnace still in use, but I'm sure there are a few somewhere. All that's left of mine is the grate, now a cold air return for the furnace. They have the same issues as floor furnaces—hot grates, etc. But if you've got one and it's working for you, go ahead and keep it. Which brings us to installing a piped furnace if you didn't have one before. It's fairly easy to run new ducts in a one-story bungalow, a little harder if there's a second floor since you have to figure out some way to get them up there. Most ducting is round, although you can get rectangular ducting that will fit inside a two-by-four wall; but a stud bay will have to be opened in order to run it. Closets can be handy for running ducts, as can clothes chutes, although I'm fond of clothes chutes and don't really like using them for this purpose. There are now furnaces that can hang from the floor joists in a crawl space, provided there's enough room, and furnaces that can be installed in the attic if the crawl space isn't big enough. (But don't let them talk you into putting the registers in the ceiling; make them run a chase from the attic down to the basement so the registers can be in the floor or wall as they ought to be.) Both salvage and reproduction registers are readily available, so you won't have to use modern-looking ones.

Hot water and steam heat have a lot of technical issues that are too complex to go into here, but it's entirely possible to get a new boiler and keep the existing radiators. I refer you to Dan Holohan's fine books on the subject of with it, and it is the basis for all forms of mechanical refrigeration that we use today, which is why I am now able to cease writing for a moment and run down to the refrigerator to get a nice cold soda.

In 1902, a young engineer named Willis Carrier was waiting for a train in the fog. While contemplating the fog, he experienced some sort of "engineering satori" concerning the relationship between temperature, humidity, and dew point. Shortly after that, he designed his first air-conditioning system for a printing company in Brooklyn, New York, and took out a patent in 1906 for his first device, "An Apparatus for Treating Air." In 1915, he banded together with some friends and formed his own company. Most of the early air-conditioning systems were installed in factories, businesses, retail stores, and movie theaters. In the late 1920s, Carrier began developing smaller air conditioners for smaller businesses, and it was a short step from there to residential systems introduced in 1928. One problem with these air-conditioning units was that they sucked a lot of electricity, and the average bungalow usually had a 30-amp

service with only a couple of circuits, so you had to upgrade the electrical service to even have one. Besides the central units, there were window or console units that could cool one room. Initially these resembled refrigerators, but, as most of them were bought by rich people, pretty soon the companies started tarting them up and wood-graining them to look like radios. Unfortunately, the Depression and then the demands of World War II stopped residential air conditioning in its tracks, but after the war, demand began to pick up again. Today, the majority of homes in hot climates have either room or central air conditioning.

PIPE DOWN

Indoor plumbing is the very basis of modern civilization and is the one aspect of it that few of us would be willing to give up. Conveniently, not much has changed in the DWV (drain-waste-vent) and water supply pipes since the late nineteenth century, except for the introduction of plastic piping, a few design modifications, and new code requirements.

hydronic heat. Salvaged cast-iron radiators are perfectly usable, and they're one of the very few things you're allowed to sandblast in order to remove paint. Reproductions of old-style cast-iron radiators are also available because no obsessive person would even consider modern radiators. It's also possible to retrofit radiant floor heating under existing wood floors, and if you have to retile the bathroom floor, there are electric mats that can be installed under the tile to heat the floor.

Central air conditioning is easy to install if ducts are already in place. If there aren't, the choices are these: install conventional ducts, install high-velocity mini-ducts, or use wall- or window-mounted air conditioners. All of these choices suck in one way or another. Installing

conventional ducts is easy enough in a one-story bungalow, but running them to the second floor involves taking out walls, going through closets, building chases, etc. Window air conditioners are just plain ugly. Wall-mounted "mini-splits" or "ductless" systems have units mounted high on the wall or in the ceiling, and they suffer from the same "white plastic" syndrome as thermostats. The small outlets of the high-velocity systems, though touted as unobtrusive, I personally find to be MORE obtrusive than a conventional register because they DID have conventional registers back then, but they did not have little round plastic outlets. But then it's weird to have radiators AND registers. So this is one of those questions that has no easy answer.

COMPROMISE SOLUTION
Given the current prices for natural gas, oil, and electricity, one could hardly be blamed for wanting to put in the most efficient heating and cooling system possible. Each system has pros and cons—hydronic heating (in floor or radiators) has a higher initial cost and is somewhat slow to heat up after it's been off for a while, but it gives a lovely even heat and your pets will thank you. And if you put it in under the floors, you'll be able to walk around in your socks in the middle of winter. But if you also want air conditioning, there will be no ducts. Forced air has a lower up-front cost, furnaces are avail-

able that are up to 90 percent efficient, and it's easy to put in central air at the same time. But if there hasn't been central heat previously, you will have to find places (if any) to run the ducts to the upper floor. It's easy to replace an existing gravity furnace with a new forced-air furnace and new smaller ducts. As mentioned earlier, there are furnaces that can be hung in crawl spaces or installed in attics.

If there's no choice but to have window air conditioners, they are somewhat less obtrusive if installed in a wall instead, and try to at least keep them off the front façade of the house.

Water enters the house either from a public water main or a source on the property. City water is usually delivered through a meter and a main shutoff valve. The meter may be in the basement or crawlspace or outdoors near the property line. If it is outdoors, a buried pipe usually runs from there to the house. Sometimes there is a main shutoff valve near where the line enters the house or near the meter; sometimes the shutoff valve is at the meter itself. After entering the house, the main supply line splits in two, one remaining cold and going to the cold water outlets, the other going off to the water heater and thence to the various hot water outlets.

The DWV pipes use gravity to channel wastewater and solid wastes to the main house drain, which connects to the sewer line or septic tank (thus the plumbers' adage: "S—t flows downhill"). The vent pipes disperse the sewer gas into the atmosphere and maintain air pressure in drainpipes and fixture traps (traps are curved sections in the drainpipes that remain water-filled to prevent gases from coming up through the drains). Every house has a main soil stack (usually in the vicinity of a toilet, since toilets require the biggest drainpipes), which serves as the primary drainpipe below the level of the fixtures, and as a vent above the fixtures. Drainpipes from other fixtures and branch drains from other bathrooms connect to the main stack. A second bathroom on a branch drain away from the main stack will have a secondary vent stack of its own. Often the main soil stack is found inside a deeper-than-normal wall (two-by-fours wouldn't accommodate it) or in a specially built chase (a diagonal corner in a bathroom or a recess into an adjoining closet); however, in a house that's seen a lot of remodeling, particularly if bathrooms were added, the soil stack may be running up an outside wall, and in warm climates this was sometimes done when the house was originally built.

Pipes of extruded lead, first used about 1850, had drawbacks, including heaviness and a tendency to sag, causing leaks (at the time, there was no knowledge of the dangers of lead poisoning). Later in the nineteenth century, cast iron, galvanized iron, copper, and brass replaced lead except in certain applications. It is still possible to remove an old toilet and find a lead "closet bend" leading to the drainpipe. All these (except lead) materials are still in use. Recently, plastic piping, either PVC (polyvinyl chloride—the white stuff) or ABS (acrylonitrile butadiene styrene—the black stuff) has been added to the list, as well as flexible plastic tubing (PEX), which is used extensively in Europe but has yet to find wide acceptance in the United States. Cast iron was used for drain/waste/vent piping in most bungalows because that's pretty much all they used at the time, although lead pipes were still being sold.

Copper supply pipes are still the highest quality and also the most expensive pipes one can have. The soldered joints (solder is metal that melts at a fairly low temperature and flows into the spaces between the pipe and the fitting,

making it watertight) require more skill to put together, and the copper itself is expensive. But copper pipes don't corrode like galvanized metal and therefore last a very long time. The industry is working on fittings for copper that don't require soldering, but change comes very slowly when you are dealing with plumbing. It is usually a good idea (and easy) to replace galvanized pipes if the wall is open for some other reason. If pipes are being replaced, it is worthwhile to use copper; however, where copper joins with existing galvanized pipes, be sure to use a *dielectric fitting*, which separates the two different kinds of metal to prevent galvanic corrosion (a wild orgy of molecular exchange between dissimilar metals).

In most early-twentieth-century houses, supply pipes are likely to be galvanized steel. Rather than solder, galvanized pipes are threaded and they use threaded fittings. Watertightness is enhanced through the use of "pipe dope" on the threads (or these days, Teflon tape). Galvanized pipe has gotten a bad name because, after seventy or eighty years, interior corrosion tends to restrict water flow, reducing water pressure; eventually, corrosion will make it all the way through the pipe wall, causing leaks. (The iron in galvanized pipes is also responsible for the pinkish residue that builds up on the walls of bathrooms that are not well ventilated; after the water evaporates, small amounts of iron remain.) Hot water pipes tend to corrode more, and horizontal runs of pipe collect more crud than vertical runs. This does not necessarily mean that all the pipes need replacement. Sometimes replacing only the hot water pipes will work wonders to restore water pressure.

Non-galvanized steel, or "black iron" pipe, was used for natural gas lines in the house, running from the gas meter to the water heater, stove, furnace, and, later, the gas dryer. More recently, the introduction of corrugated stainless steel tubing (CSST), which is flexible, can be run like electrical wiring, and requires fewer fittings, has begun to be used for gas lines, at least in new construction. It can only be run by plumbers that have been trained in its use, whereas black iron pipe and fittings are available at hardware stores nationwide.

Plastic pipe is a more recent development. Either PVC (white) or ABS (black) is commonly used (there seem to be regional differences). Plastic pipe joints and fittings are glued, making it easier to work with than copper. It is not as rigid as metal pipe and tends to sag in horizontal runs if not supported. In some localities, plastic pipe is not allowed by code, while in others, it is required. PVC can only be used for cold water lines (thus its use in automatic sprinkler systems).

Let me digress into the Vinyl Rant. Vinyl (polyvinyl chloride or PVC) emits toxic compounds during its entire lifecycle, from manufacture to use to disposal. Dioxins are the number-one risk from PVC production and disposal. Dioxin is one of the most toxic chemicals ever produced and causes cancer in smaller doses than any other chemical. The U.S. Environmental Protection Agency suggests that there is no safe level of dioxin exposure. In addition, PVC manufacturing plants release thousands of pounds of other carcinogenic chemicals into the environment every year, including ethylene dichloride and vinyl chloride. Dioxins also have impacts on the endocrine, reproductive, and immune systems.

PVC requires either *plasticizers* or *stabilizers* to be functional. Plasticizers are used to make the vinyl flexible for use in flooring, shower curtains, and the like. The most common stabilizers are called *pthalates*. Stabilizers are used to slow deterioration of the PVC from heat or sunlight, and include lead, cadmium, and organotins, which are potentially toxic heavy metals.

Pthalates are released into the air over time and can also be absorbed through the skin. Asthma has been linked to the pthalates released by vinyl flooring. Pthalates have also been implicated in birth defects.

Lead dust is released from PVC products as they deteriorate in sunlight. Organotins, which cause immune system damage, can leach out of PVC pipes into the drinking water.

Vinyl chloride is also a known carcinogen. One of the largest exposures to vinyl chloride for most people is the "new car smell" that is produced by offgassing PVC dashboards, door panels, seats, and other parts.

As more and more PVC is used in building products, a new hazard has arisen. When PVC burns, it produces hydrogen chloride and dioxin. Hydrogen chloride is lethal when inhaled, and people in burning buildings are often killed by toxic fumes before the flames reach them. (This is what the newscasters are talking about when they say someone died of "smoke inhalation.") Burning vinyl-sided buildings will also release these toxic compounds into the surrounding neighborhood.

At the end of its useful life, PVC is the least recyclable of all plastics, the many different additives making recycling impractical and expensive. PVC can also contaminate the recycling of other plastics: One PVC bottle can contaminate a batch of 50,000 PET bottles and render them unrecyclable. There is no safe disposal method for vinyl. If buried in a landfill, it will leach toxic chemicals into the groundwater, and if burned it releases dioxins, heavy metals, and other chlorine compounds that contaminate the air, water, and land.

PVC is also unavoidable. Here is a partial list of products that contain PVC: vinyl siding, gutters and drainpipes, water supply pipes, sewage pipes, drainage pipes, electrical conduit pipes; electrical wiring (Romex, insulation on metallic-sheathed cable wires), telephone wiring, data cables, and cable sheathing for video, TV, and stereo; vinyl doors and windows; large appliances (PVC shelving, cables, door gaskets); lamp and extension cords, lampshades; computer, fax, and printer casings and cables; vinyl flooring; carpets and mats (vinyl backing); furniture (imitation leather and other parts); miniblinds and shower curtains; food packaging and cling film; tablecloths, placemats, and aprons; shoes and boots; luggage; raincoats and patent vinyl clothing; toys, baby furniture, bibs, and diaper covers; garden hoses, garden furniture, tarpaulins, pool toys, and inflatable/noninflatable pools; cars (dashboards and door panels, upholstery, etc.); packing tape, ring binders, clipboards, organizers, and writing pads; medical items (IV bags, catheters, etc.); and LP records (they don't call it "vinyl" for nothing).

So you probably don't want any more of it in your house than you already have. End of rant.

DRAIN OF TERROR

I know, I already used that pun in *Bungalow Bathrooms*, but it's so bad I thought I'd use it again. The water coming in through the supply pipes also needs an escape route once it has served its purpose, and the DWV (drain-waste-vent) system allows the used water and other waste to make their way to the sewer or septic tank while maintaining air pressure in the system, preventing the contamination of clean water with used water and guarding against sewer gas by venting it through the roof. The subject of much experimentation in the nineteenth century, the DWV system hasn't changed much since then. In the early twentieth century, visible drainpipes were usually nickel- or chrome-plated brass or copper; once inside the wall, cast-iron drainpipes were generally the rule, though some of the smaller vent or drainpipes may be copper or brass. Cast-iron joints came together with "hub" or "bell and spigot" fittings joined with molten lead and oakum (hemp or jute impregnated with asphalt). Nowadays, this method has been replaced by neoprene gaskets held by adjustable stainless-steel clamps.

IN HOT WATER

All of this plumbing would not have become nearly as popular without the invention of easier ways to get hot water to the tubs, sinks, and showers. Indeed, hot and cold running water and indoor toilets are pretty much the hallmark of Western civilization. For centuries, if you wanted hot water it had to be heated in the fire or on the stove (introduced in the 1820s). Some of the early water-heating products were scary: a sheet-metal bathtub with an open-flame gas burner underneath, or heaters attached to one end of the tub with no flue to carry off the combustion gases. Eventually hot water tanks or boilers attached to the stove became the most common way to heat water. This method continued well into the twentieth century. Another method is what we would now call an instantaneous water heater, which uses gas burners to heat the water as it flows through a coiled pipe. Known as "geysers" in Britain, the first of these was

This, my friends, is the largest instantaneous water heater that was manufactured by Ruud, made for commercial buildings, schools, and in this case, a really large Arts and Crafts home in Hollywood, California. Made of cast iron with gilded Art Nouveau decoration, it stands about 5 feet high and is about 18 inches in diameter, whereas the typical Ruud water heater was about 3 feet high and a foot in diameter.

invented in 1868 by Benjamin Maughan. Lacking important safety features such as a pilot light or a thermostat, it had a tendency to blow up, but these flaws were eventually corrected. This kind of water heater continues to be more common in Europe than in the United States. Edwin Ruud invented the first automatic storage water heater in 1889. In 1894, Herbert S. Humphrey invented a wall-mounted instantaneous water heater, and began the Humphrey Water Heater Company in 1899. Ruud's company bought him out in 1913 and continued manufacturing the instantaneous heaters for several more decades. Many of them were quite beautiful with Art Nouveau casting and nickel trim, and many are still in use. If you have an old one that's still working, you should keep it—they are works of art. But Ruud also manufactured the automatic storage heater, which for some reason became more popular. These have been likened to leaving your car running all the time in case you might want to go somewhere. Instantaneous heaters are becoming more popular currently because they take up less space and save energy. They also have draw-backs; although they produce an endless supply of hot water, it's an all-or-nothing proposition; a trickle of hot water is not possible. The invention of the temperature and pressure release valve in the late 1930s eliminated the danger of water heater explosions and made them safer for home use. Most water heaters were installed in the kitchen next to the stove, but by now many of them have been moved to the basement or the utility porch.

The exhibit of the Pittsburg Water Heater Company is only one of 200 *permanent* exhibits maintained the year around at the vast Building Material Exhibit in Chicago.

Ah, the family gathers round to admire their Pittsburg water heater—Father with his pipe, Grandfather with his cane, Mother with Little Brother clinging to her skirts, and Sis wearing a rather daring and fashionable bicycling outfit. No doubt Mother is thinking, "These teenagers today have no sense of decency! Going out in public half-naked! What ever shall I do with her?"

CURRENT EVENTS

By the time bungalows were being built, most city and sub-urban dwellers had access to electricity. Rural areas lagged behind, partly because the power companies were reluctant to build lines out to isolated farms; many rural areas were not electrified till the 1930s or after.

Nonetheless, the large majority of bungalows were built with electricity. The power line came in from the utility pole to a weatherhead atop a pole called the mast. This came through the roof either into a wall or on the outside of the house and down to the electric meter. There was often a main shutoff at the meter. Sometimes the fusebox was next to the meter in a recessed box on the side of the house (a box that was often lined with asbestos sheet). Or the fuse-box could be located in the basement, service porch, closet, or some other location inside the house. There might also be sub-panels within the house that also contained fuses. The fuses themselves screwed into porcelain sockets. Early on,

Hot Water Like Cold Water

ready in abundance at a mere turn of a faucet—as much or as little as wanted, at any time, for any pur-pose—and cheaply heated by gas, the economical fuel, is the service provided by a

HUMPHREY

Automatic Gas Water Heater

Simple—Durable

Fit the health, time and fuel conservation needs of today—*Guaranteed.*

Made by

HUMPHREY COMPANY
Div. of Ruud Mfg. Co.

KALAMAZOO, MICH., U. S. A.

Ruud must have continued to manufacture instantaneous heaters under the Humphrey name as well as their own, since this ad appeared in the August 1918 *American Builder*. The ad stated that the heater "Fit the health, time, and fuel conservation needs of today—Guaranteed." That would be true of instantaneous heaters today as well.

the amount of power available (called the size of the service) was 30 amps at 120 volts, and there were only two to four circuits. The circuits were protected from overloading by 15- or 20-amp fuses. Fuses work by melting a "fusible link" when too much current flows; a solder-like wire inside the fuse heats up and melts, cutting off power to the circuit. Starting in the 1930s, circuit breakers began to replace fuses, and service increased to 60 amps. At this point, breakers (or fuses) of more than 20 amps were used to protect circuits other than lights and plugs, like built-in wall heaters. A circuit breaker is essentially a switch that senses when there is too much current and then opens to interrupt the circuit. The minimum service installed today is 100 amps, and many new houses have 200-amp services.

From the fusebox, wiring ran to the various outlets and fixtures on separate wires. This is called *knob-and-tube* wiring because the wires were supported by porcelain knobs to hold them away from the framing members as well as porcelain tubes wherever they pierced the framing members.

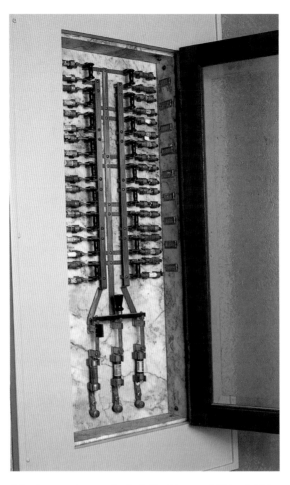

A fusebox can be a work of art, like this one at "Artemisia" in Hollywood, California. Lined in marble for fire protection (asbestos was a more common lining), cartridge fuses are lined up in copper mounts and each circuit is labeled with a small brass plate at the side.

In a knob-and-tube system, the hot wire (the one that carries the current to the various outlets) and the neutral wire (the one that returns the current to the fusebox, completing the circuit) ran separately, typically parallel (about 12 to 18 inches apart), only coming together to be connected to the outlet or fixture. Where wires ran from the last knob to the fixture or outlet, a heavy woven cotton tubing impregnated with tar, called *loom,* was slipped over each wire to offer protection from damage. Wire splices in a knob-and-tube system are soldered and wrapped first with rubber and then with friction tape. (There should be a knob on each side of the connection.) Splices were made in the open; no junction boxes were used. This was okay when the wiring was installed, and is still fine for these original splices because of the solid way they were made. Any subsequent or new splice has to be made in a junction box. Connections to the fixture wires were made with porcelain wire nuts.

With modern wiring (generally post World War II), all connections are made with wire nuts inside of an electrical box, but in knob-and-tube systems, often only the outlets (plugs) had boxes, the lighting wires often emerging directly from a stud or ceiling joist without a box. The boxes were primarily metal, although Bakelite boxes began to be used after the invention of Bakelite in 1910. Unlike today, there weren't a zillion electricity-sucking appliances connected to the system, only a few lights and plugs and the occasional electric appliance like an electric iron or a toaster. In many homes, it was necessary to unscrew the light-bulb from the fixture socket in order to screw in a plug so it could be used to plug something in. On an average, each room had only a couple of lights and a couple of plugs.

Loomex, the predecessor of today's nonmetallic sheathed cable (generically called Romex, though that is a trade name) became available in the late 1920s. Originally consisting of two wires in an asphalt-impregnated cotton jacket, it was later changed to include a ground wire, and the sheathing was changed to plastic in the 1970s. Armored cable, generally called BX (another trade name), though properly called AC, was invented about 1900 by Harry Greenfield and Gus Johnson. It had an insulation of rubber and braided cotton covering the wires, surrounded by a spiral steel armor. It had begun to gain acceptance by 1910 and came into widespread usage by the 1920s and 1930s. Knob-and-tube began to be phased out in the 1940s as being too labor intensive.

In some areas, metallic conduit was installed and loose wires run through it. This conduit could be *heavywall* (similar to galvanized-iron water pipe) or *thinwall* (also known as *EMT*—electrical metallic tubing). Houses wired using conduit are easy to rewire—pull out the old wire and pull in the new—but can be harder to modify, especially if they have heavywall conduit.

As more electrical appliances came into being, the few circuits began to get overloaded. People tired of replacing blown fuses began to replace the fuses with oversize fuses to keep that from happening, or they used pennies or metal slugs to bypass the fuse entirely. This led to damaged wiring and electrical fires. To prevent this, fuses can be replaced with *Type-S fuses,* which are tamper-proof and cannot be replaced with a larger-size fuse. Even if there are circuit breakers, fuses were often used to provide additional protection for motors like those for furnace fans and pumps.

The insulation on knob-and-tube or nonmetallic cable can be damaged, whether by overheating, age, or chewing by rodents (which is why I like to run BX cable for everything). This increases the risk of fire and electrical shock.

Low-voltage wiring was also run in many bungalows, mainly for doorbells, phone lines, and thermostats. These days, low-voltage wiring also includes wiring for burglar alarms, smoke detectors, computer networks, stereo speakers, television, and so on. A doorbell circuit requires a transformer to convert the "line voltage" electricity from the power company to the 16 to 24 volts used by the doorbell, buzzer, or chime. The bell transformer was usually installed in the attic, basement, or closet. Sometimes the transformer was built into the fusebox.

Since radio was the main form of entertainment at the time, some bungalows had special outlets for plugging in the radio antenna. These were sometimes separate or were combined with a regular electrical outlet. They connected either to an antenna on the roof or to a wire strung between insulators in the attic, basement, or crawl space.

Many modern light-fixture instructions make reference to 60- or 90-degree wiring; what this refers to is the temperature rating of the insulation on the wire in degrees Celsius (60 degrees C = 140 degrees F; 90 degrees C = 194 degrees F). Nonmetallic cable rated 90 degrees C is labeled NM-B, and 60 degrees is called NM. Why does this matter? Because incandescent lightbulbs get very hot and could possibly melt the insulation on the wiring—that's why most modern fixtures have fiberglass insulation between the canopy and the wall or ceiling.

OUTLET MALL

Very early receptacles had sockets that took the threaded Edison bases still found on lightbulbs, and the electrical cords that fit these had the bases on the end instead of the prongs we are used to. These were way too easy to stick your finger into, causing shock, so they were replaced by slotted outlets. The Edison receptacles in old systems had only one outlet instead of the two that are standard now, although there were two outlet receptacles as well. Initially they were made of porcelain. After 1910, the receptacles were also made of Bakelite, which only came in dark brown. Outlets could also be installed in the floor. These outlets had two equal slots for plugs, unlike modern polarized or grounding (three-hole) outlets. Grounding outlets were introduced in the 1950s but didn't become universal until the 1970s. Ground Fault Circuit Interrupter (GFCI) outlets were intro-

duced in 1971. They are now required in kitchens, bathrooms, laundry rooms, garages, and outdoors—anywhere there is electricity and water in the same place. Arc Fault Circuit Interrupters (AFCI), which protect against certain kinds of arcing caused by loose connections, are now required in bedrooms; these are only available as a breaker to be installed in the panel, not as individual outlets.

SWITCHED AT BIRTH

In the infancy of residential electricity, lights had to be turned on and off at the fixture, either with a "key" or knob at the socket or with a pull string. That's why they hung lower than fixtures do now—so you could reach them. Around the turn of the century, push-button switches came into use; these had porcelain bodies with screws for attaching wires on the front and were housed in steel boxes. Why

In my view, there should never be more than two light switches together; after that it becomes confusing. But here there are nine, mounted vertically. It's also more difficult to tell if a horizontally oriented light switch is on or off, so these have been provided with helpful red lights that are illuminated when the switch is on. Labels below each switch help make sense of which ones are which.

Luminous Electric Light Buttons

Hunting for an electric light button or pendant in a dark room is an exasperating job. Consequently luminous pendants and buttons have a strong appeal to the house owner. Herewith are illustrated a pendant and a button that can readily be located in the dark. And strange as it may seem, considering the enormous cost of this material, they are made with radium—not of, but with radium. The process of producing this material is exceptionally complicated, but it suffices to say that the particles of radium used in the manufacture are infinitesimally small. The luminous material with which the buttons and pendants are treated, however, is declared to retain its luminescence permanently.

Find It in the Dark.

porcelain bodies and steel boxes? Take the switch plate off one sometime and watch the spark that happens when you push the button—don't want that happening inside the wall! Inside the box, the actual switch mechanism was made of brass. Push-button switches were made of hard rubber or Bakelite with mother-of-pearl inlay on the top button. Three-way switches were also made, allowing one to turn off the lights from either end of a hall or from the top or bottom of the stairs. Starting around the 1920s,

Left: Radium (discovered in 1898) could be used to coat buttons for light switches and pulls for pendant lights so one could find them in the dark. I don't think it caught on; most buttons were simply inlaid with mother-of-pearl.

Facing: Yup, it's a really early dimmer switch, written up in the February 1919 *American Builder.* I assume one chain was longer than the other was so one could tell them apart.

ELECTRICAL

OBSESSIVE RESTORATION

Knob-and-tube wiring is safe if the insulation is intact, the circuits aren't overloaded or overfused, and no one has made any funky modifications. Unfortunately, the K&T has often been tapped into in various ways with splices not in junction boxes, inappropriate-size wires, and so forth. Sometimes people just cut off live wires without bothering to disconnect them—I can't tell you how many live wires I've found hanging inside walls, buried in plaster, or under Sheetrock. Or the lack of outlets has caused people to use taps and extension cords to increase the number in any one receptacle, overloading the circuit, or two-prong ungrounded outlets have been replaced with three-prong outlets without bothering to ground them. It used to be you could run a ground wire from the outlet to the nearest water pipe, but now it has to be run all the way back to the panel, at which point you might just as well run new wire. Or you could put in a two-prong outlet; they are safe as long as you only plug two-prong things into them and you don't use adapters to make grounded plugs work in them. (A brown two-prong receptacle is hard to find—apparently the manufacturers think everything is white or ivory now.) All of these things can be dealt with—fuses can be replaced with Type-S fuses to prevent overfusing, small areas of deteriorated wiring can be repaired (heat shrinkable tubing works wonders), new circuits can be run or outlets added, the panel can be upgraded from fuses to circuit breakers with a larger service—and adding circuits will take some of the load off the existing K&T. Of course, if you get a larger service, you may have to argue with the utility company,

which generally has lots of rules about where the meter can be and how high it has to be, and they're pretty unlikely to let you put it back in the recessed box where the old one was. Just don't let them make you put it on the front façade.

And you could do all these things, which are all a good idea if you are going to keep the existing K&T, and it will all be for naught. Why? Because your insurance company doesn't care. As far as they are concerned, knob-and-tube wiring is unsafe and no amount of proof from people who know better will convince them otherwise. (As mentioned earlier, a study in California found that over a ten-year period not a single electrical fire was caused by knob-and-tube wiring.) If you already have a policy, you will be lucky if they renew it. If you sell your house, even though you have a policy, it will be a miracle if the buyers are able to get one. If you just bought the house and are trying to get a policy—good luck. If you do manage to get one, it will be expensive. And if you decide to rewire the house to modern code, better do it with a permit because they will want you to prove it.

It is generally a good idea to rewire things if you have walls open and can do so. It's also a good idea to run any other wiring you might care to run at the same time, including phone, data, alarm, doorbell, etc. And an even better idea is to install a piece of 1-inch thinwall steel conduit or Schedule 40 PVC conduit (but you know how I feel about PVC) to be used as a chase later in case you decide to run some other wiring between floors. (You might want to cap it off at both ends to keep vermin out.) As I mentioned earlier, I like to rewire using armored

Saving Electric Current

There is a neat little device that will appeal to the thrifty housewife. It is a device that will allow her to save electric current, and still have a light in the room. This is a socket with a chain attached, a pull of which will dim the light. This not only saves current, but ofttimes provides just the illumination necessary, as, for instance, in the children's sleeping room, or in the bath room, or the sick room. It has only been within the last few years that these fixtures have been inexpensive enough to become in general use, altho Edison discovered the principle a long time ago.

Electric Fixture Shuts Off Most of the Light and Saves Current.

these began to be supplemented or replaced by Bakelite toggle switches similar to the ones still in use today. Switches were generally mounted on the wall near a door; sometimes they were cut into the door casing. Predating the push-button switch, there were also surface-mounted switches with knobs that turned clockwise; these were usually about 2 inches in diameter.

RUN FOR COVER

Cover plates for the early outlets and switches were either cast or stamped brass. It could be plated with nickel for kitchens and bathrooms. Later on, plates made from Bakelite and other plastics were also used, though switches in the formal rooms continued to have brass plates.

cable because rodents can't chew it, but possibly I'm more paranoid than most people are. The code actually dictates where you can run nonmetallic cable and what kind. If the walls aren't open, then the wires will have to be "fished." Fishing is tedious, and you won't find many electricians willing to do it, or many that are willing to do it with minimal damage to the finished surfaces of the house. Actually, you might not want to be paying their hourly rate to have them do it with minimal collateral damage. I guarantee that the wall you need to fish the wire through will have fallen plaster keys, diagonal blocking in a really inconvenient place, and many other hindrances. Thus, fishing wires is the perfect job for homeowners (actually two people make it somewhat easier)—you can do the tedious part and pay the electrician to do the hookups. Make sure the electrician is willing to do this since the electrician will be responsible for all the wiring, whether they ran it or not. Nonetheless, it is likely that much plaster patching will be necessary afterward, especially if you had to go across the studs or the joists. Let me just mention right here that one of the finest tools for cutting holes in lath and plaster is a mini-router or a spiral saw (one popular brand is Rotozip), or

if you have more money to spend, the Fein Multimaster.

However, even if you have to rewire, you will still be able to have push-button light switches, which are being reproduced with mother-of-pearl inlay (although now it's faux). Some are even UL listed. They don't make the really satisfying "thunk" that the old ones do (more of a soft "click"), but they also don't put out sparks.

Old outlets were usually installed sideways in baseboards. Modern outlets are often installed vertically in the wall instead. GFCIs are the most obtrusive, but you can get around that by putting a GFCI breaker on the circuit, allowing the use of regular outlets. You can also install a GFCI in an out-of-the-way location, hook some cable to the "load" terminals on the GFCI, and then run cable from there to the outlet to be protected. If you have to put in a GFCI outlet, there are some available with the TEST/RESET buttons the same color as the outlet, which are somewhat more subtle than the red and black buttons on most of them. GFCI outlets usually won't fit in the smaller boxes used for old wiring—you can either put in a junction box to splice into the old wiring and then run a new piece of cable to the outlet, or replace the existing box with a larger "old work" box.

COMPROMISE SOLUTION

Rewiring your house to modern code and upgrading the service to 200 amps is probably a good idea, and it will do wonders for your insurance rates. You can put in switched plugs to turn on lamps or put your computer on a dedicated circuit. You can still use the reproduction push-but-

ton switches—they even make a dimmer switch. If you prefer, you can use toggle switches instead, especially for a bungalow built in the 1920s. I draw the line at modern switches, though—no "decora" switches, no sliding dimmers, and no "motion-detector" switches (although I could see these being useful in the basement or the attic).

TIMELINE OF ELECTRICAL WIRING TECHNOLOGY

Earliest: 30-amp, 120-volt service. Electric meter, main disconnect, a knife switch in a box (earliest: wood, sometimes with asbestos lining; later: steel box). Three or four fuses, either in exposed blocks or a fusebox, supplying two to four circuits. Early on, the neutral was fused! Each room had a pendant, keyed lamp socket. That's it! No wall switches, no receptacle outlets! Either knob-and-tube wiring (with no junction boxes for pendant fixtures) or steel conduit with tiny junction boxes.

Next: Receptacle outlets added, one or two per room. At first, Edison style; later, twin-blade nonpolarized. Surface-mounted light fixtures, with a wall switch (turn button or push button).

1910s and 1920s: Armored cable (BX) used instead of K&T in more expensive houses or in areas that required it (for greater fire safety). Steel boxes used for devices and as junction boxes in BX or conduit systems.

Late 1920s to early 1930s: 60-amp, 120-volt services. Toggle switches and flat-bladed receptacles. No more fused neutrals.

Late 1930s to mid-1940s: 60-amp, 120- and 240-volt services. K&T still commonly used, although thin-wall steel conduit (EMT) or heavywall steel conduit was used in more expensive homes or in very strong union towns (EMT is still required in Chicago!).

Post–World War II to mid 1950s: K&T rare, BX common. Toggle switches displace push buttons. Nylon replaces porcelain and Bakelite for switches and receptacles. Fuseboxes still very commonly installed. Loomex nonmetallic cable begins to be used.

Late 1950s to mid-1960s: Service size 100 amps, 120 and 240 volts is state of the art. Loomex common, some with small ground wire (18 gauge). Bakelite or fiberglass boxes used for devices and as junction boxes. Circuit breakers becoming common. Polarized receptacles appear.

Late 1960s to early 1970s: Services of 150 amps, 120 and 240 volts serve "modern all electric" homes. Circuit breakers common. GFI receptacles first required. Plastic insulation on conductors of Loomex cable, and then modern NM cable (with plastic sheath as well). Full-sized grounding wire in NM. PVC boxes common.

These dates can vary by 10 to 20 years or more, depending on the cost of the house and local requirements.

(Because I don't really understand electricity and basically think it's a form of magic, I want to thank Cliff Popejoy of Apex Electrical in Sacramento for most of this very fine information.)

SMOKE ALARMS

Smoke detectors and carbon monoxide detectors could very well save your life, and smoke alarms are required. In some jurisdictions, smoke alarms have to be hard-wired, especially in new construction, while in others, battery-operated models are okay. They are required in bedrooms, outside sleeping areas, in basements, and there should be at least one on each level of the house. That's all swell except for one thing: all smoke alarms are made of white plastic! And unlike white plastic thermostats, which can be disguised in a lovely wooden box, a smoke alarm has to have air circulation around it, and it has to be placed on or near the ceiling. And everywhere you turn there are warnings not to paint them, although one suspects that may be manufacturers covering themselves in case some idiot paints one in a way that clogs all the holes and then subsequently dies in a fire, and then the idiot's family sues the manufacturer for not making it perfectly clear that smoke alarms shouldn't be painted. Thus, I would say that if you choose to paint one, it will have to be entirely at your own risk.

There is, however, absolutely no reason that they have to be made of white plastic except that it's easier, and apparently the manufacturers have some belief that all ceilings are white. I think there is a niche market just waiting to be exploited—manufacturing colored smoke detectors. In the meantime, buy the smallest and least obtrusive ones you can find.

SECURITY COUNSEL

Was it safer in the early twentieth century? Nostalgia makes it seem so. Publications of the time showed stereotypical masked burglars in ads for locks or tamper-proof coal-chute doors, but no one seemed concerned about windows being smashed or doors kicked in, let alone drive-by shootings. (Well, except for gangsters in Chicago.) Still, the abandonment of inner cities and inner-ring suburbs as the twentieth century advanced means that some bungalow neighborhoods are, shall we say, a "security challenge." Nonetheless, I don't think that is any excuse for putting yourself and your family behind bars instead of the criminals.

Certainly it's a good idea to have modern deadbolts on the doors, and vulnerable door or window glass can be replaced with laminated glass. Motion-detector lights are a fine idea, and having a dog (if you like dogs) is an excellent deterrent. Work with your neighbors to set up a neighborhood watch if possible; it's far better for neighbors to watch out for each other than to hole up in their houses behind bars and security doors and razor wire.

And don't even start with me about how dangerous your neighborhood is. I'm from Oakland—we're the poster child for bad neighborhoods.

MODERN TECHNOLOGY

One of those kinds of discussions that only Arts and Crafts people ever have is "What would Stickley do with a computer?" And there seems to be two camps: the "Oh, he'd just stick it out on a library table" camp and the "No, he would have designed a special piece of furniture for it" camp.

In no way am I saying there's a right answer to the question, but in many ways the struggle to have both technology AND art IS the central question of the original movement as well as the Arts and Crafts Revival. And this being 2005, not 1905, we have to come up with our own answer because some of the technology we have now is nothing Gus could have even imagined. If you think we're alone in this, here's a quote from Oscar Wilde, sometime in the nineteenth century:

> The circumstances with which you must surround your workmen are those of modern American life, because the designs you have now to ask for from your workmen are such as will make modern American life beautiful. The art we want is the art based on all the inventions of modern civilization, and to suit all the needs of nineteenth century life.

I myself tend toward the "special piece of furniture" camp for a couple of reasons. One of them is the difference in attitudes toward utilitarian objects at the beginning of the twentieth century compared to today. In the early twentieth century, even functional objects were ornamented and made of real materials like metal and wood, not plastic.

Another reason is that Arts and Crafts is not just a philosophy, it's also an aesthetic, and while an iMac may be fine looking, it doesn't exactly have an Arts and Crafts aesthetic. At least an iMac has some kind of aesthetic, though—the design, if you could call it that, of most modern technology could be summed up completely by the word "gray." But take a look at the tangle of cords and wires on the back of your computer for the real reason—do you really want that hanging off the back of a nice oak desk in your den?

Back in the early twentieth century, the man of the household would retire from the after-dinner festivities and retreat to his study in order to do manly things, like reading the newspaper or paying the bills or smoking a cigar. Nowadays it is just as likely to be the woman of the household. And the study may still contain bookcases and a desk, but instead of a typewriter there will be a computer, and that will entail at least a monitor, a CPU, a keyboard, a mouse, and a printer. But more likely it will also entail more than one printer, a notebook computer, scanner, copier, fax machine, cradle for the PDA, ZIP drive, battery backup, router, USB hub, cable or DSL modem, webcam, speakers, surge protectors, regular phone, cordless phone, cell phone charger, lamp, file cabinet, Rolodex, CD storage, paper shredder, and a copy of *Office 2003 for Dummies*. (At least, that's what I have.) Many of these things will require wires and power cords and the dreaded transformers (that's assuming the kids have their own computers).

And that's why Gus would have designed a special piece of furniture, because it just wouldn't be very artful to put all that junk out on a library table. Heck, there wouldn't even have been room for all of it.

So we of the twenty-first century have the computer desk and the computer armoire. The fact that you can get a "Mission-style" computer desk almost anywhere is either a sign that the Arts and Crafts Revival has succeeded or it's the end of the world as we know it—you decide.

Ah, you say, but what about wireless? I have a wireless keyboard and mouse! I have Bluetooth! I have Centrino! There is Wi-Fi! I surf the Internet on my back porch! That's maybe half of you—the other half is going "What the heck is Centrino?" All well and good till the computer battery runs down, and then you have to plug it in somewhere. That and the teenage kid next door keeps hacking into your network. Nonetheless, wireless technology will have far less impact on your bungalow and be much easier than fishing CAT-5 (or whatever number it's up to by the time you read this) through your walls.

FRESH AIR AND PROTECTION!

The Ives Window Ventilating Lock

A Safeguard for Ventilating Rooms, allowing windows to be left open at the top, the bottom, or both top and bottom, with entire security against intrusion.

Descriptive circular mailed on application.

THE H. B. IVES CO.

SOLE MANUFACTURERS

NEW HAVEN - - CONNECTICUT

The H. B Ives Company still manufactures this ventilating window lock, though this advertisement is from 1915.

In the early twentieth century, the living room was to be the center of home life, with the family gathered around the hearth. They would play board games or parlor games, read, play musical instruments, and women would do needlework. They might even listen to 78s on the gramophone or listen to the radio. They would even, God forbid, talk to each other. We're more likely to turn on the stereo.

A stereo tends to be very high-tech looking and usually black or silver, though there's no reason, really, why they couldn't come in hammered copper. Then they have speakers, which have to be somewhere else. These are fairly easy to disguise because they are either small or they are actually made out of wood, and you can in fact get Arts and Crafts–style speakers. They can also be built in. The stereo components themselves can go in a cabinet or a closet.

For entertainment, we prefer to watch TV. In fact, it's pretty much replaced the fireplace as the center of home life, whether you think that's good or bad. But it's not just the TV. It's the VCR and the DVD player and the DVR and the video game console, and the remote controls and joysticks and whatever goes with all of these. Often the stereo and a computer are hooked into it as well. And that is why the entertainment center was invented. Now you could just throw a lovely piece of hand-embroidered linen over the TV when you're not using it—that is an option. In fact, I think slipcovers might be a lovely idea—they could be stenciled with Arts and Crafts mottoes. Or perhaps we need to get new twenty-first-century mottoes. I think an appropriate motto for the TV might be "The two most plentiful elements in the universe are hydrogen and stupidity." On the other hand, you could have custom cabinetry built for the TV and all its little electronic friends, with pullout shelves that make it easy to get to the wiring and a plasma TV that's flat so you can hang a tapestry in front of it when you're not watching. And of course, it's easy enough to keep all the remotes in a lovely box of some sort. Or perhaps a hand-embroidered linen bag. Naturally, it will have to go on a side table or maybe on the library table positioned behind the settle, because no proper Arts and Crafts house would have a coffee table.

In 1915, the phone would have been in the hall or maybe the kitchen. Now we have phones everywhere. About all you can do if you want to hide them is recess them into the wall. Of course, it is still possible to buy old phones that have been rewired to plug into modern phone jacks. But we have lost the muscle memory required to pick up a candlestick phone with both hands.

In an ideal world, there would be a built-in place to keep the cat litter box (which would be fully waterproofed and ventilated) and a large closet into which you could roll the fully decorated artificial Christmas tree until the following year.

I am struck by just how ugly many of the elements of contemporary life really are and how out of place they look in an Arts and Crafts interior. Beauty is not really part of the equation anymore for most technological things. It is difficult to live a simple existence in the face of cultural pressures and to choose only the technology that is actually helpful to us.

Beneath a cover set into the floor of this Seattle bungalow is a box containing an electrical outlet, a coaxial cable outlet for the TV, and stereo speaker wires. The cutout provides a conduit for the wires as well as a way to remove the cover.

Much of the technology that has come about in the last century is useful—I certainly don't intend to give up the computer that allowed me to rewrite this paragraph several times with ease. (On the other hand, I still feel free to curse it when it decides to change the typeface of parts of the document all on its own!) But I often think we have become enamored of bells and whistles for which we have no real use, and altered our houses, our lives, and even the outer environment in unfortunate ways in order to make room for them. It isn't a new struggle. Back in 1904, Charles Keeler wrote,

> Eliminate in so far as possible all factory-made accessories in order that your dwelling may not be typical of American commercial supremacy, but rather of your own fondness for things that have been created as a response to your love of that which is good and simple and fit for daily companionship.

Technology has made our lives better in many ways. Oscar Wilde understood this, saying,

> Do you think, for instance, that we object to machinery? I tell you we reverence it; we reverence it when it does its proper work, when it relieves man from ignoble and soulless labor, not when it seeks to do that which is valuable only when wrought by the hands and hearts of men. And let us not mistake the means of civilization for the end of civilization; steam-engine, telephone and the like, are all wonderful, but remember that their value depends entirely on the noble uses we make of them, on the noble spirit in which we employ them, not on the things themselves.

STEWARDSHIP

"When they discover the center of the universe, a lot of people will be disappointed to discover they are not it."
—Bernard Bailey

William Morris was a historic preservationist. In 1877, he founded the Society for the Protection of Ancient Buildings, an organization that is still in existence. Historic buildings continue to be pulled down, manufacturing continues to poison the environment, old-growth trees are clear-cut, and farmland paved over, all in the name of profit. In every town, there are and have been property owners or developers or city councils or bureaucrats or colleges or businesses perfectly willing to demolish one bungalow or a hundred in the name of "progress."

That the bungalows pictured in this book are still here to be photographed means that they were preserved. They were not bulldozed to make way for parking lots or office buildings or strip malls or mini-mansions. They did not have all of their historic fabric removed in order to install the latest fad in décor or architecture from some decade or other, or if they did, someone took the trouble to restore them back to what they once were and what they were supposed to be.

Above: A flat screen TV is far easier to hide than the typical bulky television. This one hangs on the wall above custom-built fir cabinetry in a Seattle bungalow. Pullout shelves provide access to the various electronic components, while closed cabinets provide storage for all the DVDs, videos, games, and so forth.

Left: At the Pierpont Inn in Ventura, California, a television has been hidden behind doors above the fireplace, thus combining the period and the modern focal points of a living room in one place.

A candlestick phone has its own tiled niche, complete with a light, in the kitchen of a Berkeley home. The lightbulb is a reproduction of an Edison bulb.

An annunciator (an early sort of intercom) was used to communicate with the servants at the Duncan-Irwin House in Pasadena. The lights are labeled so the servants would know from which room the call was coming.

In most places, bungalows aren't even considered to be historic or worth preserving. They are rarely protected by law, even in cities and towns that may have some kind of historic preservation regulations or guidelines. (The majority of towns and cities have nothing.) They are regarded by many people as little more than shacks. Even in jurisdictions with historic preservation regulations, interiors are not protected. Their only protection comes from caring and knowledgeable owners.

Up until now, the mainstream preservation movement has primarily concerned itself with what could be termed "trophy buildings": city halls, courthouses, mansions, historic theatres, hotels, residences designed by famous architects, etc. All of these are eminently worth preserving. But while those buildings were being fought for, thousands of modest buildings were lost to the wrecking ball, and continue to be lost. Few people have stepped up to defend the Arts and Crafts bungalows, working-class Victorians, historic gas stations, small commercial buildings, old warehouses, and other modest buildings. A huge number of these buildings have been lost, buildings that represent a large part of our history, the history of ordinary people who built them, worked in them, lived in them—that is our real history, not the history of wars and politicians and great events. We are told this is the price of progress. It isn't. As Russell Baker said, "Usually, terrible things that are done with the excuse that progress requires them are not really progress at all, but just terrible things."

And we can no longer afford to throw away the now irreplaceable materials and craftsmanship that went into those buildings. To do so is an affront to the labor and artistry of those who built them. These buildings ARE the old-growth forests we cut down, the stones we quarried, the metals we mined, and the bricks we fired. The tiniest bungalow contains several hundred board feet of old-growth timber—it is an insult to the trees that gave their lives to send that wood splintered and useless to a landfill.

The destruction of historic buildings robs us all of something important. It is theft, pure and simple. It may be disguised with lofty pronouncements about bettering the community or that it will achieve some praiseworthy goal, but it is still theft.

You are only a caretaker for your house, a curator, if you will; the house was there before you, and if it is lucky, it will be there after you are gone. Think carefully about what you do, try to remember that the universe does not revolve around you, and try not to do anything that some later owner will be cursing you for, as you may be cursing some previous owner right now.

Most books and magazines and television decorating shows are constantly bombarding you and advising you to "express yourself," to have "state-of-the-art" whatever. Bad advice is rampant. Manufacturers of appliances, vinyl windows, plumbing fixtures, or laminate flooring do not make money except by convincing people to throw out whatever they've got and buy whatever is being offered. Of course no one tells you to repair your windows, refinish your floors, or keep using your old sink with the separate taps—there's no money in that. They want you to buy an internet-ready refrigerator instead. And the contractors who come to your house, by and large, are not interested in saving your original kitchen and helping you figure out how to fit in a dishwasher when they can get you to pay them $100,000 to rip it all out and put in a fumed oak Arts and Crafts Revival kitchen with stainless-steel appliances and can lighting.

Of course you can express yourself in your house. Just don't express yourself ON your house. You can have any kind of furniture, rugs, artwork, lamps, plants, books, or other movable and removable things you want. You can indulge your love of red in towels, sheets, rugs, upholstery, throws, pillows, art, flowers, even wall color—you don't need to paint the fireplace tile red.

And if you would really prefer a contemporary house or a mid-century modern house, or a Victorian— then buy one. Don't make your bungalow into something it's not (that goes for other houses as well.) I'm really tired of seeing people try to turn a ranch house into a bungalow. If you want to have Arts and Crafts stuff, fine, but let the house be what it is, whatever that happens to be.

Besides, a bungalow is the best house in the world.

A built-in telephone stand in the upstairs hallway of Charles and Henry Greene's Bolton House in Pasadena holds a candlestick phone. A woodcarving decorates the upper door.

RESOURCES

WHAT IS A BUNGALOW?
Aladdin Built In A Day House Catalogs online
http://clarke.cmich.edu/aladdin/Aladdin.htm

The Arts and Crafts Society
www.arts-crafts.com
(734) 358-6882

The William Morris Archive
www.marxists.org

APPLIANCES
Floodsaver
www.floodsaver.com
(866) 341-7674

ART TILE
Duquella Tile
www.tiledecorative.com
(866) 218-8221

Handcraft Tile
www.handcrafttile.com
(877) 262-1140

Maine Coast Art Tile
www.MaineCoastArtTile.com
(207) 797-4595

Meredith Art Tile
www.meredithtile.com
(330) 484-1656

Mosaic Rock Rugs
www.rockrugs.com
(303) 910-2198

Motawi Tileworks
www.motawi.com
(734) 213-0017

Native Tile and Ceramics
www.nativetile.com
(310) 533-8684

North Prairie Tileworks
www.handmadetile.com
(612) 871-3421

Pewabic Pottery
www.pewabic.com
(313) 822-0954

Laird Plumleigh
www.lairdplumleigh.com
(760) 436-1831 phone/fax

Terra Firma Art Tile
www.terrafirmaarttile.com
(803) 643-9399

TrafficMaster Stainproof Grout
www.trafficmasterstainproofgrout.com

Trikeenan Tileworks
www.trikeenan.com
(603) 352-4299

Winters TileWorks/Artistic License
www.artisticlicense.org
(510) 533-7624 / (415) 922-7444

ATTICS: INSULATION
Air Krete
www.airkrete.com
(315) 834-6609

Atlas Roofing Corporation
www.atlasroofing.com

Bonded Logic, Inc.
www.bondedlogic.com
(480) 812-9114

Garrison Specialty Chemicals
www.soyfoam.com

GreenFiber
www.greenstone.com
(800) 228-0024

Igloo Cellulose
www.cellulose.com
(514) 694-1485

Insulstar
www.insulstar.com
(866) 678-5283

International Cellulose Corporation
www.celbar.com
(800) 444-1252

Polyisoncyanurate Insulation Manufacturers Association (PIMA)
www.pima.org
(703) 684-1136

Woolbloc Insulation
www.woolbloc.com
64-3-546 4387

ATTICS: INSULATION, RADIANT BARRIER
Horizon Energy Systems
www.savenrg.com
(602) 867-3176

Hy-Tech Thermal Solutions
www.hytechsales.com
(866) 649-8324

Innovative Insulation Inc.
www.radiantbarrier.com
(800) 825-0123

Reflectech
www.reflectech.com
(601) 799-6998

Smart Foils
www.smartfoils.com
(800) 492-6333

U-B-Kool
www.u-b-kool.com
(619) 275-6919

ATTICS: LADDERS AND STAIRS
Atticap Corp.
www.draftcap.com
(888) 292-2229

Calvert USA, Inc.
www.CalvertUSA.com
(866) 477-8455

Resource Conservation Technology Inc.
www.conservationtechnology.com
(410) 366-1146

ATTICS: SKYLIGHTS
Solar Innovations
www.solarinnovations.com
(800) 618-0669

Velux
www.velux.com
800) 88-VELUX

Bristolite Skylights
www.bristolite.com
(800) 854-8618

Creative Structures
www.creativeconservatories.com
(800) 873-3966

Glass House Conservatories
www.glasshouseusa.com
(800) 222-3065

Roto Frank of America
www.roto-roofwindows.com
(800) 243-0893

Solar Innovations
www.solarinnovations.com
(800) 618-0669

Sun-Tek Manufacturing, Inc.
www.sun-tek.com
(407) 859-2117

Velux
www.veluxusa.com
(800) 88-VELUX [888-3589]

Albert Wagner and Son, Inc.
www.albertwagnerandson.com
(773) 935-1414

ATTICS: FANS
Fan-Attic
www.fan-attic.com
(877) FAN-ATTIC [326-38842]

Tamarack Technologies (attic fans)
www.tamtech.com
800) 822-5932

ATTICS: GABLE VENTS
European Attic
www.europeanattic.com
(800) 632-9408

Fan-Attic
www.fan-attic.com
(408) 254-6661

Kimball Design
www.kimballdesigns.com
(870) 326-4326

The Whitfield Group, Inc.
www.whitfieldvents.com
(903) 291-WOOD [9663]

VERMIN
Contech (motion-activated sprinklers)
www.scatmat.com
(800) 767-8658

BASEMENTS
Décor by Madrid
(basement pole covers)
www.madridinc.com
(562) 404-9941

Dricore
www.dricore.com
(866) 976-6374

Preservation Resource Group, Inc.
www.prginc.com
(800) 774-7891

Saniflo
www.saniflo.com
(800) 363-5874 CANADA
(800) 571-8191 USA

BATHS
Ceramic Tool Company
www.ceramictool.com
(800) 236-5230

Mr. Shower Door
www.mrshowerdoor.com
(800) 633-3667

BEDS (Murphy)
Create-A-Bed, Inc
www.wallbed.com
877) 966-3852

Flying Bed Company
www.flyingbeds.com
(888) 892-4645

Murphy Bed Company
www.murphybedcompany.com
(800) 845-2337

BUILT-INS
McGeehan's Cabinets
(fold-up nook)
www.pockettable.com
(513) 897-1360

CAT BATHROOMS
Harrisworks
www.catlitterfurniture.com
(310) 793-1777

Hawks Will Custom Woodwork
www.hawkswillwoodwork.com
(336) 468-8099

CatsPlay.com
www.catsplay.com
www.lovethatcat.com
(412) 366-7545

CEILING FANS
Fanimation
www.fanimation.com
(888) 567-2055

Vintage Fans, LLC
www.vintagefans.com
(817) 431-6647

Woolen Mill Fan Company
www.architecturalfans.com
(717) 382-4754 phone/fax

CLOSETS
Architectural Products by Outwater LLC (closet rod lighting)
www.outwater.com
http://www2.archpro.com/
cgi-bin/worderc?confc=B2C
(800) 835-4400

CURTAINS, WINDOW COVERINGS, CURTAIN HARDWARE
Archive Edition Textiles
www.archiveedition.com
(877) 676-2424

Arts and Crafts Period Textiles
www.textilestudio.com
(510) 654-1645

J. R. Burrows and Co.
www.burrows.com
(800) 347-1795

Craftsman Interiors
www.craftsmaninteriors.com
(877) 374-7843

Glyders
www.glyders.com
(928) 505-1070

Handwerk Shade Shop
www.thehandwerkshop.com
(503) 659-0914

Liberty Valances and Curtains
www.libertyvalances.com
(973) 857-4114

Rejuvenation
www.rejuvenation.com
(888) 401-1900

Charles Rupert, The Shop
www.charles-rupert.com
(250) 592-4916

Ann Wallace & Friends
www.annwallace.com
(213) 617-3310

Wellspring Textiles
www.wellspringtextiles.com
(508) 746-1847

DOORS
A&A Millwork
www.aamillwork.com
(612) 721-1111

Caoba Doors
www.caobadoors.com
(800) 417-3667

CraftsmanDoors.com
www.craftsmandoors.com
(866) 390-1574

Crisp Door & Window
www.crispdoor.com
(281) 540-5551

Custom Glass Doors
www.customglassdoors.com
(832) 445-0686 / (281) 324-1131

Doors by Decora
www.doorsbydecora.com
(800) 359-7557

Fevreco Door Products
www.fevreco.com
(520) 844-1099 fax

Fine Doors LLC
www.finedoors.com
(800) 395-3667

Floating World Wood Design
www.perceptionofdoors.com
(828) 230-0134

Great Northwest Door Company
www.greatnwdoors.com
(800) 895-3667

H.I.C. Window and Door
www.homeideacenter.com
(615) 371-8080

The Hidden Door Company
www.hiddendoors.com
(877) 218-5434

Historic Doors
www.historicdoors.com
610) 756-6187

Homestead Hardwoods
www.homesteadhardwoods.com
(419) 684-9582

Hull Historical
www.hullhistorical.com
(800) 990-1495 / (817) 332-1495

International Door & Latch
www.internationaldoor.com
(541) 686-5647

Jurs Architectural Glass
(800) 679-9772

Karona, Inc.
www.karonadoor.com
(800) 829-9233

Madawaska Doors Inc.
www.madawaska doors.com
(800) 263-2358

Millwork Specialties
www.millwork-specialties.com
(800) 592-7112
(718) 768-7112

**Northstar WoodWorks
Incorporated**
www.northstarww.com
(360) 384-0307

Omega Too
www.omegatoo.com
(510) 843-3636

Pinecrest, Inc.
www.pinecrestinc.com
(612) 871-7071

Public Lumber Company
www.hardwoodint.com
(313) 891-7125

Select Millwork Company
www.selectmillwork.com
(800) 349-2056.

Sheppard Doors & Glass LLC
www.beveldoor.com
(832) 644-2444
(713) 807-1444

Signamark (interior doors)
www.signamark.com
(800) 803-8182

Simpson Door Company
www.simpsondoor.com
(800) 952-4057

Touchstone Woodworks
www.touchstonewoodworks.com
(330) 297-1313

TruStile Doors LLC
www.trustile.com
(888) 286-3931

Upstate Door
www.upstatedoor.com
(800) 570-8283

Victoriana East
www.victorianaeast.com
(856) 546-1882
(856) 910-1887

Vintage Woodworks
www.vintagewoodworks.com
(903) 356-2158

W G H Woodworking
www.wghwoodworking.com
(520) 798-1133

YesterYear's Vintage Doors
www.vintagedoors.com
(800) 787-2001

DOORS: SCREENS
Combination Door Company
(wood storm/screen doors)
www.combinationdoor.com
(920) 922-2050

Great Northwest Door Company
www.greatnwdoors.com
(800) 895-3667

Hull Historical
www.hullhistorical.com
(817) 332-1495

Phantom Screens
www.phantomscreens.com
(604) 855-3654

Touchstone Woodworks
www.touchstonewoodworks.com
(330) 297-1313

Upstate Door
www.upstatedoor.com
(800) 570-8283

Victoriana East
www.victorianaeast.com
(856) 546-1882
(856) 910-1887

Vintage Woodworks
www.vintagewoodworks.com
(903) 356-2158

Wooden Screen Door Company
www.woodenscreendoor.com
(207) 832-0519

**YesterYear's Vintage Doors
and Millwork**
www.vintagedoors.com
(800) 787-2001

DOORS: HARDWARE
(see also HARDWARE)
The Brass Knob
www.thebrassknob.com
(202) 332-3370

Direct Door Hardware
www.directdoorhardware.com
(877) 852-9449

William J. Rigby Com.
www.wmjrigby.com
(607) 547-1900

DOORS: POCKET DOOR HARDWARE
Blaine Window Hardware
www.blainewindow.com
(800) 678-1919

G-U Hardware
www.g-u.com
(800) 927-1097

Hettich America
www.hettichamerica.com
(800) 438-8424

L. E. Johnson Products
www.johnsonhardware.com
(219) 293-5664

ELECTRICAL
Classic Accents
(pushbutton switches)
www.classicaccents.net
(800) 245-7742

Lightning Switch
www.lightningswitch.com
(757) 624-2134

ELEVATORS, DUMBWAITERS
Access Industries
www.dreamelevator.com
(800) 829-9760

Auton Motorized Systems
www.auton.com
(661) 257-92823

Cemcolift
www.cemcolift.com
(800) 962-3626

Concord Elevator
www.concordelevator.com
(800) 661-5112

W. B. Fowler
www.wbfowler.com
(800) 290-8510

Inclinator
www.inclinator.com
(800) 343-9007

Miller Manufacturing, Inc.
www.silentservant.com
(800) 232-2177

National Wheel-O-Vator
www.wheelovator.com
(800) 968-5438

Residential Elevators
www.residentialelevators.com
(800) 832-2004

Ultimate Die Corp.
(813) 620-8847

Waupaca Elevator Company
www.waupacaelevator.com
(800) 238-8739

EPOXY CONSOLIDANTS
Abatron
www.abatron.com
(800) 445-1754

Advanced Repair Technology
www.advancedrepair.com
(607) 265-9040

Conserv Epoxy
www.conservepoxy.com
(973) 579-1112

Epoxy Heads
www.epoxyheads.com
(866) 376-9948

Gougeon Bros.
www.westsystem.com
(989) 684-7286

Protective Coating Company
www.pcepoxy.com
(610) 432-3543

Rot Doctor, Inc.
www.rotdoctor.com
(206) 364-2155

System Three
www.systemthree.com
(800) 333-5514

FINISHES
Bonakemi
www.bonakemi.com
(800) 574-4674

Howard Products, Inc.
www.howardproducts.com
(800) 266-9545

Shellac.Net
www.shellac.net
(866) 339-2933

FINISHES: PENETRATING OIL
Penofin
www.penofin.com
(800) 736-6346

Sutherland Welles, Ltd.
www.tungoilfinish.com
(800) 322-1245

Waterlox
www.waterlox.com
(800) 321-0377

FIREPLACES, CHIMNEYS, MANTELS
Ahrens Chimney Technique
www.ahrenschimney.com
(800) 843-4417

Amvic, Inc.
www.amvicsystem.com
(877) 470-9991

Andiron Technologies
(Eco-Fire grates)
www.ecofire.com
(650) 330-1051

Architectural Ornament
www.architectural-ornament.com
(800) 567-3554

Archive Designs (hoods)
www.archivedesigns.com
(541) 607-6581

Burton Mouldings
www.burton-mouldings.com
(888) 323-8926

Dearborn Heater/Burge Hardware
(radiant heaters)
www.dearbornheater.com
(817) 535- 0838

Fires of Tradition
www.firesoftradition.com
(519) 770-0063

Golden Flue
www.chimneys.com
(800) 446-5354

Guardian Chimney Liner
www.guardianinc.com
(800) 545-6607

Heat-Fab
www.heat-fab.com
(800) 772-0739

Hennis Enterprises
www.hennisenterprises.com
(888) 643-2879

Homesaver Chimney Liners
www.homesaver.com
(866) 466-3728

Mantels of Yesteryear
www.mantelsofyesteryear.com
(888) 292-2080

Moberg Fireplaces
www.mobergfireplaces.com
(503) 227-0547

Northern Roof Tiles
www.northernrooftiles.com
(888) 678-6866

Protech Systems, Inc.
www.protechinfo.com
(800) 766-3473

Solid/Flue Chimney Systems
www.solidflue.com
(800) 444-3583

Supaflu Chimney Restoration
www.supaflu.com
(800) 788-7636

Superior Clay Corporation
www.superiorclay.com
(800) 848-6166

Summit Views (goodwood® firelogs)
www.summitviews.com

Town and Country Fireplaces
www.townandcountryfireplaces.net

The Victorian Fireplace Shop
www.thevictorianfireplace.com
(866) 427-2625

FLOORING: CARPETS
Family Heirloom Weavers
www.familyheirloomweavers.com
(717) 246-2431

J. R. Burrows and Co.
www.burrows.com
(800) 347-1795

Jax Arts and Crafts Rugs
www.jaxrugs.com
(859) 986-5410

The Persian Carpet, Inc.
www.persiancarpet.com
(800) 333-1801

FLOORING: RESILIENT
Armstrong World Industries
www.armstrong.com

Forbo Industries
www.themarmoleumstore.com

LaBelle Studios (floor cloths)
www.labellestudios.com
(888) 889-3409

FLOORING: TILE (see also ART TILE)
American Restoration Tile
www.restorationtile.com

FLOORING: WOOD
Bear Creek Lumber
www.bearcreeklumber.com
(800) 597-7191

Duluth Timber Company
www.duluthtimber.com
(218) 727-2145

Fine House, Ltd.
www.finehouse.net
(540) 436-3180

Granville Manufacturing Company
www.woodsiding.com
(802) 767-4747

Heartwood Pine
www.HeartwoodPine.com
(800) 524-7463

Hoffmeyer's
www.hoffmeyersmill.com
(877) 644-5843

Housatonic Hardwoods, Inc.
www.hhardwoods.com
(800) 924-5684

Jefferson State Forest Products
www.jeffersonstateproducts.com
(530) 628-1101

Launstein Hardwood Floors
www.launstein.com
(888) 339-4639

Manomin Resawn Timbers
www.mrtimbers.com
(888) 207-6072

Natural Wood Flooring, Inc.
www.naturalwood.net
(800) 726-7463

Old Wood LLC
www.douglasfirfloors.com
(505) 454-6007

Pacific Heritage Wood Supply
(877) 728-9231
www.phwood.com

Rare Earth Hardwoods
www.rare-earth-hardwoods.com
(800) 968-0074

Scotland Neck Heart Pine, Inc.
www.snheartpine.com
(800) 826-8117

TerraMai
www.terramai.com
(800) 220-9062

What Its Worth, Inc.
www.quartersawnantiquepine.com
(512) 328-8837

Windfall Lumber
www.windfalllumber.com
(362) 352-2250

STAIN AND ODOR REMOVAL
ExStink
www.pinkexstink.com
(877) 397-8465

Mister Max (Anti-Icky Poo)
www.mistermax.com
(800)745-1671

Non-Scents, Ltd.
www.deodoroc.com
(604) 580-0060

Urine-Off
www.urine-off.com
(877) 874-6363

ZeoCrystal
www.zeocrystal.com
(800) 936-6367

GLASS: ART GLASS
Theodore Ellison Design
www.theodoreellison.com
(510) 532-7632

Lyn Hovey Studio
www.lynhoveystudio.com
(617) 261-9897

Little/Raidl Design Studios
www.sonic.net/little-raidl
(707) 632-5569

Naughty Squirrel Stained Glass
www.naughtysquirrelstainedglass.com
(505) 301-7603

Brian McNally
www.brianmcnallyglassartist.com
(805) 687-7212

Anne Ryan Miller Glass Studio
www.anneryanmillerglassstudio.com
(812) 988-9766

Sybaritic Studios
www.sybariticstudios.com
(262) 635-8267

Two Fish Art Glass
www.TwoFishArtGlass.com
(708) 366-6800

Unique Art Glass
www.uniqueartglass.net
(425) 481-6046

Wallis Stained Glass
www.jackwallisdoors.com
(270) 489-2613

GLASS: RESTORATION GLASS
AGW Window Glass
www.homestead.com/oldstyleAGW/oldstyleAGW.html
(410) 435-0300

Bendheim (new cylinder glass)
www.bendheim.com

Fairview Glass (old glass)
www.fairviewglass.com
(301) 371-3364

HARDWARE
Al Bar Wilmette Platers
(hardware restoration)
www.albarwilmette.com
(800) 300-6762

Mitchell Andrus
www.mitchellandrus.com
(908) 647-7442

Architectural Iron Company
(sash weights)
www.architecturaliron.com
(800) 442-4766

Arts and Crafts Hardware
www.arts-n-craftshardware.com
(586) 772-7279

Australian Global Services
www.aussieglobe.com
(888) 222-8940

Baldwin Hardware
www.baldwinhardware.com
(800) 566-1986

Ball and Ball
www.ballandball.com
(800) 257-3711

Bungalow Metal
(hardware restoration)
www.bungalowmetal.com
(888) 205-3444

Cabin 26
www.cabin26.com
(800) 264-2210

Charles Locksmith, Inc.
www.charleslocksmith.com
(866) OLD-KEYS

Classic Accents
www.classicaccents.net
(734) 284-7661

Craftsmen Hardware Company, Ltd.
www.craftsmenhardware.com
(660) 376-2481

Crown City Hardware
www.crowncityhardware.com
(800) 950-1047

Ed Donaldson Hardware Restorations
www.eddonaldson.com
(717) 249-3624

Doorbell Factory
www.doorbellfactory.com
(800) 390-7449

Eugenia's Antique Hardware
www.eugeniaantiquehardware.com
(800) 337-1677

FMG Designs
www.fmgdesigns.com
(773) 761-2957

Griffin Brothers and Company
  (hardware restoration)
www.griffinbros.com
(860) 678-9007

Hamilton Decorative Collection
www.hamiltondeco.com
(866) 900-3326

Historic Houseparts
www.historichouseparts.com
(888) 558-2329

House of Antique Hardware
www.houseofantiquehardware.com
(888) 223-2545

Knob Gallery
www.knobgallery.com
(888) 921-KNOB

Lee Valley Tools (stop adjusters)
www.leevalley.com
(800) 871-8158

Liz's Antique Hardware
www.lahardware.com
(323) 939-4403

Old Rose Hardware
www.oldrosehardware.com
(800) 508-0022

Paxton Hardware
www.paxtonhardware.com
(800) 241-9741

Phelps Company
  (brass window hardware)
www.phelpscompany.com
(802) 257-4314

Phoenix Lock Co.
www.phoenixlock.com
(800) 471-3087

Pullman Manufacturing Co.
www.pullmanmfg.com
(585) 334-1350

Rejuvenation
www.rejuvenation.com
(888) 401-1900

William J. Rigby Co.
www.wmjrigby.com
(607) 547-1900

Swan Picture Hangers
www.swanpicturehangers.com
(530) 865-4109

Van Dyke's Restorers
www.vandykes.com
(800) 787-3355

Vintage Hardware
www.vintagehardware.com
(408) 246-9918

Web Wilson
www.webwilson.com
(800) 508-0022

HEAT: MINI-DUCTS

Energy Saving Products, Ltd.
www.hi-velocity.com
(708) 453-2093

Spacepak
www.spacepak.com
(413) 566-9571 (U.S.)
(905) 625-2991 (Canada)

Unico System, Inc.
www.unicosystem.com
(800) 527-0896

HEAT: HYDRONIC

**A-1 New and Used Plumbing
  and Heating Supplies**
  (antique radiators)
A1plumbing@rcn.com
(617) 625-6140

Applied Radiant Technologies
www.appliedradiant.com
(215) 258-0932

Burnham Hydronics
  (antique style radiators)
www.burnham.com
(717) 397-4701

Dan Holohan Associates
www.heatinghelp.com
(800) 853-8882

Hydronic Alternatives Inc.
www.hydronicalternatives.com
(413) 543-8733

InFloor Radiant Heating, Inc.
www.infloor.com
(800) 588-4470

Orbit Radiant Heating
www.orbitmfg.com
(800) 522-3986

Radiantec
www.radiantec.com
(800) 451-7593

RadiantMax
www.radiantmax.com
(800) 572-7831

Radiant Technology
www.rtisystems.com
(800) 784-0234

Shafter Bros, Inc.
www.oldcastironradiators.com
(800) 361-1778

Warmboard
(831) 685-9276
www.warmboard.com
(831) 685-9276

Warmly Yours
www.warmlyyours.com
(800) 875-5285

Zurn Plumbing Products Group
www.zurn.com
(800) 872-7277

**HEAT: REGISTER COVERS,
  RADIATOR COVERS**

Architectural Grille
www.archgrille.com
(800) 387-6267

Cape Cod Air Grilles
www.ccairgrilles.com
(800) 547-2705

Central Radiator Cabinet Company
www.Eradiatorcovers.net
(800) 733- 1713

Classic Wood Vents
www.classicvents.com
(800) 545-8368

Grate Vents
www.gratevents.com
(815) 459-4306

Mission Woodworking
www.missionwoodworking.com
(877) 848-5697

Monarch Products
www.monarchcovers.com
(201) 507-5551

Overboards
www.go-overboard.com
(877) 466-8372

Prairie Woodworking
www.prairie-woodworking.com
(612) 724-6805

Reggio Register Company
www.reggioregister.com
(978) 772-3493

Wolf Radiator Enclosures
www.eradiatorcovers.biz
(800) 519-8602

**The Wooden Radiator
  Cabinet Company**
www.woodenradiatorcabinet.com
(800) 817-9110

LIGHTING

AamscoCraftsmen Lighting Ltd.
  (reproduction antique bulbs), Ltd.
www.aamscocraftsmenhardware.com
(800) 221-9092

Antique Lighting Company
www.antiquelighting.com
(800) 224-7880
(660) 376-2481

Arroyo Craftsman
www.arroyocraftsman.com
(626) 960-9411

Aurora Studios
www.aurorastudiosoldcalifornia.com
(860) 928-1965

Brass Light Gallery
www.brasslight.com
(800) 243-9595

Revival Lighting
www.revivallighting.com
(509) 747-4552

Cherry Tree Design
www.cherrytreedesign.com
(800) 634-3268

Classic Accents
(pushbutton switches)
www.classicaccents.net
(734) 284-7661

Conant Custom Brass, Inc.
www.conantcustombrass.com
(800) 832-4482

Continuum Antiques and Collectibles
www.oldlamp.com
(508) 255-5813

Craftsmen Lighting, Ltd.
www.craftsmenhardware.com
(660) 376-2481

Desert Craftsmen
www.desertcraftsmen.com
(623) 935-4495

Eclectic Revival
www.eclecticrevival.com
(416) 766-5500

Elcanco, Ltd.
www.elcanco.com

EvergreenStudios
www.evergreenstudios.com
(360) 352-0694

Genuine Antique Lighting
www.genuineantiquelighting.com
(617) 423-9790

Griffin Brothers and Company
(lighting restoration)
www.griffinbros.com
(860) 678-9007

Steven Handelman Studios
www.stevenhandelmanstudios.com
(805) 962-5119

Historic Lighting
www.historiclighting.com
(626) 303-4899

The Lamp Shop
(lamp parts)
www.lampshop.com
(603) 224-1603

Luminaria Lighting
www.luminaria.com
(800) 638-5619

Mica Lamp Company
www.micalamps.com
(818) 241-7227

MicaLight
(mica sheets)
www.micalight.com
(310) 416-1225

Mission Spirit
www.missionspirit.com
(208) 623-1211

Mission Studio
www.missionstudio.com
(866) 987-6549

New Metal Crafts
www.newmetalcrafts.com
(800) 621-3907

Old California Lantern Company
www.oldcalifornia.com
(800) 577-6679

Old House Lights
www.oldhouselights.com
(218) 834-5399

Old Pasadena Vintage Lighting
www.oldpasadenavintagelighting.com
(626) 396-0843

Paxton Hardware (lamp parts)
www.paxtonhardware.com
(800) 241-9741

P. W. Vintage Lighting
www.pwvintagelighting.com
(413) 644-9150

Rejuvenation Lamp and Fixture
www.rejuvenation.com
(888) 401-1900

Renaissance Antique Lighting
(800) 850-8515
www.antique-lighting.com

Revival Lighting
www.revivallighting.com
(509) 747-4552

Schoolhouse Electric Co.
www.schoolhouselectric.com
(800) 630-7113

Stone Standard (cloth covered wire)
www.stonestandard.com
(210) 738-1060

Sundial Wire (cloth covered wire)
www.sundialwire.com
(413) 582-6908

Turn of the Century Lighting
www.tocl.on.ca
(888) 527-1825

Victorian Revival
www.victorian-revival.com
(416) 789-1704

Vintage Hardware
www.vintagehardware.com
(408) 246-9918

Vintage Lights
www.vintagelights.com
(206) 932-9184

Waterglass Studios
www.waterglassstudios.com
(250) 384-1515

West End Light
www.westendlight.com
(707) 745-4150

MAGAZINES
American Bungalow
www.ambungalow.com
(626) 355-1651

Fine Homebuilding
www.taunton.com
(800) 477-8727

Old House Interiors
www.oldhouseinteriors.com
(800) 462-0211

Old House Journal
www.oldhousejournal.com
(800) 234-3797

Style 1900
www.style1900.com
(609) 397-4104

MILLWORK, MOLDINGS, PANELING
Architectural Millwork
www.archmillwork.com
(800) 685-1331

Bear Creek Lumber
(800) 597-7191
www.bearcreeklumber.com

A Crown Specialty Moldings
www.crownspecialtymoldings.com
(608) 751-2040

Deschenes and Cooper Architectural Millwork
www.expertmillwork.com
(860) 599-2481

Fat Andy's Hardwoods
www.fatandys.com
(800) 962-5529

Georgia-Pacific
  (beadboard paneling)
www.gpplytanium.com
(800) 284-5347

Hull Historical Millwork
www.hullhistorical.com
(817) 332-1495

Jimmy's Cypress
www.jimmys-cypress.com
(888) 245-1050

Maple Grove Restorations, LLC
www.maple-grove.com
(860) 742- 5432

McCoy Millwork
www.mccoymillwork.com
(888) 236- 0995

Museum Resources
www.museum-resources.com
(804) 966-1800

New England Classic (paneling kits)
www.newenglandclassic.com
(888) 880-6324

Old World Mouldings
www.oldworldmouldings.com
(631) 563-8660

Pacific Heritage Wood Supply
www.phwood.com
(877) 728-9231

Pioneer Millworks
www.pioneermillworks.com
(800) 951-9663

Ryan Wholesale, Inc.
www.ryanwholesale.com
(800) 799-3237

**Scotland Neck
  Heart Pine, Inc.**
www.snheartpine.com
(800) 826-8117

San Francisco Victoriana
www.sfvictoriana.com
(415) 648-0313

T and H Industries
www.tandh.com
(727) 573-7989

Talarico Hardwoods
www.talaricohardwoods.com
(610) 775-0400

**Victorian Architectural
  Millworks, Inc.**
www.victoriantrim.com
(773) 237-6272

Windfall Lumber
www.windfalllumber.com
(360) 352-2250

PAINT
Auro
www.aurousa.com
(888) 302-9352

Bioshield Paints
www.bioshieldpaint.com
(800) 621-2591

The Faux Store
(800) 270-8871
www.fauxstore.com

Johnson Paint Company (calcimine)
www.johnsonpaint.com
(617) 536-4244

The Muralo Company (calcimine)
www.muralo.com
(800) 631-3440

PAINT REMOVAL: CHEMICALS
**American Building
  Restoration Products**
www.abrp.com
800) 346-7532

Back To Nature Products (Ready-Strip)
www.ready-strip.com
(800) 211-5175

W. M. Barr and Company (Citristrip)
www.citristrip.com
(800) 235-3546

Dumond Chemicals (Peel Away)
www.dumondchemicals.com
(212) 869-6350

Fiberlock Technologies (Lemon Peel)
www.fiberlock.com
(800) 342- 3755

Franmar Chemical (Soy-Gel)
www.soysolvents.com
(800) 538-5069

K and E. Chemical Company
www.klenztone.com
(800) 331-1696

Napier Environmental Technologies
  (Removall)
www.removall.com
(800) 663-9274

Soyclean
www.soyclean.biz
(888) 606-9559

PAINT: INFRARED
Paint Peeler
www.paintpeeler.com
(800) 613-1557

Viking Sales, Inc.
www.silentpaintremover.com
(585) 924-8070

PAINT: MECHANICAL
American International Tool, Inc.
  (Paint Shaver)
www.paintshaver.com
(800) 932-5872

Preservation Resource Group
  (Pro-Prep scrapers)
www.prginc.com
(800) 774-7891

PLASTER
American Clay
  (clay-based plaster)
www.americanclay.com
(866) 404-1634

Charles Street Supply
  (plaster washers)
  (800) 382-4360

Master of Plaster
(800) 352-5915
www.masterofplaster.com

Med Imports
  (Terramed clay wall coating)
(866) 363-6334

Nu-Wal Restoration System
www.nu-wal.com
(800) 247-3932

TK Coatings, LLC
  (Krack-Kote)
www.tkcoatings.com
(800) 827-2056

Wassmer Studios
  (plaster moldings)
www.wassmerstudios.com
(800) 923-4234 x 105

PRESERVATION
**National Trust
  for Historic Preservation**
www.nationaltrust.org
(800) 944-6847

Preservation Directory
www.preservationdirectory

STAIRS
Automatic Tubing Corp.
www.atcbrass.com
(718) 383-0100

Stair World
www.stairworld.com
(800) 387-7711

Zoroufy Stair Rods
www.zoroufy.com
(608) 833- 9026

STENCILS, WALL DECOR

Craftsman Interiors
www.craftsmaninteriors.com
(360) 297-3755

Helen Foster Stencils
www.bungalowborders.com

Hurley Century Arts
www.cjhurley.com
(503) 234-4167

Trimbelle River Studio and Design
www.trimbelleriver.com
(866) 273-8773

VENTILATION

American Aldes Ventilation Corp.
www.americanaldes.com
(800) 255-7749

Fantech
www.fantech.com
(800) 747-1762

WALLPAPER

Bradbury and Bradbury
www.bradbury.com
(707) 746-1900

J. R. Burrows and Co.
www.burrows.com
(800) 347-1795

Burt Wallpapers
www.burtwallpapers.com
(707) 745-4207

Carol Mead Designs
www.carolmead.com
(707) 747-0223

Carter and Company/ Mt. Diablo Handprints
www.carterandco.com
(707) 554-2682

Charles Rupert, The Shop
www.charles-rupert.com
(250) 592-4916

Trustworth Studios
www.trustworth.com
(508) 746-1847

Wolff House Art Papers
www.wolffhouseartpapers.com
(740) 392-4947
(800) 843-4417

WINDOWS: FIBERGLASS

The Duxton Company
www.duxtonwindows.com
(204) 339-6456

Fiberglass Windows
www.fiberglasswindows.com
(617) 269-6397

WINDOWS: MISCELLANEOUS

Window Restoration Systems
www.steamstripper.com
(207) 725-005

WINDOWS: SCREENS

Air-Tite Storm Windows
www.airtitestormwindows.com
(800) 722-4424

Connecticut Screen Works
www.connscreen.com
(203) 741-0859

Euroscreen
www.eurollscreen.com

Grabill Windows and Doors
www.grabillwindow.com
(810) 798-2817

Heirloom Screen Door Company
www.heirloomscreendoors.com
(541) 426-4811

Old Fashioned Windows and Millwork
www.oldfashionedwindows.com
(973) 589-3181

Rollaway Disappearing Screens
www.rollaway.com
(888) 526-4111

Screen Technology Group
www.wovenwire.com
(800) 440-6374

Victoriana East
www.victorianaeast.com
(856) 546-1882

Vintage Woodworks
www.vintagewoodwork.com
(250) 386-5354

WINDOWS: SHUTTERS

Alternative Timber Structures
www.alternativetimberstructures.com
(208) 456-2711

Ament Shutters
www.amentshutters.com
(715) 829-7686

Doors by Decora
www.doorsbydecora.com
(800) 359-7557

Fevreco Door Products
www.fevreco.com
(520) 844-1099

Fine Doors LLC
www.finedoors.com
(800) 395-3667

H. Hirschmann, Ltd.
www.hhirschmannltd.com
(802) 438-4447

H.I.C. Window and Door
www.homeideacenter.com
(615) 371-8080

Karona, Inc.
www.karonadoor.com
(800) 829-9233

Millwork Specialties
www.millwork-specialties.com
(718) 768-7112

Pinecrest, Inc.
www.pinecrestinc.com
(612) 871-7071

Public Lumber Company
www.hardwoodint.com
(313) 891-7125

S. A. Shutter Mill
www.sashuttermill.com
(877) 675-7861

Select Millwork Company
www.selectmillwork.com
(269) 349-7841

Snugg Harbor Woodworking
www.snuggharbor.com
(800) 424-7778

Upstate Door
www.upstatedoor.com
(800) 570-8283

Vixen Hill
www.vixenhill.com
(610) 286-0909

Withers Custom Shutters
www.withersind.com
(843) 376-0013

W.G.H. Woodworking
www.wghwoodworking.com
(520) 798-1133

YesterYear's Vintage Doors and Millwork
www.vintagedoors.com
(800) 787-2001

WINDOWS: STORM—INTERIOR

Citiquiet
www.citiquiet.com
(212) 874-5362

The Energy Doctor
www.northerntropic.com
(800) 408-5554

Innerglass
www.stormwindows.com
(800) 743-6207

Rusco Windows and Doors
www.ruscons.com
(902) 456-5259

Soundproof Windows
www.soundproofwindows.com
(877) 800-3850

Thermopress Corporation
www.thermopress.com
(804) 355-9147

Window Saver Company
www.windowsaver.com
(800) 321-WARM

WINDOWS: STEEL

Seekircher Steel Window Repair
www.design-site.net/seekirch.htm
(914) 725-1904

WINDOWS: WOOD

Aaron Wood Windows, Inc.
www.aaronwoodwindows.com
(604) 538-4618

American Heritage Window Rebuilders
www.vintagewindows.com
866) 866-3973

Bagala Window Works
www.bagalawindowworks.com
(207) 878-6306

Bear Wood Windows
www.bearwoodwindow.com
(888) 704-2709

Bergerson Cedar Windows
www.bergersonwindow.com
(800) 240-4365

Caoba Doors
www.caobadoors.com
(215) 747-6577

Custom Trades International
www.customtrades.com

Custom Window Company
www.customwindow.com
(800) 255-1920

Grabill Windows and Doors
www.grabillwindow.com
(810) 798-2817

Hawk Retrofit, Inc.
www.hawkretrofit.org
(410) 757-0895

H. Hirschmann, Ltd.
www.hhirschmannltd.com
(802) 438-4447

H.I.C. Window and Door Company
www.homeideaccenter.com
(615) 371-8080

Hoffmeyer's
www.hoffmeyersmill.com
(877) 644-5843

Horner South Florida Millwork
www.southfloridamillwork.com

Hull Historical
www.hullhistorical.com
(800) 990-1495

Jarrett, Inc.
www.jarrett-windows.com
(800) 533-5097

Joseph Millworks
www.josephmillworks.com
(541) 894-2347

Kronenberger and Sons Restoration, Inc.
www.kronenbergersons.com
(800) 255-0089

Marlowe Restorations
www.marlowerestorations.com
(203) 484-9643

Millwork Specialties
www.millwork-specialties.com
(800) 592-7112

Old Fashioned Windows and Millwork
www.oldfashionedwindows.com
(973) 589-3181

Reilly WoodWorks
www.reillywoodworks.com
(631) 208-0710

Restoration Works, Inc.
www.restorationworksinc.com
(815) 937-0556

Re-View
www.re-view.biz
(816) 741-2876

Sabana Windows
www.sabanawindows.com
(305) 825-1256

The Sash Window Workshop
www.sashwindow.com

Smith Restoration Sash
www.smithrestorationsash.com
(401) 351-1222

Tradewood Industries
www.tradewoodindustries.com
(800) 410-0268

Weston Millwork Company
www.westonmillwork.com
(816) 640-5555

Wewoka Window Works
www.wewokawindowworks.com
(405) 257-2839

The Window Man
www.thewindowman.com
(902) 462-4576

Wood Windows
www.woodwindows.com
(610) 896-3608

Woodstone
www.woodstone.com
(802) 722-9217

THE UNABASHED FAVORITISM SECTION

Apex Electrical Contracting
www.apexelectricalcontracting.com
(916) 443-6644

Artistic License
www.artisticlicense.org
(415) 922-7444

The Crafted Home
www.thecraftedhome.com
(303) 860-8444

Ivy Hill Interiors
ltaylor@serv.net
(206) 243-6768

Laurie Crogan
(linoleum inlay)
www.inlayfloors.com
(310) 474-1821

Robyn Einhorn, Murphy Bed Expert
robyn_e@hotmail.com

Through The Woods Fine Wood Flooring
Dennis Prieur
4532 West Kennedy Boulevard
Suite 288
Tampa, FL 33609
(813) 232-3985

BIBLIOGRAPHY

PUBLICATIONS
"If we knew what we were doing it would not be called research, would it?" —Albert Einstein

The Aladdin Company. *Aladdin Homes: "Built in a Day" Catalog #29.* Bay City, Michigan, 1917. Reprint: Mineola, New York: Dover Publications, 1995.

Brown, Henry Collins. *Book of Home Building and Decoration.* Garden City, New York: Doubleday, Page, and Company, 1912.

The Building Brick Association of America. *One Hundred Bungalows.* Boston, Massachusetts: 1912. Reprint: Mineola, New York: Dover Publications, 1994.

Duchscherer, Paul, and Keister, Douglas. *The Bungalow: America's Arts and Crafts Home.* New York: Penguin Books, 1995.

Duchscherer, Paul and Keister, Douglas. *Outside the Bungalow: America's Arts and Crafts Garden.* New York, New York: Penguin Books, 1999.

Gordon, Liz, and Terri Hartman. *Decorative Hardware.* New York: HarperCollins Publishers, 2000.

Gordon-Van Tine Company. *Gordon-Van-Tine Homes.* Davenport, Iowa, 1923. Reprint: Mineola, New York: Dover Publications, 1992.

Hodgson, Fred T. *Practical Bungalow and Cottages for Town and Country.* Chicago: Frederick J. Drake and Company, 1906.

Keith, M. L. *Keith's Magazine on Home Building, July 1918.* Minneapolis, Minnesota.

King, Anthony D. *The Bungalow: The Production of a Global Culture.* London, England: Routledge and Kegan Paul, 1984.

Lancaster, Clay. *The American Bungalow.* New York: Abbeville Press, 1985. Republication: Mineola, New York: Dover Publications, 1995.

Lewis Manufacturing Company. *Lewis Homes: Homes of Character.* Bay City, Michigan, 1923.

Loizeaux Lumber Company. *Loizeaux's Plan Book #7.* Plainfield, New Jersey, 1927. Reprint: Mineola, New York: Dover Publications, 1992.

Maire, F. *Modern Painter's Cyclopedia.* Chicago: Frederick J. Drake and Company, 1934.

Makinson, Randall L. *Greene and Greene: The Passion and the Legacy.* Salt Lake City, Utah: Gibbs Smith Publisher, 1998.

Morgan. *Building with Assurance.* Chicago: Morgan Woodwork Organization, 1921.

Moss, Roger W. *Paint in America.* New York: John Wiley and Sons, 1994.

Norman, Donald A. *Emotional Design: Why We Love (or Hate) Everyday Things.* New York, New York: Basic Books, 2004.

Parry, Linda. *William Morris.* London, England: Phillip Wilson Publishers, in Association with the Victoria and Albert Museum, 1996.

Pfeiffer, Bruce Brooks. *Frank Lloyd Wright: Selected Houses.* Tokyo, Japan: A.D.A. EDITA Tokyo Company, Ltd, 1991.

Prentice, Helaine Kaplan and Blair, and City of Oakland Planning Department. *Rehab Right.* Oakland, California: City of Oakland, 1978. Reprint: Berkeley, California: Ten Speed Press, 1986.

Radford, William A. *Radford's Artistic Bungalows.* Chicago: Radford Architectural Company, 1908. Reprint: Mineola, New York: Dover Publications, 1997.

Ray H. Bennett Lumber Company. *Bennett Homes: Better-Built Ready-Cut.* North Tonawanda, New York, 1920. Reprint: Mineola, New York: Dover Publications, 1993.

Sears Roebuck and Company. *Honor-bilt Modern Homes.* Chicago: 1926. Reprint: Mineola, New York: Dover Publications, 1991.

Smith, Bruce, and Alexander Vertikoff. *Greene and Greene Masterworks.* San Francisco: Chronicle Books, 1998.

Stickley, Gustav. *Craftsman Homes.* New York: Craftsman Publishing Company, 1909. Reprint: Mineola, New York: Dover Publications, 1979.

Stickley, Gustav. *More Craftsman Homes.* New York: Craftsman Publishing Company, 1912. Reprint: Mineola, New York: Dover Publications, 1982.

Vanderwalker, F. N. *Interior Wall Decoration.* Chicago: Frederick J. Drake and Company, 1924.

Wilhide, Elizabeth. *William Morris: Décor and Design.* London, England: Pavilion Books Limited, 1991.

Wilson, Henry L. *A Short Sketch of the Evolution of the Bungalow: From Its Primitive Crudeness to Its Present State of Artistic Beauty and Cozy Convenience.* Los Angeles, n.d. Reprint: Mineola, New York: Dover Publications, 1993.

Winter, Robert. *The California Bungalow.* Los Angeles: Hennessey and Ingalls, Inc., 1980.

WEB ARTICLES AND ADDRESSES
"For a list of all the ways technology has failed to improve the quality of life, please press three." —Alice Kahn

Faragher, John Mack. "Bungalow and Ranch House: The Architectural Backwash of California," *Western Historical Quarterly* 32, no. 2 (summer 2001): 149. www.historycooperative.org/journals/whq/32.2/faragher.htm

Morris, William. "The Lesser Arts of Life." An Address Delivered in Support of the Society for the Protection of Ancient Buildings. London, 1882. www.burrows.com/morris/lesser.html

Morris, William. The William Morris Internet Archive. http://www.marxists.org/archive/index.htm

Nagengast, Bernard. "An Early History of Comfort Heating," *The Air Conditioning, Heating, & Refrigeration News,* 2001.

Phillips, Kerry. *What Is a Bungalow?* Sacramento Bungalow Heritage Association, 2003.

Turrell, Colleen. "Storm Windows Save Energy." *Home Energy Magazine Online,* July/August 2000. www.homeenergy.org/archive/hem.dis.anl.gov/eehem/00/0007contents.html

Wilson, Elmina T. *Modern Conveniences for the Farm Home.* U.S. Department of Agriculture, Farmer's Bulletin No. 270, transcribed by Debbie Clough Gerischer. Washington, D.C.: Government Printing Office, 1906.

http://iagenweb.org/history/mc/mcmp.htm

www2.cr.nps.gov/tps/briefs/brief21.htm

www.antiquedoorknobs.org/mineral%20knobs.htm

www.ashrae.org/content/ASHRAE/ASHRAE/ArticleAltFormat/2003627101234_326.pdf

www.batcon.org/home/default.asp

www.buginfo.com

www.cdc.gov/ncdod/diseases/hanta/hps/index.htm

www.cloudglass.com/holophane.htm

www.codecheck.com/wiring_history.htm#bx

www.csia.org/homeowners/chimfire.htm

www.dearbornheater.com/RADIANT%20FIRE.htm

www.ehsni.gov.uk/built/buildings/advice_window.shtml

www.findaproperty.com/cgi-bin/story.pl?storyid=3553

www.fpl.fs.fed.us/documnts/techline/crawl_space_ventilation.pdf

www.greensmiths.com/bees.htm

www.heatinghelp.com/newsletter.cfm?Id=38

www.hhinst.com/Artcellulose.html

www.hhinst.com/Artfiberglass.html

www.historicnewengland.org/wallpaper/essays/1890.htm

www.inventors.about.com/library/inventors/bltools.htm

www.mistermax.com

www.naturalgas.org/overview/history.asp

www.nofma.org/finishing3.htm#B

www.oikos.com/esb/30/atticvent.html

www.oldhousejournal.com/magazine/2004/april/spring_balance.shtml

www.outdoorlite.com/us-lighting-history.html

www.picasusa.org

www.primesourcebp.com

www.pscleanair.org/burning/indoor/index.shtml#more

www.rumford.com/contents.html#written

www.seatekco.com/bx.htm

www.taunton.com/finehomebuilding/pages/h00160.asp